MICHAEL HELTZER

THE INTERNAL ORGANIZATION OF THE KINGDOM OF UGARIT

THE INTERNAL ORGANIZATION OF THE KINGDOM OF UGARIT

(Royal service-system, taxes, royal economy, army and administration)

BY

MICHAEL HELTZER

1982

DR. LUDWIG REICHERT VERLAG · WIESBADEN

Acknowledgement is gratefully made to The Applied Research Co.
University of Haifa Ltd. and
to the Publications Committee of the University of Haifa
for lending their support to the publication of this book.

CIP-Kurztitelaufnahme der Deutschen Bibliothek

Heltzer, Michael:
The internal organization of the Kingdom of Ugarit: (royal service-system, taxes, royal economy, army, and administration) / by Michael Heltzer. – Wiesbaden: Reichert, 1982.
ISBN 3-88226-107-X

FOREWORD

The present monograph was typed and edited with the financial support of the Commission of Basic Research of the Israeli Academy of Sciences and of the Research Authority of the University of Haifa. Mr. U. Thon and the Editorial Committee of the University gave their help in the subsidizing of the edition, as well as good advice, which made the appearance of the monograph in print possible.

Mrs. A. Aronson contributed in the editing and typing of the manuscript.

The useful discussions, which I had with my colleagues, Professors B. Oded (Haifa), E. Lipinski (Leuven), G. Wilhelm (Saarbrücken, now Hamburg) and C. Zaccagnini (Bologna) helped me to achieve a better understanding of some very complicated questions.

Dr. Ludwig Reichert, the publisher, cooperated with deep understanding during all stages of work on the manuscript, till its publication.

I am very indebted to all these highly esteemed persons.

Naturally, the full responsibility for any possible misunderstandings and mistakes is my own.

Michael Heltzer

Haifa, May 1982.

CONTENTS

ABBREVIATIONS AND BIBLIOGRAPHY

ACF	Annuaire du Collège de France
AdF	Anuario de Filologia, Barcelona
AfO	Archiv für Orientforschung
AHW	*W. von Soden*, Akkadisches Handwörterbuch; Wiesbaden, 1959-1981
AION	Annali, Istituto Orientale, Napoli
Aistleitner, a	*J. Aistleitner*, Untersuchungen zur Grammatik des Ugaritischen, Berlin 1954
Aistleitner, b	*J. Aistleitner*, Lexikalisches zu den Ugaritischen Texten, AOH, 9, 1960, pp. 29-34
Aistleitner, c	*J. Aistleitner*, Die Mythologischen und Kultischen Texte aus Ras Shamra, Budapest, 1959
AJA	American Journal of Archaeology
AJSR	Association of Jewish Studies Review
Albright, a	*W.F. Albright*, Dwarf Craftsmen in the Keret Epic and Elsewhere in North-West Semitic Mythology, IEJ, 4, 1954, pp. 1-4
Albright, b	*W.F. Albright*, Specimens of Late Ugaritic Prose, BASOR, 150, 1958, pp. 36-38
Albright, c	*W.F. Albright*, Baal-Zephon, Festschrift für A. Bertholet, Tübingen, 1950, pp. 4-14
Albright, d	*W.F. Albright*, Two Little Understood Amarna Letters from the Middle Jordan Valley, BASOR, 89, 1943, pp. 7-17
Albright, *Moran*, e	*W.F. Albright, and W.L. Moran*, Rib-Adda of Byblos and the Affairs of Tyre (EA 89) JCS, 4, 1950, pp. 163-168
Al-Khalesi, a	*Y.M. Al-Khalesi*, Tell al Fakhar (Kurruḫanni), a *dimtu*-Settlement, Excavation Report, "Assur" 1/6, 1977, pp. 1-42
Alt, a	*A. Alt*, Die Behandlung Kriegsgefangener Frauen und Kinder, WO, 2, 1954, pp. 15-18
Alt, b	*A. Alt*, Hethitische und aegyptische Herrschaftsordnung in unterworfenen Gebieten, FuF, 25, 1949, No. 21/22, pp. 249-251 (Kl. Schr., Bd. III, pp. 99-106)
Alt, c	*A. Alt*, Hohe Beamte in Ugarit, "Studia Orientalia *J. Pederseni* dicatae" Kopenhagen, 1954, pp. 1-11
Alt, d	*A. Alt*, Menschen ohne Nahmen, ArOr, XIX, 1950, pp. 9-24 = (Kl. Schr. III, pp. 198-213)
Amadasi, a	*M.E. Amadasi*, L'iconografia del carro de guerra in Siria e Palestina, Roma, 1965
AnSt	Anatolian Studies, London

AOAT	Alter Orient und Altes Testament
AOF	Altorientalische Forschungen
AOH	Acta Orientalia ... Hungarica
Archi, a	*A. Archi*, Citta e territoria in Siria e in Anatolia. Mari-Ugarit-Hattusa, DdA. IX-X, 1976-77, pp. 75-107.
ARMT	Archives royales de Mari, Textes, Transcription Translation... Paris
ARMT, VII	*J. Bottéró*, Textes économiques et administratifs, Paris, 1957
ARMT, X	*E. Dossin*, Correspondance féminine, Paris, 1978
ARMT, XVIII	*O. Rouault*, Mukannišum, l'administration et l'économie palatiales de Mari, ARMT, XVIII, Paris, 1977
ArOr	Archiv Orientalní
AS	Assyriological Studies, Chicago
Astour, a	*M. Astour*, The Merchant Class of Ugarit, RAI, XVIII, München, 1972, pp. 12-26
Astour, b	*M. Astour*, Place Names, RSP, II, pp. 251-369
Astour, c	*M. Astour*, *Ma'ḫadu*, The Harbour of Ugarit, JESHO, 13, 1970, pp. 113-127
Astour, d	*M. Astour*, New Evidence on the Last Days of Ugarit, AJA, 69, 1965, pp. 253-258
Astour, e	*M. Astour*, Les étrangers à Ugarit et le statut juridique des Habiru, RA, 53, 1959, pp. 70-76
Astour, f	*M. Astour*, The Kingdom of Siyannu-Ušnatu UF, XI, 1979, pp. 13-28
Astour, g	*M. Astour*, review of Heltzer, a, JNES, 39, 1980, pp. 163-167
AT	*D.J. Wiseman*, The Alalakh Tablets, London, 1953
AUSB	Annales Universitatis Scienticarum Budapestiensis de Rolando Eötvös Nominata, Sectio Historica
Avigad, a	*N. Avigad*, The Governor of a City, IEJ, 26, 1977, pp. 178-182
Barkay, a	*G. Barkay*, A Second Bulla of a *Śar Ha'īr*, "Qadmoniyot", X, 1977, pp. 69-71
BASOR	Bulletin of the American Schools of Oriental Research
Bass, a	*G. T. Bass*, Cape Gelidonia, A Bronze Age Shipwreck, Philadelphia, 1967
BE	Babylonian Expedition of the Pennsylvania University
BeO	Bibbia e Oriente
Berger, a	*P. R. Berger*, Die Alašia-Briefe Ugaritica 5. Noug. NRN 22-24, UF, 1, 1969, pp. 217-221
Berger, b	*Ph. R. Berger*, Zu den "akkadischen" Briefen Ugaritica, V, UF, II, 1970, pp. 285-294
Bin-Nun, a	*Sh. Bin-Nun*, The Tawananna in the Hittite Kingdom, Heidelberg, 1975
BM	Baghdader Mitteilungen

BMB	Bulletin du Musée de Beyrouth
BMes	Bibliotheca Mesopotamica, Undena Publications, Malibu.
BO	Bibliotheca Orientalis
Bogoslovsky, a	*E, S. Bogoslovsky*, Property and Ex-Officio Possessions in Ancient Egypt, VDI, 1979, No. 1, pp. 3-23 (Russian, English summary)
Bonfante, a	*G. Bonfante*, Étymologie du mot Grec ἀλαζών BSL, 37 (1936), pp. 77-78
Bordreuil-ʿAjjan, a	*P. Bordreuil, L. ʿAjjan*, Lexicographie Ougaritique: *ḪṬM*.CTA, 16.VI, 8; *MĠRT*, PRU, II, 40 : 18, Sem, 28, 1978, pp. 5-6
Bordreuil, b	*P. Bordreuil*, Nouveaux textes économiques et cunéiformes alphabétiques de Ras Shamra-Ougarit (34e Campagne 1973). Sem. 25, pp. 19-29
Bordreuil-Caquot,	*P. Bordreuil, A. Caquot*, Les textes en cunéiformes alphabétiques découvertes en 1977 à Ibn Hani, "Syria" LVI, 1979, pp. 295-315
Borger, b	*R. Borger*, Assyrisch-Babylonische Zeichenliste, AOAT, 33, Neukirchen-Vluyn, 1978
Borger, a	*R. Borger*, Weitere Ugaritologische Kleinigkeiten, III. Hebraisch *MḪWZ* (Psalm 107, 30) UF, I, 1969, pp. 1-3
Bottéró, a	*J. Bottéró*, Ḫabiru, RlA, IV, 1972, pp. 14-27
Bounni, a	*A. Bounni*, Résidence royale ugaritique à Ras Ibn Hani, CIEU, 1979
Boyd, a	*J.L. Boyd*, A Collection and Examination of the Ugaritic Vocabulary Contained in the Akkadian Texts from Ras-Shamra (Diss. Univ. Microfilms) Chicago, 1975
Boyer, a	*G. Boyer*, La place des textes d'Ugarit dans l'histoire de l'ancien droit orientale in *G. Boyer*, "Mélanges G. Boyer", II, Paris, 1965, p. 111-152
Boyer, b	*G. Boyer*, Royauté et droit public dans les textes d'Ugarit, "Mélanges G. Boyer", II, Paris, 1965, pp. 153-167
Brin, a	*G. Brin*, On the Title "*bn hmlk*" "Lešonēnu" 31, 1966, No. 1, pp. 5-20, no. 2, pp. 85-96 (Hebrew)
Brin, b	*G. Brin*, The Title *bn (h)mlk* and its Parallels, The Significance and Evolution of an Official Title, AION, 19, 1969, pp. 433-465
BSL	Bulletin de la Société de Linguistique de Paris
BSOAS	Bulletin of the School of Oriental and African Studies
BSSAV	Beiträge zur sozialen Struktur des Alten Vorderasiens, 1, Berlin, 1971
Buccellati, a	*G. Buccellati*, Due Noti di Testi Accadici di Ugarit: MAŠKIM-*sākinu*, OA, II, 1963, pp. 223-228
Buccellati, b	*G. Buccellati*, Cities and Nations of Ancient Syria, Rome, 1967

Buchholz, a — *H.G. Buchholz*, Der Kupferhandel des zweiten vorschristlichen Jahrtausends in Spiegel der Schriftforschung, "Minoica" Festschrift *J. Sundwall*, Berlin, 1958, pp. 92-115

Buchholz, b — *H.G. Buchholz*, Talanta, Neues über Metallbarren der ostmediterranen Spätbronzezeit, "Schweizer Münzblatter" 16, 1966, H.62, pp. 58-72

Buchholz, c — *H.G. Buchholz*, Metallurgie, in pp. 142-154 in "Kunst Sardiniens" Karlsruhe, 1980

Butz, a — *K. Butz*, Ur in altbabylonischer zeit als Wirtschaftsfaktor, OLA, 5, 1979, pp. 257-409

CAD — Chicago Assyrian Dictionary

Calders i Artis, a — *T. Calders i Artis*, El Carro de Guerra en Ugarit en el Segundo Milenio a.C. AdF, 3, 1977, pp. 167-193

Caquot-Masson, a — *A. Caquot and E. Masson*, Tablettes ougaritiques du Louvre, Sem, 27, 1977, pp. 5-19

Caquot, b — *A. Caquot*, Correspondance de ʿUzzin, fils de Bayaya, (RS, 17.63 et 17.117), U.VII, pp. 389-398

Caquot, c — *A. Caquot*, ACF, 75, (1975-76), pp. 426-429

Cassin, a — *E. Cassin*, Nouveaux documents sur les Ḫabiru, JA, 246, 1958, pp. 225-236

Cassin, b — *E. Cassin*, Techniche della Guerra e Strutture Sociali in Mesopotamia nella seconda Metà del II Millenio, RSI, 1965, pp. 445-455

Cassin, c — *E. Cassin*, Le Palais de Nuzi et la Royauté d'Arrapḫa, PR, pp. 373-392

Cazelles, a — *H. Cazelles*, Hébreux, Ubru et Hapiru, "Syria" 35, 1958, pp. 198-207

CḪ — Codex Ḫammurabi

Chadwick, a — *J. Chadwick*, The Mycenaean World, Cambridge 1976

CIEU — Colloque International d'Études Ugaritiques, Lattaqie, 1979 (Summaries of Reports)

CIS — Corpus Inscriptionum Semiticarum

CNI — Christian News of Israel

Collon, a — *D. Collon*, A New Look at the Chronology of Alalakh Level VII, AnSt. 27, 1977, pp. 127-131

CTA — *A. Herdner*, Corpus des Tablettes cunéiformes alphabétiques découvertes à Ras Shamra-Ugarit de 1929 à 1939, T. I et II, Paris, 1963

Curto, a — *S. Curto*, The Military Art of the Ancient Egyptians, Torino, 1971

Cutler-Macdonald — *B. Cutler - J. Macdonald* (cf. *Macdonald-Cutler*)

Daddi-Pecchioli, a — *F. Daddi Pecchioli*, Il Ḫazan(n)u nei testi di Hattusa, OA, 14, 1975, pp. 93-136

Daddi-Pecchioli, b — *F. Daddi-Pecchioli*, Il ^{LÚ}KARTAPPU nel regno Ittita, SCO, 27, 1976, pp. 169-191

Dalley, a — *S. Dalley*, Old Babylonian Trade in Textiles at Tell Al Rimah, "Iraq", 39, 1977, pp. 155-159

Dandamayev, a — *M. Dandamayev*, Rev. on Weisberg, a, VDI, 1972, No. 2, pp. 129-135 (Russian)

Dandamayev, b — *M. Dandamayev*, State and Temple in Babylonia in the First Millennium B.C., OLA, VI, 1979, pp. 589-596

DdA — Dialoghi di Archeologia

De Jong Ellis, a — *M. De Jong Ellis*, Taxation in Mesopotamia, The History of the Term *miksu*, JCS, 26, 1974, pp. 211-250

Del Olmo Lete, a — *G. Del Olmo Lete*, Notes on Ugaritic Semantics I, UF, VII, 1975, pp. 89-102

Del Olmo Lete, b — *G. Del Olmo Lete*, The Ugaritic War Chariot, A New Translations of KTU 4.392 (PRU.V, 105) UF, 10, 1978, pp. 47-51

Del Olmo Lete, c — *G. Del Olmo Lete*, Quantity Precision in Ugaritic Administration Texts, UF, XI, 1979, pp. 179-186

Delcor, a — *M. Delcor*, Le personnel du temple d'Astarte à Kition d'après une tablette phénicienne (CIS 86 A et B) UF, 11, 1979, pp. 147-169

Deller, a — *K. Deller*, Die Rolle des Richters in neuassyrischen Prozessrecht, Studi in onore *E. Volterra*, VI, 1972, pp. 639-653

Diakonoff, a — *I. M. Diakonoff*, Some Remarks on I 368, ArOr, 47, 1979, pp. 39-41

Diakonoff, b — *I. M. Diakonoff*, *Muškênum* and the servicelandholding on royal lands at the time of Chammurabi, "Eos" 48, 1956, pp. 37-62 (Russian, English summary)

Diakonoff, c — *I. M. Diakonoff*, Die hethitische Gesellschaft, MIOF, XIII 3, 1967, pp. 313-366

Diakonoff, d — *I. M. Diakonoff*, Hurrisch und Urartäisch, München, 1971

Diakonoff, e — *I. M. Diakonoff*, Die Arier im Vordern Orient: Ende eines Mythos, Or, 41, 1972, pp. 91-120

Diakonoff, f — *I. M. Diakonoff*, A Babylonian Political Pamphlet from about 700 B.C., AS, XVI, 1965, pp. 345 ff.

Dietrich-Loretz, a — *M. Dietrich, O. Loretz*, SSAU, I, WO, III, 1966, pp. 194-212

Dietrich-Loretz, b — *M. Dietrich, O. Loretz*, *Pilku-Ilku* "Lehnspflicht, UF, IV, 1972, pp. 165-166

Dietrich-Loretz, c — *M. Dietrich, O. Loretz*, ANŠT und (M)INŠ(T) im Ugaritischen, UF, IX, 1978, pp. 47-50

Dietrich-Loretz, d — *M. Dietrich, O. Loretz*, SSAU, V, UF, I, 1969, pp. 37-64

Dietrich-Loretz, e — *M. Dietrich, O. Loretz*, SSAU, IV, ZA, 60 1970, pp. 88-123

Dietrich-Loretz, f — *M. Dietrich, O. Loretz*, Epigraphische Problemen in KTU, 4.609, 10-11; UF, X, 1978 (1979), p. 423

Dietrich-Loretz, g — *M. Dietrich, O. Loretz*, Untersuchungen zur Schrift und Lautlehre des Ugaritischen (I). Der Ugaritische Konsonant ġ. WO, IV, 2, 1968, pp. 300-315

Dietrich-Loretz-Sanmartin, h — *M. Dietrich, O. Loretz, J. Sanmartin*, Die Verteilung der Rationen in PRU.V, 105 (= RS. 18.130), UF, VI, 1974, p. 468

Dietrich-Loretz, i — *M. Dietrich, O. Loretz*, Der Vertrag zwischen Suppiluliuma und Niqmandu, Eine politische und kulturhistorische Studie, WO, III, 1966, pp. 206-245

Dietrich-Loretz, j — *M. Dietrich, O. Loretz*, Die Schardana in den Texten von Ugarit, Festschrift *H.E. Stier*, Münster, 1972, pp. 35-42

Dietrich-Loretz, k — *M. Dietrich, O. Loretz*, SSAU, II, WO, V, 1969, No. 1, pp. 57-97

Dietrich-Loretz, Sanmartin, l — *M. Dietrich, O. Loretz, J. Sanmartin*, Brief über die Auswirkung einer Razzia (RS.19.11 = PRU.V, 114), UF, VII, 1975, pp. 532-533

Dietrich-Loretz, Sanmartin, m — *M. Dietrich, O. Loretz, J. Sanmartin*, Das Ritual, RS.1.5.-CTA.33, UF, 7, 1975, pp. 525-528

Dietrich-Loretz, Sanmartin, n — *M. Dietrich, O. Loretz, J. Sanmartin*, Die Texteinheiten in RS 1.2 = CTA 32 und RS.17.100-CTA Appendice I, UF, 7, 1975, pp. 141-146

Dietrich-Loretz, o — M. Dietrich, O. Loretz, Das "Seefahrende Volk" von Šikila (RS.34.129), UF, X, 1978, pp. 53-56

Dietrich-Loretz, p — *M. Dietrich, O. Loretz*, Einzelfragen zu Wörtern aus den Ugaritischen Mythen und Wirtschaftstexten, UF, XI, 1979, pp. 189-198

Dijkstra-de Moor, a — *M. Dijkstra, J. de Moor*, Problematical Passages in the Legend of Aqhâtu, UF, VII, 1975, pp. 171-215

Dijkstra, b — *M. Dijkstra*, Does Occur the Verb HBṬ in CTA, 4, III, 21?, UF, VIII, 1975, p. 565

DISO — *Ch. Jean. J. Hoftijzer*, Dictionnaire des inscriptions sémitiques de l'ouest, Leiden, 1965

Donner, a — *H. Donner*, Art und Herkunft des Amtes der Königinmutter im Alten Testament, "Festschrift *J. Friedrich*", Heidelberg, 1959, pp. 105-145

Drenkhahn, a — *R. Drenkhahn*, Die Handwerker und ihre Tätigkeit im Alten Ägypten, Wiesbaden, 1976

DV — Drevni'i Vostok, Jerevan

EA — *J.A. Knudtzon*, Die El-Amarna Tafeln, VAB 2, Leipzig, 1915

Edzard, a — *D.O. Edzard*, Altbabylonisch *nawûm*, ZA, NF 19(53), 1959, pp. 168-173

EI — Eretz-Israel, Jerusalem *(Non-Hebrew Section)

Eissfeldt, a — *O. Eissfeldt*, Neue Keilalphabetische Texte aus Ras-Schamra-Ugarit, Berlin, 1965

Eissfeldt, b — *O. Eissfeldt*, Kultvereine in Ugarit, U. VI, pp. 187-195

Eissfeldt, c — *O. Eissfeldt*, Etymologische und archäologische Erklärung alttestamentlicher Wörter, OA, 5, 1966, pp. 171-176

EM — Encyklopedia Miqrait-Encyclopaedia Biblica (Hebrew) — Jerusalem 1955-1982

Epstein, a — *Cl. Epstein*, A New Appraisal of Some Lines from a Long-known Papyrus, JEA, 49, 1963, pp. 49-56

ESS — *M. Dietrich, O. Loretz*, Die Elfenbeininschriften und S-Texte aus Ugarit, AOAT, 13, Neukirchen-Vluyn, 1976

Farber, a — *W. Farber*, Kampfwagen, RlA, V, 5/6, pp. 344-351

Faulkner, a — *R.O. Faulkner*, Egyptian Military Organization, JEA, 39, 1953, pp. 32-47

Fauth, a — *W. Fauth*, Sonnengottheit (^{d}UTU) und "Königliche Sonne" (^{d}UTU^{ši}) bei den Hethitern

Fensham, a — *F.C. Fensham*, The Semantic Field of *kly* in Ugarit, JNSL, VII, 1979, pp. 27-30

Fenton, a — *T.L. Fenton*, The Claremont 'MRZḤ' Tablet, Its Text and Meaning, UF, 10, 1977, pp. 71-75

Fenton, b — *T.L. Fenton*, *Sōken*, EM, V, pp. 55-56

Finet, a — *A. Finet*, Le *ṣuḫārum* à Mari, XVIII RAI, München 1972, pp. 65-72

Fisher, a — *L.R. Fisher*, The Claremont Ras Shamra Tablets, Roma, 1971

Foster, a — *B.R. Foster*, Humor and Cuneiform Literature, JANES, 6, 1974, pp. 69-83

Freydank, a — *H. Freydank*, Untersuchungen zur sozialen Struktur in Mittelassyrischen Zeit, AOF, 4, 1976, pp. 111-130

Freydank, b — *H. Freydank*, Zwei Verpflegungstexte aus Kār-Tukulti-Ninurta, AOF, I, 1974, p. 55ff.

Friedrich, a — *J. Friedrich*, Hethitisches Wörterbuch, Heidelberg, 1952

Frost, a — *H. Frost*, The Stone-Anchor of Ugarit, U.VI, P. 1969, pp. 235-245.

Frost, b — *H. Frost*, Mediterranean Harbours and Ports of Call in the Bronze and Iron Ages, RSJB, 32, 1974, pp. 35-41

Frost, c — *H. Frost*, Egypt and Stone Anchors: Some Recent Discoveries, MM, 65, 1979, pp. 137-162

Frost, d — *H. Frost*, The Stone-Anchors of Byblos, MuSJ, 45, 1969, pp. 425-442

FuF — Forschungen und Fortschritte

FWG — Fischers Weltgeschichte, 1966

Gaál, a	*E. Gáal*, The Economic Life of Alalaḫ in the XVIII-XVIIth Centuries B.C., AUSB, v. 13, 1972, pp. 279-300
Gaál, b	*E. Gaál*, *Pūrum* Lands and Houses in Alalaḫ, "Oikumene", 2, 1978, pp. 145-148
Gaál, c	*E. Gaal*, The "*Eperum*" in Alalaḫ, AUSB, 17, 1976
Galling, a	*K. Galling*, Beschriftete Bildsiegel des 1. Jahrtausends v. Chr. ZDPV, 64, 1941, pp. 121-202
Gardiner, a	*A. Gardiner*, The Kadesh Inscriptions of Ramesses II, Oxford, 1960
Garelli, a	*P. Garelli*, Les Assyriens en Cappadoce, Paris 1963
Garelli, b	*P. Garelli*, Les temples et le pouvoir royal en Assyrie du XIVe au VIIe siècle, RAI, XX, 1972, pp. 116-124
Garelli, c	*P. Garelli*, Hofstaat (Assyrisch) RlA, IV, pp. 446-452
Gaster, a	*Th.H. Gaster*, A Phoenician Naval Gazette, PEFQS, 1938, No. 2, pp. 105-121
Gelb, a	*I. Gelb*, The Ancient Mesopotamian Ration System, JNES, pp. 230-243
Gelb, b	*I. Gelb*, Household and Family in Early Mesopotamia, OLA, 5, Leuven, 1979, pp. 1-98
Gelb, c	*I.J. Gelb*, *Homo Ludens* in Early Mesopotamia, St.Or. 46, 1976, pp. 43-76
Gelb, d	*I. Gelb*, The Word for Dragoman in the Ancient Near East, "Glossa" 2, 1968, pp. 93-104
Gibson-Driver, a	*J.C.L. Gibson, G.R. Driver*, Canaanite Myths and Legends, Edinburgh, 1977
Ginsberg, a	*H.L. Ginsberg*, The Legend of King Keret, BASOR, Supplementary Studies, 2-3, New Haven, 1946.
Giorgadze, a	*G.G. Giorgadze*, Očerki po socialno-ekonomičeskoi istorii Chettskovo gosudarstva, Tbilisi, 1973 (Studies in the social and economic history of the Hittite state — Russian)
Glaeseman, a	*R.R. Glaeseman*, The Practice of the King's Meal in Mari: A System of Food Distribution in the 2nd Millenium B.C., 1978 (Univ. of California Dissert., Los Angeles)
Goetze, a	*A. Goetze*, The City Khalbi and the Khapiru People, BASOR, 79 (1940), pp. 32-34.
Goetze, b	*A. Goetze*, Warfare in Asia Minor, "Iraq", 25, 1963, pp. 124-130
Goetze, c	*A. Goetze*, Remarks on the Ration Lists from Alalakh, JCS, 13, 1959, pp. 34-38
Goetze, d	*A. Goetze*, Hittite Courtiers and their Titles, RHA, XII, 54, 1952, pp. 1-24
Goetze, e	*A. Goetze*, Ugaritic *mdrġl*, JCS, I, 1947, p. 72
Gomi, a	*T. Gomi*, On the Dairy Productivity at Ur in the Late Ur III Period, JESHO, 23. 1980, pp. 1-40

Gordon, a — *C.H. Gordon*, Review on PRU, V, JSS, XI, 1967, pp. 110-111

Gordon, b — *C.H. Gordon*, *'ḥdym* = *ILTÊNŪTU* "Pair". Studies in the Bible, presented to *M.H. Segal*, Jerusalem. 1964 (English section), pp. *5-*9

Gordon, c — *C.H. Gordon*, Ugaritic Guilds and Homeric Δημιοεργοι, Studies, presented to *H. Goldman*, New-York, 1976, pp. 136-143

Gray, a — *J. Gray*, The Legacy of Canaan, Leiden, 1957

Gray, b — *J. Gray*, Canaanite Religion and Old Testament Study in the Light of New Alphabetic Texts from Ras Shamra, U.VII, pp. 79-108

Greenfield, a — *J.C. Greenfield*, *našû-nadānu* and its Congeners. Ancient Near Eastern Studies in Memory of *J.J. Finkelstein*, 1977, pp. 88-91

Greenfield, b — *J. Greenfield*, Ugaritic Lexicographical Notes, JCS, 21, 1967, (1969), pp. 89-93

Greenfield, c — *J.C. Greenfield*, The *Marzeaḥ* as a Social Institution, "Wirtschaft und Gesellschaft in Alten Vorderasien", Budapest 1976

Güterbock, a — *H.E. Güterbock*, rev. of *Friedrich*, a, "Oriens" 10, 1957, pp. 350-362

Güterbock, b — *H.G. Güterbock*, The Hittite Temple According to Written Sources, XX RAI, 1977, Leiden, 1975, pp. 125-132

Güterbock, c — *H.E. Güterbock*, Lexicographical Notes, II, RHA, 22, fasc. 74, 1964, pp. 95-97.

Haase, a — *R. Haase*, Eine hethitische Prozessurkunde aus Ugarit, RS.17.109, UF, III, 1971, pp. 71-74

Haase, b — *R. Haase*, Zum Recht von Ugarit, RIDA, XI, 1964, pp. 3-17

Haase, c — *R. Haase*, Anmerkungen zum ugaritischen Immobilienkauf, ZA 24, 1967, pp. 196-210

Hammond, a — *Ph. Hammond*, An Ammonite Stamp Seal from Amman, BASOR, 160, 1960, pp. 41-43

Harris, a — *R. Harris*, The Organization and Administration of the Cloister in Ancient Babylonia, JESHO VI, 1963, pp. 121-157

Hawkins, a — *D. Hawkins*, Karkemiš, RlA, V, pp. 426-446

Helck, a — *W. Helck*, Die Beziehungen Ägyptens zu Vorderasien im 3. und 2. Jahrtausend v. Chr. Wiesbaden, 1962

Helck, b — *W. Helck*, Militär (Personal, Organisation), LA, IV, 1980, pp. 127-134

Held, a — *M. Held*, *mḫṣ/mḫš* in Ugaritic and other Semitic Languages, JAOS, 79, 1959, pp. 169-178

Heltzer, a — *M. Heltzer*, The Rural Community in Ancient Ugarit, Wiesbaden, 1976

Heltzer, b — *M. Heltzer*, Goods, Prices and the Organization of Trade in

Ugarit (Marketing and Transportation in the Eastern Mediterranean in the Second Half of the IIth Millenium B.C.E.), Wiesbaden, 1978

Heltzer, c — *M. Heltzer*, The Royal Economy in Ancient Ugarit, OLA, 6 1979, pp. 459-496

Heltzer, d — *M. Heltzer*, Review on PRU, II, VDI, 1961, No. 1, pp. 158-167 (Russian)

Heltzer, e — *M. Heltzer*, *A. Charsekin*, New Inscriptions in Phoenician and Etruscan from Pyrgi, VDI, 1965, No. 3, pp. 108-131 (Russian)

Heltzer, f — *M. Heltzer*, The Datation of the Undated Texts from Ugarit, PS, XI, 1964, pp. 3-8 (Russian, English Summary)

Heltzer, g — *M. Heltzer*, Soziale Aspekte des Heereswesens in Ugarit, BSSAV, I, pp. 123-132

Heltzer, h — *M. Heltzer*, Ugarito-Akkadian Etymologies (*mūdū/md*), SJ, II, Moscow, 1965, pp. 335-367 (Russian-English Summary)

Heltzer, i — *M. Heltzer*, On the Akkadian Term *rêšu* in Ugarit, IOS, IV, 1974, pp. 4-11

Heltzer, j — *M. Heltzer*, Slaves, Slaveowning and the Role of Slavery in Ugarit, VDI, 1968, No. 3, pp. 85-95 (Russian-English Summary)

Heltzer, k — *M. Heltzer*, Some Problems of the Military Organization of Ugarit (Ugaritic *ḫrd* and Middle-Assyrian *ḫurādu*), OA, XIX, 1979, pp. 245-253

Heltzer, l — *M. Heltzer*, On the Ownership of the Pasture Lands in Ugarit (Hebrew) SHJPLI, III, 1974, pp. 9-13

Heltzer, m — *M. Heltzer*, Penalties for Non-Performance of Obligations (the term *nayyālu* in Ugarit), VDI, 1971, No. 2, pp. 78-84 (Russian-English Summary)

Heltzer, n — *M. Heltzer*, Zur Bedeutung des Ausdrucks "die *ṣibbiru*-Felder" in Ugarit, OLP, VIII, 1977, pp. 47-55

Heltzer, o — *M. Heltzer*, Service-Landholding in Ancient Ugarit, (Russian) LAMMD, IX, 1967 (1968), pp. 183-208

Heltzer, p — *M. Heltzer*, The Word *ṣṣ* in Ugaritic (About the Occurrence of Salt-Taxes in Ugarit) AION 18, 1968, pp. 355-362

Heltzer, q — *M. Heltzer*, "Royal Dependents" (*bnš mlk*) and Units of the Royal Estate (*gt*) in Ugarit, VDI, 1967, No. 2, pp. 32-47 (Russian, English Summary)

Heltzer, r — *M. Heltzer*, Nouveaux textes d'Alalakh et leur importance pour l'histoire sociale et économique de l'Orient ancien, VDI, 1956, No. 1, pp. 14-27 (Russian)

Heltzer, s — *M. Heltzer*, Problems of Social History, OAC, IX, 1969, pp. 37-43

Heltzer, t — *M. Heltzer*, Review on "Ugaritica, V, VDI, 1971, No. 1, pp. 183-208 (Russian)

Heltzer, u — *M. Heltzer*, *Dimtu-gt-pyrgos* — An Essay about the Non-Etymological Sense of these Terms, JNSL, VII, 1979, pp. 31-35

Heltzer, v — *M. Heltzer*, Royal Administration and Palace-Personnel in Ugarit (Russian), LAMMD, 10, 1970, pp. 230-283

Heltzer, w — *M. Heltzer*, The Social and Political Struggle in Byblos of the Amarna Period, VDI, 1954, No. 1, pp. 23-30 (Russian).

Heltzer, y — *M. Heltzer*, The Organization of Craftsmanship in Ugarit (Russian), PS, 13, 1965, pp. 47-60

Heltzer, A — *M. Heltzer*, The Metal Trade of Ugarit and the Problem of Transportation of Commercial Goods, "Iraq", 39, 1977, pp. 203-211

Heltzer, B — *M. Heltzer*, A Recently Discovered Phoenician Inscription and the Problem of the Guilds of Metal-Casters (I International Congress of Phoenician Studies, Roma, 1979) (in print).

Heltzer, C — *M. Heltzer*, Review on PRU, V, VDI, 1966, No. 3, pp. 191-205

Heltzer, D — *M. Heltzer*, Some Questions Concerning the Sherdana in Ugarit, IOS, IX (in press)

Heltzer, E — *M. Heltzer*, A Heavy Canaanite (?) Scolding in an Akkadian Text from Ugarit, RA, 67, 1973, pp. 164-165

Heltzer, F — *M. Heltzer*, Temple Landownership in Ancient Ugarit, LAMMD, VI, 1964, pp. 153-162 (Russian)

Heltzer, G — *M. Heltzer*, Zum Hauskauf in Ugarit, UF, 11, 1979, pp. 365-370

Heltzer, H — *M. Heltzer*, On Tithe Paid in Grain in Ugarit, IIj, 25, 1975, pp. 124-128

Heltzer, I — *M. Heltzer*, An Old Aramean Seal-Impression and Some Problems of the History of the Damascus Kingdom (International Conf. on Arameans and Aramaic, January 1980, Bar-Ilan University, Ramat-Gan) (in press)

Heltzer, J — *M. Heltzer*, Mortgage of Land Property and Freeing from it in Ugarit, JESHO, 19, 1976, pp. 89-93

Heltzer, K — *M. Heltzer*, Once More on Communal Self-Government in Ugarit, VDI, 1965, No. 2, pp. 3-13 (Russian)

Heltzer, L — *M. Heltzer*, Some Northwest Semitic Epigraphic Gleanings from the XI-VI Centuries B.C., AION, v. 21, 1971, pp. 183-198

Heltzer, M — *M. Heltzer*, A Note on the *aluzinnu* in Ugarit, AfO, 27, 1980, p. 409

Heltzer, N — *M. Heltzer*, The Suteans (with a contribution by *Sh. Arbeli*), Naples, 1980 (1981)

Heltzer, O and S	*M. Heltzer*, ḪZR in den Verwaltungstexten aus Ugarit, UF, XII, 1980, pp. 410-412
Heltzer, P	*M. Heltzer*, Vessels of the King of Karchemish in Ugarit, (in print)
Heltzer, Q	*M. Heltzer*, La signification de *unṯ/unuššu* à Ougarit, Sem. 30, 1980, pp. 5-12
Heltzer, R	*M. Heltzer*, Der ugaritische Text KTU, 4.751 und das kollektive Fest(?)-Mahl der Dienstleute des Königs, UF, XII, 1980, pp. 413-415
Heltzer, T	*M. Heltzer*, The *mdrġl(m)* and the UN-*tù* men in Ugarit (in print)
Heltzer, U	*M. Heltzer*, On the Meaning of the Term *ubdit/updt* in Ugarit, JNSL, IX (in print)
Heltzer, V	*M. Heltzer*, The Inscription on the Nimrud Bronze Bowl No. 5 (BM.91303) PEQ, 1982, pp. 1-6
Henshaw, a	*R.A. Henshaw*, The Office of *ŠAKNU* in Neo-Assyrian Times, I, JAOS, 87, 1967, pp. 517-525, II, JAOS, 88, 1968, pp. 461-483
HG	*A. Ungnad*, *J. Kohler*, *P. Koschaker*, Hammurabis Gesetz, II-VI, Leipzig, 1909-1923
Hillers, a	*D.R. Hillers*, A Hebrew Cognate of *unuššu/unṯ* in Is 33:8, HTR, 64, 1971, pp. 257-259
Horwitz, a	*W.J. Horwitz*, The Ugaritic Scribe, UF, XI, 1979, pp. 389-394
HSS	Harvard Semitic Series
HTR	Harvard Theological Review
HUCA	Hebrew Union College Annual
Hurst, a	*A. Hurst*, A propos des forgerons de Pylos, SMEA, V, 1968
Huss, a	*W. Huss*, Die Stellung des *rb* im karthagischen Staat, ZDMG, 129, 1979, pp. 217-232
IEJ	Israel Exploration Journal
IFPCO	*M.G. Guzzo Amadasi*, Le iscrizioni Fenicie e Puniche delle Colonie in Occidente, Roma, 1967
IH	Ras Ibn Hani
Imparati, a	*F. Imparati*, Una Concessione di Terre da Parte di Tudhaliya IV, RHA, 32, 1974 (1977), pp. 1-209
Imparati, b	*F. Imparati*, *É duppas*, LÚ*tuppanuri*, "Athenaeum" Pavia, XLVII, 1969, pp. 154-159
Imparati, c	*F. Imparati*, "Signori" e "figli del re", Or, 44, 1975, pp. 80-95
IOS	Israel Oriental Studies
Ismail-Müller, a	*B.K. Ismail*, *M. Müller*, Einige bemerkenswerte Urkunden aus Tell al Faḫḫar zur altmesopotamischen Recht-Social und Wirtschaftsgeschichte, WO, IX/1, 1977, pp. 14-34
Ivanov, a	*V.V. Ivanov*, Urartian *MARI*, *Hurrian MARIANNE*, Hayasan, *MARIJA*, PAS, III, 1979, pp. 101-112 (Russian-English Summary, p. 271)
JA	Journal Asiatique

JANES	Journal of the Ancient Near Eastern Society of Columbia University
Jankovska, a	*N.B. Jankowska*, Communal Self-Government and the King of the State of Arrapḫa, JESHO, 12, 1969, pp. 233-282
Jankowska, b	*N. Jankowska*, The "Old Palace" and the *DIMTU* of Potters in Arrapḫa, DV, III, 1978, pp. 218-229 and 274-276 (Russian-English Summary)
Jankowska, c	*N.B. Jankowska*, L'autonomie de la communauté à Ougarit (garanties et structure) VDI, 1963, No. 3, pp. 35-55
Janssen, a	*J.J. Janssen*, Kha'emtôre, a well-to-do Workman, OudMed, LVIII, 1977, pp. 221-232
Janssen, b	*J.J. Janssen*, The Role of the Temple in the Egyptian Economy during the New Kingdom, OLA, 6, II, Leuven, 1979, pp. 505-516
JAOS	Journal of the American Oriental Society
JARCE	Journal of the American Research Center in Egypt
JCS	Journal of Cuneiform Studies
JEA	Journal of Egyptian Archaeology
JESHO	Journal of the Social and Economic History of the Orient
JIVUF	Jahresbericht des Instituts für Vorgeschichte der Universität Frankfurt am Main
JNES	Journal of Near Eastern Studies
JNSL	Journal of the Northwest Semitic Languages
Jordan, a	*B. Jordan*, The Athenian Navy in the Classical Period, Berkeley, 1975 (University of California. Publications, Classical Studies Vol. 13)
JSS	Journal of Semitic Studies
KAI	*H. Donner*, *W. Röllig*, Kanaanäische und aramäische Inschriften, I-III, Wiesbaden, 1964
Kammenhuber, a	*A. Kammenhuber*, Die Arier im Vorderen Orient, Heidelberg, 1968
Kammenhuber, b	*A. Kammenhuber*, Die Arier im Vorderen Orient und die historischen Wohnsitze der Hurriter, Or, 46, 1977, pp. 129-143
KAR	*E. Ebeling*, Keilschrifttexte aus Assur religiösen Inhalts, Leipzig, 1919
Kendall, a	*T. Kendall*, Warfare and Military Matters in the Nuzi Tablets (Dissert. Brandeis University, 1975)
Kestemont, a	*G. Kestemont*, Les travaillers dans le monde Hittite, OA, XVII, 1978, pp. 17-28
Kestemont, b	*G. Kestemont*, Diplomatique et droit international en Asie occidentale, 1600-1200 av. J.C., Louvain, 1974
Kestemont, c	*G. Kestemont*, Le traité entre Mursil II de Hatti et Niqmepa d'Ugarit, UF, 6, 1974, pp. 83-127
Kienast, a	*B. Kienast*, Rechtsurkunden in Ugaritischer Sprache, UF, XI, 1979, pp. 430-451
Kitchen, a	*K.A. Kitchen*, The King List of Ugarit, UF, 9, 1977 (1978), pp. 131-142

Kition — *M. G. Guzzo Amadasi* et *V. Karageorghis*, Fouilles de Kition, III, Inscriptions Phéniciennes, Nicosia, 1977

Klengel, a — *H. Klengel*, Die Palastwirtschaft in Alalaḫ, OLA, 6, 1979, pp. 435-457

Klengel, b — *H. Klengel*, Geschichte Syriens im 2. Jahrtausend v.u.Z., I-III, Berlin, 1965-1970

Klengel, c — *H. Klengel*, Königtum und Palast nach den Alalaḫ-Texten, PR, pp. 273-282

Klengel, d — *H. Klengel*, Zur ökonomischen Funktion der Hethitischen Tempel, SMEA, XVI, 1975, pp. 181-200

Kl. Schr. — Kleine Schriften

Komoroczy, a — *G. Komoroczy*, Zu den Eigentumsverhältnissen der altbabylonischer Zeit, Das Problem der Privatwirtschaft, OLA, 6, 1979, pp. 411-422

Korošec, a — *V. Korošec*, The Warfare of the Hittites from the Legal point of View, "Iraq" 25, 1963, pp. 159-166

Kozyreva, a — *N. V. Kozyreva*, The Countryside in the Kingdom of Larsa (Russian, English Summary), VDI, 1975, No. 2, pp. 3-17

Kraus, a — *F. R. Kraus*, Der "Palast", Produzent und Unternehmer im Königreiche Babylon nach Hammurabi (ca. 1750-1600 v. Chr.), OLA, 6, Leuven, 1979, pp. 423-434

Kraus, b — *F. R. Kraus*, Staatliche Viehhaltung in altbabylonischen Lande Larsa, Amsterdam, 1966

Kraus, c — *F. R. Kraus*, Akkadische Wörter und Ausdrücke, X-XI, RA, 70, 1976, p. 165-172

Kristensen, a — *A. L. Kristensen*, Ugaritic Epistolary Formulas, UF, IX, 1978, pp. 143-158

KTU — *M. Dietrich*, *O. Loretz*, *J. Sanmartin*, Die keilalphabetische Texte aus Ugarit, I Neukirchen-Vluyn, 1976

KUB — Keilschrift-Urkunden aus Boghazköi

Kühne, a — *C. Kühne*, Mit Glossenkeil markierte fremde Wörter in Akkadischen Ugarittexten, I, UF, VI, 1974, PP. 157-167, II UF, VII 1975, pp. 253-260

Kümmel, a — *H. M. Kümmel*, Ugaritica Hethitica, UF, 1, 1969, pp. 159-163

Labat, a — *R. Labat*, Manuel d'Épigraphie Akkadienne, Paris, 1976

LÄ — Lexikon der Ägyptologie, Wiesbaden

LAMMD — Lietuvos TSR Aukstųjų Mokyklų Moksliniai Darbai, Istorija, Vilnius

Landsberger, a — *B. Landsberger*, Studien zu den Urkunden aus der Zeit des Ninurta-tukulti-Aššur, AfO, X, 1935-36, pp. 148-152

Landsberger, b — *B. Landsberger*, Remarks on the archive of the soldier Ubārum, JCS, 9, 1955, p. 121 ff.

Landsberger, c — *B. Landsberger*, Nachtrag zu *aspu* "Schleuder", AfO, 19, 1969, 1960, p. 66

Landsberger, d — *B. Landsberger*, Brief des Bischofs von Esagila an König Asarhaddon, Amsterdam, 1965

Laroche, a — *E. Laroche*, Glossaire de la langue hourrite, I-II) RHA, 34, 1976 (1979); 35 1977 (1979)

Laroche, b	*E. Laroche*, Textes de Ras Shamra en Langue hittite, U.V., 1968, pp. 769-784
Leemans, a	*W.F. Leemans*, rev. of *F.R. Kraus*, *b*, JESHO, 12, 1969, pp. 341-343
Leemans, b	*W.F. Leemans*, The *Asiru*, RA, 55, 1962, pp. 57-76
Lehmann, a	*G.A. Lehmann*, Der Untergang des Hethitischen Grossreiches und die neuen Texte aus Ugarit, UF, 2, 1979, pp. 39-73
Lemaire, Delavault, a	*B. Delavault*, *A. Lemaire*, La tablette ougaritique RS. 16.127 et l'abréviation "Ṭ" en nord-ouest sémitique, Sem. 25, 1975, pp. 31-41
Lettinga, a	*J. Lettinga*, rev. *R. de Langhe*, Les textes de Ras Shamra-Ugarit, I-II, Leuven, 1945, BO, 5, p. 42
Levy, a	*J. Levy*, Neubräisches und chaldäisches Wörterbuch über die Talmudim und Midraschim, I-IV, Leipzig, 1889
Lilliu, a	*G. Lilliu*, Sculture della Sardegna Nuragica, 1966
Limet, a	*H. Limet*, Le travail du Metal au pays de Sumer au temps de la IIIe dynastie d'Ur, Paris, 1961
Lipinski, a	*E. Lipinski*, Le Poème royal du Psaume LXXXIX, 1-5, 20-389, Paris, 1967
Lipinski, b	*E. Lipinski*, *SKN et SGN* dans le sémitique occidental du Nord, UF, V, 1973, pp. 191-207
Littauer-Crouwel, a	*M.A. Littauer*, *J.H. Crouwel*, Kampfwagen (Archäologisch), RlA, V, 5/6, pp. 344-351
Liver, a	*J. Liver*, Mydwt wmšqlwt, EM, IV, 1962, pp. 846-888
Liverani, a	*M. Liverani*, Storia di Ugarit nell'eta degli archivi politici, Roma, 1962
Liverani, b	*M. Liverani*, *Kbd* nei testi amministrativi di Ugarit, UF, II, 1979, pp. 89-108
Liverani, c	*M. Liverani*, Il Corpo di Guardia del Palazzo Reale di Ugarit, RSO, 44, 1969, pp. 191-198
Liverani, d	*M. Liverani*, Ville et campagne dans le royaume d'Ugarit. Essay d'analyse économique, CIEU, Lattaqie, 1979 (2 pages without pagination)
Liverani, e	*M. Liverani*, Le Chene de Sherdanu, VT, 27, 1977, pp. 212-216
Liverani, f	*M. Liverani*, La Royauté syrienne de l'Age du Bronze récent, PR, XIX RAI, Paris, 1974
Liverani, g	*M. Liverani*, Il fuoroscitismo in Siria nella tarda eta del bronzo, RSI, 77, 1969, p. 315-336.
Liverani, h	*M. Liverani*, Economia delle Fattorie Palatine Ugaritiche, DdA, 1979, No. 2 (appeared late in 1980), pp. 57-72
Liverani, i	*M. Liverani*, Communautés de village et palais royal dans Syrie du IIe millénaire, JESHO, XVIII, 1979, pp. 146-164
Loding, a	*D. Loding*, A Craft Archive from Ur (University of Pennsylvania Dissertation) 1974
Loretz, a	*O. Loretz*, Zu Ug. UNṮ, und He. ʾN(W)Š, UF, 8, 1976, pp. 449

Loretz, b — *O. Loretz*, Ugaritisch-hebräisch *ḫb/pṯ, bt ḫpṯt-ḥpšj, byt hḥpšj/wt*, UF, VIII, 1976, pp. 129-132

Loretz, c — *O. Loretz*, Die hebräischen Termini *Ḥpšj* "Freigelassen, Freigelassener" und *Ḥpšh* "Freilassung", UF, IX, 1977, pp. 163-167

Loretz, d — *O. Loretz*, Die *ASIRUM*-Texte, I, UF, X, 1978, pp. 121-160

Loretz, e — *O. Loretz - W. Mayer*, Hurrisch *parašš* – "treniertes Pferd", ZA, 69, 1979, pp. 188-191

Macdonald, a — *J. Macdonald*, The Unique Personnel Text KTU.4.102, UF, X, 1978 (1979), pp. 161-173

Macdonald-Cutler, b — *J. Macdonald - B. Cutler*, Identification of *Na'ar* in the Ugaritic Texts, UF, VIII, 1976, pp. 27-35

Macdonald-Cutler, c — *B. Cutler - J. Macdonald*, The Unique Ugaritic Text UT 113 and the Question of "Guilds", UF, 9, 1976 (1977), pp. 13-30

Maddoli, a — *G. Maddoli*, ΔΑΜΟΣ e ΒΑΣΙΛΕΣ, Contributo alla Studia delle origini della polis, SMEA, 12, 1970, pp. 7-57

Magnanini, a — *P. Magnanini*, Le iscrizioni fenicie dell'Oriente, Testi, Traduzioni, Glossari, Roma, 1973

Malamat, a — *A. Malamat*, Early Israelite Warfare and the Conquest of Canaan, Oxford 1978, 23 p.

Malamat, b — *A. Malamat*, Conquest of Canaan: Israelite Conduct of War according to Biblical Tradition, *RIHM*, No. 42, pp. 25-52

Margalit, a — *B. Margalit*, A Matter of "Life" and "Death" Neukirchen-Vluyn, 1980 (AOAT.206)

Margalit, b — *B. Margalit*, Studia Ugaritica, II, UF, 8, 1976, pp. 137-192

Masson-Sznycer, a — *O. Masson, M. Sznycer*, Recherches sur les Phéniciens à Chypre, Geneve-Paris, 1972

Matouš, a — *L. Matouš*, Verkauf des "Hauses" in Kaneš nach I 568, ArOr, 47, 1979, Pp. 33-39

Mayer, a — *W. Mayer*, Nuzi-Studien I (Die Archive des Palastes und die Prosopographie der Berufe) 1978, Neukirchen-Vluyn, AOAT 205/1

Mendelsohn, a — *I. Mendelsohn*, Guilds in Babylonia and Assyria, JAOS, 60, 1940, pp. 68-72

Mendelsohn, b — *I. Mendelsohn*, Guilds in Ancient Palestine, BASOR, 80, 1940, pp. 17-21

Mendelsohn, c — *I. Mendelsohn*, Free Artisans and Slaves in Mesopotamia, BASOR, 89, 1943, pp. 25-29

Meyer, a — *E. Meyer*, *Pyrgos* "Wirtschaftsgebäude", "Hermes", LV, 1920, pp. 100-102

WHLI — *J. Liver* (ed.), The Military History of the Land of Israel in Biblical Times, Tel-Aviv 1973 (Hebrew)

Milano, a — *L. Milano*, Kly nel Lessico Amministrativo del Semitico di Nord-ovest, VO, I, 1978, pp. 83-97

Millard, a — *A. Millard*, Königsiegel, RlA, VI (1981), pp. 135-140

Miller, a — *P.D. Miller*, Ugaritic *ĠZR* and Hebrew *'ZR* II, UF, II, 1970, pp. 158-175

MIOF — Mitteilungen des Instituts für Orientforschung

MM The Mariners Mirror, London
Moran, a W. L. Moran, Ugaritic *ṣîṣûma* and Hebrew *ṣîṣ* "Biblica" 39, 1958, pp. 69-71
MSL *B. Landsberger*, Materialien zum sumerischen Lexicon, Roma
Muhly, a *J. D. Muhly*, Copper and Tin, The Distribution of Mineral Resources... in the Bronze Age, Hamden, Conn. 1973
Muhly, b *J. D. Muhly*, Supplement to Copper and Tin, Hamden, Conn. 1976
Muntingh, a *L. M. Muntingh*, Status of a Free Ugaritic Female, JNES, 25, 1967, pp. 102-112
MUSJ Mélanges de l'Université Saint-Joseph, Beyrouth
Na'aman, a *N. Na'aman*, A New Look at the Chronology of Alalakh Level, VII, AnSt, 26, 1976, pp. 136-139
NF Neue Folge
NKTU *O. Eissfeldt*, Neue keilalphabetische Texte aus Ras Schamra-Ugarit, Berlin, 1965
Noel-Giron, a *M. Noel-Giron*, Cachet Hebraïque, JA, Ser. XI v. XIX, 1922, pp. 62-63
Nougayrol, a *J. Nougayrol*, Guerre et paix à Ugarit, "Iraq" 25, 1969, pp. 110-123
Nougayrol, b *J. Nougayrol*, Note on Heltzer, E, RA, 68, 1974, p. 95.
OA Oriens Antiquus
OAC Oriens Antiquus Collectio
Oelsner, a *J. Oelsner*, Zur sozialen Lage in Ugarit, BSSAV, pp. 118-123
OLA Orientalia Lovaniensia Analecta, Leuven
Olivier, a *J. P. J. Olivier*, Notes on the Ugaritic Month Names, II JNSL, II, 1972, pp. 53-59
OLP Orientalia Lovaniensia Periodica
OLZ Orientalistische Literaturzeitung
Oppenheim, a *A. L. Oppenheim*, A Note on *ša rêši*, JANES, 5, 1973, pp. 325-334
Oppenheim, b *A. L. Oppenheim*, Note on Oppenheim, a, RA, 68, 1974, p. 95
Or Orientalia, Roma
Otten, a *H. Otten*, Aufgaben eines Bürgermeisters in Ḫattusa, BM, 3, 1964, pp. 85-95
Oud Med Oudheidkundige Mededelingen uit het Rijksmuseum van Oudheden te Leiden
Palmer, a *L. R. Palmer*, La struttura della societa micenea in *M. Marazzi* (ed.) La societa Micenea, Roma, 1978, pp. 133-141
Palmer, b *L. R. Palmer*, War and Society in a Mycenaean Kingdom, "Armées et fiscalité dans le monde antique", Paris, 1978, pp. 35-62
Pardee, a *D. Pardee*, The Ugaritic Text 147 (90), UF, VI, 1974, pp. 277-278
PAS Peredneaziatskij Sbornik
Passow, a *F. Passow*, Handwörterbuch der griechischen Sprache, Darmstadt, 1970
PdP La Parola del Passato
PEFQS Palestine Exploration Fund, Quarterly Statement

PEQ — Palestine Exploration Quarterly

Pettinato, a — *G. Pettinato*, Il Commercio Internationale di Ebla: Economia Statale e Privata, OLA, V, Leuven 1979, pp. 171-233

Pini, a — *M.G. Pini*, Su due termini riguardanti il carro nei testi di Ugarit, OA, 15, 1976, pp. 107-114

Poljakova, a — *G.F. Poljakova*, Socialnopolititscheskaja struktura pilosskovo obshtshestva (The socio-political structure of the Pylos society) (Russian), Moscow, 1978

Postgate, a — *J.N. Postgate*, Land-Tenure in the Middle Assyrian Period, A Reconstruction, BSOAS, 34, 1971, pp. 496-520

Postgate b — *N. Postgate*, Neo-Assyrian Royal Grants and Decrees, Roma, 1969

Postgate, c — *J.N. Postgate*, The Economic Structure of the Assyrian Empire. "Mesopotamia" 7, Kopenhagen, pp. 193-221

PR — Le Palais et la Royauté (Archaeologie et civilisation) XIX RAI, Paris, 1974

Preisigke, a — *F. Preisigke*, Die Begriffe πυργος und στηγη bei der Hausanlage, "Hermes" LIV, 1969, pp. 423-432

PRU, II — *Ch. Virolleaud*, Le palais royal d'Ugarit, II, Paris, 1957

PRU, III — *J. Nougayrol*, Le palais royal d'Ugarit, III Paris, 1955

PRU, IV — *J. Nougayrol*, Le palais royal d'Ugarit, IV, Paris, 1956

PVU, V — *Ch. Virolleaud*, Le palais royal d'Ugarit, Paris, 1965

PRU, VI — *J. Nougayrol*, Le palais royal d'Ugarit, VI, Paris, 1970

PS — Palestinskij, Sbornik

Pugliese-Carratelli, a — *G. Pugliese-Carratelli*, I Bronzieri di Pilo Miceneo, SCO, XII, 1963, pp. 242-254

RA — Revue d'Assyriologie

Rabin, a — *Ch. Rabin*, Hittite words in Hebrew, in "Studies in the Bible presented to *M.H. Segal*", Jerusalem, 1964

Rabin, b — *Ch. Rabin*, Hittite Words in Hebrew, Or 32, 1963, pp. 113-139

RAI — Rencontre Assyriologique Internationale

Rainey, a — *A.F. Rainey*, ^{LÚ}MAŠKIM at Ugarit, Or. 35, 1966, 426-428

Rainey, b — *A.F. Rainey*, Gleanings from Ugarit, IOS, 3, 1973, pp. 34-62

Rainey, c — *A.F. Rainey*, A Social Structure of Ugarit, Jerusalem, 1967 (Hebrew)

Rainey, d — *A.F. Rainey*, Institutions, Family, Civil and Military, in RSP, II, 1975, pp. 71-107

Rainey, e — *A.F. Rainey*, *Ašīru* and *asīru* in Ugarit and the Land of Canaan, JNES, 26, 1967, 296-301

Rainey, f — *A.F. Rainey*, The Military Personnel of Ugarit, JNES, 24, 1963, pp. 17-27

Rainey, g — *A.F. Rainey*, The Scribe in Ugarit. His Position and Influence, "The Israel Academy of Sciences and Humanities, Proceedings," III, 4, Jerusalem, 1968, pp. 139-146

Rainey, h — *A.F. Rainey*, A Front Line Report from Amurru, UF, 3, 1971, pp. 131-149

Rainey, i — *A.F. Rainey*, Reflections on the Battle of Qedesh, UF, 5, 1973, pp. 280-282

Rainey, j — *A.F. Rainey*, Organized Religion of Ugarit, CNI, 15, 1969, No. 1, pp. 16-24

Rainey, k — *A.F. Rainey*, El Amarna Tablets 359-379, Neukirchen-Vluyn, 1969

Renger, a — *J. Renger*, Interaction of Temple, Palace and "Private Enterprise" in Old Babylonian Economy, OLA, 5, 1979, pp. 249-256

Renger, b — *J. Renger*, Örtliche und zeitliche Differenzen in der Struktur der Priesterschaft Babylonischer Tempel, XX, RAI, Leiden, 1972 (1975), pp. 108-115

Renger, c — *J. Renger*, Hofstaat, RlA, IV, pp. 435-446

RES — Répertoire d'Épigraphie Sémitique

Reviv, a — *H. Reviv*, More about the "*Maryannu*" in Syria and Palestine, SHJPLI, III, 1972, pp. 7-23 (Hebrew, English summary)

Reviv, b — *H. Reviv*, Škbt "'nšy hnwym" (*ṣabū namê*) wmrkybyh b'llẖ (The strata of *ṣabū namê* and its elements in Alalaẖ), Shn. I, Jerusalem, 1975 (Hebrew)

Reviv, c — *H. Reviv*, Some Comments on the *Maryannu*, IEJ, 28, 1972, pp. 218-228

RGTC — Répertoire Géographique des Textes Cunéiformes, Bd.6. *G.F. Del Monte und J. Tischler*, Die Orts- und Gewässernamen der hethitischen Texte, Wiesbaden, 1978

RHA — Revue Hittite et Asianique

RIDA — Revue Internationale des Droits de l'Antiquité

RIHM — Revue Internationale d'Histoire Militaire, Tel-Aviv

Rinaldi, a — *G. Rinaldi*, Osservazioni sugli elenchi ugaritici *šd ubdy*, *ubdy*. "Mélanges *E. Tisserant*, I, Vaticano, 1964, pp. 343-349

RlA — Reallexikon der Assyriologie

Röllig-von Soden, a — *W. von Soden*, *W. Röllig*, Das Akkadische Syllabar, 3 Auflage, Roma, 1976

Römer, a — *W.H. Ph. Römer*, der Spassmacher im Alten Zweistromland. Zum "Sitz im Leben" altmesopotamischer Texte, "Persica" VII, 1977, pp. 43-68

RS — Ras Shamra

RSI — Rivista Storica Italiana

RSJB — Recueil Societé Jean Bodin

RSO — Rivista degli Studi Orientali

RSP — *L.R. Fisher* (ed) Ras Shamra Parallels, I, Roma, 1972, II, Roma 1975

Saffirio, a — *L. Saffirio*, Razioni e salari in natura nell'antico Egitto, "Aegyptus" LVII, 1977, pp. 14-78

Salonen, *E*, a — *E. Salonen*, Die Waffen der alten Mesopotamier, Helsinki, 1965

Salonen, b — *A. Salonen*, Die Wasserfahrzeuge in Babylonien, Helsinki, 1939

Salonen, d — *A. Salonen*, Der Abschnitt "Wagen" der 5. Tafel der Serie ḪAR-*ra* = *ḫubullu*, StOr XI/3, 1945

Salonen, e — *A. Salonen*, Hippologia Accadica, Helsinki, 1953

Salonen, f	*A. Salonen*, Die Landfahrzeuge des alten Mesopotamien, Helsinki, 1954
Salonen, g	*A. Salonen*, Jagd und Jagdtiere im alten Mesopotamien, Helsinki, 1976
Sanmartin, a	*J. Sanmartin*, Zu Ug. *ADR* in KTU.1.17.VI 20-23, UF, 9, 1977, pp. 371-373
Sasson, a	*J. Sasson*, Canaanite Maritime Involvement in the Second Millennium B.C., JAOS, 86, 1966, pp. 126-136
Sasson, b	*J. Sasson*, The Military Establishments at Mari, Roma, 1967
Schaeffer, a	*C.F.A. Schaeffer*, Remarques sur les ancres en pierre d'Ugarit, U. VII, Paris, 1978, pp. 371-381
Schaeffer, b	*C.F.A. Schaeffer-Forrer*, Épaves d'une bibliothèque d'Ugarit, U. VII, pp. 399-474
Schaeffer, c	*C.F.A. Schaeffer*, Soixante-quatorze armes et outils en bronze dédiés au grand-prêtre d'Ugarit, U. III, p. 250-272
Schaeffer, d	*C.F.A. Schaeffer*, Épées du Roi d'Ugarit, U. III, pp. 276-279
Schaeffer, e	*C.F.A. Schaeffer*, Une épée de bronze d'Ugarit partout le Cartouche du Pharaon Mineptah, U. III, P. 1956, pp. 169-178
Schmitz, a	*B. Schmitz*, Untersuchungen zum Titel *SꜢ*-NJŚWT "Königssohn", Bonn, 1976
Schulman, a	*A.R. Schulman*, Military Rank, Title and Organization of the Egyptian New Kingdom, München, 1964
Schulman, b	*A.R. Schulman*, The Egyptian Chariotry, A Reexamination, JARCE, II, 1963, pp. 75-98
Schulman, c	*A.R. Schulman*, Some observations of the Military Background of the Amarna Period, JARCE, III, 1964, pp. 51-69
Schwarzenberg, a	*C. Schwarzenberg*, L'organizzazione feudale di Ugarit secondo le tavolette giuridiche provenienti dagli scavi archeologici (Archivi del Palazzo Reale) di Ras Shamra, RIDA, III-11, 1964, pp. 19-44
SCO	Studi Classici e Orientali, Pisa
SDB	Supplement au Dictionnaire de la Bible, fasicule, 52-53, Paris, 1979. Ras-Shamra, pp. 1124-1466
Sem	"Semitica"
SHJPLI	Studies in the History of the Jewish People and the Land of Israel, Haifa (Hebrew)
Shn	Shnaton, An Annual for Biblical and Ancient Near Eastern Studies, Jerusalem (Hebrew)
SJ	Semitskije Jazyki, Moscow
SMEA	Studi Micenei e Egeo-Anatolici
Speiser, a	*E.A. Speiser*, Akkadian Documents from Ras Shamra, JAOS, 75, 1955, pp. 154-165
Sperber, a	*D. Sperber*, On the pyrgos as a Farm-Building, AJSR, I, 1976, pp. 359-361
SSAU	*M. Dietrich*, *O. Loretz*, Zur sozialen Struktur von Alalaḫ und Ugarit.
St.Or	Studia Orientalia, Helsinki
Tarragon, a	*J.M. de Tarragon*, Le culte à Ugarit, Paris, 1980

TCL	Textes Cunéiformes de Louvre
ThLG	Thesaurus Greacae Lingue, Graz, 1954
Thureau-Dangin, a	*Fr. Thureau-Dangin*, Trois Contracts de Ras Shamra, "Syria" XVIII, 1937, pp. 245-255
Thureau-Dangin, b	*Fr. Thureau-Dangin*, Un Comptoir de Lain Pourpre à Ugarit d'après une Tablette de Ras Shamra, "Syria" XV, 1934, pp. 137-145
Thureau-Dangin, c	*Fr. Thureau-Dangin*, Une lettre assyrienne à Ras Shamra, "Syria", 16, 1935, pp. 188-193
Thureau-Dangin, d	*Fr. Thureau-Dangin*, Nouvelles lettres d'El-Amarna, RA, 19, 1922, pp. 91-94, 102-103
Tjumenev, a	*A. I. Tjumenev*, Gosudarstvennoje choziaistvo drevnevo Sumera, Moskva-Leningrad 1956 (State-Economy of Ancient Sumer, Russian)
Tritsch, a	*Tritsch*, Flüchtlinge in Ugarit, Abhandlungen des 24. Orientalisten-Kongresses, München, 1957 (1959)
Tsevat, a	*M. Tsevat*, Allalakhiana, HUCA, 29, 1958, pp. 109-134
Tsevat, b	*M. Tsevat*, Marriage and Monarchical Legitimacy in Ugarit and Israel, JSS, III, 1958, pp. 237-243
U. III	Ugaritica, III, Paris, 1956
U. V	Ugaritica, V, Paris, 1968, (*Cl. F.-A. Schaeffer* (ed.)), The Akkadian texts are published by *J. Nougayrol.*
U. VI	Ugaritica, VI, Paris, 1969
U. VII	Ugaritica, VII, Paris, 1978
UF	Ugarit-Forschungen
Ullendorf, a	*E. Ullendorf*, Ugaritic Marginalia, IV, EI, 14, 1978, pp. *19-*23
Urie, a	*D. M. L. Urie*, Officials of the Cult at Ugarit, PEQ, 80, 1948, pp. 42-47
Urman, a	*J. Urman*, *G^e bîrā*, EM, II, 1954, pp. 402-403
UT	*C. H. Gordon*, Ugaritic Textbook, Rome, 1965
VAB	Vorderasiatische Bibliothek
van den Branden, a	*A. van den Branden*, L'iscrizione fenicia su un sarcofogo conservato un tempo al Museo di Nicosia, BeO, No. 116-117, 1978, pp. 97-111.
Vanel, a	*A. Vanel*, Six "ostraca" phéniciens trouvés au temple d'Echmoun, près de Saida, BMB, 20, 1967, pp. 45-95
van Seters, a	*J. van Seters*, The Hyksos, A New Investigation, London, 1966
VDI	Vestnik Drevney Istorii
Veenhof, a	*K. R. Veenhof*, Aspects of Old Assyrian Trade and its Terminology, Leiden, 1972
Vinnikov, a	*I. N. Vinnikov*, Some Observations on the Language of the Ugaritic *Krt*-Epic. Proceedings of the XXVth Congress of Orientalists, Moscow, 1960 (1962), pp. 321-327 (Russian)
Vir. Dan	*Ch. Virolleaud*, La légende phénicienne de Danel, Paris, 1936
Virolleaud, a	*Ch. Virolleaud*, Cinq tablettes de Ras Shamra, RA, 38, 1941, pp. 1-12
VO	Vicino Oriente, Roma

von Soden, a	*W. von Soden*, Unregelmässige Verben im Akkadischen, ZA, 50 (16), 1952, pp. 163-181
VT	Vetus Testamentum, Leiden
Waetzold, a	*H. Waetzold*, Untersuchungen zur Neusumerischen Textilindustrie, Roma, 1972
Watson, a	*W.G.E. Watson*, An Allocation of Horses (PRU V, Text 105), UF, VI, 1974, p. 497
Weidner, b	*E. Weidner*, Hof und Harem-Erlasse assyrischer Könige aus dem 2. Jahrtausend v. Chr. AfO, 17, 1956, pp. 257-293
Weisberg, a	*D.B. Weisberg*, Guild Structure and Political Allegiance in Early Achaemenian Babylonia, New Haven, 1967
Wilhelm, a	*G. Wilhelm*, *ta/erdennu*, *ta/urtannu*, *ta/urtānu* UF, II, 1970, pp. 277-282
Wilhelm, b	*G. Wilhelm*, Zur Rolle des Grossgrundbesitzes in der hurritischen Gesellschaft, RHA, 36, 1978 (1980), pp. 205-213
Wiseman, a	*D.J. Wiseman*, Supplementary Copies of Alalakh Tablets, JCS, 8, 1954, pp. 17-20
Wiseman, b	*D.J. Wiseman*, Ration Lists from Alalakh VII, JCS, 13, 1959, pp. 22-30
WO	Welt des Orients
WUS	*J. Aistleitner*, Wörterbuch der ugaritischen Sprache, Berlin, 1963
Xella, a	*P. Xella*, Sul Ruola dei *ĠZRM* nella Societa Ugaritica, PdP, CL, 1973, pp. 194-202
Yadin, a	*Y. Yadin*, The Art of Warfare in Biblical Lands, New York, 1963
Yamashita, a	*T. Yamashita*, Professions, RSP, II, 1975, pp. 41-68
Yeivin, a	*S. Yeivin*, Ḥrmš wmgl, "Lešonēnu" 24, 1959-60, pp. 44-46 (Hebrew)
Yeivin, b	*S. Yeivin*, The Rise of Egyptian Military Power under the New Kingdom, MHLI, pp. 12-16 (Hebrew)
Yeivin, c	*S. Yeivin*, Canaanite and Hittite Strategy in the Second Half of the Second Millennium B.C.E., MHLI, pp. 27-32 (Hebrew)
Yeivin, d	*S. Yeivin*, The Israelite Conquest of Canaan, MHLI, pp. 59078 (Hebrew)
Yeivin, e	*Sh. Yeivin*, Pqydwt, EM, VI, 1971, pp. 549-575
Yoffee, a	*N. Yoffee*, The Economic Role of the Crown in the Old Babylonian Period, BiMes, V Malibu, 1977
ZA	Zeitschrift für Assyriologie
Zaccagnini, a	*C. Zaccagnini*, Note sulla Terminologia Metallurgica di Ugarit, OA, 9, 1970, pp. 315-324
Zaccagnini, b	*C. Zaccagnini*, The Rural Landscape of the Land of Arrapḫe, Roma, 1979
Zaccagnini, c	*C. Zaccagnini*, Pferde und Streitwagen in Nuzi, Bemerkungen zur Technologie, JIVUF, 1977, pp. 21-38
Zaccagnini, d	*C. Zaccagnini*, Lo scambio dei doni nel Vicino Oriente durante i secoli XV-XIII, Roma, 1973
ZDMG	Zeitschrift der Deutschen Morgenländischen Gesellschaft

ZDPV Zeitschrift des Deutschen Palästina-Vereins

ZUL *M. Dietrich, O. Loretz, J. Sanmartin*, Zur Ugaritischen Lexikographie, VII, UF, V, 1973, pp. 79-104; VIII UF, V, 1973, pp. 105-117; XI, UF, VI, 1974, pp. 19-38; XII, UF, VI, 1974, pp. 36-46

PREFACE

The main task of the present monograph is to give a general description and investigation of the system of the royal service in Ugarit and the royal economy, including its agricultural branch, and the various crafts which were involved in royal service. The military organization, temple organization and its personnel, and finally the royal administration and palace personnel are also included. The functions and organization of the royal authority will conclude the monograph.

Up to now a comprehensive monographic work in this field has been lacking and only the recent brief summary of political and socio-economic history of Ugarit, by *M. Liverani* (SDB, pp. 1295-1348), seems to be the first very useful attempt in this direction.

Our monograph is the third in a series which, first, considered the state and the development of the community-village in Ugarit (*Heltzer*, a), and, second, the development of trade and its organization in that country (*Heltzer*, b).

The present investigation is based upon a large number of articles and monographs written by various scholars, as well as our own published papers. For the sake of brevity we sometimes turn the reader's attention to these existing works, summarizing them only where it is necessary for the understanding of general information. Naturally, such questions which are reinvestigated as the result of new data or scholarly achievement are given in more detail.

As has been pointed out in our previously published studies,[1] the population of Ugarit, according to information based on PRU IV, 17.238,[2] was divided into three main groups: a) sons of Ugarit (*mârē*^{al} *Ugarit*), i.e., the main group of people — the peasants of the villages; b) servants of the king (*ardē šarri*) and c) servants of the servants of the king (*ardē*^{MEŠ} *ardē*^{MEŠ} *šarri ša* ^{mat}*Ugarit*) of Ugarit. The first group was discussed in our study of the

---

[1] Especially *Heltzer*, a, pp. 4-6 and *Heltzer*, b, p. 123. *Heltzer*, c, pp. 459-496; and recently, *Liverani*, SDB 53, p. 1333.

[2] *Heltzer*, a, pp. 3-6.

rural community,[3] the second and third groups will be analyzed in the present work. As previously mentioned,[4] slaves were not included in these groupings and must be considered separately.

---

[3] *Heltzer*, a.
[4] *Heltzer*, a, p. 5.

CHAPTER I

Ardē šarri-bnš mlk (bunušu malki) ROYAL SERVICEMEN, AND THEIR SERVICE

The *ardē*^{MEŠ} *šarri*, "royal servants," are found in an Akkadian tablet PRU, IV, 17.238. What was the Ugaritic counterpart of this term? We find the answer in lexicographic tablets from Ugarit which contain quadrilingual glossaries and give us the following information:

Akkadian	*Hurrian*	*Ugaritic*	
a-mi-lu	*tar-šu-wa-an-ni*	*bu-nu-šu* [1]	"man"

We also find here:

zi-ka-ru	*tu-ru-ḫi*	*da-ka-ru* [2]	"man, male."

A comparison of these two terms shows that *bunušu* means "man" in a social sense, while *dakaru* is simply a "male".[3] Therefore, *bunušu* has a social and not merely a biological sense.[4] One should quote here KTU 2.33.

The author of this letter says, addressing the king: (33) *w.mlk.b'ly.bnš* (34) *bnny*, "and the king, my Lord, made out of me (*bnny*, lit. "created me") a man." He acknowledges that he owes his social position of *bnš* of the king. KTU 4.169, dealing with military equipment, mentions (5) *ṯryn śśwm* (6) *ṯryn. aḥd.d.bnš*, "(5) armour for horses, (6) one armour for a man," thus contrasting the horses' and the man's (*bnš*) armour. KTU.4.40,[5] which deals with crews of ships, *ṣb'u 'anyt*, indicates for each crew the name of the village on the coast and the number of "men" (*bnšm*) who served on board.

---

[1] U. V, 130 (RS. 20. 149), II, 5′, 8′; 131 (RS.20.426Gt), 7′; 137 (RS.20.123t) II, 31′. *Laroche*, a, p. 258; *Heltzer*, c, p. 473.

[2] U. V, 137, III, 5; *Heltzer*, c, p. 478; *Laroche*, a, p. 274.

[3] *Heltzer*, c, p. 478.

[4] *Ibid* and *Aistleitner*, a, p. 90.

[5] *Heltzer*, c, p. 478-9 with the previous literature given.

Here, *bnšm* corresponds to Akkadian *mâru*^{MEŠ} *âl GN*, "sons of the village/town GN", i.e., members of a certain community.[6]

But dealing with the *arad šarri*, which is likely to correspond to *bnš mlk*, we must take text KTU 3.2:[7] (1) From the present day, (2) *Ammistamru*, (3) son of *Niqmepa*, (4) king of Ugarit, (5) gave the house of *Anndr*, son of (6) [*A*]*gytn*, *bnš* (7) of the king, which is in the village *Riš*, (8) [and g]ave (it) (9) [*to ʿb*]*dmlk*, (10) son of *Amtrn*, (11) [and to] his sons for (12) [ev]er. Nobody (13) shall take it (away) from them. (14) This house is in the hands of (15) *ʿbdmlk*, (16) son of *Amtrn*, (17) and in the ha[nds] of his sons forever, (18) [and] there is no *unṯ*-service from it."[8] It is a legal act by which the king transferred a land and a house from one person to another.[9] This allows us to equate *arad šarri* with *bnš mlk* and to translate that expression as "royal servant" or "royal dependent."

The *bnš mlk* appear in a number of other texts. We must first look at KTU 4.609 which deserves closer investigation:

1 *spr.ḥpr.bnš mlk.b yrḫ Iṯtb*[*nm*]
2 *Ršpab.rb.ʿšrt.mryn*
3 *Pġdn.Ilbʿl.Krwn.Lbn.ʿdn*
4 *Ḫyrn.Mdʿ*

---

5 *Šmʿn.rb ʿšrt.Kkln.ʿbd.Abṣn*
6 *Šdyn.Unn.Dqn*

---

7 *ʿbdʿnt.rb ʿšrt.Mnḥm.Ṯbʿm.Sḫr.ʿzn.Ilhd*

---

8 *Bnil.rb ʿšrt.Lkn.Ypʿn.Ṯ*[ ]*xab*

---

9 *yṣhm.bd.Ubn.Krwn.Tġd.Mnḥm*

---

10 *ʿpṯrm.Šmʿrgm.skn qrt.* - - - - - - - -[10]
11 *Ḥgbn.Šmʿ(šmʿrgm).skn.qrt*

---

[6] Cf. also *Liverani*, SDB, p. 1333-1334; 1338-39; and *Yamashita*, a, p. 46, where the essence of the question remains unanswered, despite the existence in 1975 of the studies explaining it.

[7] Cf. *Heltzer*, c, p. 479.

[8] *unṯ* — cf. Ch. II, pp. 16-22.

[9] Cf. also KTU 3.5, 16-18 *bnš bnšm l.yqḥnn.bd.Bʿln*, "nobody (lit. no man among men) shall take (it) away from the hands of *Bʿln*."

[10] Text erased.

12 *ṅgr krm.ʿbdadt.Bʿln.Ypʿmlk*

13 *ṯġrm.Mnḥm.Klyn.ʿdršp.Ġlmn*
14 [*A*]*bġl.Ṣṣn.Ġrn*

15 *šib.mqdšt.ʿbmlk.*[11] *Ṯṯpḥ.Mrṭn*

16 *ḫḏġlm.Il*[ ]*n.Pbn.Nḏbn.Sbd*

17 *šrm.Ṯ*[ ]×*.Ḫpn*

18 *ḥrš.b*[*htm*. . . .]*qn.ʿbdyrḫ.Ḥdṯn.Yʿr*
19 *Abdʿl.*[ ]×*.Ḥdṯn.Yḥmn.Bnil*

20 *ʿdn.w.Ildgn.ḥṭbm*

21 *tdġlm.Iln.Bʿln.Alḏy*

22 *Tdn.Ṣrṯ*[ ]×*t.ʿzn.Mtn.N*[ ]*lg*

23 *ḥrš qṭn*[.]*Dqn.Bʿln*
24 *Ġltn.ʿbd.A*[ ]×*n*

25 *nsk.ḥḏm.Klyn*[.]*Ṣ*[*d*]*qn.ʿbdilt.Btl*
26 *Annmn.ʿdy.Klby.Dqn.*

27 *ḥrṯm.Ḫgbn.ʿdn.Ynḥm*

28 *ḥrš.mrkbt.ʿZn.Bʿln.ṯb*[ ]×*lnb.Trtn*

29 [ ]*kmm.Klby.Kl*[ ]*y.Dqn*[ ]
30 [ ]×*ntn.Artn.Bdn*[.] *Nr* ×[ ]
31 *ʿzn.w Ymd.šr.bd Ansny*

32 *nsk.ksp*[.]*Amrtn.Kṯrmlk*
33 *Yḥmn.Aḫmlḳ.ʿbdrpu.Adn.Ṯ*[ ]×[ ]
34 *Bdn.Qln.Mtn.Ydln*

35 *bʿl tdtt.Tlgn.Ytn*

36 *bʿl tġpṯm.krwn.Ilšr.Agyn*

37 *Mnn.šr.Ugrt.Ḏkr.yṣr*

38 *Tgġln.ḫmš.ddm*

---

[11] Scribal omission instead of *ʿb<d>mlk*.

39 [ ]× *n.ḫmš.ddm*
(Lines 40-50 illegible)
51 *ṯṯ.l.ʿšrm.bn[š.mlk].ḫzr.lqḥ.ḥp[r]*
52 *ʿšt.ʿšrh.bn[š.mlk.]ḫ.zr.*

---

53 *bʿl šd*

1 "List of food-rations[12] (of the) king's men (royal servants) in the month of *Iṯtbnm.*[13]

---

2 *Ršpab*, the elder of ten (man),[14] the *maryannu*[15]
3 *Pġdn, Ilbʿl, Krwn.Lbn, ʿdn* 4 *Ḫyrn, Mdʿ*

---

5 *Šmʿn*, the elder of ten (man),[14] *Kkln, ʿbd, Abṣn,* 6 *Šdyn Unn, Dqn*

---

7 *ʿbdʿnt*, the elder of ten (man),[14] *Mnḥm, Ṯbʿm, Sḫr, ʿzn, Ilhd.*

---

8 *Bnil*, the elder of ten, *Lkn, Ypʿn, Ṯ*[ ]× *ab*[16]

---

9 Heralds[17] at the disposition[18] of *Ubn* — *Krwn, Tġd, Mnḥm*

---

10 *ʿpṯrm*[19] — *Šmʿrgm, sākinu*[21] (superintendant) of the village;
11 *Ḥgbn, Šmʿ* — *sākinu* of the village[20]

---

12 Guards[21] of the vineyard-*ʿbdat*; *Bʿln, Ypʿmlk*

---

13 Gatekeepers[22] — *Mnḥm, Klyn, ʿdršp, Ġlmn* 14 *[A]bġl, Ṣṣn, Ġrn*

---

15 Water-drawers[23] of the sanctuary — *ʿbdmlk, Ṯṯpḥ, Mrṭn*

---

[12] *ḥpr* — Akk. *epru*, "food ration"; UT. p. 398, No. 887.

[13] On the Ugaritic months cf. *Olivier*, a, pp. 53-59; *Iṯtbnm*, possibly August-September.

[14] Cf. below Ch. VIII, pp. 152-154.

[15] Cf. below Ch. VI, pp. 111-115.

[16] One(?) or two(?) persons.

[17] Root *ṣwh*, "to shout", Akk. *nāgiru*, cf. Ch. VIII.

[18] Lit. "in the hands."

[19] ZUL, VII, p. 95 and *Dietrich-Loretz*, f, p. 423; cf. in *Heltzer*, c, note 190 where *E. Lipinski* proposes that the name containes the theophorus element *ṯrm —šarruma.*

[20] Cf. Ch. VIII, pp. 150-152.

[21] St. cstr. pl.; cf. UT.

[22] Cf. below, Ch. IX, pp. 169-170.

[23] *š'b*, UT, p. 486, No. 2366.

16 Arrow-smiths[24] *Il*[ ]*n. Pbn, Nḏbn, Sbd*

17 Singers — *Ṯ*[ ]×, *H̱pn*

18 H[ouse]builders[25] [ ]*qn.ʿbdyrḫ, Ḥdṯn, Yʿr,* 19 *Adbʿl,* [ ]×, *Ḥdṯn, Yḥmn, Bnil.*

20 *ʿdn* and *Ildyn* — woodcutters[26]

21 *tdġlm*[27] — *Iln, Bʿln, Alḏy*
22 *Tdn, Ṣrṯ* [ ]×*t*[28], *ʿzn, Mtn.N*[ ]*lg*

23 *qṭn*-makers[29] [ ]*Dqn, Bʿln* 24 *Ġltn, ʿbd, A*[ ]×*n*

25 Arrow-casters — *Klyn, Ṣ[d]qn, ʿbdilt, Btn,* 26 *Annmn, Ady, Klby, Dqn*[29]

27 Ploughmen[30] — *Ḥgbn, ʿdn, Ynḥm*

28 Cartwrights — *ʿzn, Bʿln. Ṯb*[ ]×*l, Trtn*[31]

29 [ ]*kmm*'s[32] *Klby, Kl*[ ]*y, Dqn*[ ] 30 [ ]×*ntn, Artn, Bdn*[ ] *Nr* ×[ ], 31 *ʿzn*[33] and *Ymd,* the singer at the disposal of *Ansny.*

32 Silversmiths — *Amrtn, Kṯrmlk,* 33 *Yḥmn, Aḫmlk, ʿbdrpu, Adn, Ṯ*[ ]×[ ], 34 *Bdn, Qln, Mtn, Ydln*

35 *tdtt*-makers[34] — *Plgn, Ytn.*

---

[24] Cf. Ch. V, p. 92.

[25] Ch. V, pp. 86-87; *Yamashita*, a, p. 49, No. 10.

[26] Hebr. *ḥōṭēb*, "woodcutter"; *Yamashita*, a, p. 48, No. 8.

[27] *Dietrich-Loretz*, a, p. 201; ZUL, VII, p. 102; UT, p. 497, No. 2534 — exact meaning unknown.

[28] Seems to be the fourth person from the beginning of the line. No designation of profession.

[29] ZUL, VII, p. 100; artisan — Cf. *Freydank*, a, pp. 124-127.

[30] UT, p. 399, No. 905.

[31] Five persons.

[32] Profession unclear.

[33] At least 11 persons.

[34] ZUL, I, in BO, 23 (1966), p. 132 — *tdtt*, "Brustschmuck" — "pectoral" — Akk. *tudittu. bʿl/pʿl*, "to make, produce."

36 Makers of horse-clothes [35] — *Krwn*, *Ilštr*, *Agyn* 37 *Mnn*, the singer of Ugarit, *Ḏkr*-the potter.

---

38 (To) *Tgġln* — five *dd*-measures [36]

---

39 [ ] — five *dd*-measures.

(Lines 40-50 are broken and illegible — they may be, in part, at least, also a list of various measure units of food products)

51 Twenty-six [royal se]rvants. [ ] persons [37] (?) took food-rations

52 eleven [royal se]rvants [ ] persons [37]

---

53 Field-owners" [38]

We see that in the above text various professionals are listed among the "royal servants." They are divided into various groups according to their professions, receive month food deliveries and possess fields.

The other important text which mentions the *bnš mlk* is KTU 4.141. Col. I. (1) *[sp]r.bnš.ml[k.d.]bd.Adn[ʿm]* (2) *[bg]t Riš[*], "(1) [Li]st of roy[al] servants, [which (are)] at the disposal of *Adn[ʿm]* (2) at the *gt Riš[*]" [39] (Lines 3-21 list 19 personal names without the names of their fathers; lines 22-25 are totally illegible; Col. II, lines 1-23 again list 23 personal names). Col. II. (24) *ḫmšm ṯmn.kbd* (25) *tgmr.bnš.mlk* (26) *d.bd.Adnʿm* "(24) Twenty-eight in all [40] (25) (the) total of the royal servants (26) at the disposal of *Adnʿm*."

Col.III

1 *[š]bʿ.b.ḥrṯm*	"[S]even at the (*gt*) of the ploughmen (*Ḥrṯm*)
2 *[ṯ]lṯ.b.ṯġrm*	[th]ree at the (*gt*) of the gatekeepers (*Ṯġrm*)

---

[35] "Caparisons" — *E. Lipinski* in *Heltzer*, c, note 199. Akk. *epiš taḫapši*, AHw, p. 1301.

[36] *dd* — measure unit, Hebrew. *dūd*; capacity unknown; cf. *Liverani*, SDB, p. 1333.

[37] *Heltzer*, O, pp. 410-412, (with the preceding literature).

[38] Here *bʿl*, "owner," and not *b/pʿl*, "workers" (pl.st.cstr.). We see that these professionals were not agricultural workers, so they had to be the field-owners.

[39] The reconstruction *[b]n* in KTU is unconvincing. There is enough space at the beginning of the line for *b* and *g*, and the *t* is preserved. Therefore *[b.g]t*; *Gt* — Ch. IV, pp. 49-79.

[40] *Kbd* — *Liverani*, b, pp. 89-109.

3	*rb.qrt.aḥd*	One *rb* of the village[41]
4	*ṯmn.ḫzr*	Eight persons
5	*w.arbʿ.ḥršm*	and 4 builders,
6	*dt.tbʿln b.Pḫn*	which worked at *Pḫn*[42]
7	*ṯṯm.ḫzr.w.ʿšt.ʿšr ḥrš*	Twelve[43] persons and 11 builders
8	*d.tbʿln.b.Ugrt*	which worked in Ugarit.
9	*ṯṯm.ḫzr*	Twelve persons,
10	*dt.tbʿln*	which worked
11	*b.gt.Ḥrṯm*	On the *gt Ḥrtm* (of the ploughmen)
12	*ṯn.ḥršm*	Two builders,
13	*ṯn.ḥršm*	two builders[44]
14	*b.Nbkm*	at the *(gt) Nbkm*[39]
15	*b.gt.Ġl*	at the *gt* (of) *Ġl*[39]
16	[*ṯn*] *nġr mdrʿ*	[two] guards of the corn (field)
17	[*aḥ*]*d nġr.krm*	[on]e guard of the vineyard[45]
18	[ ]*psl.qšt*	[(figure)] fashioners of bows[46]
19	[*ṯl*]*ṯ.psl.ḥẓm*	[thr]ee fashioners of arrows[46]
20	[*ḥ*]*rš.mrkbt*	[(figure)] of cartwrights[46]
21	[ ]*ʿšrh* [ ]*p*	[ ] teen [of]
23	[*ḫm*]*š.ʿšrh*[ ]	[fif]teen [ ]
Col. IV		
1	*ḫmš.ʿšrh*	Fifteen
2	*šrm*	singers."

We also know other texts where the *bnš mlk*, "king's men" or "servants of the king" are mentioned in connection with various jobs or deliveries. For

---

[41] *rb* — Cf. Ch. VIII.

[42] Name of an otherwise unattested *gt*.

[43] Dual form of *ṯṯ*, "six".

[44] Twice written *ṯn ḥrṯm* — a scribal error.

[45] Cf. above KTU 4.609, 12.

[46] Cf. below, Ch. V, pp. 80-92.

example, KTU 4.144. (1) *spr.bnš.mlk* (2) *d.bd.Prṯ*, "(1) List of the royal dependents (2) which are at the disposal of *Prṯ*."[47]

KTU 4.367 (1) [*S*]*pr.bnš.mlk.d.b.Tbq*, "[L]ist of royal dependents, which are in *Tbq* (or at the *gt Tbq*)."[48] The text is only partly preserved, but we see from line 8 *yṣr.aḥd*, "one potter," that at least one professional was mentioned here.

KTU.4.370 (1) *spr.bnš.mlk.* (2) *d.taršn. ʿmsn.* "(1) List of royal dependents, (2) who were ordered by *ʿmsn* (P.N.)."[49] Lines 3-13 list 13 personal names (14) *ḥrš bhtm*, "house-builders," followed by 20 personal names in lines 15-34. (35) *ḥrš qṭn*, "*qatinnu*-workers"[50]; 9 names follow in lines 36-44, and (45) *pslm. Ṣnr*, "sculptors — *Ṣnr* — (only one person). Thus, according to the demand of *ʿmsn*, royal servants of various professions were put at his disposal.

We must take into consideration that the texts at our disposal were composed for purposes of bookkeeping only. They are lists of deliveries, accounts of royal officials, etc., and not all operations are detailed exhaustively nor are there many details given concerning the "king's men" or "royal dependents." Only the four above-mentioned texts specifically refer to the various groups of professionals listed as *bnš mlk*. However, it seems that other texts, in which people are mentioned who are at the disposal of the king, deal with the same *bnš mlk*. There are the following tablets:

Text KTU 4.339. The first line of this tablet tells us about *bnšm.dt.l.Ugrt.ṯb*, "People who are dwelling in[51] Ugarit." In lines 2-15 thirteen persons are mentioned together with their wives and other family members, and line 16 *Ṣlmn.ḥrš.mrkbt*, "*Ṣlmn* — cartwright." After the dividing line of the text we read (17) *bnšm.dt.l.mlk*, "The persons who are at the disposal of the king." Thus we see that they were the *bnšm* who were at the disposal of the king, i.e., *bnš mlk*. There are eleven personal names appearing in lines 18-28, along with the names of their wives and other family-members.

[47] Lines 3-6 mention only 29 and 48 without their names and confirm what pay they received.

[48] *Ṭbq*/*Tbq*/*Tipakku*, cf. Ch. IV.

[49] UT, p. 452, No. 1872, "shipment, load (of supplies)." We consider *ʿmsn* as a personal name; *arš*, in Ugaritic "to demand," "to choose" — *Heltzer*, e, p. 11.

[50] Cf. above and Ch. V, pp. 88-89.

[51] *ṯb* from the root *y*/*wṯb*, "to dwell", "to sit" and here appears the late Ugaritic form of 3p.Plur.Part (**ṯabū*).

Among them is (24) *Anntn.yṣr*, "*Anntn*, the potter." So among the people listed were professionals, but this is not especially noted in these lapidary tablets.

Text KTU 4.635. (1) *[bnšm.d]* [52] *bd.mlk*, "[People, who (are)] at the disposal of the king." And the second line: (2) *[bnšm.d.]bd mlkt*, "[People who (are)] at the disposal of the queen." [53] People are listed here by name "*bd* (at the disposal) of the king" (ll. 3, 57) the queen (l. 6) the vizier (*skn*) [54] (ll. 9, 11, 12, 37, 75). Among the persons listed in the text we see foreigners, people from Ašdod (*Adddy* — ll. 16, 20-27, 29-35, 38-40, 42, 44) as well as professionals: *mḫṣ* — guards [55] and a *mdrġl* — guard (l. 18).[56] The fact that professionals and foreigners are listed together who were at the disposal of the king, queen and the vizier, shows us one of the origins of the *bnš mlk* — among other people of foreign origin.

In text KTU 4.182, 56 we read: [ ]*rt.mḫs.bnš.mlk.yb'lhn.*, "[ ].. the guard, servant of the king make them." (The text tells about textiles and other goods.) [57]

We have now seen that among the *bnš mlk*, in those texts where the term is clearly used, there appear people of various categories of professions. Among them we find: a) military servicemen, such as *maryannu*, *mdrġlm* and other guards, b) administrative personnel such as elders over ten (men), heralds, *sākinu* (resp. *rb*) of the village (*qrt*), guards of the sown and vineyard, gatekeepers (of the palace?), etc., c) temple-personnel such as water-drawers of the sanctuary, singers (perhaps also palace singers), d) arrow-smiths of various kinds, housebuilders, woodcutters, *qatinnu*-makers, cart-wrights, silversmiths, makers of horse-cloths, potters, fashioners of bows, sculptors, e) people of purely agricultural professions such as ploughmen, and persons of other professions. Sometimes these *bnš mlk* are designated as

---

52 Reconstruction according to the parallel passages in the same text.

53 Possibly the queen-mother. Cf. Ch. X and text KTU 4.22 (CTA.138) (3) *b'lṣn bnš* (4) *mlkt*, "*B'lṣn*, dependent of the queen."

54 *skn*, Ch. VIII, pp. 141-149.

55 Cf. below, Ch. VI, pp. 123-124 and WUS, No. 1574, "Schleuder-oder-Schlage-waffe."

56 Cf. below, Ch. VI, pp. 115-121.

57 Cf. also the fragmentary KTU 4.766 including originally at least 12 personal names and (13) [*bn*]*š*, *d.bt.mlk*, "[The *bun*]*ušu* of the royal palace"; KTU 4.151 lists of personal names, but Col. II, (1) *tgmr* (2) *yṣḥm* (3) *ṯlṯm* (4) *aḥd* (5) *kbd* (6) *bnš mlk*, "Total-heralds 31 in all royal dependents."

being at the disposal of a certain person mentioned by name, maybe some kind of overseer or manager of royal work, maybe even the overseer of ten men. All this enables us to conclude that the numerous other alphabetic texts from Ugarit where we again see a) the above-mentioned professions in the above-given texts b) other professionals of a similar kind, and c) they are designated as being at the disposal of a certain person given by name, are referring to *bnš mlk*, "royal dependents", even in those cases where the whole term is omitted and instead only a brief designation, *bnš*, is given.

We have no specific designation for everyone of the *bnš mlk* since for a certain period of time it was accepted, following a study of *A. Alt*, that royal dependents were called according to the names of their fathers only.[58] *A. Alt* reached this conclusion in a legitimate manner, for in 1950 there were only several name-lists from Ugarit. Today we see that sometimes the same persons were mentioned in one tablet by their own name and their father's name, and in another text only according to the name of their father, "son of x." [59] This proves our thesis that the writing or omission of all the elements of a person's name in Ugarit did occur, especially if we take into account the lapidary character of the lists.

According to tablet KTU 4.125 we have the *bnšm* of various *gt*'s,[60] as well as *ḥrš anyt*, "shipwrights" (l. 1), *rʿym*, "shepherds" (l. 4), *tdġlym*,[61] 10 millers[62] together with their apprentices,[63] — (8) *ʿšr.ksdm.yd lmdhm*, "10 guards together with their apprentices, — (9) *ʿšr mḫṣm yd lmdhm*, "10 cooks or bakers", — (10) *apym*, "vineyard-workers, — (17) *gpny*[64], and "fullers" — (19) *kbsm*[65]. They all receive certain product deliveries.

Tablet KTU 4.29 mentions: (1) *khnm.tšʿ* (2) *bnšm w.ḥmr* (3) *qdšm tšʿ.bnšm. w.ḥmr*, "(1) Priests — nine (2) persons (*bnšm*) and (one) donkey (3) Diviners — nine persons and one donkey."[66]

---

[58] *Alt, d, pp. 9-24.*

[59] Cf. Ch. VII, pp. 131-136; texts where the same priests are named differently in various tablets and *Heltzer*, a, p. 31, where we see the same thing according to KTU 4.371 and 4.366.

[60] Cf. Ch. IV.

[61] Cf. above.

[62] *ksdym* — cf. Ch. V.

[63] *lmd* — UF, p. 428, No. 1385, "apprentice, pupil."

[64] Hebr. *gefen*, "vine" (Pl.st.cstr).

[65] Cf., Ch. V and *Yamshita*, a, p. 54, No. 17, Hebr. *kōbēs*; UT, p. 417, No. 1193, "launderer."

[66] *khnm* and *qdšm*, cf. Ch. VII.

Text KTU 4.277 begins with the word (1) *bnš* and in lines 1-9, 18 persons are listed by name. (9) ...*ḥrš* of bows(?) (10) *Blšš.lmd*, "the bows(?) builder (10) *Blšš*, the apprentice. Lines 11-12 contain 4 names and l. 13 *śǵr.Ilydn*, "the small one[67] *Ilgdn*." So we seen that both the *lmd(m)* and *śǵr* were persons subdued to the *bnš mlk*.

Similar problems arise from KTU 4.138. (1) *ḫmš bnšm*[ ] (2) *ḫḏǵlm bd* [*PN*], "(1) 5 *bnš*'s [ ] (2) arrowsmiths at the disposal [PN]." The following lines (3-9) give us from 1-7 *lmd(m)*, "apprentices," "at the disposal of PN" (bd PN).

KTU 4.243 talks about seeds (*dr'*) 68 and rations (*ḥpr*) of the *bnšm*. Among the recipients are the cartwrights — waggonbuilders — *ḥrš 'rq*.[69] The *bnšm*, such as shepherds (*r'ym*) appear again together with their subordinates (*yd sǵrh*).

KTU 4.618 considers *bnšm* at various *gt*'s who are mentioned together with pairs of oxen and donkeys.[70] *Bnš(m)* and their servants, dependents (*sǵrm*), are listed in the text KTU 4.343.

KTU 4.395 tells about pay (*šślmt*)[71] to *bnšm d.b.u*[ ], "People (*bnšm*), which are in (or at) [ ]." According to this text 16 people receive pay.

KTU 4.358: (1) *bt alpm* (2) *'šr bnšm*, "House of the oxen (cattleshed)[72] — 10 *bnšm*", who seemed to be the personnel of the royal economy. In lines 3-7 various numbers of people are designated at various *gt*'s and they were attached to *'dnm (yd 'dnm)*. But according to the last lines there were also (9) *arb' ǵzlm* (10) *ṯn yṣrm*, "four spinners (and) two potters,"[73] This text is especially important for the understanding of the organization of the royal economy.[74]

---

[67] Akk. *ṣeḫru*, *ṣuhārum*; Hebr. *ṣā'īr*; In Akkadian this term designates also an underprivileged person; cf. *Finet*, a, pp. 65-72.

[68] Hebr. *zera'*.

[69] *'rq* — Akk. *ereqqu*, "waggon", cf. ZUL, II; OLZ, 62, 1967, p. 545.

[70] Cf. KTU 4.222 (1) *bnšm.dt.iṯ.alpm lhm*, "Persons (dependents(?)) who have oxen." Originally there were 98 personal names but it is very difficult to tell if these are *bnš mlk*, or if they are simple villagers. The same problem arises with KTU 4.380 and 4.617 (1) [*bn*]*šm.dt i*[ ]*b.bth*, "The persons (*bunušu*) which [ ] their house," at least 82 persons are listed by name.

[71] Cf. Ch. III, pp. 43-48.

[72] Presumably for burden-cattle.

[73] *Virolleaud*, PRU, V, 127; NKTU, p. 34; UT. p. 463, No. 1955.

[74] Cf. also the fragments KTU 4.398; 4.653; 4.351.

A donkey-driver is designated as (12) *bnš ḥm[r*, "the *bunušu* of the donk[ey(s)" in KTU 1.86 which is in a bad state of preservation.

Special interest has to be paid to KTU 4.752:

1 *bnšm.d.iṯ.bd.rb.ʿprm*	"The *bnš(mlk)*, which are at the disposal of the elder (great) of the *eperu (ḫab/piru)*."[75]

Unfortunately, it is unclear what the connection of the *ḫab/piru-ʿprm* with the *bnš mlk* in Ugarit was. The following lines of the texts are:

2 *mr[ynm]ṯn*	"the *maryannu* — two
3 *ṯn[nm] aḥd*	the *šanānu* — one[76]
4 *ʿ[šrm] ṯlṯ*	the *ašīru* (overseers of ten) — three
5 *qdšm arbʿ*	diviner-priests — four
6 *khnm arbʿ*	priests — four
7 *mrʾu Ibrn aḥd*	the liaison-officers of *Ibiranu* — one[77]

Further on the text becomes illegible, but we see that the king could hand over his military elite — the *maryannu*, liaison-officers and priests to the disposal of the *rb ʿprm* — "elder of the *ḫab/piru*". This, again, shows the degree of dependence of the *bnš mlk* on the royal authorities.

The texts given above make it convenient to treat the remaining numerous Ugaritic texts[78] in which royal dependents are mentioned without the term *bnš mlk*, but are listed according to their professions and professional groups. We see that payments and deliveries were made to them, that they performed their obligations, etc. We will reintroduce them at the appropriate point in the text which deals with the organization of the royal economy and the various professional groups which the author has drawn together in a more comprehensive manner according to the larger branches into which these groups are gathered. We must emphasize that all of these groups of people, even those who were more privileged, were royal service people or "royal dependents," i.e. they, in contrast to the villagers of the kingdom derived their main or only source of income from their service, receiving payment in kind, silver, land, etc. As we saw in KTU 4.609 the

---

[75] *ʿprm — ḫab/piru* = SA.GAZ in Ugarit; cf. *Goetze*, a, pp. 32-34 and recently *Botteró*, a, pp. 14-27.

[76] Cf. Ch. VI, pp. 122-123.

[77] *mrum*, cf. Ch. VIII, pp. 154-156 and *Heltzer*, f.

[78] About 200 tablets and fragments of them in Ugaritic and Akkadian.

distributions of products were monthly. Later we will see what their obligations as subjects of the king were in general, and what they were with respect to their professions.

We must also point out that the *lmdm*, "apprentices," and *sġrm*, "small ones" or "subjects", of certain professionals belonged to the same ration systems as the *bnš mlk*. In the chapters which follow there will be an analysis of their role, as well as the role of others designated as the subjects of some professionals among the *bnš mlk*. But it seems almost certain that these subjects of the *bnš mlk* were identical to the *ardē ardē šarri*, "servants of the servants of the king," in the same way the *ardē šarri*, "servants of the king," were identical to the *bnš mlk*, "royal men" or "royal dependents."[79]

[79] Cf. also *Oelsner*, a, pp. 117-123, where the author reaches the conclusion about the existence of various groups of royal dependents but without the use of a special term designating all of them.

CHAPTER II

TAXES AND CORVÉE NOT CONNECTED WITH THE PROFESSIONAL SERVICE (BUT INVOLVING THE "ROYAL DEPENDENTS")

Royal dependents in all professional groups had to perform various corvée-work, as well as pay certain taxes to the royal authorities which were not directly connected with their professional service to the royal authorities or the obligations they shared with all the subjects of the king of Ugarit.[1] In this chapter we will discuss all known kinds of corvée and taxes and other obligations.

I. Akk. *ilku*/Ug. *hlk*.[2] Corvée — mostly placed on Ugaritic villages and villagers of the village-communities. These may, in some cases, include royal servicemen.

1. KTU 4.33. (1) *spr mḏrġlm* (2) *dt hlk b*[ ]. "List of *mḏrġlm*-guards,[3] who performed their *ilku* in [ ]." Lines 3-41 list 39 persons by name.
2. KTU 4.153. A fragment. The first preserved line relates concerning *ilk r*ʿ[*ym*]:[4] The *ilku*-corvée of the shepherds (and later the text relates about the families of the shepherds).
3. RS.34.147 (U. VII). It is possible that people of Ugariṭ or Karkemish. (2) *ša la-bi-ir* DIRIG *(neqelpu)* [iṣ]*eleppu aš-la-im* (3) *a-na a-la-ki a-ya-kam-ma*, "which like in former time (traditionally dragged by ropes the vessels on going (or performing their *ilku*-service) elsewhere." Naturally, the *ilku* of the villages is not mentioned here.

---

[1] These questions will also be treated in the chapters treating the larger branches of the professional groups of the "royal dependents."

[2] We will not consider here all the *ilku*-obligations of the villages and villagers of the Kingdom of Ugarit; cf. *Heltzer*, a, pp. 18-47; cf. also Bibl-Aram. *hālāk* — Esr. 4, 13, 20; 7, 24.

[3] Cf. *Heltzer*, g, p. 129; *Dietrich-Loretz*, a, p. 198 and Ch. VI, pp. 115-123.

[4] [*m*] — *our reconstruction.*

II. Ug. *unṯ* / Akk. *unuššu*.[5] As the author of this study has shown,[6] based on the land-transaction documents in Akkadian and Ugaritic, we must agree with the existing view that the *unṯ*/*unuššu* was performed as a corvée-service, in which the royal dependents were sometimes also involved. The *unṯ*/*unuššu*, as we see from documents PRU, III, 15.89; 15,156; 16,167; KTU 3.4; 3.2; 2.19; 3.5; 3.7; KTU 4.209; 4.86, is always connected with the "house" (*É*, *bîtu*, *bt*) whether the persons involved are royal dependents or not.[7] It is also important that in Alalaḫ of the XVth century B.C.E., the *unuššu* is always connected with "houses."[8]

The origin of the term, as shown by *Diakonoff*, is Hurrian and it is etymologically the equivalent of the Akkadian *ilku*, lit. "going."[9] But, in our opinion, in Ugarit of the XIV-XIIIth century B.C.E. at least, it received a new meaning and there are differences in the real meanings of *ilku*, *pilku* and *unuššu* as was shown above.

III. Ug. *ḫrd*/Akk. *ḫurādu*.[10] This term, as has been shown,[11] designates a temporary mobilization of the villagers of Ugarit, including the royal dependents according to their professional groups, for military service. In such a mobilization the professional groups of military professions were also included, for example the *maryannu* and *mḏrġlm*. The *ḫrd*-mobilizations concerned all the population groups (non-slave) in Ugarit. For us it is important that the royal servicemen had to participate also. Various other military obligations were also imposed on the villagers and royal professionals.[12]

---

[5] *Heltzer*, p; cf. *Heltzer*, Q, pp. 5-12; The former literature concerning *unṯ*/*unuššu* SSAU, I, WO, III, pp. 194-195; SSAU, IV, ZA, 60, 1970, pp. 99-100 and 120; *Nougayrol*, PRU, III, p. 227; WUS, p. 29, No. 325; UT, p. 363, No. 275; *Hillers*, a, pp. 252-259; *Loretz*, a, p. 449; *Boyd*, a, p. 47; *Heltzer*, c, pp. 479-480; *Liverani*, SDB, p. 1343; *Kienast*, a, pp. 443-51.

[6] *Heltzer*, Q, pp. 10-12.

[7] Cf. *Heltzer*, Q, pp. 5-12.

[8] AT, 193, 23; 198, 1; 199, 33; 200, 21; cf. *Laroche*, a, p. 284; SSAU, IV, ZA, 60, 1970, pp. 99-100 and 120.

[9] *Diakonoff*, a.

[10] The Akkadian term is also frequently attested in Middle Assyrian texts; cf. *Freydank*, a, pp. 111-115.

[11] Cf. Ch. VI, pp. 106-111 and *Heltzer*, k, pp. 245-253.

[12] Cf. Ch. VI, pp. 103-112.

We also see that the professional groups of the *bnš mlk* had to participate in the tribute payments to the Hittite king which was imposed on the villagers of Ugarit as well. KTU 4.610 has the headline (1) [*spr.*] *argmn.Špš*, "[List] of the tribute[13] of the Sun (i.e. Hittite king)." Both columns of the obverse side of the tablet contain from line 2-83 names of villages, every one of which had to pay (according to the preserved lines and figures) from 3 shekels (II, 24 *Ḫlby*) to 152 (I, 15 *Ilštmʿ*). The reverse of the text contains the listing of the professional groups of royal servicemen (*bnš mlk*). Originally in both columns (III and IV) were the names of 38 professional groups who had to pay from 2 (III, line 60) to 40[+ ×] (IV, line 47) shekels of silver (cf. also 46 shekels in III, 53). Unfortunately, only lines IV, 44-48 are legible. The professionals who had to participate in the Hittite tribute were (44) *mr*[*u i*]*br*[*n*] [×] (45) *mru skn*[14] 13[+ ×]; (46) *šrm* "singers" — 20; (47) *kbsm*, "fullers"[15] — 8 (48) [*i*]*nšt*, "royal personnel (?)"[16] — 25 (shekels of silver)."[17] (The total follows: (IV, 50-55), but it is impossible to calculate even the total sum of the payment by the professional groups.)

As the *unuššu*/*unṯ* and the *ḫrd*/*ḫurādu*-mobilization showed, so also the tribute to the Hittite king shows a third group of taxes and obligations common to both main categories of population in Ugarit.

IV. We have only a few examples of some taxes which sometimes only some groups of *bnš mlk* had to pay. Among these are the pasture-tax — *maqqādu* (MA.GAD) known from text PRU, VI, 116 (RS.17.64), where payment had to be made to the treasury by the villagers of Nanu, *aširu*-men and the *mur'u* for pasturing their cattle.[18]

V. There were certain taxes which only one group was obliged to pay. For example, a) the tamkars, some of whom were known as *tamkārē*^{MEŠ} *ša*

[13] *Heltzer*, a, pp. 31-33 with the full analysis of the text, concerning the village communities; dealing with the professional groups of the *bnš mlk*, the readings in KTU, 4.620 are improved; *argmn*, "tribute"; cf. *Pardee*, a, pp. 277-278. *Rabin*, a, pp. 136-152; the word *arkamannu* is of Hittite origin.

[14] Cf. Ch. VI and VIII, pp. 107-108 and 141-149.

[15] Cf. Ch. V, p. 90.

[16] *Dietrich-Loretz*, c, p. 50 — Akk. *nišūtu*, "Blutsverwandschaft, Sippe" — may be also "dependent palace personnel" (?).

[17] Possibly Column III line 46 has to be read [*mry*]*nm* 30[+ ×]; (47) [*n*ʾ]*rm* — 40[+ ×]; (48) [*m*]*dm* — 20[+ ×], but it is far from certain.

[18] *Heltzer*, c, pp. 476-478; *Heltzer*, l, pp. 9-13; *Rainey*, b, p. 46.

mandatti,[19] had to pay the king the "silver of their *mandattu*-obligation."[20] The *mandattu* was, in our opinion, a "compulsory gift of the tamkars — for legal protection abroad and for certain sums which they received from the royal authorities of Ugarit which carried with them an obligation towards the royal authorities.[21] But, we cannot exclude this as part of the *pilku ša tamkarūti*, "*pilku*-service of the tamkarship," expressed in the text PRU, VI, 30 (RS.18.500, 8-10).[22] b) A similar tax may have been from the *mūdū šarri* (resp. *šarrati*) which a "frind of the king (resp. queen)" had to pay and which came to 5-20 shekels of silver a year paid to the royal authorities.[23]

VI. *Ubdy* had to be paid by the *bnš mlk* for the fields that they received as grants into conditional holding on account of their service (Ch. III).[24] At least a part of these fields was attached to certain royal *gt*'s, i.e., units of the royal economy, where they had to do their farming.[25] We will see in Ch. IV that sometimes the professionals, *bnš mlk* of various professional groups, had to work on the *gt*'s not according to their profession, but in other capacities.

Thus, we see that there were a variety of taxes and obligations which the royal dependents in Ugarit had to pay or perform. These included the collective tax or corvée — the *ilku*, the individual land or other immovable tax or corvée — *unuššu*, the professional service — *pilku* (cf. below), and also the mobilization — *ḫrd*/*ḫurādu*. We also see that there were the specific obligations of some professional groups referred to above.

What happened to persons who did not perform their obligations? These persons were called *nayyālu*, literally "the (person) who did not perform his obligations."[26] This Akkadian term is known only from Ugarit and Middle-Assyrian texts.[27] In some cases the *nayyālu* were villagers, members of the

---

19 PRU, IV, 17.146, 28-29.

20 *kasap ša ma-an-da-at-ti-šu*, PRU, IV, 17.130, 21; cf. *Heltzer*, b, pp. 126-127.

21 Cf. *Heltzer*, b, pp. 128-131.

22 *Heltzer*, b, p. 124.

23 *Heltzer*, h. Table and p. 351; Ch. VIII, pp. 161-163.

24 Cf. Ch. III, pp. 23-48.

25 Cf. Ch. IV, pp. 49-79.

26 *Heltzer*, a, p. 51; Cf. another view *Kienast*, a, pp. 439-440.

27 *Postgate*, a, pp. 508-512; concerning the etymology of the word cf. *Heltzer*, m, pp. 78-84.

village-communities, and they have been treated in our previous works.[28] Now we must consider the royal dependents in those cases where they became *nayyālu*-people.

We must again consider 1. PRU, III, 15,Y, where we see that the King Arḫalbu, son of Niqmaddu II (4) *it-ta-ši bîta eqlātē*^{MEŠ} (5) *ša* ^{I}*Bin-Ḫa-at-ti-ya-ma* (6) ^{amel}*na-ya-li ù id-din-šu* (7) *a-na* ^{I}*Tup-pi-ya-na* (8) *ù ip-ṭur-šu* (9) *iš-tu* ^{amelMEŠ}*aškapūti*^{ti} (10) *ù iš-ku-un-šu* (11) *i-na* ^{amelMEŠ}*ZAG.LU*, "took (away)[29] the house and fields of *Bin-Ḫatiyama*, the *nayyālu*, and gave it to *Tuppiyanu*. And he (the king) freed him from the leather-workership and put him to the bronze-caster." So, *Tuppiyanu* has to perform his professional *pilku*. It is reasonable to suppose that the *nayyālu* deprived of the land was also one of the *bnš mlk*.

2. PRU, III, 15.145, where Ammistamru II (4) *it-ta-ši 4 ikī eqla*^{H} *ù* $^1/_3$ *ikā eqla* (5) *ù* $^5/_6$ *ikā* ^{iṣ}*karāna qa-du* ^{iṣ}*serdi*^{MEŠ}*-šu* (6) *qa-du: ḫi-i-ya-ša ša* ^{I}*Ili-ya-na* (7) *mâr Pu-uš-ma-na* ^{amel}*na-ya-li* (8) *i-na eqli: aṭ-ma-na* (9) *ù 5(?) ikī eqla*^{H} (10) *ù* $^1/_2$ *ikā* ^{iṣ}*karāna qa-du* ^{iṣ}*serdi*^{MEŠ}*-šu* (11) *[qa-du] ḫi-i-ya-šu ša* ^{I}*Ka-ar-zi* (12) $^{[amel]}$*na-ya-li i-na eqli aṭ-ma-ni* (13) *[ù i]d-din-šu-nu šarru* (14) *[a-na]Kur-wa-na mâr* ^{il}*Ba'ala-az-ki* (15) *ù a-na mâri*^{MEŠ}*-šu a-di da-r[i]-ti*, "took (away) 4 *iku* of field and $^1/_3$ *iku* field and $^5/_6$ *iku* vineyard together with its olive-grove together with living (houses)[30] of *Iliyanu*, son of *Pušmanu*, the *nayyālu* in the fields of *Aṭmanu* (place-name) and 5(?) *iku* field and $^1/_2$ *iku* vineyard together with its olive groove (11) [together]-with its living (houses) of *Kazzi*, the *nayyālu* in the fields of *Aṭmanu* and the king gave it to *Kurwanu*, son of *Baalazku* and to his sons forever." Further, we have the following passage (14) *ù píl-ka ia-nu ina eqli*^{H} *an-nu-ti*, "And there is no *pilku* service from these fields." It may be that formerly these fields were grant fund for the royal dependents and they had to perform their *pilku*-service, but the next recipient is a privileged person and he is freed from the *pilku*. So also, the *nayyālu* could be royal dependents, deprived of their grants.

3. PRU, III, 15.122. Once again Ammistamru II (4) */it-ta-ši* (5) *[bîta]-eqla*^{H} *qa-du* ^{bit}*dimti-šu* (6) *[qa-du* ^{iṣ}*s]erdi*^{MEŠ}*-šu* ^{iṣ}*karāni*^{MEŠ}*-šu* (7) *[ša A-dal-š]e-en-ni* (8) *[mâr*^{I}*...]a-na* ^{amel}*na-ya-lu* (9) *[ù eqlāt*^{MEŠ}*] al-la-ni* (lines 11-12 illegible)

---

[28] *Heltzer*, a, pp. 52-57; *Heltzer*, n, pp. 47-48.

[29] On this formula cf. *Greenfield*, a, pp. 88-89, concerning the *našū-nadānu* as a transferring formula for property, especially royal grants.

[30] Root *Ḥy/wy*, cf. *Boyd*, a, p. 14.

(13) *[ù i]t-ta-din-šu-nu* (14) ^{I}*A-mis-tam-ru šár* ^{al}*Ù-ga-ri-it* (15) *a-na* ^{I}*Kabit-ya-na* (16) *ù bîta eqla*^{H} ^{iṣ}*serdi*^{MEŠ} ^{iṣ}*karāni*^{MEŠ} (17) *ša* ^{I}*Ki-il-pi-ib-ri* ^{amel}*šatammi* (18) *i-na* ^{al}*Uḫ-nap-pi* (19) *ù it-ta-din-šu-nu* (20) ^{I}*A-mis-tam-ru mâr* ^{I}*Niq-me-pa* (21) *šár* ^{al}*Ú-ga-ri-it* (22) *a-na* ^{I}*Kabit-ya-na a-di da-ri-ti* (23) *i-na* $_{2}$*ûmi*^{MEŠ} *balāṭi gamri-šu* (24) *[amēlu ma-am-m]a-an la ì-la-qi-šu-nu* (25) *[iš-tu qâtē]* ^{I}*Kabit-ya-na* (26) *[ù* ^{I}*Kabit-y]a-nu 2 me-at kaspa* (27) *[a-na šimti*^{i}*]*^{i}*-šu it-ta-din* (28) *[a-na* ^{I}*A-m]is-tam-ri mâr* ^{I}*Niq-me-pa* (29) *[šàr* ^{al}*Ú]-ga-ri-it* (30) *[an-nu-ú] pil-ka-šu ša* ^{amel}*šatammūti*^{ti}, "Took (away) [the house], field together with its *dimtu*[31], [together wi]th its olive groves, (and) vineyards, [*of Adalše*]*nnu*, son of [ ]*anu*, the *nayyālu*, [and the fields] *Allani (?)* [lines 11-12] [and] Ammistamru the king of Ugarit [ga]ve them to *Kabityanu*. And (he took) the house, field, olive groves, vineyards of *Kilpibri*, the *šatammu* in (the village) *Uḫnappu* and Ammistamru, son of Niqmepa, King of Ugarit gave them to *Kabityanu* forever — to all his days of life.[32] [Nobod]y shall take it [from] *Kabityanu*. [And *Kabity*]*anu* shall give 200 (shekels) silver [as its pri]ce, to Ammistamru, son of Niqmepa [king of U]garit. [He] (i.e. *Kabityanu*) shall perform the *pilku*-service of the šatammuship".[33]

So *Kabityanu* received various lands for his *šatammu*-service, which the king took away from the *nayyālu*.[34]

4. PRU, III, 15.141 relates that Ammistamru II withdrew the fields of *Kurbanu*, son of *Niltanu*, the *nayyālu*, "in the fields, of *Ṣa'u* together with all his possessions. Here, it seems, we are dealing with a villager, but further on the text adds: (11) *ù eqlāt*^{MEŠ} ^{I}*Ya-qu-ri* ^{amel}*šatammi* (12) *ša i-na eqlāti*^{MEŠ} *Ṣa-i*, "And the fields of *Yaquru*, the *šatammu*, which be in the fields of *Ṣáu*." The fact that preceding this passage the text deals with a *nayyālu*, allows us to suppose that *Yaquru*, the *šatammu*, was also a *nayyālu*, i.e., someone who did not perform his obligatory service.[35] (The following lines of the text are broken.)

We come to the conclusion that just as the villager who did not perform his obligations was a *nayyālu*, and was deprived of his land-possessions, the

---

[31] *dimtu*, cf. Ch. IV, pp. 49-79.

[32] We have here a mixture of the formulae of: a) donating, b) granting for lifetime for service. The second formula is correct in this case.

[33] *šatammu*, cf. Ch. VIII, pp. 164-166.

[34] Cf. also PRU, III, 16.174; *Heltzer*, a, p. 54.

[35] Concerning the etymology of the word *nayyālu*, cf. *Heltzer*, m, pp. 83-84 and *Boyer*, a, p. 130; *Rainey*, c, p. 170, note 219 and p. 187; *von Soden*, a, p. 169 ff.

royal dependent could also be a *nayyālu* and deprived of his lands on behalf of the king.

We also have a number of cases where certain persons among the *bnš mlk*, mostly of more privileged professions, were freed from their obligations. We will deal with these cases in those chapters relating to the individual professions.

CHAPTER III

SERVICE-GRANTS AND DISTRIBUTIONS TO THE "ROYAL DEPENDENTS" (BNŠ MLK)

After considering the system of royal servicemen — the "royal dependents" (*bnš mlk*), and the various kinds of services which they performed and the taxes placed on them, we must now consider the system by which the royal servicemen were compensated, including land allotments whereby land was given into conditional holding, deliveries of silver and deliveries of various products and artifacts. In this chapter we will only consider the compensation itself, according to profession, without entering into the specifics of the service rendered by each professional group.

§1. The *pilku/ubdy* Service System

We must start by analyzing the term *pilku* which appears only in the Akkadian texts from Ugarit and has been until now unknown from the other cuneiform areas.

The *pilku* is connected always with the service of the royal dependents. The following texts supply us with the necessary data:

1. PRU, III, 16.242. King Ammistamru II declares that a certain *Arsuwanu* has (12) *...pi*]*l-ka* ^{LÚMEŠ}[*a-š*]*i-ri-ma* (13) *ú-bal* "[the *pil*]*ku*-service of the *ašīru* (overseers of working teams) he has to perform (lit. "to carry").[1]

2. PRU, III, 15.137. Ammistamru II grants land to a certain *Abdi-ḫagab* and declares: (8) *...iš-tu píl-k*[*i*] (9) ^{LÚMEŠ}*a-ši-ri-ma* (10) *šarru ú-na-kir-šu* (11) *ù il-ta-kán*^{an}*-šu* (12) *i-na* ^{LÚMEŠ}*mu-de*$_4$ *šarri*, "from the *pilku* of the *aširu*-people the king alienated him and established him as a *mūdū* of the king (friend of the king)".[2]

---

[1] *'šr(m)* = *a-ši-ru-ma* cf. Ch. VIII, pp. 152-154.

[2] On the *mūdū/md(m)* in Ugarit cf. Ch. IX and *Heltzer*, h, pp. 335-367 and recently the acceptance of such interpretation. *Liverani*, SDB, p. 1340.

3. PRU, III, 16.142. King Arḫalbu declares that (7) *ᴵTup-pi-ia-na...* (8) *pí-il-ka* (9) *ša ᴸᵁaškāpi(AŠ.GAB)* (10) *ú-ba*,[3] "*Tuppiyanu* shall perform the *pilku*-service of the leatherworker."[4]

4. PRU, III, 16.138. Ammistamru II declares that *Ilitešub* and his sons (35) *píl-ka ša-a mârè*ᴹᴱŠ *šarrati*ᵗⁱ (36) *[u]b-ba-lu a-di da-ri-ti*, "the *pilku*-service of the sons of the queen they shall perform forever."

5. PRU, III, 16.204. Ammistamru II declares that *Abdimilku* and his sons (v. 10′) ... the *pilku*-service (11′) of the sons of the queen (12′) shall perform forever". So we see that we are dealing here with a certain kind of official and not royal princes.[5]

6. PRU, VI, 31 (RS.19.985. Ammistamru II declares (22) ... *píl-ka-ma* (23) *ša ᴸᵁ́ᴹᴱŠmar-ia-nu-ti ša ᵁᴿᵁÚ-g[à-ri-it]* (24) *ub-bal ᴵQu-u-milku ù mârē-*[ᴹᴱŠ*-šu*], "the *pilku*-service of the maryannuship of Ugarit *Qumilku* and his sons have to perform".[6]

7. PRU, III, 16.348. Ammistamru II (4) *[ú-n]a-kir ᴵYa-an-ḫa-am-ma mâr Na-pa-ak-ki ù mârē*ᴹᴱŠ*-šu* (5) *i[š]-tu píl-<ki> ᴸᵁ̀ᴹᴱŠmur-í ᴵI-bi-ra-na*, "[alie]nated *Yanḫamu*, son of *Napakku* and his sons from the *pilku*-service of the *mur'u* (liaison officers) of *Ibiranu*," (i.e. of the heir to the throne *Ibiranu*, son of Ammistamru II).[7]

8. PRU, III, 16.139. Ammistamru II grants to *Kalbeya* and his sons fields, and adds (13) *ù píl-ku i-na A.ŠA MEŠ(eqlātī) šu-wa-ti ia-nu* (14) *píl-ka-ma ᴸᵁ̀ᴹᴱŠmur-u ᴸᵁ̀sākini*[8] *ú-bal*. "And there is no *pilku*-service from these fields. The *pilku*-service of the *mur'u* of the *sākinu* (vizier) he shall perform."

9. PRU, III, Fr. King Ammistamru II orders according to this fragmentary text (v. 10′) *píl-ka-ma ša ᴸᵁ̀ᴹᴱŠna-mu-ti* (11′) *[i-na]*, *ᵁᴿᵁRêši ú-bal ᴵGa-mi-rad-du u DÚMU(mârē)*ᴹᴱŠ*-šu* (12′) *[a-d]i da-ri-ti* "The *pilku*-service of *namū*-people[9] (transhumance shepherds(?)) *Gamiraddu* and his sons shall perform forever."

10. PRU, III, 16.162. Ammistamru II grants land to *Amaturuna* and adds: (24) *píl-ka-ma ša ᴸᵁ̀ᴹᴱŠša re-ši* (25) *ub-bal ša-nu píl-ku* (26) *i-ia-nu i-na*

---

[3] Scribal omission, instead of *ú-bal*.

[4] *Heltzer*, c, p. 487; 10).

[5] On the "sons of the king" cf. Ch. IX, pp. 168-169.

[6] On the *maryannu* cf. Ch. VI, pp. 111-115.

[7] On the term cf. Ch. VIII, pp. 154-156, and *Heltzer*, I (in print), *Rainey*, f, p. 18.

[8] Cf. Ch. VIII, pp. 154-156.

[9] *namū*, cf. Ch. IV, pp. 73-75.

A.ŠA(eqlāt)MEŠ-ti an-na-t[i], "The *pilku*-service of the eunuchs [10] he shall perform. Another *pilku*-service does not exist from these fields."

11. PRU, VI, 27 (RS.17.01). Ammistamru II gives a land-grant to *Abbanu* and: (30) *pil-ka LÚMEŠšatammi ú-bal*, "The *pilku*-service of the *šatammu* he has to perform." [11]

12. PRU, III, 15.122. Ammistamru II distributes land-allotments to *Kabityanu* and he has to perform the *pilku*-service of the šatammuship.

13. PRU, III, 16.173. The text is damaged, but we read in the preserved parts that "the king imposed on him the *pilku*-service of the šatammuship."

14. PRU, VI, 30 (RS.18.300). Ammistamru II grants land-allotments to *Abdiḫagab*, son of *Abutenu* and he has (9) *pil-[k]a-šu* (10) *ša LÚMEŠtamkāru (DAM.GAR)-ut-ti* (11) *ú-ub-bal*, "his *pilku*-service of the tamkarship (royal trader, or merchant) [12] he shall perform."

15. PRU, III, 15.123. King Niqmepa grants land-allotments to Anantenu and he has (16) ... *pil-ka* (17) *[š]a LÚMEŠUN-tù ub-bal*, "The *pilku*-service of the *UN-tù*-guard he shall perform." [13]

16. PRU, III, 15.Y. King Niqmepa makes the above-mentioned *Tuppiyanu* (No. 3), who was made an *aškāpu* (leatherworker) by his brother and predecessor Arḫalbu perform for his land-allotments (10) *pil-ka LÚMEŠZAG.LUti ú-bal*, "The *pilku*-service of the bronze-caster [14] he shall perform."

Additionally, we have a number of exemptions from the *pilku*-service, but the composition of the text or its state of preservation prevents us from drawing any conclusions. [15]

In the sixteen documents quoted above, we see that only royal servicemen, i.e., "royal dependents" (*bnš mlk*), are mentioned. These belong to military professions — *maryannu* and *UN-tù*; artisans — bronzesmiths,

---

[10] Cf. *Heltzer*, i, pp. 4-11 and Ch. IX, pp. 170-173.

[11] We do not know the exact functions of this official in Ugarit. In various places and periods the *šatammu* had to perform different functions and services; cf. AHW, p. 199. Ugaritic counterpart unknown.

[12] Cf. *Heltzer*, b, pp. 123-124.

[13] Concerning the identity of UN-*tù*/Ug. *mdrġlm* cf. Ch. VI, pp. 115-121 and *Heltzer*, T (in print).

[14] Ugar. *nsk tlṯ* — *Heltzer*, c, p. 491 (19) and *Zaccagnini*, a, pp. 315-324; Ch. V, pp. 93-95.

[15] Cf. PRU, III, 16.147 where King Niqmepa declares *Ariradu*, son of *Abdinergal* (17) *iš-tu pil-ka-šu-nu za-ki* "from their *pilku*-service they are free (lit. "pure").

leatherworkers; agricultural personnel — *namū*, merchant-tamkars; administrative personnel — *aširu*, *mur'u*, *šatammu*, eunuchs of the palace or court. We also see that their *pilku* service was connected with their professions, and that they received land-allotments. We may thus conclude that the *pilku*-service was a universal feature among the *bnš mlk* of all professional groups dependent on the king of Ugarit.[16]

What do we know about the terms connected with land-allotments which are found in the alphabetic texts from Ugarit?

The term *ubdy* is always connected with the fields or land-plots allotted by the king to *bnš mlk* of various professional groups.[17] We have the following texts:

1. KTU.4.110. (1) *šd.ubdy.Ilštmʿ* (2) *dt.bd.skn*, "The *ubdy*-fields of (the village) *Ilštmʿ*, which are at the disposal (lit. in the hands) of the *sākinu* (vizier).[18] Lines 3-12 are a listing of 12 fields in the hands of 12 persons of the *gt Prn* and the lines 5-22 — 5 fields in the hands of 5 persons at the *gt Mzln.*[19] So we see that these 17 fields at two *gt*'s were under the supervision of the *sākinu*.

2. KTU.4.103. (1) *ubdy mdm*, "The *ubdy* (fields) of the *mūdū* (friends of the king)".[20] Lines 2-6 mention 5 fields according to the formula "*sd bd x*" (("One) field to x(PN)"; Line 7 [*ub*]*dy.mrynm* "The [*ub*]*dy* (fields) of the *maryannu*." Lines 8-19 list 13 fields according to the formula "*sd x bd y*", "The field of x(PN) to y(PN)". So we have seen that in one case fields are distributed and in the other case they are redistributed. Possibly, those people from whom the fields were alienated did not perform their service-obligations, and they were the so-called *nayyālu*[21]. In one case (14) [*t*]*n. šdm.bd.Gmrd* "[Tw]o fields to *Gmrd*" are given and (11) [*š*]*d.bn.Ilṯtmr bd Tbbr* (12) [*w*]*šd.nḥlh.bd Tṯmd* "The [fie]ld of *bn Ilṯtmr* to *Tbbr* [and] the field of his heir to *Tṯmd*." So we see that even the heir of the father served in the royal service for his father's lifetime. Line 20 [*ubd*]*y.mrim*, "The [*ubd*]*y*

---

[16] On the etymology of the word *pilku* cf. below.

[17] *Heltzer*, c, p. 463; *Liverani*, SDB, pp. 1343-1344; more about the term and its etymology, cf. below.

[18] *Heltzer*, c, p. 463, esp. note 84.

[19] On the *gt*. cf. Ch. IV.

[20] Cf. above, note 2.

[21] Cf. Ch. II, pp. 16-22 and *Heltzer*, a, pp. 52-57.

(fields) of the *mur'u*-officers," and lines 21-30 talk about 9 persons receiving 10 fields. Of them 9 fields are redistributed and only one (l. 29) is given directly to a certain *bn P'ṣ*. In line 23, *Gmrd* receives two fields (*ṯn.šdm*). Line 30 [*ubdy*]*'šrm*, "the [*ubdy*] fields of the *ašīru* (overseers of the teams of ten)." Lines 31-36 deal also with distribution and redistribution of the fields. Line 37 [*u*]*bdy mri Ibrn*, "The *ubdy*-(fields) of the *mur'u* officers of *Ibiranu*" (i.e. the prince *Ibiranu* at the regnal period of Ammistamru II). Lines 39-40 speak about the redistribution of one field to a *ṯġr*, "gatekeeper." Line 41 [*u*]*bdy šrm*, "The *ubdy*-(fields) of the singers" (of the palace of temple)", and in lines 42-43, two fields are redistributed. Line 44 [*u*]*bdy.nqdm* "The *ubdy*-(fields) of the shepherds," tell us about (45) *ṯlṯ.šdm d.n'rb.gt.Npk*, "3 fields which entered (to the disposal) of *gt Npk*", i.e. we have here the same dependency of such fields from the units of the royal agricultural economy — the *gt*, with whom the service-fields were connected. Line 48 tells us about the *ubdy*-fields of the *trrm*[22] and 5 fields (lines 49-53) are redistributed. Line 54 [*ubdy mḏ*]*rġlm*, "the [*ubdy* fields of the *mḏ*]*rġlm-guards." Additionally we learn also about the fields of the mḫṣm*-guards.[23]

But with this text the mentioning of the *ubdy*-fields is not limited and we have a big list where this term appears.

3. KTU.4.7. mentions *ubdy trrm*, "the *ubdy*-(fields) of the *trrm*," where 19 fields are distributed.

4. KTU.4.309. (1) *spr.ubdym.b.Uškn*, "List of the *ubdy*-fields (or persons having the *ubdy*-fields) in the (village) *Uškn*." 30 persons are here mentioned by name.

5. KTU.4.389. mentions at least 11 *ubdy*-fields.[23]

6. KTU.4.631. *Spr.ubdy.Art*, "List of the *ubdy*-(fields) in (or of) (the village) *Art*. 20 fields are listed and distributed and redistributed. 13 fields are given to various persons whose professions are not designated; 7 of these are given *l.qrt* — "to the village," i.e. the village of *Art* was responsible for their use and performance of the service attached to the fields due the royal authorities.[24]

---

22 Term designating a certain professional group — meaning is unclear.

23 The left side of each line is broken, the words *šd ubdy* appear on the right side, the minimal figure for a number of lines are totally damaged; line 5 [ ]*bn Kxn ṯlṯm ksp b*[ ] "... 30 (shekels) silver in [ ]."

24 A thorough analysis of this text, *Heltzer*, r, pp. 51-53.

7. KTU.4.692. (1) *ubdy-yṣḥm*, "The *ubdy*-(fields) of the heralds"[25] 6 fields are redistributed. The second part of the text (l. 8 ff.) mentions *yṣḥm* by name without designating whether they had fields or not.

8. KTU.4.244. The text is in a bad state of preservation. The words *ubdy* and *krm*, "vineyard" are mentioned as well as *krm ubdy*, "vineyard of *ubdy*" (ll. 6, 9, 10). In various villages (*Art*, *Liy*, *Mgdly*, *Qmnz*, *Ykn'm*, *Ḥly*, *Ull*, *Ary*, *Ṯlrby*, etc.) we see certain numbers of *ubdy*-vineyards in the hands of various persons. Line 9 *ṯlṯ.krm.ubdym.l.mlkt.b.'nmky* [ ], "three *ubdy*-vineyards of the queen in the (village) *'nmky*[ ]." Even if we take only the preserved parts of the text, there are 139+x vineyards. At least some persons were the *maryannu*-charioteers.

9. KTU.4.164. (1) *ṯlṯ.mat* (2) *šb'm.kbd* (3) *zt.ubdym* (4) *b.Mlk*, "370 at all[26] olives of *ubdy* in (the village or at the *gt*) of *Mulukku.*"[27]

10. KTU.4.183.[28] (1) [*ḥrš.*]*bhtm.b'l šd*, "housebuilders-possessors of a field,"[29] and besides the "housebuilders" there also appear "singers," (*šrm*), *mḏrġlm*-guards, *qatinnu*-makers,[30] *b'l tġpṯm* — "makers of horse-cloths" or "caparisons,"[31] *ḥrš mrkbt*, "chariot-builders," *'bdm* — a certain group of agricultural workers in the royal economy,[32] *nsk ksp* — "silversmiths,"[33] *nsk ṯlṯ* — "bronzesmiths" (or coppersmiths), etc. The word *ubdy* is here for some reason not mentioned in the text.

11. KTU.4.222. Here we see, despite the bad state of preservation of the tablet, in lines 17-21 the formula, *šd x bd y*, "field of x(PN) to y(PN),"

---

[25] Ug. *ṣwḥ*, "to shout," cf. Ch. VIII, pp. 163-164.

[26] In such and similar contexts *kbd*, not "heavy" but accepting *Liverani*, b, pp. 89-108, "at all."

[27] It is not clear whether these are measures of olives, or olive-trees, or land-plots with olive-trees.

[28] Beginning from this text and further on we present the texts where the word *ubdy* could be partly damaged or where it was not included. Mostly, these are texts where fields are distributed to various professional groups of *bnš mlk* or it is designated that these persons have fields at their disposal.

[29] From the original 25 personal names written, only 12 are fully or partly legible.

[30] Cf. Ch. V, pp. 88-89 and *Heltzer*, c, p. 487; *Freydank*, a, pp. 124-127.

[31] Cf. Ch. V, pp. 83-84, and *Heltzer*, c, p. 482, 3).

[32] Ch. IV, p. 65, *Heltzer*, c, pp. 467-475.

[33] Ch. V, pp. 92-93.

and where among the recipients are again the "bronzesmiths" and the "horsegrooms" (*kzym*).[34]

12. KTU.4.282. Among the distributed fields, at least *širm* (measure) is in the hands of a priest *khn*, who also belonged, in Ugarit, to the *bnš mlk*. 30 fields are distributed.[35]

13. KTU.4.340. Under consideration are distributions of salt-bearing plots by the royal authorities.[36]

14. KTU.4.344. A very similar text to the preceeding concerning salt-bearing plots distributed among royal servicemen.

15. KTU.4.356. In line 1-6, 16 persons receive fields as the result of their redistribution. The professional group is not designated.

16. KTU.4.357. 32 persons receive 37 fields. Only in one case (line 24) do we see the words *šd.bd.dr.khnm*, "a field to a family of priests."[37]

17. KTU.4.399. Originally 19 lines, partly damaged. The tablet mentions persons who receive fields, and possibly the villages where the fields are located.

18. KTU.4.416. This text deals with groups (not individuals) of the *maryannu*, *mur'u*, *ʿšrm-ašīru*-overseers of teams of ten, *nqdm* — shepherds, *khnm* — priests, *ṯnnm-šanānu* — warriors,[38] and *inšt* — a certain group of workmen(?) — at least *bnš mlk*."[39] In line 1, after the professional group and the figure, is the designation *GAN.ME*, "fields". Possibly this is identical to the *ubdy*-fields. Certain numbers appear after each designation of professional groups.

19. KTU.4.423. All 24 lines of the tablet, which are partly preserved, deal with redistribution of fields. Professions and *ubdy* are not designated.

20. KTU.4.424. (1) *spr.šd ri*[*šym(?)*], "List of the fields of the villa[gers of *Riš?*].[40] The text deals with *šdm*, "fields" and *krm(m)*, "vineyards, and beginning from line 4 with the same type of lands at the village of *Ypʿ*.

---

[34] Cf. Ch. VI, p. 124 Akk. ^{LU}*kîzu*, cf. WUS, p. 146, No. 127; UT, p. 418, No. 1215; AHW, p. 496a, "Diener", "servant", term always connected with persons dealing with horses; Alalaḫ — *Giacumakis*, a, p. 83, "youth, squire, attendant", *Salonen*, a, p. 231, "Horsegroom".

[35] On the measure-units of these fields of *Liverani*, a, p. 99.

[36] On these fields, cf. *Heltzer*, p, pp. 355-362; *Moran*, a, pp. 69-71; *Liverani*, SDB, p. 1318.

[37] Cf. Ch. VII, pp. 131-139.

[38] *šanānu*/*ṯnnm* cf. Ch. VI, pp. 122-123.

[39] *inšt* — cf. above, Ch. I, pp. 3-15.

[40] Reconstruction dubious.

21. KTU.4.425. The tablet is damaged. At least 16+x fields were redistributed. No mention of professions.

22. KTU.4.609. It is a very large text, containing individuals of various professions, who are all designated a *b'l šd*, "owners (possessors) of a field." At the same time, the text does not deal with the distribution of fields especially, but it is a ration-tablet of the *bnš mlk* in the month of *Ṯṯbnm*.[41]

We see that the term *ubdy* is connected with field allotments to people in royal service and were royal dependents in Ugarit. It is clear that the *ubdy*-fields were delivered to these individuals in exchange for their service. It is important to clarify the real etymology of this term and its meaning, and exactly what was connected with it.

There have been different opinions about the semitic origin of the word *ubdy*.[42] But only *Güterbock*, in 1957, proved that the origin of the word was Hittite — *u-ba/pa-ti* — which appeared in Old Assyrian texts from Kültepe and in Hittite texts of the imperial period. He translates it according to *Friedrich*, "fief, feudal holding(?)". At the same time he connects it with dependent land-plots or territories.[43] It is very important for us that in the imperial Hittite texts, contemporary to the Ugaritic ones, we see a connection with (a) lands and (b) their holders or possessors.

Of special interest in this connection is the term attested in the Old-Assyrian texts from Kül-Tepe (Kanish) in Asia Minor — *upatinnu(m)*.[44] The word has the following meaning in the Old-Assyrian text I.568, where a certain (3) *Ašet* (4) the *alaḫinnum*[45] (and) *Ḫištašḫu* the (5) *rab ṣābim* ("commander of men (soldiers)), *Ušḫata*, (6) *Asu*, *Kulakula*, *Ḫašui* (7) and *Ḫapuala* as the representative of (8) the *upatinum* (*ki-ma ú-pá-ti-nim*) (9) which *Ašet*, *alaḫḫinum*, (10) to *Buzasu*, son of *Pušuken* (11) sold (12) *i-dí-nu-ma ši-im* (13) *bi-tim A-še-e-et* (14) *ú a-wi-lu a-ni-ú-tim* (15) *ša-bu-ú*, "(and) with the price of the house *Ašet* and these people (persons) are satisfied." On the envelope

41 Cf. this text in Ch. I, pp. 3-15. on the Ugaritic months cf. *Olivier*, a, pp. 53-59.

42 With references to the previous literature, *Heltzer*, a, pp. 67-68 and note 15. *Rainey*, c, p. 32 and 120-121; *Rinaldi*, a, pp. 343-349; UT, p. 349, No. 17.

43 *Güterbock*, a, p. 360; cf. also *Friedrich*, a, p. 325.

44 a) *Matouš*, a, pp. 33-39, esp. the text pp. 34-35, line 8 and envelope ll. 14 and 24; b) TCL, XXI, 214, 12 — cf. *Garelli*, a, p. 69, note 2; c) the partly published text by *E. Bilgiç* (inaccessible to me) and quotation according to *Matouš*, a, p. 38, note 61; cf. also AHW, p. 1423.

45 The discussion on the word *alaḫḫinu*, cf. below, Ch. V, pp. 80-81.

ll. 21-25 these same persons appear again *ki-ma ú-pá-ti-nim*, "as representatives of the *ú-pá-ti-num*". We see that the *upatinnum* appear as a collective body, which could sell a house or possibly other property. These people were not the entire *upatinum*, but acted only as its representatives.

At the same time in TCL XXI, 214 we have the expression "(11) Or somebody (12) or an *upatinu* (13) or his *tamkar* (merchant)"[46] from which we can draw the conclusion that the *upatinu* could even have "his *tamkar*." Thus the *upatinu* might have been a single person and not a collective.

Concerning the tablet partly published by *E. Bilgiç*,[47] we find that a certain *Kurdumu*, son of *Izku-iptur* "*ana upatinnum išqul*" "paid (lit. weighted) to the *upatinnum* 45 shekels of silvers, the price of a slave." The *upatinnum* here could be a collective group and *L. Matouš*[48] points out that "*upatinnum* means a group of native persons, which worked and lived in the communal economy." But this point of view does not coincide with the above-mentioned opinions of *Güterbock*, *Friedrich* and *von Soden*. *E. Laroche*[49] also designates the Hittite root *upati-* "'fief' and analogue," concerning the personal name *Upatiaḫšu* from Kanish, *I. M. Diakonoff*[50] expresses the opinion that this is the Hurrian *ub-adi* (and not *upati*) and that this is the Hurrian (term) for "service" or "obligation connected with the holding of communal land."

We can draw the following conclusions: a) The *upatinnum* may have been Hittite or possibly Hurrian, therefore the term may have belonged to both languages, whatever its origin. b) The *upatinnu* may have been collectives or individuals who had to perform certain duties. c) This does not change the fact that the *ubdy* in Ugarit was connected with landholdings, on behalf of the royal authorities, by "royal dependents" (*bnš mlk*) of various professions, and thus we see that this term entered Ugaritic via Hittite or Hurrian, contemporary to the Ugarit archives, i.e., in the XIV-XIIIth century B.C.E.

Another point arising from the Ugaritic *ubdy* and the Hittite *upati* (including the local term in Asia Minor at the beginning of the II millenium B.C.E. *upatinnu(m)*), where we have the voiceless *p* instead of *b*,

---

[46] (11) *lu ma-ma-an* (12) *lu ù-pá-ti-nu lu tamkār-šu*.

[47] Cf. note 44.

[48] *Matouš*, a, p. 38.

[49] *Laroche*, a, p. 296.

[50] *Diakonoff*, a, pp. 40-41.

allows us to understand an Ugaritic text which was impossible to interpret up to now — KTU.4.264.

1	*spr.updt*	1	List of the *updt*-people,
2	*ʿd bd.mlkytn*	2	which are at the disposal of
			Mlkytn (Milkiyatanu)

3	*kdrl*	3	*Kdrl*
4	*slṯmg*	4	*Slṯmg*
5	*adrdn*	5	*Adrdn*
6	*llwn*	6	*Llwn*
7	*ydln*	7	*Ydln*
8	*ldn*	8	*Ldn*
9	*tdġl*	9	*Tdġl*
10	*ibr kyṯ*	10	*Ibrkyṯ*

In this case the *updt* seems to be the voiceless variant of *ubd* — and the *-t* as the ending of the word seems to be the feminine plural used as a nom. collectivum. We thus understand the word as referring to a group of people who were obliged to perform their service for their *ubdy*.[51] it is also designated that they were at the disposal (lit. "in the hands") of *Milkiyatanu*, who had to be a royal official. Eight persons listed only by their names follow after the dividing line of the text.[52]So these persons were obliged by their *ubdy*. Some of these personal names also appear sporadically in other texts, but only the tablet KTU.4.147 is of special importance in this regard.

1	*ʿd[rš]p*	1	"d[*rš*]*p*
2	*pqr(?)*	2	*Pqr(?)*
3	*ṯġr*	3	(the) gatekeeper [53]
4	*ttġl*	4	*Ttġl* [54]
5	*ṯn yṣḥm*	5	two heralds [55]

[51] We cannot accept the view of *M. Sznycer* (SDB, p. 1423), that the *updt* were a separate professional group.

[52] More on the etymologies of these names and the structure of the texts cf. *Heltzer*, U (in print).

[53] *ṯġr*-"gate-keeper," cf. Ch. IX, pp. 169-170.

[54] Graphic variant of *Tdġl*.

[55] Cf. Ch. VIII, pp. 163-164.

6	*slṯmg*	6	*Slṯmg*
7	*kdrl*	7	*Kdrl*
8	*wql*	8	*Wql*
9	*adrdn*	9	*Adrdn*
10	*prn*	10	*Prn*
11	*ʿbdil*	11	*ʿbdil*
12	*ušy.šbnt*	12	*Ušy*. The woman of the village, *Šbn* [56]
13	*aẖt.ab*	13	the sister of the father [57]
14	*krwt*	14	*Krwt* [58]
15	*nnḏ*	15	*Nnḏ*
16	*mkl*	16	*Mkl*
17	*kzġb*	17	*Kzġb*
18	*iyrḏ*	18	*Iyrḏ*"

First, we see that *Ttġl* was a *ṯġr* "gate-keeper", and "two heralds" also appear in this text. Both these professions are known to be among those of the *bnš mlk* (cf. above). But, we also see that four of the personal names in KTU.4.264 are identical to names in KTU.4.147.

KTU.4.264.		KTU.4.147.	
3	*Kdrl*	7	*Kdrl*
4	*Slṯmg*	6	*Slṯmg*
5	*Adrdn*	9	*Adrdn*
9	*Tdġl*	4	*Ttġl*

This is not an accident. These four names comprises 50 % of the personal names in KTU.4.264. We see that one of them, according to KTU.4.147, *Td/tġl*, was a gate-keeper "*ṯġr*" and it seems that the other names were royal dependents, including the two "heralds", *yṣḥm*. This confirms our interpretation that the *updt*-people were those who had the *ubdy*-field (*šd ubdy*) as a holding from the king, and that they were persons obliged by the *ubdy*-holding.

[56] *Šbn* (Akk. *URUŠubbani*) a name of a village in the Kingdom of Ugarit; *šbny* — the *niṣbe*, "the man of *Šbn*"; *Šbnt*, scribal defect fem. of the *niṣbe* instead of **Šbnyt*.

[57] Perhaps the sister of the father of *Ušy*. This line explains and amends the previous line.

[58] *Krwt* — **Kurwatu* is the personal name of this woman, fem. from the well-known Ugaritic name *Krw/Krwn* = *Kurwanu*.

Another related text is KTU.4.12. The first line is half broken, but it may have contained either a personal name or possibly [*ub*] [*x*]*y*. In lines 2-13, seventeen people are listed by personal names or by the names of their fathers (*bn x* — "son of x"). In two cases, (2) [ ]*lw.nḥlh*, "[PN] and his descendent (heir)", even descendents are mentioned. The tablet concludes after the last dividing line: (14) *ubdit* (15) *bn k*[*x*]*n* (16) *bn Nẓril*, and we see that the last two people, at least, were *ubdit*. It is very likely, that the *b* in *ubdit* is an interchange with the voiceless *p* of the previous text and that the '$_2$ = *i* before the *t* seems to be a *plene* spelling-variant of the same word. Thus at least two persons mentioned in the tablet, *bn K*[*x*]*n* and *bn Nẓril*, were *ubdy* (if not all the other people mentioned as well), and they are designated here as people who had to perform their service for these holdings.

The important thing in the analysis above is first, the etymological connection of *ubdy-updt-ubdit-* which demonstrates, on the one hand, that lands were given for service, and on the other hand that persons connected with the service were connected with the land, which they received for their service *updt*/*ubdit*. From text KTU.4.147 we clearly see that among the *updt* were some people designated as *ṯġrm* and *yṣḥm*, i.e. members of the professional groups of royal dependents in Ugarit. We saw at the beginning of our explanation that in the Akkadian texts from Ugarit the service connected with the profession of representatives of various professional groups of the *bnš mlk* of the kingdom in agricultural, craft, priestly, military and administrative professions, delivered services known as *pilku* in exchange for the lands they received from the king. We can thus reach the next very important conclusion that *ubdy* (resp. *updt*/*ubdyt*) = *pilku*.

As we discussed above, the term *ub*/*pdy* is of Hittite Origin and without further knowledge from the Hittitological side [59] it is a term, connected with some obligations deriving from certain lands at the time, which could be individual or collective. The established fact of the proximity of the terms *ubdy*/*pilku* allows us a better opportunity to clarify the etymology of the term *pilku*.

There are not many explanations of the term *pilku*. *J. Nougayrol* (PRU, III, p. 226) connected this term with *ilku* — corvée-service, known from the

[59] *Imparati*, a, p. 107, *uppa-(ubba-)*, "lasciar portare" "to cause, to bring, to deliver" = Akk. *šūbultu* according to *A. Goetze*, i.e. to deliver some taxes or service.

whole cuneiform area, and gives it as a lexical variant of the term *ilku*.[60] *Speiser*[61] connects the term, contrary to his predecessors, with the Biblical Hebrew *prk* — corvée, and the Akkadian verb *palāku*, "to delimit, divide" also "to measure".[62] He also adds that the Middle-Hebrew and Aramaic *plg*, "part, share" must be taken into consideration. *Dietrich* and *Loretz*[63] return to the earlier explanation, holding that *pilku* is a certain variant of *ilku*.

But the fact that we have a clear semantic (not etymological) equation of *pilku-ubdy*[64] gives us a new approach to the problem. The reason for this is that we know now the meaning of *ubdy* so we can search for a meaning of the word *pilku* which is close to that of *ubdy*. The AHW puts the *pilku* in Ugarit under *pilku II* (p. 863b) deriving it from *pa+ilku*. At the same time we see there the *pilku I* (p. 863a and b) and the word comes from *palāku*, "to delimit, divide" and *pilku* is in this case translated as "delimitation, district".[65] In almost all the cases we have this term connected with fields or other lands which were measured or delimited and therefore we can translate the *pilku*, in the case of Ugarit, as "delimited land-plot" or "land-plot", "parcel allotment."

It is important that *(šd)ubdy* means the field which the *bnš mlk* received for his professional service, and at the same time *updt/ubdit* means the service by itself, or is used to designate the persons obliged with this service. In the spelling, we have only variants and we see that the term which denoted the service-allotments came to refer to the persons obliged with it. It seems that the same can be said about *pilku*. Etymologically, originally this was the term designating the land-plot, or the delimited allotment and so the term came to refer to the service from this plot or "allotment" or "parcel".

This enables us better to understand the whole system and forces us, in investigating further, to consider the *pilku* and *ubdy* as the same thing. This

---

60 Cf. also *Nougayrol* in PRU, VI, p. 154.

61 *Speiser*, a, pp. 161-162.

62 Idem, p. 162.

63 *Dietrich-Loretz*, b, p. 165-166.

64 *Heltzer*, u, pp. 31-35, where we deal with semantic coincidences in a near field to the present issue.

65 "Abgrenzung, Gebiet."

also widens our understanding of the taxes and service obligations in Ugarit and gives us a much broader basis for study than we have had till now.

But, in our opinion, the facts we have succeeded in proving here have a much broader importance. For to progress any further we must consider the verb *palāku(m)*. According to the AHW, p. 813b, it means "to delimitate (a plot, district)".[66] We see here also *pa-la-ku ša pil-ku*, "to divide (delimit) of the *pilku*." The OB period shows us the expression as connected with "parts of fields," *x ikū eqlam pa-la-ka-am*, "x *ikū* of field are divided?", etc. In the middle-Babylonian period we meet the expression *ana pilki ip-lu-uk*, "into parcels divided (?)". From here we see that the verb *palāku* is always connected with fields or agricultural land.[67]

By all means, then, we have shown that the terms *ubdy* in Ugaritic and *pilku* in Akkadian from Ugarit are identical and this helps us to understand better the whole royal service system of the kingdom of Ugarit.

It is very important to note that in this system were involved service-men, "royal dependents", beginning from the highest ranks as *md(m)/mūdū*, "friends of the king," the military servicemen of various groups, agricultural professionals, working in the royal real estate, various professions of artisans, priests and other temple personnel, as well as administrative personnel and overseers of teams of ten (workmen) *ʿšrm* = *rb ʿšrt*.[68] Naturally, we do not know the exact sizes of the distributed fields, or very much about manpower engaged there. Our sources have been silent until now about these. What happened to persons who lost their *pilku/ubdy* allotments is also unclear.

We also know that such features like land-allotments to royal dependents, or groups dependent on the king but named otherwise and not fully identical, were common to the Ancient Near East and its vicinity. It is not our task to analyze these features elsewhere, but in the chronologically proximate societies of the IIth millenium B.C.E. Here we see a complicated system of land-allotments for royal servicemen in the Old-Babylonian state,[69] in the Hittite Empire in the period contemporary to the Ugaritic King-

[66] "(Gebiet) abteilen; 1) aB a) "Feldteile".

[67] All this causes us to reconsider the terms τέμενος in Homeric times as well as *temena* in Linear B Greek and the Sumerian TEMEN and the word *temennu* in Old-Babylonian times, which will be done elsewhere.

[68] Cf. more about this in the chapters dealing with various branches of the economy and administration.

[69] *Diakonoff*, b, pp. 41-56.

dom.[70] A system similar and closely geographically related to the Ugaritic one existed in Alalaḫ in the XVth century B.C.E.[71] But it is not so well-illustrated in the documents from Ugarit and as we see in Alalaḫ, several professional groups appear there as united into larger entities according to their position inside the system of royal service. We do not see any more precise classification in Ugarit. A similar system existed also in the New-Kingdom Egypt.[72] Otherwise, we recognize in the texts of the Linear B script in Pylos and Knossos, contemporary to our Ugaritic texts, references to professionals in royal service who received their lands from the king.[73] This is despite the large number of questions concerning the understanding of these texts.

§2. Deliveries of Silver to the Royal Dependents

Now we must consider the payments of silver to the various groups of royal people. Since we have not exact dating of the texts, we do not know exactly the periodicity of all of them. So we shall consider the texts in general, taking first the tablets written in Akkadian since they are easier to understand correctly, and there is also a greater variety of the Akkadian texts which give us material and standard formulae found elsewhere. Even after comparisons have been made, however, we still do not know whether the silver deliveries were of a sporadic or regular nature.[74]

1. PRU, III, 11.878: 10 persons designated as *aklu*, "overseers", possibly identical to *ʿšrm/rb ʿšrt/ašīru*, "overseers of ten" received 62 shekels of silver. The average for one person is 6.2 shekels.

2. PRU, III, 11.839: 3 *šanānu* listed by name receive 247 shekels of silver (average 82 $^{1}/_{3}$) and *mur'u*-officer received 18 $^{1}/_{2}$ shekels.

---

[70] *Diakonoff*, c, pp. 318-345; *Imparati*, a.

[71] *Dietrich-Loretz*, d, pp. 37-64; *Dietrich-Loretz*, e, pp. 121-123. *Klengel*, a, pp. 435-457; the *pūrum*, land-distribution system among royal servicemen in Alalaḫ seems also to be similar to a certain degree to the Ugaritic *ubdy*-system, *Gaal*, b, pp. 145-148.

[72] *Bogoslovsky*, a, pp. 3-23.

[73] *Poljakova*, a, pp. 17-26 and 256-258; *Palmer*, a, pp. 133-141.

[74] More precisely about the details concerning every professional group in the silver-delivery texts, in the chapters concerning various groups of the royal dependents. The severely damaged and almost illegible tablets are not included in our study.

3. KTU.4.38: Priests (*khnm*)[75] receive 6 shekels; *qdšm*-diviners — 6 shekels; *mkrm*-tamkars — 6 shekels; *mdm-mūdū*, "friends of the king" — 6; *inšt* — 6; *ḥrš bhtm*, "housebuilders", — 6.

4. KTU.4.69: The *mur'u*-officers, no less than 36, receive more than 130 shekels[76]; 14 *khnm*, "priests", — 84 shekels; 54 *maryannu*-warriors — 240 shekels; their subjects, *bdl mrynm* — 4 persons — 140 shekels of silver; 9 *mru skn-mur'u* of the *sākinu* are also among the recipients. 8 *mru* of *Ibrn* (the prince *Ibiranu*) receive 32 shekels;[77] 10 *mḏrġlm*-guards receive 75 shekels and 3 of their subjects (*bdl mḏrġlm*) — 6 shekels of silver.

5. KTU.4.71: 3 *kbśm*, "fullers,"[78] receive 12 shekels of silver and 3+3 *ʿbdm* — a kind of agricultural workers[79] receive small quantities of silver.

6. KTU.4.98: 3 cartwrights (*ḥrš mrkbt*) receive 6 shekels of silver; 1 *qatinnu*-maker — 1 shekel; and 1 shepherd (*nqd*) and one *nsk* ("metal-caster") 2 and 4 shekels respectively.

7. KTU.4.99: A group of priests receive 16 shekels; *md(m)/mūdū*, "friends of the king", — 4 shekels; the number of the persons involved is unknown, but among the recipients are also the *inšt*, *mur'u* of the *sākinu*, *mur'u* of *Ibiranu* the *mḏrġlm*-guards, the *kbśm*, the *ʿbdm*, the *ʿšrm (aššīru)*, the "(workers) of the royal *gt*" — *gt mlkym*, the *yqšm*, "fowlers," *trrm*, horse-grooms (*kzym*), silversmiths (*nsk ksp*), the *mḫṣm*-guards, *kšdm*, "millers" (?),[80] *pslm*, "sculptors", *yṣḥm*, "heralds".

8. KTU.4.745: 2 shekels of silver receive the *šanānu*-warriors; 3 shekels the *mur'u*-officers, 2 shekels the priests, 2 shekels the tamkars (*mkrm*); 2 the cartwrights (*ḥrš mrkbt*); 2 the *qatinnu*-makers, 2 the *nqdm* (shepherds); 3 the *nsk(m)* (metal-casters); 2 the silversmiths (*nsk ksp*); and 2 *nʿrm*, lit. "youths," but certainly meaning here some subjects of another group mentioned above.[81]

---

[75] The group is given as a whole.

[76] Col. III, 11-12 and IV, 1-31.

[77] Col. V, 17-26.

[78] Cf. Ch. V, p. 90.

[79] Cf. Ch. IV, p. 65.

[80] Cf. Ch. V, pp. 90-91.

[81] Cf. also the text-fragments KTU.4.439; 4.69; 4.71; 4.126 as well as the tablets where it is unclear whether there is under consideration silver-delivery or deliveries of some other kind of product. KTU.4.105; 4.124; 4.134; 4.155; 4.182; 4.215; 4.245; 4.263; 4.332; 4.412; 4.485; 4.681; 4.692.

We find in the above texts distributions of silver to administrative and military personnel, priests, artisans and workers of the royal agricultural economy, i.e., practically all kinds of groups of *bnš mlk*. We see from this that not only land-allotments were received as payment, but nothing is known about the regularity of the distributions, whether they were sporadic or regular. We must only add that, by themselves, the silver deliveries are a much rarer feature for the IIth millenium B.C.E. than land-allotments or deliveries of products and artifacts. Possibly it confirms the fact that Ugarit was a highly developed trading center for the whole area.

§3. Distribution of Natural Products and Artifacts

In order to understand the whole system of payments to the royal dependents we must concern ourselves with the distribution of products. At least theoretically, although not always the case, we can state the following: the deliveries were divided into *ḥpr*, "rations,"[82] at the time of work of the royal dependents, and other kinds of deliveries. Naturally, inedible artifacts belonged not to the rations, but to the deliveries such as land-allotments and silver distributions. For a better understanding we shall begin again from the Akkadian tablets. We must consider here the professions of the persons receiving deliveries, the kind of products or artifacts, the periodicity of distribution and the kind of things distributed.[83]

1. PRU, III, 16.257[84]: The tablet deals with deliveries of jars of oil (*karpat šamnu*) to various professional groups, where the persons are listed by name. Accordingly, 17 tamkars receive from 1-20 jars. Among them, also their subjects (*bidaluma* -*bdlm*); 28 *ašīru* (*ʿšrm*) receive from 1-10 jars and 6 of their subjects (^{LÚMEŠ}*muš-ke-nu-tum*) ^{LÚMEŠ}*a-ši-ru-ma*,[85] 18 priests —

---

[82] Akk. *eprum*/*iprum*, AHW, p. 385a; CAD, I, pp. 166-168, esp. p. 168, 2′f. EA 155, 20 *jānu iṣṣē jā*<*nu*> *mē jānu tibnu jānu ip-ru jānu šammu*, "There is no wood, no water, no food, no fodder". It is also possible to compare this with *eperum* from Alalaḫ, as the territory, from which food products were received (*Gaal*, c, pp. 3-14).

[83] The texts, speaking about deliveries to persons, where we cannot see what their profession was, or where we are not sure that the person was a royal dependent, are not included.

[84] The text is partly broken.

[85] Possibly identical with the *bdlm*/*bidaluma*.

1-5 jars; 8 *ša naqi*[86] — 1-5 jars to each one; 9 *UN-tù (mḏrġlm)*[87] — 2-4 jars, as well as 3 of their subjects (*LÚ MEŠmuš-ke-nu-tum LÚ MEŠUN-tù*); 10 *mur'u* of the *ušriyannu* (— of the heir — *mur'u Ibirana*)[88] — 1-5 jars; 3 *nuḫatimmu* ("bakers" or "cooks") — 1 jar a piece; 8 ZAG.LU *siparri* (= *nsk ṯlṯ*, "bronzecasters") — 1-3 jars.

2. U.V.99 (RS.20.425): A group of *ittinu* (= *ḥrš bhtm*, "housebuilders") receive 4 jars of oil and 5 of wine; a group of weavers (*išpāru*) — 1 jar of wine.

3. KTU.4.38: We have here a monthly delivery "in the month of *Rêš-karāni*"[89]; the tamkars (*mkrm*) receive 3 GUR grain and 6 sheep; priests (*khnm*) receive the same quantities, as do the housebuilders (*ḥrš bhtm*); the *qdšm*-diviners and the "friends of the king" (*mdm*) receive 1 GUR grain and 2 sheep; the *inšt* receive 2 GUR and 5 sheep.

4. KTU.4.128: The text deals with deliveries to various individuals as well as for cattle destined for fattening; the units of measure are *dd*'s.[90] The *mḫṣm*-guards receive 20 *dd* of grain; the *kbsm* ("fullers") 2 *dd*'s; the gate-keepers (*ṯġrm*) receive 1 *dd*.

5. KTU.4.149: The text deals with distributions of wine to temples, single persons and professional groups. The *maryannu* receive 8 jars (*kdm*).[91]

6. KTU.4.175: Delivery by *dd*-units to individuals and "royal dependents". The shepherds (*r'ym*) receive 2 units.

7. KTU.4.213:[92] The *mḏrġlm*-guards receive 140 jars of wine; the *gzzm*, "sheep-shearers" receive 20 jars.

8. KTU.4.216: The text deals with the deliveries of wine. The housebuilders (*ḥršm*) receive 3 jars; the *ḫzrm* (male-personnel) receive 1 jar;[93] the *maryannu*-warriors receive 5; the *mḏrġlm*-guards receive 4; the *ṯrtnm-šerdana*-warriors receive 1 jar.[94].

---

86 Meaning of the term is unclear.

87 On the identity of these terms cf. Ch. VI, pp. 115-121.

88 Cf. Ch. VIII, pp. 154-156.

89 (13) *i-na arahrêš karāni* = Ug. *rišyn*. Cf. *Olivier*, a, pp. 53-59; ZUL, XI, pp. 28 ff.

90 UT, p. 384; No. 643; *Liverani*, SDB, p. 1333.

91 Ll. (9) *kd.l.mrynm* (10) *šb'.yn* (11) *l mrynm b yṯb mlk*, "(1) jar to the *maryannu; 7 jars to the maryannu* at the royal seat (palace)." It seems that the delivery was made at the time of service of these *maryannu*.

92 Cf. Ch. IV, pp. 77-78, where the text is given.

93 Cf. below in this chapter and *Heltzer*, S, pp. 410-412.

94 Cf. Ch. VI, pp. 125-127 and *Heltzer*, D (in print).

9. KTU.4.230:[95] 4 jars of wine are received by the *maryannu*-warriors; 2 jars by the *mḏrġlm*-guards.

10. KTU.4.243: We know that "shepherds" (*rʿym*) and their apprentices (*sġrm*) received certain amounts of grain. 12 units were received by the "cartwrights" (*ḥrš ʿrq*).[96] All this is designated as *ḥpr bnšm* "ration(s) of the men", i.e., the royal dependents.

11. KTU.4.263: The whole text deals exclusively with the delivery to tamkars (*mkrm*) and they receive 1 *parīsu* and 2 *lth* units of grain.[97]

12. KTU.4.269: The text deals with various professionals partly listed by their names. 5 *myṣm* and 5 of their apprentices (*lmdhm*) received a certain amount of grain as rations (*ḥpr*); the "sheep-shearers" (*gzzm*) received 30 *dd* units of spelt (*kśmm*) and 6 *dd* of wheat (*ḥṭn*); 1 *dd* was received by a woodcutter (*ḥṭb*). We also see that it was a monthly delivery.[98]

13. KTU.4.352: Delivery for various professionals and unspecified individuals. 248 units (oil?) were received by the bronzesmiths.[99]

14. KTU.4.377: Groups of professionals and other single persons received deliveries.[100] The *maryannu* receive 28 *dd* of grain.

15. KTU.4.387: Groups of professionals and single persons receive the following: 10 *dd* of grain are given to the bakers (*apym*) of the village *Riš*; 4 *dd* to the *md(m)* "friends of the king"; 80+x *dd* to the *mḏrġlm*-guards. We also see that this was a monthly delivery.

16. KTU.4.609. All the professional groups mentioned in this text receive the *ḥpr* ("rations") in the month of *Iṯtbnm*.[102]

---

[95] Total. $^{(13)}$ *ḫmšm.ḫmš* $^{(14)}$ *kbd tgmr* $^{(15)}$ *yn.d.nkly*, "55 (jars) at all (is the) total of supply-wine" (*kly/nkly* cf. *Milano*, a, pp. 83-97 and *Fensham*, a, pp. 27-30, where the word *kly/nkly* is translated as "preserved, prepared", which does not contradict our translation).

[96] Cf. Ch. V, pp. 87-88.

[97] Cf. on this measure and esp. *lth* in Ugarit, *Heltzer*, R, pp. 413-414.

[98] $^{(10)}$ *tgmr kśmm.b.yrḫ.Iṯtbnm*, "Total: spelt in the month of *Iṯtbnm*." *myṣm* — we have to accept the original reading and not the "corrected" (*mḫṣm*) — cf. *Liverani*, h, p. 68 "caseificatori" "dairymen" possibly "cheesemakers" (cf. Ch. IV, p. 75).

[99] *sbrdnm*, cf. Ch. V, pp. 93-95.

[100] Also donkeys mentioned (*ḥmrm*) and the personnel dealing with them.

[101] *b yrḫ* [*x*] mentioned several times in the text.

[102] Cf. the full text Ch. I, pp. 4-8.

17. KTU.4.636. According to this text *akl*, "food", is delivered to *'bdym* (a group of agricultural workmen) at various *gt*'s.

Again we see all kinds of professions: military, priestly, administrative, agricultural and artisans. It is very important that sometimes these are particularly referred to as rations, or monthly rations. This proves that such deliveries were made during the time of active service. It also gives us the monthly delivery for one person.[103]

We have another text, KTU.4.751, according to which the *mḏrġlm*-guards received meat, flour, spices, beverage, and fruit and sweets from a common feast-meal.[104] This is, up to now, the only text revealing a delivery for a collective meal of royal dependents, in this case *mḏrġlm*.[105]

Our documentation about rations to royal dependents from Ugarit is far from being so rich as the data from the big temple-royal economies from Mesopotamia during the Ur III period.[106] At the same time, our data from Ugarit is much broader than from Alalaḫ of the VIIth level (XVIII-XVIIth century B.C.E.) and its IVth level. (XVth century B.C.E.)[107] It is interesting to note that in Ugarit the dependent status of the service-people is always underlined. The Ugaritic documentation is more precise than the Middle-Assyrian documentation of more or less the same period[108] or from the Hittite Empire.[109]

Naturally, such a system of distributions and allotments existed in other places, but not in the same form as in Ugarit. In the Old-Babylonian kingdom the distribution system was more in the form of wages,[110] and

---

[103] The figures given by *Liverani*, d, that the yearly production of one working person was 60 *dd* and his consumption reached 12 *dd* are not realistically calculated from the data we have. Until now the figures and the texts by themselves are too lapidary for such conclusions.

[104] More about this text, *Heltzer*, R, pp. 413-415.

[105] On Mari cf. *Glaeseman*, a.

[106] *Tjumenev*, a, pp. 379-413, *Gelb*, a, pp. 230-243, *Gelb*, b, pp. 11-24.

[107] *Heltzer*, r, pp. 23-25; *Klengel*, a, pp. 439-441 (with the previous bibliography given).

[108] *Freydank*, a, pp. 127-130.

[109] *Giorgadze*, a, pp. 9-131. The Hittite sources give only the possibility to state that there existed, sometimes, a similar system of product-distributions; on land-allotments *Imparati*, a; cf. also *Kestemont*, a, pp. 17-28.

[110] *Yoffe*, a, pp. 31-43 and 143-144; cf. also *Kraus*, a, pp. 423-434.

working teams existed in the state-economy more on the basis of slavery or as prisoners of war. In Egypt we know of the ration system, also, for labour-gangs, and also stabile distributions to the workers of the Theban necropolis.[111]

Otherwise, it seems that the distribution systems in Pylos and Knossos, according to the Linear B tablets were based on very similar principles as the Ugaritic system.[112]

§4. Some Other Kinds of Distributions

We must now consider the widely discussed question of distribution of two items *šʿrt* and *ššlmt*. For, in order to understand these terms, we must consider the texts where they appear and analyze them.

These are the following Ugaritic alphabetic texts: *a*) KTU.4.46; *b*) KTU. 4.131; *c*) KTU.4.144; *d*) KTU.4.153; *e*) KTU.4.378; *f*) KTU.4.395; *g*) KTU. 4.630; *h*) KTU.4.705.

a) ....[113]

1	[ ]*bn. š*[*šlmt*]	"[....]*bn*[114] *š*[*šlmt*]
2	*bnš.Iwl*[.*š*]*šlmt*	The man.... *š*[*šlmt*]
3	*Šdyn.ššlmt*	*Šdyn* the (or "a") *ššlmt*
4	*Prtwn šʿrt*	*Prtwn* wool (or barley)[115]
5	*Tṯn.šʿrt*	*Tṯn*. wool (or barley)
6	*ʿdn.šʿrt*	*ʿdn* wool (or barley)
7	*Mn.n šʿrt*	*Mnn* wool (or barley)
8	*Bdn.šʿrt*	*Bdn* wool (or barley)
9	*ʿpṯn.šʿrt*	*ʿpṯn* wool (or barley)

[111] *Saffirio*, a, pp. 30-73. The author takes into account all possible documentary sources in this field and sometimes gives us also daily rations of working teams for the period of the New Kingdom. Cf. also *Janssen*, a, pp. 226-231; *Janssen*, b, pp. 509-513.

[112] *Poljakova*, a, pp. 258-266; *Chadwick*, a.

[113] The beginning of the text is not preserved.

[114] End or beginning of a personal name.

[115] Hebr. *ś^{e}ōrā* "barley" and *śēʿarā*, "hair" Akk. *šārtu* "hair". Only in the case when the name of the Ugaritic village *Šʿrt* is written in Akkadian by the Sumerian sign SIG "wool" we are sure that it is not barley.

10 *ʿbd.yrḫ šʿrt*	*ʿbdyrḫ* wool (or barley)
11 *Ḫbd.ṯr.yṣr.šʿr*<*t*>	*Ḫbdṯr* the potter wool (or barley)
12 *Pdy.yṣr šʿrt*	*Pdy*, the potter wool (or barley)
13 *Atnb.ḥrš* 14 *ʿrq šʿrt*	*Atnb*, the cartwright wool (or barley)."

We have seen here that among the people mentioned are at least three who were royal dependents and, it seems, so were the other people.

b) 1 *lqḥ.šʿrt*	"(People who) took wool[116]
2 *Urḫ.ln.kkrm*	*Urḫln* two talents
3 *w.rṭd.kd.šmn*	and *Rṭd* (1) jar oil
4 .....*drt.b.kkr*	]*drt* by talent
5 *Ubn.ḫṣ kkr*	*Ubn* 1/2 talent
6 *kkr.lqḥ Ršpy*	(1) talent took *Ršpy*
7 *Tmrtn.bn.Pnmn* 8 *kkr*	*TMrtn*, son of *Pnmn* (1) talent
9 *bn.Sgṯtn* 10 *kkr*	*Bn Sgṯtn* (1) talent
11 *Ilšpš.kkr*	*Ilšpš* (1) talent
12 *bnʿgltn* 13 *kkr.w*[ ]	*Bn ʿgltn* (1) talent and [ ]
14	.........."

This text gives only the personal names and wool. Except for wool we know of only one person who also took 1 jar of oil. In this case it is difficult to conclude that this is a ration, perhaps it is a natural payment, or a distribution of wool to spinners or weavers. The forthcoming analysis has to give an answer. At least we know that it is wool.

c) 1 *spr.bnš.mlk*	"List of royal dependents,
2 *d.bd.Prṯ*	which are at the disposal of *Prṯ*
3 *tšʿ.l.ʿšrm*	29 (persons)
4 *lqḥ.ššlmt*	took[121] (the) *ššlmt*
5 *ṯmn.l.arbʿm*	48 persons
6 *lqḥ.šʿrt*	took wool (or barley)."

[116] The word *kkr*, "talent" in the following lines shows that it was wool, and not "barley" — measured by other units of measure used in measuring grain.

Here the numbers are given, not according to individual persons, but designated are also the total number of the people, but not the quantities of the *ššlmt* and *šʿrt*. We also see that the people were royal dependents at the disposal of a certain (official) *Prṯ*.

d) . . . .[117]

1	*ilk.rʿ[ym(?)*]	"The *ilku*-service[118] of the she[pherds]
2	*Aršm.bʿl [aṯt]*	*Aršm*, — husband ? of a [wife](?)
3	*Tṯḫ.bʿl.aṯt*	*Tṯḫ*, husband ? of a wife(?)
4	*Ayab.bʿl aṯt*	*Ayab*, husband ? of a wife(?)
5	*Iyṯr. bʿl aṯt*	*Iyṯr* husband ? of a wife(?)[119]
6	*Ptm.bʿl ššlmt*	*Ptm*, owner ? of *ššlmt*[120]
7	*ʿdršp.bʿl ššlmt*	*ʿdršp*, owner ? of *ššlmt*
8	*Ṯtrn.bʿl ššlmt*	*Ṯtrn*, owner ? of *ššlmt*
9	*Arśwn.bʿl ššlmt*	*Arśwn*, owner ? of *ššlmt*
10	*Ḥdṯn.bʿl ššlmt*	*Ḥdṯn*, owner ? of *ššlmt*
11	*Ssn.bʿl ššlmt*	*Ssn*, owner ? of *ššlmt*"

So we see different persons, 4 of them are *bʿl aṯt*, 6 of them are *bʿl ššlmt*, and all are connected with the *ilku*-service of the shepherds *rʿ[ym]*. Only the following analysis can show us what the real connection of the *ilku* was with the shepherds, the *bʿl aṯt* and *bʿl ššlmt*.

We must remember that the numbers are given not according to individual persons in text *c* but designated also are the total numbers of people. However, the quantities of the *ššlmt* and *šʿrt* are not. We see that these people were royal dependents at the disposal of a certain (official) *Prṯ*.

e) 1	*spr.rʿym*	"List of shepherds
2	*lqḥ.šʿrt*	which took wool (or barley):
3	*Anntn*	*Anntn*
4	*ʿdn*	*ʿdn*

[117] The beginning of the tablet is not preserved.

[118] Ch. II, p. 16.

[119] Or "Owner of a woman"(?).

[120] *ššlmt* — cf. below; possibly also that *bʿl*, "owner" is here a recipient of *ššlmt*, "pay", as well as instead of *pʿl* can be "worker", and then "worker for pay," i.e., "hired workers,"(?) but cf. below for a more trustworthy view.

[121] Plural, 3. pers. perfect.

5 *Sdrn*	*Sdrn*
6 *Mzln*	*Mzln*
7 *Ḫyrn*	Ḫyrn
8 *Ṯ'ln*	*Ṯ'ln*
9 [*'š*]*rm.ṯn.kbd*	22 in all
10 *śġrm*	apprentices
11 *lqḥ.ššlmt*	took (the) *šślmt*"

We see in this text a very interesting thing. Six shepherds listed by name took the *š'rt* and 22 of their apprentices (*śġrm)* took the *šślmt*. *(The latter are listed only as a total.) What is the difference in the overall analysis of texts of these types?*

f) 1 *bnšm.d.b.u*[ ]	"(Royal) people[122] which are at (or in) the *u*[ ].
2 *tš'.dt.tqḥ*[*n*] 3 *š'rt*	Nine (of them), which took wool (or barley)
4 *šb' dt tqḥn* 5 *šślmt*	Seven of them, which took *šślmt*."

So we see here the following things: 16 *bnš mlk* were at the *u*[ ], and their payment or rations were differentiated. One group took the "wool" or "barley", the other the *šślmt*.

g) 1 *aḥd kbd* 2 *arb'm.b.ḫzr* 3 *lqh.š'rt*	"41 in all of the males[123] (persons) took wool (or barley)
4 *ṯṯ 'šrh.lqḥ* 5 *ḫlpnt*	16 (persons) took *ḫlpnt*[124] garments
6 *ṯṯ.ḥrṯm* 7 *lqḥ š'rt*	6 plowmen took wool
8 *'šr.ḥrš* 9 *bhtm.lqḥ* 10 *š'rt*	10 housebuilders took wool
11 *arb'.* 12 *ḥrš qṭn* 13 *lqḥ š'rt*	4 *qatinnu*-makers took wool
14 *ṯṯ.nsk.ḥẓm* 15 *lqḥ.š'rt*	6 arrow-casters took wool"

---

[122] Abridge from *bnš mlk*.

[123] Cf. *Heltzer*, S, pp. 410-412. — *ḫzr* = *ġzr*, "male" in late non-literary Ugaritic.

[124] UT, p. 402, No. 968, "in any case hair" possibly similar to *š'rt*, "wool", ZUL, I, BO, 23, p. 129, "a kind of tunic"; cf. also *Dijkstra-Moor*, a, p. 212 and *Heltzer*, b, p. 39, No. 88 and note 303; *Eissfeldt*, a, p. 24.

This text is very interesting and important in order to understand the whole series of texts. We see a) that *š'rt* is wool, for *ḫlpnt* — a garment — cannot be made from barley; b) the scribe made a mistake. The total number of persons of various professions in lines 4-14 is 42, but in line 1-2, 41 are mentioned; c) this shows us that *š'rt* is wool, but in one case there were woolen textiles or garments; d) that *ḫzr*, "persons, males" is the collective designation of those who took the *ḫlpnt*-garments (or textiles), the plowmen, the housebuilders, the *qatinnu*-makers and the arrow-casters; e) all these were people of productive professions.

The analysis of the seven texts given above gives us some additional data:

a) The fact that in *b* and *g*, *š'rt* appears, as it does in many texts from Ugarit, shows that in the remaining texts it is also wool. We see, thus, that it was a wool delivery.

b) The recipients, according to these texts, were mostly *bnš mlk*, named by profession or name, or by both elements together. Thus wool deliveries were made to *bnš mlk*. (Cf. also KTU.4.705). However, we do not know for what purpose the wool deliveries were made.

It is not less important that the counterpart of *š'rt* is the *ššlmt*. What is the meaning of this term? We have no idea of what elements the *ššlmt* consists. It appears in *a*, 1-3 (together with *š'rt*); *c*, 3-4 (together with *š'rt*); *d*, 6-11 (without *š'rt*); *e*, 9-11 (together with *š'rt*); *f*, 4-5 (together with *š'rt*). In all cases where *š'rt* is also mentioned the people (*lqḥ*) took it. In the case of *d* — *b'l ššlmt* — is given.

What kind of payment or delivery was this? The existing dictionaries show it as follows: *Aistleitner* uses first of all the basic text, *d*, and there *b'l aṯt* appears with *b'l ššlmt*. Therefore, he understands it as "garment"(?) or "a kind of concubine."[125] *Gordon*[126] connects it with "rendering (service or taxes)", but he does not enter into the whole question of its meaning. The most recent works do not give any definitive answer, either.[127]

More convincing are the interpretations of *Dietrich* and *Loretz*,[128] who understand it as a "garment", for it appears together with *š'rt*, "wool."

[125] WUS, p. 317, No. 2699 comparing with Akk. *ša šelemtu*.

[126] UT, p. 490, No. 2424, *šlm*, p. 491 (*šaf'el*).

[127] *Macdonald*, a, pp. 166, 167, polemizing with *Muntingh*, a, pp. 100-107, where the word is translated "concubine"; *Rainey*, d, p. 77, No. 6 "*ššlmt*-woman".

[128] ZUL, I, BO, 23, p. 132.

At the same time in *bʿl ššlmt* they explain *bʿl* as *pʿl*, "Hersteller" = "producer, maker." In such a case they have to interpret *aṯt*, not as "woman", but according to AHW, p. 80, *asâtu I*, "Zügel" — "rein", "bridle (of horses)". Later, the same authors, together with *Sanmartin*,[129] return to their former point of view, concurring with *C.H. Gordon*s interpretation, "a devoted and sacred woman."[130]

We accept the former point of view of *Loretz-Dietrich-Sanmartin* and understand the *ššlmt* as a certain garment, or possibly, textile, and possibly one not made from wool. Otherwise there would be no difference between *šʿrt* and *ššlmt*. It also seems that we have to accept the interpretation of *aṯt*, in this case, not as "woman", but as "rein" or "girdle of the horse." Then we can propose a new interpretation of the whole text of *d*.

1 The *ilku*-service of the shep[herds]

---

2 *Aršm* producer of reins (girdles)
3-5 In all these lines *Ttḫ*, *Ayab*, *Iyṯr* appear in the same function.

---

6 *Ptm*, producer of *ššlmt* (garments or textiles)
7-11 *ʿdršp*. *Ṯtrm*, *Arśwn*, *Ḥdṯn* and *Ssn* appear in the same function.

After a correct interpretation of this text we can see that it has something in common with deliveries. Thus, along with the *ubdy* and *ḥpr*-ration, there were deliveries of wool and textiles (*šʿrt* and *ššlmt*) which were general terms and they were made to individuals or to certain groups of population.

We have seen, therefore, that the *bnš mlk* benefitted in Ugarit from: a) land-allotments (*ubd(y)-pilku*, and the service for it, b) silver distributions, c) distributions of various products (grain, oil, wine) and d) possibly from the distribution of wool and textiles.

We can now approach the study of the royal economy and its personnel.

---

[129] ZUL, VIII, p. 115, No. 65.

[130] *Gordon*, a, pp. 110-111 together with the unrealistic proposals.

CHAPTER IV

THE ROYAL AGRICULTURAL ECONOMY

§1. The *gt*

In discussing the royal economy, and to begin with the agricultual branch, we must begin with the primary unit — the *gt*. This Ugaritic term has its Akkadian counterpart *dimtu(m)*, within phonetically *di-im-tu(m)*, *dim-tu(m)* and sometimes with the determinative GIŠ*(iṣu)*, designating that it was made of wood, or sometimes with the determination *É(bîtu)* "house", showing that it was a building. It is often spelled in Sumerian as AN.ZA.QAR. Its primary meaning is, without any doubt, "tower".[1]

It is not our task here to deal with the *dimtu*, when it appears as a "tower" or a part of the city fortifications or as a "siege-tower", known from the Old Akkadian to Neo-Assyrian times. In our case we see special meaning when the word *dimtu* appears in an agricultual context, beginning from the Old Babylonian times.[2] Thus, we know in Sippar, "an orchard together with the *dimtum* "GIŠ.SAR.*qa-dum di-im-tim*, *eqel* (A.ŠÀ *dimtim* "field of a *dimtum*") i.e., a field, which had a *dimtu* appears frequently in Old Babylonian texts from various Mesopotamian towns.[3]

The term *dimtu* appears also frequently in Nuzi and there the term has many meanings. Sometimes, we see that it is connected with a garden, well, house, or with land-ownership[4] or as an administrative district.[5] In Nuzi (Arrapḫa) in the XVth cent. B.C.E. this term also had more than one meaning. According to the definition of *N.B. Jankowska*[6] the term *dimtu*

---

[1] CAD, D, pp. 144a-147a, AHW, pp. 170b-171a — with most of its meanings and the respective *Belegestellen*.

[2] Cf. CAD, D, p. 144b 2′a′, p. 145a (3) b1′.

[3] BE 6/1, 62, 5, 11 (= HG, III 451); 70, 7 (= HG III, 412), 77, 2 = HG, III 526) and other numerous places.

[4] AHW, 171a4; CAD, D, 144b 1, 2′c′ p. 145b3.

[5] CAD, D, p. 146, 3b.

[6] *Jankowska*, a, p. 238; *Jankowska*, b, pp. 218-229, 274-276.

designated there: "(a) fortified dwelling of an extended family commune; (b) the extended family commune itself; (c) the territory of its possessions, including its buildings and fields in their totality." Possibly, one was a settlement — *Kuruḫḫanni.*[7] As *Zaccagnini* points out, the term *dimtu* in Nuzi had a broader sense. According to his documentary study, *dimtu* had the meaning of a settlement, surrounded by fields and orchards. Sometimes it may have been a fortified manor/farmhouse together with all of its economic buildings and fields. But the real sense of the word in Nuzi could be broader according to *Zaccagnini.*[8]

The above-said gives clear evidence that the word *dimtu* with it primary meaning, "tower", could have developed various meanings in various places and for various reasons. Sometimes it may have had different meanings in the same period and region. This forces us to reconsider the term as it appears in the Akkadian texts from Ugarit[9] from the XIV-XIIIth cent. B.C.E. and first of all land transactions. Our attention will be directed to the spelling of the word *dimtu*, and to the other elements of the agricultural economy, which appear together with the *dimtu*.

The number of cases which we will consider here, and where the *dimtu* is mentioned, is thirty-one.[10] Twenty-nine cases belong to the reign of Ammistamru II, i.e. to the central part of the XIIIth cent. B.C.E. In nineteen cases, the determinative *É (bîtu)* "house" "building" appears before the word *dimtu*, and it is beyond any doubt that the *dimtu* was a certain building. The texts under consideration do not deal always with houses of single peasants, and the person from whom the land was taken or to whom it was given did not necessarily have to live there. Therefore, it is of special interest that in the texts PRU, III, 15.123; PRU, VI, 27 and 32 we see that under consideration was *bît* [*x qa*]-*du eq*[*lāti*^{MEŠ}-*šu*] *qa-du* ^{bit}*dimāti*^{KIMEŠ}-*š*[*u*] *qa-du* ^{is}*serdi*^{MEŠ}*š*-[*u*] *qa-d*[*u kir*]*i-šu qa-du gab-bu mim-*

---

[7] *Al-Khalesi*, a, pp. 1-42; *Ismail-Müller*, a, pp. 14-34.

[8] *Zaccagnini*, b, pp. 47-52.

[9] CAD, D, p. 144b, 1a211′, p. 145a (b) 2′.

[10] PRU, III, 15.127, 4-7; 15.132, 4-7 and 8-11; 15.139, 11-13; 15.140, 4-8; 15.141, 7-9; 15.155, 6-9 and 12-14; 16.138, 3-6, 7-10, 11-12, 13-14, 15-17 and 24-25; 16.154, 4-7; 16.178, 3-6; 16.201, 6-13; 16.204, 5-7, 9-10, 12-14 and 15-18; 16.254C, 4-5; 16.254F, 4-8; 16.261, 6-14; 16.343, 4-6 and 10-12; 16.353, 7-8, PRU, VI, 27 (RS 17.01) 3-5; 29 (RS 17.147), 4-9; 31 (RS 19.98), 5-10; 56 (RS.17.121) V. 3′-5′.

ma-šu[11] "the house of X (pers. name) with [his] fiel[ds], with his *dimtu* (buildings),[12] with h[is] olive groves, with its vineyar[d], with [his] orchar[ds], and with all what he has." These three texts give us evidence that the *dimtu* was not considered as a living-house (or "tower" resp.). In twelve cases[13] we find after the word *dimtu*, the determinative KI, which designates here a certain area (space).[14] Perhaps here we have the proof that the *dimtu* were not one building, but sometimes consisted of several buildings, dispersed in the same area and possibly that the KI.MEŠ in PRU, VI, 31, 6 gives evidence in favour of such an understanding.[15]

Perhaps of secondary importance is the fact that in most texts the word *dimtu* appears after the word *eqlu* "field" and precedes all other kinds of land (cf. above). In five cases[16] this order is not followed and the *dimtu* is mentioned between the other kinds of productive land and in one case (PRU, III, 16.254C, 4) precedes even the *eqlu* "field". But all this produces the best evidence that the *dimtu* was organically incorporated into the whole complex of the agricultural economy of a single family or patronymy. It is possible that the *dimtu* sometimes consisted of more than one building. All this evidence makes the translation of the term, in this case, as "tower" dubious. But we may take another meaning in this case. In the texts U, V, 96 (RS.20.12) and 95 (RS.20.01) we find among the other *dimtu* names *Tagabira* and *Mabari*. These two *dimtu* are known also from the alphabetic Ugaritic texts as *Tgbr(y)*[17] and *M'br*[17]. But here the *dimtu* appear not as a particular building, but as the primary unit of the royal economy. These units were dispersed throughout the whole territory of the kingdom of Ugarit. The interesting thing here is that the Ugaritic term, an exact counterpart of the Akkadian *dimtu* in this sense, was *gt*.[18] But this is a

---

[11] According to PRU VI, 32, 5-10 — other texts are very similar.

[12] The plural sign in the case when we have only one complex of land after the sign KI is unique.

[13] PRU, III, 16.138, 4, 9, 11, 13, 16, 25; 16.201, 8; 16.261, 12; 16.204, 6, 13, 17; PRU, VI, 31, 6.

[14] Cf. also *Kühne*, a, I, p. 164, note 41; II, p. 255, note 40.

[15] PRU, III, 15.132, 4-7 and 8-10; 16.154, 4-7; 16.204, 9-10; 16.254C, 4-5.

[16] KTU, 4.271, 7; U.V 96, 5-6 and 13-17, 23-24.

[17] KTU, 4.243, 12-13, U.V.9, 7-9 and 20-22.

[18] AHW, p. 171, 5b, "Gutsbezirk" — "area of real estate", cf. also *Heltzer*, c, and below, *Heltzer*, a, pp. 8-15; *Heltzer*, g, pp. 37-43; *Heltzer*, q, pp. 32-47.

counterpart not in the linguistic sense, but only according to its meaning. These are equivalent terms — one in Akkadian, the other in Ugaritic. The word *gt* has nothing in common with the literary meaning "tower" — *dimtu*. In biblical Hebrew, the word *gat* means "oil or wine-press". It seems also that the vocalization of *gt* in Ugaritic has to be **gattu*, and the root here is **gnt*.[19] Thus we see that *gat* and *dimtu* have no linguistic proximity. We must note that also in the OT the meaning of the word *gat* is not limited to "oil or wine-press". Thus, in Jud. 6:11, we read that Gideon was "threshing wheat on the *gat*, for to hide it from the Midianites."[20] This passage is very important, for it relates about events at the end of the second millennium B.C.E., chronologically close to the texts from Ugarit of the XIIIth cent. B.C.E. The *gat* appears also as a storage-place of agricultural products in Joel 4:13. And in Jes. 5:2 we again have the word "tower" in Hebrew coinciding in a certain way with its first meaning in the agrarian texts of Ugarit. On the other hand, *yeqeb* has a very close relation to the sense of *gat*. So we see that here it did not have to be necessarily a "watch-tower,"[21] but an economic unit or building, depending on what context it appears in. The equivalence of the terms *dimtu/gt* in Akkadian and Ugaritic results also from the text U.V. 96 and 95 (RS.20.12 and 20.101) where well-known Ugaritic *gt*, such as *Śi-ka-ni-ma*[22] (*Sknm*) and *Ma-ba-ri (M'br)*, are called *dimtu*. However, in the administrative texts, written mostly in Ugaritic, the term *gt/dimtu* is connected with the royal economic system.

Although the kingdom of Ugarit included about 200 villages, the number of *gt* known from the documents published amounts only to 78.[23] Of these,

---

[19] Cf. also *Kühne*, a, p. 163, note 36.

[20] ... *ḥobēṭ ḥiṭṭīm bag-gat lᵉhānis mip-pᵉnē Midyān*.

[21] Cf. *Heltzer*, u, pp. 31-35 where the etymologies and similar features from other societies and periods are given; *Preisigke*, a, pp. 423-432; *Meyer*, a, pp. 100-102; *Sperber*, a, pp. 359-361.

[22] The correct reading *Sí-kà-ni-ma*, and equivalence to the Ugaritic *Sknm* was proposed by *E. Lipinski*, instead of the reading of *Nougayrol*, *Zi-qa-ni-ma* (U.V) which has no equivalent in Ugaritic spelling.

[23] We have used here only the Akkadian texts given below and the Ugaritic administrative texts in which a concrete *gt* is mentioned or in which the name of a *gt* appears. Passages are also taken into account in which the word *gt* is omitted before the name of a particular *gt*, but the general context shows that this is indeed a *gt*; a slightly out-of-date list of the Ugaritic villages and *gt*, cf. *Heltzer*, a, pp. 8-18;

30 names coincide with the names of known villages: *Alḫb*,[24] *Ar*(^{URU}*A-ri?*),[25] *Atlg*(^{URU}*A-tal-lig*),[26] *Ilštmʿ*(^{URU}DINGIR-*iš-tam-ʾi*),[27] *Ipṯl*,[28] *Ulm*-(^{URU}*Ul-la-mi*),[29] *Bir*(^{URU}*Bi-i-ri*),[30] *Gbʿly*(^{URU}*Gi-Ba-la*, ^{URU}*Gi*$_5$-^{d}*U-la*, ^{URU}*Gi*$_5$*-Ba-a-li-ia*),[31] *Gwl*(*Gu-wa-li*),[32] *Gnʿy*(^{URU}*Ga-ni-ia*),[33] *bît Du-me-te*(*Dmt*) (?)[34], *Zbl*,[35] *Ḥdṯt*(^{m}*Ḫu-da-ši*),[36] *Ḫldy*(^{URU}*Ḫu-ul-da*),[37] *Ṭ/Tbq*(^{URU}*Ṭi/Te-ba-qu*),[38] *Yknʿm*(^{URU}*Ia-ku-na-me*),[39] *Yny*(^{URU}*Ia-na*),[40] *Yʿny*(^{URU}*Ia-a-ni-ia*),[41] *Knpy* (*Ka-an-na-pi-ia*),[42] *Mlk*(^{URU}*Mu-lu-uk-ku*),[43] *Mʿbr*(*Ma-ba-ri*),[44] *Mʿrby* (^{URU}*Ma-ʾa-ra-ba*),[45] *Mṣbt*(^{URU}*Ma-ṣi-bat*),[46] *Mril*(^{URU}*Ma-ra-ila*),[47] *Nḫl*,[48]

---

more or less all the names of the Ugaritic villages together with a commentary, *Astour*, b, pp. 251-369. Our list of *gt*'s is here slightly revised compared with *Heltzer*, c, pp. 460-462; cf. also *Liverani*, SDB, pp. 1341-1342.

[24] KTU.4.243, 16.

[25] KTU.4.382, 15; KTU.4.139, 5.

[26] KTU.4.618, 27; KTU.4.625.

[27] KTU.1.80, 11; KTU.4.382, 15, 26, 33; *Astour*, b, p. 264, No. 14, p. 352, No. 152.

[28] KTU.4.125, 11; 4.213, 19; 4.397, 5; 4.618, 7, 25; 4.625, 13.

[29] KTU.4.213, 9-10; 4.307, 2; 4.618, 9, 26; 4.625, 4; *Astour*, b, p. 269, No. 17; p. 367, No. 195.

[30] KTU.4.313, 12-13; 4.625, 15; 4.636.2; *Astour*, b, p. 269; No. 18; 346, No. 133.

[31] KTU.4.618, 28; 4.380, 6; 4.386, 2; 4.365, 6.

[32] KTU.4.213, 18; 4.397, 7; 4.618, 4, 24; 4.623, 11.

[33] KTU.4.213, 22; 4.382, 14; *Astour*, b, p. 274, No. 26; *Astour*, b, p. 347, No. 139.

[34] PRU, VI, 122 (RS.21.203); the determinative *bît* (É) may indicate that *Dumati* is a *gt*/*dimtu*; *Astour*, b, p. 346, No. 136 and p. 27, No. 33 and not as *Astour*, f, p. 17.

[35] KTU.4.213, 13; *Astour*, b, p. 284, No. 38.

[36] KTU.4.213, 12; 4.243, 22; U.V. 95, 4 (RS.20.01); *Astour*, b, p. 276, No. 29.

[37] KTU.4.636, 10.

[38] KTU.4.213, 5; 4.243.10.

[39] KTU.4.307.

[40] KTU.4.320, 2.

[41] KTU.4.243, 26; 4.296, 14.

[42] KTU.4.243, 18; 4.271, 1; 4.296, 10; *Kühne*, a, II, pp. 253-256.

[43] KTU.4.105, 5; 4.161, 1-4; 4.750, 13.

[44] KTU.4.243, 12; U.V.96, 7, 20 (RS.20.12).

[45] KTU.4.213, 8; 4.307, 3.

[46] KTU.4.345, 1-2; *Astour*, b, p. 302, No. 64, p. 356, No. 19 164-165.

[47] KTU.4.345, 8-9.

[48] KTU.4.243, 24; 4.296, 9.

Np/bk(m)(Na-ap/pa-ki-ma),[49] *Sġy*,[50] *ʿnmky(*^{URU}IGI*-ma-ka-(ia))*,[51] *ʿnqpat (*^{URU}IGI*-qáp-at)*,[52] *Ġl(=Ḫly?)*, ^{URU}*Ḫi/Ḫu-li)*,[53] *Rqd(*^{URU}*Riq-di)*,[54] *Šdm*,[55] *Šlmy(*^{URU}*Šal-me-ia)*,[56] *Šʿrt(*^{URU}SIG*)*,[57] *Šrš(*^{URU}*Šu-ra-šu)*,[58] *Ṯlṭ(Śld*, ^{URU}*Sú-la-ṭa/i)*,[59] *Ṯm(*^{URU}*Šúm-me)*,[60] *Ṯpn/Šbn(*^{URU}*Šu-ba-nu)*,[61] *Ṯrmn*.[62]

The following 39 *gt* names do not coincide with names of known villages: *Al*,[63] *Aġld*,[64] *bn Il*,[65] *(dimtu of)Ilumilku(*^{m}DINGIR-LUGAL*)*,[66] *Irbṣ*,[67] *Bʿln*,[68] *Gbry*,[69] *(dimtu)Gal-ni-um*,[70] *Glʿd*,[71] *Gpn*,[72] *Dprnm*,[73] *Ḥṣb*,[74] *Ḥrṯm*,[75], *Yṡd*,[76] *bn.Ksb/d/u*,[77] *Krr*,[78] *Mzln*,[79] *Mlkt*,[80] *Mnḥm*,[81] *Mġrt*,[82] *Ngr*,[83]

---

[49] KTU.4.103, 45; 4.141, 12-14; 4.269, 19; 4.638, 3; *Kühne*, a, II, pp. 258-260.

[50] KTU.4.213, 15; 4.625, 7.

[51] KTU.4.243, 28; U.V.96, 3-4 (RS.20.12) (INIM.ME.IGI is also possibly *ʿnmky*); *Astour*, b, p. 309, No. 77; p. 353, No. 153.

[52] KTU.4.296, 1.

[53] KTU.4.141, III, 15; 4,200, 8; 4.243, 14; 4.320, 8; 4.636, 15; *Kühne*, a, I, pp. 166-167.

[54] KTU.4.397, 11.

[55] KTU.4.320, 18; *Astour*, b, p. 306, No. 72.

[56] KTU.4.382, 20; *Astour*, b, p. 330, No. 101; p. 364, No. 186.

[57] KTU.4.382, 25; *Astour*, b, p. 331, No. 103; p. 365, No. 189.

[58] KTU.4.397, 9; *Astour*, b, p. 334, No. 106; p. 366, No. 191.

[59] KTU.4.96; *Astour*, b, p. 364, No. 183.

[60] KTU.4.424, 13 ^{URU}*Šum-me*, against ZUL, VII, pp. 82-83.

[61] KTU.4.89, 3; 4.213, 21; 4.382.28; 4.618, 1-3, 23; *Astour*, b, p. 339, No. 115.

[62] KTU.4.243, 20-21; 4.296, 8-10; 4.139, 9.

[63] KTU.4.382, 27.

[64] KTU.4.382, 32.

[65] KTU.4.297, 3 and possibly also PRU, VI, 29 (RS.17.147), 3 [Á.Š]À^{MEŠ}(?) *e-la-ya*.

[66] U.V.95 (RS.20.01), 14.

[67] KTU.4.122, 1; 4.125, 13; KTU.4.200, 9-10; KTU.4.358, 5.

[68] KTU.4.358, 6; 4.636, 5.

[69] KTU.4.296, 12-13.

[70] U.V.95, 13 (RS.20.01).

[71] KTU.4.125, 2; *Astour*, b, p. 275, No. 28.

[72] KTU.4.358, 7-8.

[73] KTU.4.175, 9; cf. *Kühne*, a, I, p. 163, Akk. TI-BI-*ra-ni-ma* = *Dipran(ima)*.

[74] KTU.4.409, 7.

[75] KTU.4.141, III, 1, 11; 4.618, 21; 4.625, 17; *Astour*, a, p. 276, No. 30.

[76] KTU.4.139, 7.

[77] KTU.4.297, 6.

[78] KTU.4.139, 9.

[79] KTU.4.110, 15-21; 4.307, 1.

Nḫry,[84] *Nṯṯ*,[85] *Sknm*,[86] *ʿmq*,[87] *ʿṯrt*,[88] *Pḫn*,[89] *Psḥn*,[90] *Pri*,[91] *Prn*,[92] *Ṣbʳ/k*,[93] *Rbt*,[94] *Špšyn*,[95] *bn.Tbšn*,[96] *Tgbry* and *Ta-ga-bi-ra*,[97] *Tgyn*,[98] *Trġnds*,[99] *Ṯġrm*,[100] *Ṯryn*.[101]

The names not coinciding with village names are derived at least partly from agricultural terms (*Gpn*, "vineyard"), personal names (*bn Il*, *bn.Tbšn*, *Ilumilku*, *Mnḥm*, *Špšyn*), or professional names (*Ḥrṯm*, "ploughmen"; *Ngr*, "herald", or "carpenter"; *Mlkt*, "the queen"), or *ṯġrm* "gates" or "gate-keepers". They are virtually as numerous as the names coinciding with those of villages. However, it should be borne in mind that new village names may appear in documents still to be published. Besides, we have no exact datation within the XIV-XIIIth centuries B.C.E. and it is therefore possible that at least a few *gt* did not exist during all this period. Still, these considerations do not change the general picture.

---

80 KTU.4.142, 1-2.

81 KTU.4.139, 4.

82 KTU.4.125, 18; *Astour*, b, p. 301, No. 63; *Bordreuil-ʿAjjan*, a, p. 6.

83 KTU.4.125, 3.

84 KTU.4.89, 1; *Astour*, b, p. 305, No. 71; p. 359, No. 171.

85 KTU.4.409, 8; KTU.1.75, 1, 5.

86 KTU.4.213, 1-3; 4.243, 7-9; U.V., 96, 1, 18-19 (RS.20.12).

87 KTU.4.625, 9-10; *Astour*, b, p. 277, No. 31.

88 KTU.4.125, 5-6; 4.696, 6; *Astour*, b, p. 277, No. 32.

89 KTU.4.141, III, 5.

90 KTU.4.96, 12.

91 *gt bn Pri*; KTU.4.297, 1-2.

92 KTU.4.110; 3-14.

93 KTU.4.400, 1-2.

94 KTU.4.125, 10.

95 KTU.4.213, 20; 4.297, 4.

96 KTU.4.96, 1-8.

97 KTU.4.271, 7; U.V.96 (RS.20.12), (13) *T[ák!]-ka-bar-ia*, according to *E. Lipinski* and (16) *Ta-ka-bi-ra-ia*. *E. Lipinski* sees it as different from *Ta-ga-bi-ra*-U.V.96 and 23, but we consider it as the same *gt*.

98 KTU.4.97, 5-6; 4.643, 9.

99 KTU.4.141, III, 2.

100 KTU.4.141, III, 11.

101 KTU.4.636, 1; cf. also the passages where the name of the *gt* is completely illegible; KTU.4.111, 9; 4.118, 8, 10; 4.120, 1; 4.139, 2, 8; 4.213, 20; 4.271, 2, 3; 4.297, 5; 4.345, 7; 4.358, 4; 4.400, 5, 10, 18; 4.405, 5; 4.574, 2; 4.636, 20, 25, 31; 4.696, 3, 4, 5, 9; 4.733, 3.

It should be added that some large villages contained two or three *gt*. Thus, in KTU.4.110, which deals with *ubdy*-fields,[102] we read: (1) *šd.ubdy. Ilštmʿ* (2) *dt.bd.skn*, "the *ubdy*-fields (pl.st.cstr.) of (the village of) *Ilštmʿ* which are at the disposal (lit. "in the hands") of the *sākinu* ("vizier, superintendent") (Cf. Ch. VIII). Lines 3-11 follow the pattern *šd* PN *b.gt Prn*, "the field of PN at *gt Prn*." And lines 15-22 have in five passages: *šd* PN *l.gt.Mzln*, "the field of PN (belonging) to *gt Mzln*." Since a *gt Ilštmʿ* is also known in KTU.1.80, this village had at least three *gt: Ilštmʿ*, *Prn*, and *Mzln*. It also seems to be in the tablet KTU.4.643.9 [ ]*xyb b.Bqʿt b gt Tgyn*, "[ ]*xyb* (PN) in (the village) *Bqʿt* at the *gt Tqyn*." So we see that the *gt Tgyn* was in the village of *Bqʿt*. Or, text KTU.4.244 relates that (1) *spr*[.]*šd. Ri*[*šym*] (2) *krm.w.šdm*[ ] *x*[ ] (3) *b.gt.Ṯm x*[ ]... "List of fields of the [people] of *Riš*. Vineyard and fields (or two fields) at the *gt Ṯm x*[ ]." The meaning seems here to be that the *gt Ṯm x*[ ] was at the village of *Riš*.

Therefore we can see here that even in these cases, where names of the villages coincide with the name of the *gt*'s we have to do with two different things. And we think that these *gt* were the primary units of the royal economy. But we would abstain from the more exact term "agricultural farms (*gt*) of the palace", as *M. Liverani* calls them.[103]

The activities and functions of the *gt* ought now to be examined.

I. KTU.4.625 tells us about stocks of agricultural tools in various *gt*: *Atlg*, *Ulm*, *Sġy*, *ʿmq*, *Gwl*, *Ipṯl*, *Bir*, *Ḥrṯm*. The text follows the same pattern for each *gt*: (1) *b.(gt) Atlg.ṯlṯ.ḥrmṯt.ṯṯm* (2) *mḫrhn.nit.mit.krk.mit* (3) *mṣd. ḫmšm.mqb.ʿšrm*, "at the (*gt*) of (the village of) *Atlg*: three (metal) sicles,[104] the price(?)[105] of which is sixty; *nit*,[106] (one) hundred; *krk*,[107] (one)

---

[102] Cf. Ch. III, pp. 26-37.

[103] *Liverani*, d, (without pagination), and *Liverani* SDB, p. 1341.

[104] The respective numbers for the other *gt* are: 16, 5, 5, 8, 6, 10, and 5. Cf. Deut. 16, 9; 23, 26. On the origin of the word, see *Yeivin*, a; *Ch. Virolleaud* (PRU, V, p. 63) *Eissfeldt*, a, p. 23; cf. also ZUL, VII, p. 79-80; PRU, VI, 141 (RS 19.112), *2 ^{URU}ḫa-ar-me-ša-tu ^{GIŠ}eleppāti^{MEŠ}*, "2 *ḫarmešātu* of the ship". (Cf. Ch. V). The determinative URUDU shows that the text refers to metal sickles. Akkadian spelling of the Ugaritic word is used here.

[105] *Mḫrhn* appears only in this passage of the text. The view which holds that it means "price" is not convincing, despite the lack of another interpretation. Though *Dietrich*, *Loretz*, and *Sanmartin* refer also to the structure of the text (ZUL VII, 79),

hundred; adzes,[108] fifty; trimmers (hedge cutters),[109] twenty." Some other — badly damaged — texts in Ugaritic and Akkadian seem to be similar accounts of stocks of agricultural tools.[110] KTU.4.625 ends up as follows: (19) *b.Ḫrbġlm.Ġlm[n]* (20) *w.Trhy.aṯth* (21) *w.Mlky.bnh* (22) *Ily.Mrily. tdgr*, "in (the village of) *Ḫrbġlm* (akk. *URUḪurbaḫulimi*), *Ġlmn* and *Trhy*, his wife, and *Mlky*, his son. *Ily*, man from (the village of) *Mril*, the *tdgr*."[111]

Consequently, agricultural tools were stored in the *gt* and certain persons were responsible for them.

II. Cattle is also found in the *gt*, as appears from several texts. KTU.4.89 mentions (1) *ṯlṯ.ṣmdm* (2) *b.Nḫry.* (3) *ṣmdm.b.Ṯp[n]* (4) *aḥdm.b.gt x[ ]*,

---

one can hardly accept that the price of three sickles amounted to 60 shekels of silver. Therefore, the proposal made in *Liverani*, h, p. 62-63 that *mḫr* is a certain accepted unit of price or standard measure — possibly shekels of copper (bronze) has to be accepted.

106 At the other *gt* the number of the *n'it* is: 6, 1, 1, 1, 1, 1, and 1. The exact meaning is not clear. *Greenfield*, b, p. 93, "an implement used in digging trenches for damming water". Cf. also *nit* in PRU, V, 53, 3 and *ni'itu (ša)qātē* in PRU, VI, 142 (RS.19.135), 2; 157 (RS.19.235, 1, 5; 168 (RS.21.199), 2, 11; *(ša)qātē* may indicate that it was a handworked tool. Cf. *Liverani*, h, p. 62 on the basis of the Sumerian ninda/inda Akk. *ittû* — Hebr. *'ēt* "shovel" — this proposal seems convincing.

107 At the other *gt*: 1, 1, 1, 1, 1, 1, and 1. According to *Greenfield*, b, 92-93, it designated "some sort of binding instrument" or "an instrument used for irrigation", with preference for the latter. Earlier interpretation are rejected by *Greenfield* as based on inexact readings of medieval commentaries to Talmudic literature. Cf. also PRU, VI, 157, 2 (2(?) *ku-ri-ka-a[t]*). 12(1 *ku-ri-ku*); 168, 5(2 *ku-ri-[ka-at]*); cf. *Liverani*, h, p. 62.

108 At the other *gt*: 2, 1, 1, 1, 1, 1, and 1. Hebrew *ma'ăṣad*. Cf. *Greenfield*, b, 92; PRU, V, 43, 3; PRU, VI, 142, 3 ([x] *URUDU.MEŠma-ṣa-du-maMEŠ*); 137, 15 (1 *ma-ṣa-du*). We see from the determinative URUDU, "copper", that the tool was made from metal; cf. CAD, M, p. 329a.

109 At the other *gt*: 2, 1, 1, 1, 1, 1, and 1. Translation according to *Greenfield*, 92; root *nqb*. Cf. also PRU, VI, 14, 9, 13; 142, 5; 157, 4 (3 *ma-qa-bu-ma* URUDU*MEŠ*). 12 (2 *ma-qa-bu-ma*); 168, 3 (4 *ma-qa[-bu-ma]*). 9 (1 *ma-qab-bu*). It is important to note that, at least once, *mqb* is designated as being made out of copper or bronze (URUDU); cf. CAD, M, p. 252 b.

110 KTU.4.632; PRU, VI, 142; 157; 168. Some additional tools are listed.

111 *Tdgr* is a personal name according to UT, p. 497, No. 2532. The word can be understood also as a term designating as an unknown profession, perhaps of some kind of "secretary."

"(1) Three teams (of beasts) (2) at *(gt) Nḫry*; (3) two teams [112] at *(gt) Ṯpn*; (4) two single (beasts) [113] at the *gt* [ ]". KTU.4.618 is composed according to the following pattern: (1) *[b].gt.Ṯpn.ʿšr.ṣmdm* (2) *w.ṯlṯ.ʿšr.bnš* (3) *yd.Ytm. yd.rʿy ḥmrm*, "[at] *gt Ṯpn*, ten teams (of beasts of burden) and thirteen men with *Ytm* (PN), with the assherd". This text lists thereafter several teams of beasts of burden in the *gt* of *Gwl* (ll. 4-6), *Ipṯl* (ll. 7-8), *Ulm* (ll. 9-12), *Ḫrṯm* (ll. 21-22), and in four additional unidentified *gt*. The beasts of burden are mentioned together with the workmen of the *gt*.[114]

KTU.4.358 relates: (1) *bt alpm* (2) *ʿšr.bnšm*, "the oxen shed: ten men". Here, again, the oxen are mentioned with the working personnel.

The remaining lines show the same situation in some *gt*: (4) *ʿšr.b.gt.* [ ], "ten at *gt* [ ]"; (5) *ṯn.ʿšr.b.gt.Irb[ṣ]*, "twelve at *gt Irb[ṣ]*"; (6) *arbʿ.b. gt.Bʿln*, "four at *gt Bʿln*"; (7) *ʿšt.ʿšr.b.Gpn* (8) *yd.ʿdnm*, "eleven at *(gt) Gpn* with *ʿdnm*." And (9) *arbʿġzlm* (10) *ṯn yṣrm*, "four spinners,[115] two potters."

KTU.4.367 contains the headline: *[s]pr.bnš.mlk.d.b.Ṭbq*, "[l]ist of the king's men (royal dependents) who are at *(gt) Ṭbq*". The text is badly damaged, but the last line (l. 10) says: *w.ʿšrm.ṣmd.alpm*, "and twenty oxen teams". These oxen were used for ploughing, as appears from the headline of the partly destroyed tablet KTU.4.122: *[ḥr]ṯm.b.gt.Irbṣ*, "[plou]ghmen at *gt Irbṣ*." Thereafter follow at least thirty personal names.[116]

KTU.4.296 states: (8) *ṯlṯ.alp.ṣpr.dt.aḥd* (9) *ḥrṯh.aḥd.b.gt.Nkl* (10) *aḥd.b. gt.Knpy.w.aḥd.b.gt.Ṯrmn*, "three branded [117] oxen, which their ploughmen took: one at *gt Nḫl*, one at *gt Knpy*, and one at *gt Ṯrmn*". The text, which is partly broken, relates further that single oxen (*alp aḥd*) were taken to various *gt* (ll. 11-15). These oxen received fodder, as appears from KTU.4. 636: (1) *[sp]r.akl[. .b.gt]*, *Ṯryn*, "inventory of food (fodder) [at *gt*] *Ṯryn*".

---

[112] Dual. Several texts mention *ṣmd(m)* of beasts of burden. Although they are likely to refer to the royal economy, they cannot be connected with a concrete *gt*.

[113] *E. Lipinski* proposes *aḥdm* is the opposite of a pair, contrary to UT, p. 354, No. 126; and *Gordon*, b, pp. 5-9, "pair" compared with Akk. *iltênūtu*.

[114] On the *gt* personnel, see below; cf. *Liverani*, h, p. 67, where the proportion between the beasts and workmen is given.

[115] UT, p. 463, No. 1955.

[116] Cf. also KTU.4.175, where we read in the broken text: *ddm.gt.Dprnm l ḥrṯm*, "two *dd*(-measures) from *gt Dprnm* for the plowmen" (ll. 9-10).

[117] Cf. Akk. *ṣapārum*: AHW, p. 1082a, D4, "Viehmarke einritzen" ("to brand the cattle mark").

The text is divided into seven sections [118] and mentions respectively *gt Bir*, *gt Bʿln*, *gt Ḫldy*, *gt Ġl*, *x*, *x*, and *x*.[119] Let us look at one of these passages: (5) *tgmr.akl.b. gt*[.] *Bʿln* (6) *tlṯ.mat.ṯṯm.kbd* (7) *ṯṯm.ṯṯ.kbd.ḥpr.ʿbdm* (8) *šbʿm. drt.arbʿm drt.lalpm*, "(5) total of food (fodder) at *gt Bʿln*: (6) three hundred and sixty (measures) in all [120] (7) sixty-six (measures), in all, (as) food rations [121] of the *ʿbdm* [122] (8) seventy (measures) of millet (?) forty (measures) of millet (?) for the oxen". The other sections of the text are similar, varying only in the quantities mentioned. An analogues combination of personnel and cattle is found in U, V, 95 (RS.20.01): (14) *12 napšātu*^{MEŠ} *11 alpu*^{MEŠ} *3 imērū*^{MEŠ} *i-na dimti* ^{m}*Ilu-milki*, "12 persons, 11 oxen, 3 donkeys at the *dimtu* (= *gt*) of *Ilu-milku*".

Oxen and donkeys of burden were not the only kind of cattle located at the *gt*. We know that there were also sheep, geese and fattening cattle. Many texts give evidence to this effect,[123] but only KTU.4.296 refers to the *gt*. We have already seen that this text dealing with royal economy lists oxen distributed to different *gt*. Two other sections of the same tablet sum up: (5) *tgmr.uz.Ġrn.arbʿ.mat*, "total: geese (at the disposal) of *Ġrn* four hundred"; (6) *tgmr.uz.Aḫmn.arbʿ.mat* (7) *arbʿm kbd*", "total: geese (at the disposal) of *Aḫmn*, four hundred and forty, in all." Besides fattening cattle, geese were thus fattened in the *gt*, in order to provide meat for the court and, possibly, for religious offerings.[124]

Additional data are found in KTU.4.213 which inventories various agricultural products from different *gt*. The summing up of products gives an

---

[118] Lines 2-4, 5-9, 10-14, 15-19, 20-24, 25-29, 30-33.

[119] The *gt* was in the broken part of the line.

[120] The meaning of the word *kbd* in administrative texts, *Liverani*, b, p. 89-108.

[121] Akk. *iprum*. The proportion of the rations of fodder, oxen, seeds and rations of workers analyzed in *Liverani*, h, p. 59, but without using all the possible reconstructions of the text.

[122] Some kind of working personnel of the royal economy, but not slaves; see below.

[123] (1) *alpm mrim*, "fattening oxen," (2) *ṯṯ ddm l ṣin mrat*, "six *dd*(-measures) for fattening small cattle", etc. The same text mentions deliveries of food made for men on royal service. See also *KTU 4.129*, (1) *ṯn rʿy.uzm*, "two gooseherds", etc.; cf. KTU.4.275 where fodder for cattle is mentioned in a broken tablet, and KTU 4.247, 16-17, 20-21 where *alp.mri* and *uz.mrat* are listed.

[124] Naturally it is impossible to compare the Ugaritic data with the abundance of information from the Ur III period, cf. *Gomi*, a, pp. 1-42.

indication about deliveries to various royal dependents: (30) *ʿšrm.yn.mṣb xxḥxx.l.gzzm*, "twenty (measures) of stored wine[125]... for the shearers (of sheep)". Also, KTU.4.269 refers to these matters: (26) *ṯṯ.ddm.l.gzzm*, "six *dd*(measures) for the shearers". The relatively well-preserved line 45 of KTU.4.243 gives similar information: [ ]*nkly.l.rʿym.šbʿm.l.mitm.dd*, "[ ] *nkly*; for the shepherds, two hundred and seventy *dd*(measures of grain)".[126]

Lines 8-18 mention also the *myṣm* — the "dairy-men (cheesemakers)" with their apprentices, who also seemed to receive their rations. The *gt* was thus the place where fattening cattle and geese, as well as beasts of burden, were concentrated for the needs of the royal economy.[127]

III. The *gt* was also a storage centre for the agricultural products that were to be distributed to royal dependents of various professional groups and to villagers when these were bound to the corvée. Also the fodder for the royal cattle and geese was stored and distributed in the *gt*.

The texts list different products. Thus, KTU.4.143 refers to olives: (1) *b.gt. mlkt.b.Rḥbn* (2) *ḫmšm.mitm.zt*, "at the *gt* of the queen by the (river) *Raḫbānu*[128]: two hundred and fifty (measures) of olives" (or "olive-trees"). KTU.4.213 is composed according to the following pattern: (1) *ḫmš.ʿšr.yn.ṭb* (2) *w.tšʿm.kdm.kbd.yn.d.l.ṭb* (3) *w.arbʿm.yn ḫlq.b.gt.Sknm*, "(1) fifteen (jars of) good wine, (2) and ninety jars, in all, of wine that is not good, (3) and forty (jars) of spoiled wine at *gt Sknm*". The other parts of the text refer to similar quantities of wine at the *gt* of *Ṭbq*, *Mʿrby*, *Ulm*, *Ḥdṯt*, *Zbl*, *Sġy*, *Gwl*, *Ipṯl*, *S*[..], *Ṯpn*, *Gnʿy*.[129] Further on, there is a list of deliveries for various purposes.

---

[125] UT, p. 436, No. 1525: "term modifying wine"; WUS, p. 212, No. 1831: "Wein aus dem Keller", i.e. "lagered, stored wine", see also ZUL, VIII, in UF 5 (1973).

[126] Many shepherds appear in various texts where the word *gt* does not occur, cf. below and *Liverani*, h, p. 68-69.

[127] For some similar features in ancient Larsa and Ur in the XIXth and at the beginning of the XVIIIth century B.C.E., see *Kraus*, b, 1966; review *Leemans*, a, pp. 341-343; *Butz*, a, pp. 346-360; in Alalaḫ, cf. *Gaal*, a, pp. 280-3.

[128] *Raḫbānu* is a river according to Akkadian texts from Ugarit; cf. PRU, III, p. 267; PRU, VI, p. 147; *Astour*, b, p. 329, No. 99; p. 361, No. 176.

[129] Lines 4-5, 6-8, 9-10, 11-12, 13, 14-15, 16-18, 19, 20, 21, 22-23, respectively; on this text cf. *Lemaire-Delavault*, a, pp. 34-38.

KTU.4.243 deals with other products. The sections preserved give the following picture:[130] (12) *b.gt.Mʿbr.arbʿm.l.mit.drʿ.w.ṯmnym*[.]*drt* (13) *w.ʿšrm. l.mit.dd.ḥp*[*r.*]*bnšm*, "(12) at *gt Mʿbr*, one hundred and forty (measures) of seeds, and eighty (measures) of millet (?),[13] and one hundred and twenty *dd* (measures as) rations for the (king's) men (*bnšm*)". We find varying quantities of the same products also in the *gt* of *Sknm*, *Ṭbq*, *Ġl*, *Alḫb*, *Knpy*, *Ṯrmn*, *Ḥdṯt*, *Nḫl*, *Yʿny*, *ʿnmky*.[131] The remainder of the text deals with deliveries to individuals and gives their total.

KTU.4.269 inventories various supplies: (1) *spr.ḥpr.bt.k*[ ] (2) *tšʿ.ʿšrh. dd.l.bt*[ ], "(1) list of rations of the house of [ ], (2) nineteen *dd*(-measures) for the house [ ]". Also, deliveries to various persons mentioned by name and to professional groups taken as a whole body (4 and 26 *gzzm*, "shearers", 8 *myṣm*, "diary-men" etc.) are inventoried. Follows the total of the text: (30) *tgmr.kśmm.b.yrḫ Iṯtbnm* (31) *šbʿm.dd.ṯn.kbd* (32) *tgmr ḥṭm.šbʿ.ddm* (33) *ḫmš.dd.šʿrm* (34) *kdm.yn* (35) *kdm.ḥmṣ*, "(30) The total of spelt[132] in the month of I*ṯtbnm*[133]: (31) seventy-two *dd*, in all. (32) The total of wheat: seven *dd*; (33) five *dd* of barley; (34) two jars of wine; (35) two jars of vinegar". *Gt. Nbk* (l. 19) was among the stores from which deliveries of products were made. Another example is given by *KTU.4.271*: (1) *tgmr.akl. b.gt.Knpy.alp* (2) *tgmr.akl.b.g*[*t x .a*]*lp*, "(1) The total of food at *gt Knpy*: (one) thousand; (2) the total of food at *g*[*t x*, (one) th]ousand", etc. In the partly preserved lines, four other *gt*, at least, are mentioned, among them *gt Tgbry* (ll. 7 and 9).

KTU.4.345 (2) contains an account of *gt Mṣbt* (ll. 1-2), *Ḥxmi* (l. 7), and *Mril* (l. 9). Spelt (*kśmm*), wheat (*ḥṭm*), and barley (*šʿrm*) are mentioned.

According to the lines remaining from the fragmentary text KTU.4.397, farm produce was kept at *gt* [*Ip*]*ṯl* (l. 5), *Gwl* (l. 7), *Šrš* (l. 9), *Rqd* (l. 11), and: (12) *mit.tšʿm.*[*kb*]*d.ddm* (13) *b.gt.Bir*. KTU.4.400 lists five *gt*, but only *gt Trġnds* as legible in line 15. Large quantities of wheat, spelt, barley, and wine are referred to. KTU.4.636, in which products for the working personnel and fodder for oxen are inventoried, has been considered above.

---

[130] Lines 1-2, 3-4, 5-6 disallow the reading of the name of the *gt*.

[131] Lines 7-9, 10-11, 14-15, 16-17, 18-19, 20-21, 22-23, 24-25, 26-27, 28-29.

[132] *kśmt*: UT, p. 422, No. 1283.

[133] On the Ugaritic months, see *Olivier*, a, p. 53-59; ZUL, XI, p. 28 ff.; *Liverani*, h, p. 59.

IV. The fields and other lands distributed by the king to various royal dependents as conditional holdings (*ubdy*) were also attached to a *gt*, as first appears from KTU.4.110 (1) *šd.ubdy.Ilštm'* (2) *dt.bd.skn*, "(1) The *ubdy*-fields of (the village of) *Ilštm'*, (2) which are at the disposal of the *sākinu*." (Cf. above). Thus, the superintendent was responsible for the royal *ubdy*-fields. Lines 3-14 are composed according to the pattern: *šd* PN*(b)gt.Prn*, "the field of PN (at) *gt Prn*". Twelve fields are mentioned. The formula *šd* PN *l.gt.Mzln*, "The field of PN (belonging) to *gt Mzln*," is used in reference to five fields in lines 15-22. Also KTU.4.103 deals with "*ubdy*-fields" for various professionals who were on royal service. Among them, under the title (44) [*u*]*bdy.nqdm*, "the tenures of the shepherds", one reads: (45) [*ṯlṯ*]. *šdm.d.n'rb.gt.Npk*, "[three] fields that form part of (lit. "entered") *gt Npk*". Thus, these fields were attached to the *gt*. A text similar to it is the badly preserved KTU.4.424: (1) *spr*[.]*šd.Ri*[*šym (?)*] (2) *krm* [.*w*].*šdm* [.] '*x*[ ] (3) *b gt Ṯm x*[ ]*l tyn*[ ], "(1) List of the fields of [the people of (the village of)] *Ri*[*š*]. (2) Vineyard [and] fields [ ] (3) at *gt Ṯ*[ ]". Here, as in *Ilštm'*, the fields and vineyards of royal dependents living in *Riš* may have been attached to *gt Ṯm*[ ]. The lines preserved list further on: (4) [ ].*krm.b.Yp' l.Y'dd*, "vineyard in *Yp'* for *Y'dd*", and (23) *krm.Ib?*[*r*]*d*. *b.bn.Ndbn*, "vineyard of *Ib*[*r*]*d* for *bn.Ndbn*".[134] There are also some data about olive-trees in KTU.4.164 (1) *ṯlṯ.mat* (2) *šb'm.kbd* (3) *zt.ubdym* (4) *b Mlk*, "(1-2) in all, three hundred and seventy (3) olive-trees (or '[measures of] olives') of tenures at (*gt* /?/) *Mlk*." The lapidary style of the text does not allow us to give an undisputed translation. At least two interpretations are possible: a) olives from 370 olive-trees or 370 measures of olives were received for pressing at *gt Mlk*, or b) these olives came from landholdings attached to *gt Mlk*, like there were fields attached to *gt Mzln* and to *gt Prn*, according to KTU.4.110.

In any case, these texts enable us to conclude that lands held in consideration of service rendered to the king were connected with the units of the royal economy.

---

134 Cf. also the fragment KTU.4.120: *spr.gt. r*[ ] (l. 1), "List of *gt R*[ ]", and *šd.dr*[ ] (l. 3), "field *dr*[ ]". Some personal names, *gt*, and the word "field" (*šd*) are mentioned in the fragmentary text KTU.4.638. In PRU, VI, 56 (RS.17.121), vineyards (^{GIŠ}GEŠTIN^{MEŠ}) and fields (A.ŠA^{MEŠ}) are connected in lines 5′, 7′, 9′ of reverse with *Na-pa-ki-ma (Npkm)*. Maybe the text is of the same kind.

§2. The Manpower of the *gt*

I. The texts contain also some data concerning the special *ġt* personnel. These people are counted together with other royal dependents, but distinguish themselves from other crafts because of their profession connected with the *gt*. They are called *bnš gt*, "the personnel[135] of the *gt*". One also finds *bdl gt* and *gt mlkym*, literally, "*gt* of royal men".

KTU.4.96 reads (1) *bdl.gt.bn.Tbšn* (2) *bn Mnyy.Šʿrty*, etc., "(1) the *bidalūma* of *gt bn-Tbšn*: (2) *bn Mnyy*, man of *Šʿrt*," etc. In all, seven persons are referred to. Two *bidalūma* are mentioned "at *gt bn-Ṯlṭ*", *b.gt.bn.Ṯlṭ* (ll. 9-11), and one "at *gt Psḥn*.", *Ilḏ.b.gt.Psḥn* (l. 12). The purpose of the text is not clear. The headlines of KTU.4.99 are broken, but the text lists professional groups of royal dependents. Since a numeral stands after each group, this text concerns payments or deliveries. Line 5 mentions *gt. mlkym*. The same *gt. mlkym* appears in a list of professional groups in KTU.4.126.

KTU.4.125 mentions the *bnš gt*. Line 20 makes it clear that various professional groups or single persons receive grain which is measured in GUR. Among them one finds:

2	*bnš.gt.Glʿd*	*4*,	"the personnel of *gt Glʿd* — 4 (GUR)";
3	*bnš.gt.Ngr*	*4*,	"the personnel of *gt Ngr* — 4 (GUR)";
6	*bnš.gt.ʿṯtrt*	*1*,	"the personnel of *gt ʿṯtrt* — 1 (GUR);
11	*bnš.gt.Ipṯl* [ ],		"the personnel of *gt Ipṯl* [ ]";
15	[*bnš.g*]*t*, *Ir*[*bṣ*],		"the personnel of *gt Ir*[*bṣ*]";
16	[*bn*]*š.gt. Rbt*[ ],		"the personnel of *gt Rbt*[ ]";
18	*bnš Mġrt 1*[+x],		"the personnel of *(gt) Mġrt* — 1[+x] (GUR)".

Owing to their lapidary style, some texts do not specify the status of the people at the *gt*. But it seems that the *bnš gt* are referred to. One reads in KTU.4.307: (1) *ṯn.b gt.Mzln* (2) *ṯn.b Ulm* (3) *Abmn.b gt.Mʿrb...* (21) *ṯn.b gt Yknʿm*, "(1) two at *gt Mzln*, (2) two at *(gt) Ulm*, (3) *Abmn* at *gt Mʿrb*,... (21) two at *gt Yknʿm*." Each of the remaining lines of the text (ll. 4-20 and 22) consists of one personal name. One should also mention KTU.4.608, already referred to in the section dealing with cattle: (1) [*b.*]*gt.Ṯpn.ʿšr, ṣmdm* (2) *w.ṯlṯ.ʿšr.bnš* (3) *yd.Ytm.yd.rʿy ḥmrm*, "(1) At *gt Ṯpn* ten teams (of beasts of

---

[135] Plur. st. cstr., here and further on; cf. also *Liverani*, SDB, pp. 1339-41; *Liverani*, d.

burden) (2) and thirteen *bnš* (3) with *Ytm*, with the assherd."[136] KTU.4.358 deals with beasts of burden, it inventories: (3) *ḫmš.bnš i.ṯt*[ ] (4) *ʿšr.b.gt.*[ ] (5) *ṯn.ʿšr.b.gt.Irb*[*ṣ*] (6) *arbʿ.b.gt.Bʿln* (7) *ʿšt.ʿšr.b.Gpn* (8) *yd.ʿdnm*, "(3) five *bnš* (?)... [ ], (4) ten at *gt*[GN], (5) twelve at *gt Irb*[*ṣ*], (6) four at *gt Bʿln*, (7) eleven at *(gt) Gpn* with *ʿdnm* (PN)".

In this context, KTU.4.382 deserves close consideration. Lines 1-18 are badly damaged, but the ends of lines 1-2 are legible: *bd.mlkt*, "at the disposal of the Queen". In lines 19, 20 and 22 appear the *gt* or villages [*A*]*ġt*, [*U*]*brʿy*, and *Ar*. One reads further: (23) *bn.Ngr*[*šp.d.yṯ*]*b.b.Ar*, "*bn Ngr*[*šp* who dwe]lls at *(gt) Ar*", (24) (also a person dwelling at *Ar*), (25) *bn.Agpṯ.ḫpṯ.d.*[*.yṯb*]*b.Šʿrt*,[137] (26) *Yly.bn.Ṯrnq*[*yṣ*]*r.d.yṯb.b.Ilštmʿ*, "*Yly*, son of *Ṯrnq*, the potter, who dwells at (*gt*) *Ilštmʿ*," (27) *Ilšlm, bn.Gsn.* [*y*]*ṣr.d.yṯb.b.gt.Al*, "*Ilšlm*, son of *Gsn*, the [pot]ter, who dwells at *gt Al*", (28) *Ilmlk.*[*bn*]. *Ktt.*[*.d.*]*yṯb.b.Šbn*, "*Ilmlk*, [son of] *Ktt*, who dwells at (*gt*) *Šbn*" (29) (one person dwelling at *gt Šlmy*), (32) *Ann*[ ]. *b*[*n*] *Pyx* [*.d.*]*yṯb.b.gt.Aġld*, "*Ann*[ ], s[on] of PN, who dwells at *gt Aġld*." Lines 33-34 list persons dwelling respectively at *Ilštmʿ* and *Syn*.[138] PRU.V.15 indicates thus that certain craftsmen, like potters, dwelled at least at some of the *gt*.

II. We now have a partial idea of various professionals working or receiving supplies at the *gt*, and we can turn to those who exercised professions proper to agriculture and received wages and deliveries from the royal stores. These workers of the royal economic units were referred to as *ʿbdm*.[139]

---

[136] Cf. also KTU.4.355 where the *bnšm* (from 2 to 20 men) are mentioned in 42 lines of the text in connection with 42 place-names, or possibly, *gt* names, but the word *gt* is not mentioned before the place-names.

[137] *ḫp/bṯ*, Akk. *ḫupšu*, a dependent or semi-dependent class of the population, AHW, p. 357 a, cf. also SSAU, 6, WO, V, 1, p. 91.

[138] *Syn*/^{URU}*Siyannu*, a town and small kingdom near Ugarit. the text was probably written when Siyannu was under Ugarit's rule, i.e., in the time of the Hittite king Mursilis II; cf. *Liverani*, a, pp. 60 and 72-73; *Klengel*, b, II, pp. 353-355 and 267-368; otherwise it could happen later, when Siyannu was again under the rule of Ugarit in the XIIIth cent. B.C.E., cf. *Heltzer*, a, pp. 58-62; *Astour*, f, pp. 13-28. Concerning the word *yṯb* "dwells" (?) we have to compare it with cases in Nuzi when people were in a certain state of dependence (*aššabūtu*) from a certain landowner and lived at a certain *dimtu* and they are called *aššabū* — *Wilhelm*, b, pp. 211-212.

[139] Cf. KTU.4.636 discussed above. The *ʿbdm* were by no means slaves, as insists

They and the other workers of the royal agricultural estate will be treated according to their professions. The texts are without exact data and prosopographic material is available to give us the possibility of reconstructing the reign of even one particular king. Therefore we shall consider every professional group in general, according to the following criteria: a) the term and its translation; b) the sources; c) the number of persons; d) the engagement in service activities and the corvée which was not necessarily connected with their craft; e) the specialized service work (*pilku*) of the agricultural workers and, if possible, at which *gt* they were located; f) deliveries from royal stores and their periodicity, if possible; g) the dwelling-places of the persons; h) references to their appurtenance to the royal dependents (*bnš mlk*); i) the hereditary character of their profession; j) land- allottments given by the king; k) other additional data.[140]

1. a) *ʿbdm*, "laborers, workers".
b) KTU.4.35, II, 2-7; KTU.4.87, 2; 4.71, III, 10-13; 4.99, 1; 4.126, 13; 4.183, II, 19-21; 4.320, 1 and 2-203; 4.332, 10-11; 4.636.
c) KTU.4.35 — 5; 4.71 — 3+x; 4.87 — group (1); 4.99 — group; 4.126 — group; 4.183 — 3(?); 4.320 — 10; 4.332 — 2; 4.646 — 6 groups.
e) KTU.4.320 — (2) *b gt yny*, "at the *gt Yny*" — persons by name (8) *b (gt)Ḥl* —5 persons by name; 4.636 — groups of *ʿbdm* at least at the *gt*'s *Bir* (l. 2), *Bʿln* (l. 7), *Ḫldy* (l. 12), *Ġl* (l. 19).
f) KTU.4.71 — silver (figures broken); 4.99 — delivery (figures broken); 4.636 — on the listed above *gt*'s — *ḥpr bnšm* in large quantities.
h) In all the lists where the *ʿbdm* are counted as a whole group they appear together with professional groups known as *bnš mlk*.
i) KTU.4.35, II (5) *ʿbd* (6) *w.nḥlh*, "*ʿbd* (PN) and his heir."
j) KTU.4.183, the *ʿbdm* together with the people of the other professional groups are designated as *bʿl šd*, "field-owners."

2. a) *ḥrṯm* — "plowmen"[141]

Liverani, h, pp. 58-59, 66-67 and 72, for we see that they had families and received land-allotments.

[140] When no data are available the paragraphs concerned will not be mentioned.

[141] WUS, p. 108, No. 980; UT, p. 399, No. 908, common semitic Hebr. *ḥāraš*, Arab. *ḥaraṯa*, "to plow." Akk. *erēšu*; cf. *Heltzer*, q, p. 32-33; *Yamashita*, a, p. 50, No. 11, but contrary to his opinion the word has no other additional sense.

b) KTU.4.65; 4.106;[142] 4.122; 4.175, 9-10; 4.296, 8-10, 15; 4.609, 27;[143] 4.630, 6-7.[144]

c) KTU.4.65; 2-14 — 13 persons by name; 4.106 — 22 persons by name; 4.122 — 28+x persons by name; 4.175 — group; 4.609 — 3 persons by name; 4.630 — 6 persons.

e) 4.122 — *gt. Irbṣ*; 4.175 — *gt Dprnm*; 4.296, lines 8-10, 15 and 17 cf. above on cattle on the *gt*. — plowmen worked with oxen on the *gt*'s *Nẖl*, *Knpy* and *Ṯrmn*. Plowmen at two additional unrecognizable *gt* are mentioned (lines 15 and 17).

f) 4.175, (9) *ddm gt Dprnm* (10) *l.ḥrṯm*, "2 *dd*-measures (from the) *gt Dprnm* to the plowmen", 4.609 in the month of *Iṯtbnm*; *ḥpr bnšm*, "rations of the royal dependents." Measure *dd*; 4.630 — *s'rt*, "wool".

g) KTU.4.65, (6) *bn Atnb Mr*[ ] (7) *bn Sẖr Mr*[ ] (9) *bn Idrn 'Š*[ ] as well as at least the lines 10-11. It seems that the words after the personal names are the beginnings of the names of the villages, where these plowmen dwelled.

h) KTU.4.609 — the whole text concerns *bnš mlk*.

i) KTU.4.65, (10) *bn.Bly mr*[ ] (11) *wnḥlh Mr*[[145] "(11) and his heir *Mr*[ ]; 4.122 (2) *bn Šmyn* (3) *w.nḥlh*, "and his heir".

j) KTU.4.609 — all persons named in this text were *b'l šd* "field-owners."

---

[142] Although the texts KTU.4.106 and 4.122 did not fully present the line where it is written that they were *ḥrṯm*; our prosapographic comparison gives a possibility for this. (Cf. *Heltzer*, q, p. 33 — here is given a revised version according to the corrected readings of KTU).

KTU.4.65		*4.106*		*4.122*	
1	*ḥrṯm*[			1	[*ḥr*]*ṯm.bgt Irbṣ*
2	*bn Ṯmq*	20	*bn Ṯmq*	7	*bn. Ṯmq*
3	*bn.Ntp*	21	*bn Ntp*	8	*bn Ntp*
7	*bn.Atnb mr*[	9	*bn Atnb*		
9	*bn.Idrn 'š*[	1	[*bn Id*]*rn*		
12	*Ilšpš*	3	[*Ilš*]*pš*		

So we can also reconstruct line 1 of the text 4.122 and receive, undoubtedly, the information that the *ḥrṯm*, "plowmen" are listed by name. KTU.4.106 lists undoubtedly also the *ḥrṯm*. Here are given only the coinciding lines.

[143] Cf. the full text in Ch. I, pp. 3-15.

[144] Cf. the full text, Ch. III, pp. 46-47.

[145] I.e., from the same village (the person and his heir), possibly *Mr*[*il*].

Though only four passages refer explicitly to "king's fields",[146] these ploughmen are likely to have tilled royal land, and, as seen above, some of them took oxen for ploughing from or to a *gt*, as it was shown above.[147]

3. a) *gpny(m)*, "vine-dressers."
b) KTU.4.125.
c) Group.
e) The whole text relates about personnel on the various *gt*'s but we do not know which ones.
f) Receive 1+x GUR of (barley(?)).
h) The whole text refers to royal dependents.

4. a) *tmrym* — "date-palm workers."
b) KTU.4.126, 20.
c) Group.
h) The whole text lists groups of professionals of *bnš mlk*.

5. a) *nġr mdrʿ* and *nġr krm* "(sown) field-keepers (guards)" and "vineyard-keepers" (guards).
b) KTU.4.141, III, 16;[148] 4.609, 12; 4.618, 6.
c) KTU.4.141 — one *nġr mdrʿ* and one *nġr krm*; 4.609, 12 — 3 *nġr krm* by name; 4.618 — 1 person.
e) KTU.4.141 — at the *gt Ġl*; 4.618 — at the *gt Gwl*.
f) 4.609 — *ḥpr bnšm*, "ration of the *bnš (mlk)* at the month of *Iṯtbnm*.
h) All three texts deal with *bnš mlk*.
j) 4.609 — all persons mentioned are field-owners (*bʿl šd*).

Now we must turn to the professions engaged with cattle and poultry.

6. a) *gzzm* — "(sheep)shearers."[149]

---

[146] At *Gawalu (Gwl)* = PRU, III, 16.201, 11, *URUUḫnappu (Uḫnp)* = PRU, III, 16.150, 8, *URUŠuksu*, and *URUḪarmanu*, PRU, IV, 17.123, 8-9 and 12-13.

[147] But we are not sure whether this is one of the agricultural personnel on the royal estate, or an administration official. Cf. *akil eqli*, "overseer of the field" in the Akkadian texts from Ugarit (cf. Ch. VIII).

[148] Cf. the text in Ch. I, pp. 3-15.

[149] WUS, p. 65, No. 64; *Yamashita*, a, p. 47, No. 5; Hebr. *gzz*; AHW *gāzizu* "shearer"; Akkadian from Alalaḫ, *gazzu* "sheared wool", *Giacumukis*, a, p. 75. The existence of such a profession is clear, for, as we have seen in the deliveries-texts,

b) KTU.4.213 and 4.269, 4.

c) 4.213 — group; 4.269 — group.

e) 4.213 — the delivery was made at various *gt*'s; 4.269, (30) *tgmr... yrḫ Iṯtbnm*, "Total at the month *Iṯtbnm*."

f) 4.213, (30) *ʿšrm.yn.mṣb.x x ḥ x x.lgzzm*, "20 (jars) lagered wine... to the shearers"; *ṯlṯm.dd.kśmm.l.gzzm*, "30 *dd* emmer (spelt) to the shearers" (25) *ṯṯ.ddm.l.gzzm*, "6 *dd*'s to the shearers" — the preceding line speaks about wheat (*ḥṭm*).

g) 4.269 — appearance together with other professional groups known as *bnš mlk*.

7. a) *nqdm* Akk. (from Ugarit) *amelnâqidu*[150] "shepherd."[151]

b) KTU.4.68, 71; 4.126, 5; 4.369, 6-8; 4.416, 5; 4.624; 4.681; 4.745, 4; PRU, VI, 93 (RS.17.131); 131(19.35A).

c) 4.68 — group; 4.126 — group; 4.369 — group; 4.416 — ?; 4.624 — originally no less than 12 persons listed by name; 4.681 — 9+x persons; 4.745 — 2 persons(?); PRU, VI, 93 — 3 persons; 131 — group.

d) 4.68.71 — the *nqdm* give together with the *ṯnnm (šanānu)* 1 archer to a certain guard unit;[152] 4.624, (1) *[n]qdm.dt.kn.npṣhm* "The shepherds, whose ammunition[153] are in a good condition." Further, the text deals with various weapons in the hands of at least 12 *nqdm*. So we see here that they had military service. PRU, VI, 131 — deliveries of weapons — i.e., military service.[154]

f) 4.681 — possibly a kind of delivery(?); 4.745 — possibly(?) a kind of group-delivery.

h) 4.68; 4.69; 4.416; PRU, VI, 93 and 131 — the *nqdm* appear together with other groups of "royal dependents" (*bnš mlk*).

---

there is a lot of wool, *šʿrt*. The textile products were developed in Ugarit as well as sheep-breeding.

150 PRU, VI, 93, 7 (RS.17.131); 131, 9 (RS.19.35A), NA.GAD.

151 Hebr. *nōqēd*; Akk. *nāqidu*, AHW, p. 744; *Yamashita*, a, p. 63, No. 28.

152 On this text and the *ṯnnm*, Ch. VI, pp. 122-123.

153 Cf. *Heltzer*, g, p. 130, Note No. 42; WUS, No. 1824; UT, p. 446, No. 478 "clothes" is, at least in this case, unacceptable, for later various kinds of weapons are listed. ZUL, I, BO, 23, 1966, p. 131, "die Garderobe und Ausrüstung von Personen."

154 Cf. the interpretation of this text in Ch. VI, p. 105.

j) 4.416 — all groups mentioned in this text received "fields" GÁN.ME, but the figure designating the number of the fields of the *nqdm* is broken.[155]

k) 4.369, (6) *ṯmnym arbʻt* (7) *kbd.ksp* (8) *d.nqdm*, "84 in all (shekels) silver from (or 'of the') shepherds" — the text deals with farming out taxes from the villages of Ugarit, and only the *nqdm* appear here from the "royal dependents",[156] *Rb nqdm*, "elder of the shepherds" appear on the colophon of literary texts.[157]

8. a) *rʻy(m)* Akk. *rêʼu*, "shepherds".[158]

b) KTU.4.75, IV, 19; 4.125, 4; 4.129; 4.153, 1; 4.175; 4.243, 41-49; 4.374; 4.378; 4.391; 4.440; 4.493; 4.618, 3; 4.729; 4.740; PRU, VI, 118, 10 (RS.18.116); U.V.96, 8-10 (RS.20.12).

c) 4.75 — 1 by name; 4.125 — group; 4.129 — 11 *(rʻym)* by name, 2 — gooseherds and 11 *sġr(m)*, "helpers, youngsters, subjects, apprentices";[159] 4.175 — 1 person; 4.243, 45 — group, 49 — group; lines 42, 43, 44 — 1 *śġr*, "subject" in every line; 4.374 — 13 *rʻym* and 13 "subjects";[160] 4.378 — 6 shepherds by name and 22 "subjects" (*śġrm*) — (only the numbers of the men are mentioned); 4.391 — 18 "shepherds";[161] 4.440 — 5 shepherds;[162] 4.493 — 3 shepherds;[162] 4.618 —

[155] Cf. *Imparati*, a, pp. 24-25 and 30-31 about land-allotments to the GAL.NA.KAD "great shepherd" in the Hittite Empire.

[156] Cf. this text *Heltzer*, a, p. 33-34.

[157] KTU.1, 6, V (54) *spr.Ilmlk.Šbny.* (55) *lmd.Atn.Prln.rb* (56) *khnm.rb.nqdm* (57) *ṯʻy. Nqmd mlk Ugrt*... "The scribe *Ilmlk*, from the village *Šbn*, apprentice of *Atn Prln*, chief priest, elder of the shepherds, the noble of Niqmaddu, the king of Ugarit...."

[158] The term by itself has the only meaning "shepherd." The possible difference between the *nqd(m)* and *rʻy(m)* will be discussed below.

[159] The text has the following wording: (1) *ṯn.rʻy.uzm*, "two gooseherds". (2) *śġr. bn.ḫpsry.aḫd*, "*śġr*. of *bn Ḫpsry* — 1". We may understand that *bn Ḫpsry* had 1 *śġr* and lines 3-12 are also composed according to the formula "*śġr* of PN — 1" *śġr* — Cf. Ch. I and Hebrew *ṣāʻîr*, "young", "small" Akk. *ṣeḫru* and *ṣuḫāru* "young, small," but also an underprivileged person. *Finet*, a, 65-72, and by no means, as a "young aristocrate" as *MacDonald-Cutler*, b, pp. 27-35; cf. *ṣeḫrum* I, AHW, pp. 1088b-1089b, esp. C 5 and 6 where the word appears as "servant" and "subject"; p. 1109, a, *ṣuḫāru(m)* where we see the word again in the sense "servant", "employee".

[160] *rʻym, dt.bd.Iytlm*, "Shepherds who are at the disposal of *Iytlm*." (2) *Ḫyrn.w. śġrh*, "*Ḫyrn* and his subject" or (3) *śġr.bn.Prsn*, "The subject of *bn. Prsn*" (5) *Tʻln* (PN) (7) *śġr.Plṭ*, "The subject of *Plṭ*" (8) *Sdrn.w.ṯn.śġrh*, "*Sdrn* and 2 his subjects." All other lines are composed according to the line-formulae given here.

[161] The whole text — 18 lines — is composed to the formula (1) *Ḫrny.w.rʻh*,

1(?) assherd;[163] 4.729 — 4 shepherds and 22 "subjects";[164] 4.740 — at least 3 shepherds;[162] PRU, VI, 118 — number unknown;[165] U.V.96 — 2 poulty (goose-)herds, 1 shepherd, 4 oxherds.[166]

d) 4.153 — (1) *ilk.rʿ[y* "the *ilku*-service(?) of the shepherds".[167]

e) 4.125 — at a certain *gt*; 4.243 — everything is going to certain *gt*'s, but the names of those where there were *rʿym* were broken; 4.618 — at the *gt Ṯpn*; U.V. 96 — at various *gt*'s.

f) 4.125 — *rʿym* received 2 GUR of barley; 4.175 — 2 *dd*'s to the shepherds (barley?); 4.243 — (45) [*yn.d*] *Nkly*[168] concerning l.r*ʿym.šbʿm.l.mitm dd* "[wine] of consumption to the shepherds — 270 jars";[169] (49) — delivery; lines 40-44 — deliveries to the "subjects" (*śġrm*); 4.378 — the shepherds received wool (*šʿrt*) and the "subjects" *ššlmt* (garments); (Ch. III, pp. 39-43); U.V.96 — deliveries of grain.

h) Cf. Ch. I.

k) The *rʿym*, "shepherds" belonged to certain kinds. Among them were also goose-, ass-, and oxherds. Besides the *rʿym* they also had "subjects", *śġrm*, but not every subject was attached to a certain *rʿy*. The "subjects" received their deliveries separately from the "shepherds"; 4.374 — we see that the *rʿym* and the "subjects" were attached to (or at the disposal of) *Iytlm*; 4.618 — possibly a certain *Ytm* was the overseer of the assherds; 4.72 — *rʿym dt*[...] — possibly also here the shepherds were at the disposal of somebody.

"*Ḫrny* and his shepherd." (x(PN) and his shepherd). The real sense and purpose of the text is unclear.

162 Fragment. In all, 5 lines only *r*]*ʿh*.

163 (1) [*b.*].*gt.Ṯpn.ʿšr.ṣmdm* (2) *w.ṯlṯ.ʿšr.bnš* (3) *yd.Ytm.yd.rʿy. ḥmrm*, "[At] the *gt Ṯpn* 10 pairs (of oxen) and 13 people (*bnš*), together with *Ytm* (and) together with (one) assherd (or assherds — pl.st.cstr.).

164 (1) *arbʿ*, *r*[*ʿym*] (12) *ʿšrm.ṯn.ś*[*ġrm*] — these are the lines of the total of the text. The text itself (1) *rʿym dt*[ ] "shepherds which [.....]" at least partly the *śġrm* are attached to the *rʿym*.

165 Line 8 r*ʿym* in Ugaritic; the seven other lines of the text are written in Akkadian.

166 (9) LÚÙ.DAB.MUŠEN (10) LÚÙ.DAB (11) 4 LÚÙ.DAB.GUD.

167 Cf. Ch. II, p. 16.

168 Our reconstruction. *nkly* — according to *Milano*, a, and *Fensham*, a.

169 *dd* instead of *kd*. "jar".

Before we turn to the analysis of the personnel of the *gt*, we must consider the difference between the shepherds, *nqdm*, on the one hand, and the *r'ym* on the other. It is clear that they were different persons. We know about arms deliveries to the *nqdm*, but nothing about the military service of the *r'ym*. The *nqdm* received land allotments; about the *r'ym* we know of no land allotments. On the other hand, the *r'ym* had their *śġrm*, "subjects" and we read of no such people at the disposal of the *nqdm*. The *r'ym* were divided into certain subgroups according to the beasts which they had to pasture and they were more closely attached to *gt*'s than the *nqdm*. But it is also possible that, at least in part, the differences expressed here are caused by the lapidary and occasional character of our data. It is, however, clear that a certain difference existed between these two groups of "royal dependents" (*bnš mlk*). We do have at our disposal some additional data to help us analyze the difference.

The corvée to which the Ugaritic villages were bound and the taxes they had to pay in silver or in kind are quite well known. These obligations were certainly connected with the royal economy as a whole,[170] but at least a part of them were likely to be directly related to the *gt*.

Besides the sector of the royal economy which found its expression in the *gt* and the royal fields, there were royal pasture-lands. Despite the common view on the communal ownership of pasture-lands in ancient and primitive societies, it is likely that these lands were in royal hands in the kingdom of Ugarit.[171] In fact, some texts inventory large quantities of livestock, using the general formula x UDU.ME *eli* PN, "x (numeral) sheep (entrusted) to PN".[172] According to PRU, III, 16.155, six persons received various quantities of sheep and their total was 1821;[173] these sheep were "entrusted", *šu-ku-na* (l. 7). The reverse of the same text sums up "67 oxen entrusted" and the tally says that 4 persons received from 3 to 39 oxen each. The other texts also refer to sheep, goats, and oxen. According to PRU, VI, 119 (RS.19.69), fifteen goats were delivered to a certain [*-n*]*a-na* from ^{URU}*Ya-na* (*Y'ny*). Similar data are found in the other texts. The

[170] *Heltzer*, a, p. 24-47.

[171] *Heltzer*, l, p. 9-13; *Heltzer*, c, pp. 476-478, where this question is especially analyzed.

[172] PRU, III, 16.155; PRU, III, 16.274; PRU, III, 16.294; PRU, VI, 117 (RS.17.136); 118 (RS.18.116); 119 (RS.19.69); 120 (RS.19.116); 121 (RS.19.141).

[173] *1 li-im 8 me-at 21* U[DU.ME].

most interesting of these is PRU, VI, 118 (RS.18.116), lines 1′-8′ of which are preserved:

[*x*] *a*[*lpū*^{MEŠ}*eli* ^{m}...-]*na amil* ^{URU}*Na-ni-i.*
[ ] *41 alpū*^{MEŠ} *eli* ^{m}*Ta-mar-ti-nu amil* ^{URU}*Šú-la-ṭi*
[ ] *27 alpū*^{MEŠ} *eli* ^{m}*A-na-ni-ia-na amil* ^{URU}*Ia-ku-SIG*$_5$
[2]*0 (?) alpū*^{MEŠ} *eli* ^{m}*Na-pa-ri amil* ^{URU}*Ḫal-bi*
[*x*] *alpū*^{MEŠ} *eli*] ^{m}*Lu-lu-wa-na amil* ^{URU}*Ša-ḫa-qi*
[*x alpū*^{MEŠ} *eli*] ^{m}[*P*]*u-us-ḫa-na amil* ^{URU}*U-bur-a*
[*x alpū*^{MEŠ} *eli* ^{m}*Pu*]*r-ra-na mâr* ^{m}*Gu-ub-ru-na amil* ^{URU}*Na-ni-i*
[ ] *rʿym*

Lines 1′-7′ give a determined (not always preserved) number of oxen entrusted to (*eli*) persons listed by name. Two persons (ll. 1′ and 7′) were from the village of *Nanu* and one, respectively, from *Šulaṭu (Ṯlṭ)* (l. 2′), *Ya-ku-SIG*$_5$ *(Yknʿm)* (l. 3′), *Ḫalbu (Ḫlb)* (l. 4′), *Šaḫaqu (Šḫq)* (l. 5′), and *U-bur-a (Ubrʿy)* (l. 6). The remainder of line 8′ specifies in Ugaritic script that these persons were "shepherds". Since the text comes from the royal archives, it must concern the distribution of royal cattle to royal "shepherds". Perhaps the other texts dealing with distribution of cattle are of a similar kind. One reads in PRU, VI, 115 (RS.17.37): "(1) 113 sheep (2) (entrusted) to *Ḫannanu* and to *Anatenu* (3) and to his wife and to his son". The sheep were entrusted to two men (probably brothers), one of whom was married and had a son, and all these persons were responsible for the delivered cattle. This information may concern cattle of a royal *gt (dimtu)*. Unfortunately, we do not know in single cases whether the text concerns royal shepherds, who received royal flocks and pastured them on the royal pasture lands, or whether it refers to private herdsmen. In any case, it is important to know that the complex of a royal *gt*, administered by the Crown, included also wide pasture lands. PRU, VI, 116 (RS.17.64) is an important text in this respect:[174]
(1) *ṭup-pu kaspi ša* MA.GAD (2) *6 (?) kaspu ša it-ta-din* (3) *amilu*^{MEŠ} ^{URU}*Na-ni-i* (4) *3 kaspu ša* ^{LÚ}*a-ši-ru-ma* (5) *3 kaspu ša* ^{LÚ}*mur-'u-ma* (6) *kaspu an-nu-u* (7) *ša mu-qa-di-im* (8) *šair-te-e*[*ḫ*..], "(1) Tablet of the silver (payment) of the

[174] Cf. *Rainey*, b, p. 34-62 (see p. 46), with a critical view on the reading and interpretations of the legal terms appearing in this text; cf. *Heltzer*, a, p. 34 and now CAD, M, I, p. 252. *maqqadu (muqqadu)* "tax levied on pasturing (on common ground)"; and a full translation of the text.

pasture rights. (2-3) 6(?) (shekels) silver that the men of *Nanu* gave: (4) 3 (shekels) silver from the *aširu*-men[175] (5) 3 (shekels) silver from the *mur'u*-men.[176] (6) This is the silver (7) of the pasture rights (8) that remains [to be paid]".[177] It is irrelevant whether any surplus remained in the treasury, or whether this was a debt still to be solved by those who were bound to do so. The most important thing is that a) villages and b) groups of royal dependents had to pay pasture rights for their cattle.[178] This means that the pasture lands were in royal hands and were not owned by village communities or individuals. The royal treasury profited by this tax and the pasture lands therefore played a role in the royal economy. Although a similar structure can be found in only the royal economy of the kingdom of Larsa in Old Babylonian times.[179] As it is pointed out in CAD.M, p.252, the words *maqqadu* and *mu(q)qadu* in PRU, VI, 116 are considered as by-forms of the word *nāqidu* (i.e. *nqd*). And possibly we can consider here the *nāqidu (nqd)* as an Ugaritic word, written in Akkadian. We have such examples from Ugarit. In the Ugaritic text there appear certain professionals, the *yṣrm* "potters" (Ch. V), sometimes written in Akkadian *ya-ṣi-ru-ma*, and not by the Akkadian word *paḫḫāru*, "potter." The metal-casters, *nskm*, appear also as *na-si-*[*ku-ma*], and the *mr'u(m)* — royal officials are written in Akkadian *mur-'u*, without translation. Therefore, it is possible that the word *nāqidu*, written ideographically, as well as *maqqadu*, etc., were by-forms of *nāqidu* which came under the west-semitic (Ugaritic) influence, as was pointed out in the CAD. It is also possible that in the Akkadian texts of Ugarit there existed an Akkadian counterpart to this term. *F. R. Kraus* analyzed recently the Old-Babylonian term, *nawûm*, which, as he points out, is of West-Semitic origin.[180] The person designated as

---

175 *LÚMEŠa-ši-ru/ri-ma* = ugar. *'šrm* (RS.16.242 and Ch. VIII, pp. 152-154). *Rainey*, e, pp. 296-301.

176 Ug. *mru(m)*, Akk. *mur-u*; *Heltzer*, v, pp. 230-233, and Chap. VIII, pp. 154-157.

177 Cf. the translation of CAD.M., p. 252, "tablet concerning the silver of the tax levied on pasturing: six shekels which the people from the village GN have given, three shekels of silver of the *aširu*-officials, three shekels of silver of the *muru*-officials, this is the silver from the tax levied on pasturing which remains [to be paid]".

178 Cf. PRU, III, 16.153, 12: UDU.MEŠ: *ma-aq-qa-du*, pasture rights paid in sheep.

179 Cf. *Kraus*, b, and *Kozyreva*, a.

180 *Kraus*, c, pp. 172-179; cf. also *Edzard*, a, pp. 168-173.

nawûm is, according to *Kraus* a man who is "engaged at the summer-pasturing area."[181] He explains this more exactly as a shepherd who is busy with the pasturing of cattle by seasonal migration (transhumance) of the herds, which must not be confused with a nomadic way of life. This explanation of Kraus is now widely accepted.[182] As it was pointed out by Kraus and others, in the middle of the IIth millennium B.C.E., *nawûm* was spelled *namû*.[183] This term is widely known from the texts of Alalaḫ from the XVth century B.C.E.[184] *Dietrich* and *Loretz* show us that the *namû* are sometimes equated with the shepherds.[185] And as *Reviv* pointed out,[186] the *namû* were dwellers of the peripheral regions of the kingdom, engaged in cattle-breeding.

We also know that the *namû* are mentioned several times in the texts of Ugarit. According to R.S.8.208,[187] *Burianu namû* (*^{I}Bu-ri-a-nu ^{LÚ}na-mu-ú*) marries a released slave-maid *Eliawa* and pays to her former lord 20 shekels of silver.

In PRU, III, 16.148 a certain *Gamiraddu*, son of *Amatarunu*, receives at least a part[188] of the possessions of *Takḫulinu* — a very high officer at the court of Ugarit and Karchemish. (v. 6′) [ ] *^{I}Tak-ḫu-li-nu imât bîtātū ^{MEŠ}-šu eqlātu ^{MEŠ}-šu ardū^{MEŠ}-šu amâtu^{MEŠ}-šu* (7′) *[alpū^{MEŠ}]-šu imêrū^{MEŠ}-šu gab-bu mim-mu-šu* (8′) *[a-na] ^{I}Ga-mi-rad-di mâr A-[m]u-[t]-a-ru-na ù a-na mâri^{MEŠ}-šu* (9′) *[a-di] da-ri-ti ù píl-ku mim-ma ia-nu* (10′) *[i-na] nidnūti^{MEŠ} šarri an-nu-ti píl-ka-ma ša ^{LÚ}na-mu-ti* (11′) *[i-na] ^{URU}Rêšu ú-bal ^{I}Ga-mi-rad-du ù mârū^{MEŠ}-šu* (12′) *[a-d]i da-ri-ti* "[And if] *Takḫulinu* dies, his houses, his fields, his slaves, his female slaves, his [oxen], his donkeys, everything that he has — [to] *Gamiraddu*, son of *Amutaruna* and to his sons [for]ever (will be). And there is no *pilku*-service [from] these royal gifts. The *pilku*-service of the

---

181 *Kraus*, c, p. 179.

182 *Butz*, a, p. 314, 345-353; 356-358 (esp. 352-3, where *Butz* shows that there were *nâwum* at the disposal of the king; *Kraus*, a, pp. 430-432.

183 *Kraus*, c, p. 172; AHW, p. 729b, *namû* I.

184 Cf. *Giacumakis*, a, p. 100, *ṣābē namē* with the references to the texts; SSAU, II, WO, V, 1, 1969, pp. 79-93.

185 Ibid., p. 87, at least twice, but according to pp. 88-89 they were not the only social group who were shepherds, and the *namû* social group in Alalaḫ were not only shepherds and, according to p. 91, the name (pl.) are connected with the *ḫupšu*.

186 *Reviv*, b, pp. 247-282.

187 *Thureau-Dangin*, a, pp. 253-255.

188 The central part of the text is very damaged and not everything is clear.

namû-ship [in] the village *Rêšu Gamiraddu* and his sons have to perform". So we see that this was not in the city of Ugarit proper but in one of the villages.

On the one hand *Gamiraddu* had the right to inherit after *Takḫulinu* at least a part of his property and this had in itself no burden of service-obligations. Otherwise, he had to perform the *namû*-service, as well as his sons, in the village, *Rêšu*. But also here the character of the service is not shown.

We do not know any other mentioning of *namû* from the texts of Ugarit. We also lack the definitive proof that the *namû* at Ugarit dealt with transhumance pasturing. We see otherwise that the *namû* in Ugarit was in both cases a relatively wealthy man. The *nqdm* in Ugarit, (as we see, that the *rb nqdm* was at the same time the *rb khnm*, "high priest,") were also not in the lowest level in the royal service hierarchy of the *bnš mlk*. Therefore, it is possible to suppose that the *namē* and *nqdm* were identical in Ugarit and that they dealt with the pasturing of the royal and perhaps private cattle on the royal transhumance pasturing lands.

As Liverani proved, there were also *myṣm* "diary men". They belonged also to the *bnš mlk*.[189]

The *ḫupšu*- frequently mentioned in the texts from Alalaḫ[190] and in the Byblos-letters from the El-Amarna correspondence — are also mentioned here. We know quite well that they were among the lower strata of the non-slave population.[191] In Ugarit their mention is very scarce and only once do we see them in connection with the *gt*'s (cf. above, KTU.4.382, 25). Concerning their role in Ugarit we have no definitive conclusions.[192]

Speaking in general about the special staff of the *gt*, we have seen here the *bnš gt*, *bdl gt*, *gt mlkym* and the professional groups of agricultural

---

[189] KTU.4.269, 8-18 — *5 myṣm* and their 5 apprentices (*lmdh*) receive their *ḥpr* "rations', *Liverani*, h, p. 68; *myṣm* "caseificatori" as he compares with Hebr. *mīṣ* — in Prov. 30, 33.

[190] *Giacumakis*, a, p. 78.

[191] EA.77; 81, 33, 37-38; 83; 85; 112; 10-12; 114, 21-23, 55-56; 117, 90; 118, 22-23 and 37-38; 130, 39-42; on their role in Byblos of the Amarna period, *Heltzer*, w, pp. 33-39. Cf. *ḫupšu*, CAD, H, p. 241 and AHW, p. 357.

[192] *Rainey*, d, pp. 103-104. Cf. *Del Olmo Lete*, a, pp. 100-101; but the word is taken only according to its meanings in the literary texts (preceding literature given); *Loretz*, b, pp. 129-132 and *Loretz*, c, pp. 163-167.

professions. Additionally, we know that there were also hired persons — *LÚMEŠagrûti* (ḪUN.GA).[193] But their single appearance in only one text does not permit us to make further conclusions. This only shows that a lot of elements remain unknown and prevent us from completing a total picture of the real situation.

But it is clear that all these people were *bnš mlk* and received their products, silver and fields from the royal stores and treasury. We do not know everything about all the groups of professionals. For example, we do not know anything about the military service of the agriculture workers, except the *nqdm*. We also know nothing about their family life, but the appearance of members of some of the groups together with "his heir" shows that they had families. Otherwise, we know that the maximum known to us about one of these professional groups was 28+x in the case of the *ḥrṯm*, "plowmen." The other known figures of this group and the other groups are lower. It seems that the total numbers were large in general, but lack of evidence does not permit us to make any conclusions.[194] Only further publications of new tablets will widen our horizons here. By all means it is clear that even their dependent status does not show us their servile status.

III. The available sources deal also with the work of royal dependents (*bnš mlk*) who exercised non-agricultural professions at the *gt*. As seen above, KTU.4.125, books grain received from the royal stores by: a) the personnel of the *gt* (*bnš gt* GN), b) people engaged in cattle-breeding (*rʿym*), and c) handicraftsmen like *ḥrš anyt*, "shipwrights",[195] *apym*, "bakers",[196] and other artisans.[197]

---

[193] U.V., 99 (RS.20.245), 1. The hired people receive 8 jars of wine and a certain quantity of oil.

[194] Therefore we cannot understand on what data *Liverani* based his conclusions (*Liverani*, d), that the peasants of the royal forms had no family-life ("manque de vie familiale pour les paysans des fermes palatines"); and that the productive population of the *gt* was $^1/_{20}$ of the whole productive population of Ugarit. It is also impossible to understand where the data about yields in Ugarit, the living-standard of the working population, etc., comes from. Our only hope is that in the future such data will be at our disposal.

[195] Line 1: six GUR.

[196] Line 10: two GUR.

[197] Cf. the fragmentary text KTU.4.139.

In this respect, one of the best examples is given by KTU.4.141: [*sp*]*r*. *bnš.ml*[*k.d.*]*bd adn*[*'m bg*]*t* [198] *Riš*[ ] (col. I, 1-2), "Lis[t] of the kin[g's] men who are at the disposal of *Adn*[*'m*] at *gt Riš*[ ]". Col. I, 3-26 and II, 1-23 thereafter list forty-seven personal names. The summing up is found at the bottom of Col. II: (24) *ḫmšm.ṯmn.kbd* (25) *tgmr.bnš.mlk*. (26) *d.bd.Adn'm*, "(24) fifty-eight in all,[199] (25) the total of the king's men (26) who are at the disposal of *Adn'm*." Then follows col. III: (1) [*š*]*b'.b.Ḥrṯm* (2) [*t*]*lṯ.b.Ṯġrm*, "(1) seven at *(gt) Ḥrṯm*, (2) three at *(gt) Ṯġrm*"[200]; (3)*rb.qrt.aḥd*, "one elder (*rb*) of a township"; (4) *ṯmn.ḫzr* (5) *w.arb'.ḥršm* (6) *dt.tb'ln.b.Pḫn*, "(4) eight males[201] (5) and four craftsmen (6) who worked at *Pḫn*[202]"; (7) *ṯṯm. ḫzr.w.'št. 'šr.ḥrš* (8) *d.tb'ln.b.Ugrt*, "twelve[203] males and eleven craftsmen who worked at Ugarit",[204] (9) *ṯṯm.ḫzr* (10) *dt.tb'ln* (11) *b.gt Ḥrṯm*, "twelve males who worked at *gt Ḥrṯm*"; (12) *ṯn.ḥršm* (13) *ṯn.ḥršm* (14) *b.Nbkm*, "two craftsmen[205] at *(gt) Nbkm*"; (15) *b.gt.Ġl* (16) [*ṯn.*]*nġr.mdr'* (17) [*aḥ*]*d. nġr.krm*, "at *gt Ġl*, [two] field-guards, [on]e vineyard-guards." The badly preserved remainder of the text mentions *psl qšt*, "bow makers", *psl ḥẓm*, "makers of arrows", *ḥrš mrkbt*, "cartwrights", *šrm*, "singers", always in connection with a *gt* the name of which did not survive on the tablet. In consequence, royal dependents of non-agricultural professions had to work at the *gt*, at least on certain occasions. This work may have been a corvée they had to perform in addition to their professional service, but it may also have been connected with their handicraft.

There is a lot of additional information showing the connection of the "king's men" (*bnš mlk*) with the *gt*.

The above-mentioned table KTU.4.213, which reports on various quantities of products at different *gt*, has the following entry:

---

198 The restitution [*b*]*n* in KTU is unconvincing. There is enough space at the beginning of the line for *b* and *g*, and the *t* is almost completely preserved. Therefore, we propose [*b.g*]*t*.

199 The total is not clear, for there were no more than 47 personal names.

200 The *gt* of the "ploughmen" and "gatekeepers".

201 *ḫzr*, cf. above, Ch. III.

202 It might be the name of an otherwise unattested *gt*; cf. above.

203 Dual of *ṯṯ*, "six".

204 Also the city of Ugarit might have had a *gt*.

205 The twice written *ṯn.ḥršm* seems to be a scribal error.

(28) *mit.arbʿm.kbd.yn.mṣb* (29) *l.mḏrġlm*, "in all, (one) hundred and forty (jars) of stored wine for the *mḏrġlm*-guards.[206] Another text already mentioned is KTU.4.243, where *ḥpr bnšm*, "rations of (royal) *bnšm*", are reported to be distributed in various *gt*. This text books deliveries made to (2) *ḥrš. ʿrq*, "cartwrights".[207] In connection with different *gt*, KTU.4.358 lists (9) *arbʿ.ġzlm* (10) *ṯn.yṣrm*, "four spinners, two potters". Numerous other texts mention dependents in relation with the royal corvée (*pilku*), but they give only indirect evidence of these people's connection with the *gt*.

Additional data are found in U.V, 96 (RS.20.12), which mentions (ll. 1, 3, 5, 9) the *dimtu (gt)* of *Sí-kà-ni-ma*, *T[ák!]-ka-bar-ia*, *Ta-ga-bi-ra*, and *Ma-ba-ri* with, respectively, 6, 4, 1 and 5 *ardu*^{MEŠ}, "servants" (-*bnš mlk* = Akk. *arad šarri*). It is specified that they *la ša(l)-li-ma*, "did not pay" or "did not perform their duties." The second part of the text (ll. 16, 18, 20, 23) refers again to the *dimtu of Ta-ga-bi-ra-ia Sí-kà-ni-ma*, *Ma-ba-ru*, and *Ta-ga-bi-ra* in connection with 7, 8, 4, and 4 ^{LÚ}*ardu*^{MEŠ} who *šal-li-ma*, i.e., "paid" or "performed their duties". This unique text shows that duties performed or not performed at the *gt* were registered.[208]

In summary, the *gt* was the primary unit of the royal rural economy. Stores of rural products and of agricultural tools, as well as royal fattening cattle and beasts of burden, were concentrated there. The *gt* had a special rural personnel of royal dependents who had to work there. But, at least at times, also other professionals were bound to work there. The royal fields were related to the *gt* and were tilled with the means of the *gt*. The fields that the king's men received for their service were also attached to the *gt*.

What parallel features have we to such a system as the *gt* system of the royal economy in Ugarit? The comparison with the Ur-III large estates or Egyptian temple-economy is not in the right place. As we have shown, some similar features existed in Larsa. But it is better to take a smaller territorial state of the XV-XVIth century B.C.E. in the East Mediterranean. Although nothing is known which bears any similarity in Alalaḫ, the economic life of the palace had a character of a "*Hauswirtschaft*", i.e., that the palace directly controlled its whole economy while dividing it into *gt*'s. The palace

---

206 *mḏrġlm*, below, Ch. VI.

207 *ʿrq* = Akk. *ereqqu*, "cart", "waggon", as proposed in ZUL II, in OLZ 62 (1967), col. 545; in consequence, *ḥrš ʿrq* = *ḥrš mrkbt*, "cartwrights", cf. Ch. V.

208 *Heltzer*, a, p. 59.

paid all the payments to its dependent people, as well.[209] Until now we have no idea about the royal economy in other syro-palestinian states of this period, but the maritime position and central role of Ugarit in the period under consideration may prove the thesis that the economy of Ugarit was more developed, as compared with its small neighbour-states. It seems that only Mycenean society and, first of all the linear B texts from Pylos and Knossos, as far as they are today known and correctly interpreted, have a similar system of royal cattle-breeding and pasturing as well as organization of the work in the royal estate, although the organization of the royal estate was different than in Ugarit.[210]

It is important, too, that the *gt*-system was not the only element of the royal economy, and we see here also all the elements who enjoyed its products (system of *bnš mlk* of all professions) as well as the widely developed crafts organization, which will be considered in the next chapter.[211]

---

[209] *Klengel*, a, p. 435-457.

[210] *Poljakova*, a, pp. 177-212 and 258-266; a very important element in Pylos is the origin of various lands which were, in fact, in royal hands "from the people" or "of the people" (*parodamo*, *damo*), which are seen only as rudiments in the practice of Ugarit (cf. *Heltzer*, n, pp. 47-55).

[211] The brief summary concerning the royal estate in Ugarit, *Liverani*, SDB, pp. 1341-42 is generally in agreement with our conclusion.

CHAPTER V

CRAFTS AND THEIR ORGANIZATION

As seen above (Ch. I, II and III), the *bnš mlk* — "royal dependents" — system was in full conformity with the system of craftsmen in Ugarit. We have many texts concerning them and this enables us to analyze and draw certain conclusions, perhaps on a more solid basis than in our preceding works.[1] We must, of course, also consider the neighboring societies. Among them are Alalaḫ, Nuzi, the Middle-Assyrian, and if possible, the Hittite data, as well as Mycenean society (Linear B) in Greece. We can compare organizational structure between these societies. For the purposes of a systematic study our classification follows this scheme of presentation: a) the term and its translation; b) the sources; c) the number of persons; d) the engagement in service activities and the corvée that are not necessarily connected with the craft; e) the specialized service work (*pilku*) of the artisans and the delivery of raw materials from the royal stores; f) the deliveries of silver or products from royal stores and their possible periodicity; g) the dwelling-place; h) the references to their appurtenance to the royal dependents (*bnš mlk*); i) the hereditary character of their profession; j) the fields put at their disposal by the king; k) the destination of the production of the craftsmen taken from direct or indirect evidence; l) data about the organization of the professional group; m) other available data.[2]

1. a) *alḫn* — Akk. *alaḫinnu* "miller" or "administrative official".[3]

---

[1] Cf. *Heltzer*, y, pp. 47-60; *Heltzer*, c, pp. 482-496; cf. also among the preceding literature *Diakonoff*, b, pp. 37-62; *Mendelsohn*, a, pp. 60 ff.; *Mendelsohn*, b, pp. 17-21; *Mendelsohn*, b, pp. 17-21; *Mendelsohn*, c, pp. 25-29; *Gordon*, c, pp. 136-143. From the most recent works we must take into account *Sznycer*, SDB, pp. 1417-1425. Concerning the preceding period cf. *Albright*, a, pp. 1-4 and *Margaliht*, a, p. 15; 45-50 ff.

[2] When no data is available the paragraphs concerned will not be mentioned.

[3] AHW, p. 31; CAD A/1, pp. 294-296; ZUL, XI, p. 19, No. 2, personal name and designation of profession, at least according to PRU, V, 4; "miller" cf. below *kš/sd(m)*; but *alaḫinnu* — "miller" cf. *Landsberger*, a, p. 150; *Boyd*, a, p. 28,

b) KTU.4.102, 25; KTU.4.392; KTU.4.337, 11; PRU, VI, 70 (RS.17.50).

c) KTU.4.102 — 1; KTU.4.337 — 1; KTU.4.392 — a certain number; PRU, VI, 70 — 1.

e) KTU.4.392, 4-8 — the whole text relates about a certain corvée.

f) KTU.4.392; (4) *bt alḫnm.ṯlṯm.ṯṯ.kbd* (5) *tšʿ dt.tqḥ[n]* (6) *šʿrt* (7) *šbʿ.dt.tqḥn* (8) *ššlmt*, "(4)*The house of the alaḫḫinu* — at all 36 (persons) (5) Nine (of them), which took wool; (7) seven (of them) which took the *ššlmt*-garments.[4]"

g) PRU, VI, 70, (11) *URUIz-pu ISa-mu-nu mâr A-la-ḫi-ni*, "The village *Izpu-Šamumu*, son of *Alaḫinnu*."[5]

l) The term *bt alḫnm*, shows that there was a certain organized unit of the *alaḫḫinu* — men.

m) KTU.4.337, (11) *ṯlṯ.uṭbm.bd alḫn.b.ʿšrt ksp.*, "3 *uṭbm*-garments to the *alaḫḫinu* for 10 (shekels) of silver."[6] This shows that this *alḫn* had at his disposal certain sums of silver. KTU.4.102, (25) *[aṯt].w.bth.b.bt.Alḫn*, "[(one) wife] and her/his daughter in the house of the *alaḫḫinu*." This shows that they had, at least sometimes, families.

2. a) *apy(m)*,[7] *kkrdn(m)*,[8] Akk. *LÚnuḫatimmu*, *LÚka-ka-ru*,[9] "bakers"? or "cooks."

"miller" or "administrative official"; *Zaccagnini*, b, p. 79 does not translate *alaḫḫinu* from the text HSS, 4, 31, 3; *Mayer*, a, p. 117, "miller", but also based on inexact evidence; cf. also Ch. III, pp. 23-48.

[4] Cf. Ch. III on *ššlmt*.

[5] Possibly not the real name of the father but the designation of his profession.

[6] Cf. *Heltzer*, b, p. 50, No. 118.

[7] Hebr. *ʾōfe*; *Sznycer*, a, p. 1423 "boulangers"; *Mayer*, a, p. 179, "Bäcker" — Nuzi.

[8] AHW, p. 421b, *kakkartum*, "Rundbrot"; 4221 — *kakkaru* — Hebr. *kikkār*, "loaf of bread." This word is designated as of possible Hittite origin; cf. also *Laroche*, a, p. 134. Hurrian *kakkar*, "pâtisserie cultuelle"; *dann/tann* — *denn/tenn* — Hurrian suffix of *nomen actoris* as shown by *Wilhelm*, a, pp. 280-282 and so we can explain the term *kkrdn(m)* as "bakers" or "conditors" or "cooks". (This idea was given to me by Mr. *T. Kvasman* from the Heildelberg University and I owe him my deep thanks.) Cf. also AHW, p. 421a, *kakardinnu*, neo-Assyrian *karkadinnu*, "Truchseß", where the translation is not exact; CAD, K, pp. 42-43, "a baker or cook producing special dishes" and esp. p. 43a 2′ where the special tasks of the *kakkardinnu* at court or in temples are under consideration and "Possibly his task is not only to prepare special dishes (pastries?) but also to serve them to god and king; *Postgate*, b, pp. 91-93, No. 45. In the text of the time of Adad-nirā*ri III*, *the*

b) KTU.4.125, 10; KTU.4.126, 27 — *kkrdnm*; KTU.4.212, 5; KTU.4.362, 4-5; KTU.387; PRU, III, 15.131; PRU, III, 16.257, Tr. I, 2-4; PRU, VI, 93, 25 (RS.17.131).

c) PRU, III, 16.256 — 3 persons by name; 15.132 — 1 person; PRU, VI, 93 — one person; KTU.4.362 — one person; other texts — a group.

d) Maybe PRU, VI, 93.

e) Possibly KTU.4.362, (4) *d.apy*[ ]*bl* (5) *w.arb*[ʿ]*m.d.apy ʿbdh* "that the baker... and four [ ] that the baker...". Possibly, PRU, III, 15.132, *Dunuibru* is the "*kakaru* of the king" Ammistamru II [*kakaru*] *ša šarri*; "There is no *pilku* for the lands he receives," i.e. only the *pilku* of his professional service.

f) KTU.4.125 — the *apym* receive 2 GUR of grain; KTU.4.212.5 *1 apy. mi*[*t.kb*]*d* "for the baker (one) hund[red in a]ll". In both cases the bakers are mentioned together with other professional groups, i.e. it is not flour for baking; PRU, III, 16.257 — a number of jars of oil (*karpat šamni*); KTU.4.387, (26) *ʿšr.dd.l.ap*[*y*] (27) *R*[*i*]*š* "ten *dd*-measures for the bakers of (the village or *gt*) *Riš*."

g) KTU.4.387, (27) *Riš*; PRU, III, 15.132, *Dunuibri* the *kakaru* receives his fields in URU*Ḫulda* (lines 7 and 11).

h) KTU.4.126 — the *kkrdnm* appear among the other professional groups of *bnš mlk*, as well as in PRU, III, 16.257 and VI. 93.

j) PRU, III, 15, 132 — *Dunuibri* receives large amounts of land and seems to be a court official. Possibly he was one of the chief cooks or bakers of the king.[10]

3. a) Akk. *LÚMEŠaškāpū*, "leather-workers."[11]

---

karkedinnu are the contributors of various quantities of products for certain purposes; we do not agree with *Weidner*, a, p. 18, note 127 and p. 28, note 217, where the author equates the *kakardinnu* with the *sâḫiṭ šamni*, "oil-presser", without any proof; also, *Landsberger*, a, p. 151; *Mayer*, a, p. 180, *nuḫatimmu*, "Koch" — Nuzi.

[9] PRU, III, 15.132, 14 and 23. According to the reading of *Nougayrol*, *qá-qá-ru*, but the sign *qá* especially in the *Randgebiete* in the II millennium B.C.E. has to be read *kà*, cf. *Röllig - von Soden*, a, p. 32, No. 170.

[10] Cf. CAD, K, p. 43 d) 2′ about LÚ GAL.NINDA.MEŠ = *amelrab kakardinnuMEŠ*.

[11] LÚAŠ.GAB; what is the respective Ugaritic term, if it appears among the terms, designating the professional groups, is still unclear. Cf. *Mayer*, a, pp. 183-184; *askāpu* (AŠGAB) in Nuzi; Alalaḫ — *Giacumakis*, a, p. 67; *Klengel*, a, p. 439; *Gaal*, a, p. 292, 3, 4; Cf. *Salonen*, g, p. 17, *aškāpu ša qašti* "Hersteller der ledernen Teile des Bogens" = "the producer of the leather-parts of the arch."

b) PRU, III, 16.142 and PRU, III, 15.Y; PRU, VI, 93 (RS.17.131), 14; U,V, 83, 20 (RS.20.146); PRU; VI, 131 (RS.19.35A), 8.
c) PRU, III 15.Y; one person; PRU, VI, 93: two persons; U,V, 83 — one person.
d) PRU, VI, 131, the *aškāpū* receive 1 arch and 1 quiver for some guard service.
e) PRU, III, 15.Y; king *Arḫalbu* orders *Tuppiyanu* "to perform the service of a leather worker" — *pí-il-ka* (9) *sa* LÚ*aškāpi* (10) *ú-bal*; PRU, III, 15.Y: king Niqmepa "frees" *Tuppiyanu* "from the service of the leather-workers," (8) *ip-ṭur-šu* (9) *iš-tu*LÚ.MEŠ*aškāpūti*ti and orders him to be coppersmith (cf. below).
g) The *aškāpu* [ ]-*ya-nu* is designated as a man of the village *Riqdi*.
h) PRU, III, 15.Y: *pilku*, "service" of a professional group of royal dependents; PRU, VI, 93 deals with groups of *bnš mlk*.
j) PRU, III, 15.Y: *aškāpu Tuppiyanu* receives from king Arḫalbu (4) ...*bîta eqla* (5) *ša Bin-Ḫa-at-ti-ya-ma*..., "the house (and) the field of *bin-Ḫattiyama*."
k) It is difficult to propose what the leather workers supplied for there is still no recognizable information.
m) PRU, III, 16.142 and 15.Y shows us the transfer from one professional group of the *bnš mlk* to another.
4. a) *b'l tdtt*,[12] "makers of pectorals."
b) KTU.4.609, 39.
c) Two persons mentioned by name.
f) Delivery of "food rations" to "king's men" (*ḥpr.bnš.mlk*); KTU.4.609, 1: *byrḫ Iṯtbnm*, "in the month of *Iṯtbnm*".
h) KTU.4.609: *bnš mlk*.
j) KTU.4.609, 53: *b'l.šd*, "field owners."
5. a) *b'l.tġpṯm*,[13] "makers of horse-cloths" or "caparisons."
b) KTU.4.609, 36; KTU.4.183, II, 10.

---

[12] ZUL I, in BO 23 (1966), p. 132: *tdtt*, "Brustschmuck", i.e., "pectoral", like Akk. *tudittu*. *B'l*, "to make", "to produce", appears frequently in late-Ugaritic texts instead of *p'l*.

[13] As proposed by *E. Lipinski*, *Heltzer*, c, note 199. *b'l tġpṯ* = Akk. *ēpiš taḫapši* AHW, 1301.

c) KTU.4.609; three persons; KTU.4.183: one person; all mentioned by name.[14]

f) Delivery of "food rations" to "king's men" *(ḫpr.bnš.mlk)*; KTU.4.609, 1: *byrḫ Iṯtbnm*, "in the month of *Iṯtbnm*".

h) KUT.4.609, *bnš mlk*.

j) KUT.4.183, I, 1: *bʿl.šd;* KTU.4.609, 53: *bʿl.šd*, "field owners."

k) Chariot-horses were provided with various textiles from the royal stores.

6. a) *ḫḏġlm/psl ḥẓm*, "makers of arrows".[15]

b) KTU.4.141, III, 19: *psl.ḥẓm*; KTU.4.138, 2; KTU.4.154: *ḫḏġlm*; KTU 4.188: *ḫḏġlm*; KTU.4.609, 16.

c) KTU.4.141: three persons; KTU.4.138: a group; KTU.4.188: seven persons (five mentioned by name); KTU.4.609: five persons mentioned by name.

d) KTU.4.141, III, 15: work at a *gt (Ġl)*.

f) KTU.4.188, 1: *šbʿ.ḫḏġl*[*m*]; in lines 2-6, three persons mentioned by name receive a "garment" (*ḫpn*[16]) and two persons receive "wool" (*šʿrt*); KTU.4.609: delivery of rations in the month of *Iṯtbnm*.

h) KTU.4.141: *bnš mlk*; KTU.4.138: *bnšm*[ ]; KTU.4.609: *bnš mlk*.

j) KTU.4.609: *bʿl.šd*, "field owners".

k) As we see from the deliveries of arms from royal stores, they provided supplies for the royal authorities for military purposes.

m) KTU.4.138: *bd* P[N], "at the disposal of PN"; in the preserved lines, another group is designated as *bd* PN, "at the disposal of PN."

7. a) *ḥṭb(m)*, "woodcutters".[17]

b) KTU.4.609, 20.

c) Two persons mentioned by name.

f) Food rations distributed in the month of *Iṯtbnm*.

---

[14] *Krwn*, possibly the same person, appears in both texts.

[15] The terms designate makers of the non-metallic part of the arrow, for the same text KTU.4.609, 25 mentions also the *nsk ḥẓm*, "arrowsmith"; *ḫḏm* = *ḥẓm* — corruption possibly under Hurrian influence; Alalaḫ — *Gaal*, a, pp. 20-21; 3.2.2. — the arrows were made from reeds.

[16] *Ch. Virolleaud*, PRU V, 65: "horse-cloth"; UT, p. 403, No. 990: "a kind of garment"; CAD 6, H, p. 238: "*ḫupanu*-objects".

[17] Hebr. *ḥōṭēb*; *Yamashita*, a, p. 48, No. 8; cf. also *Mayer*, a, p. 183, *ampannuḫlu* "*ampannu*-Holzarbeiter", which could have the meaning of woodworker, in general something similar to the carpenter(?); *Klengel*, a, p. 439, note 19; LÚ^{MEŠ} *qi-ib-bi* "firewoodmen", from Alalaḫ, *Giacumakis*, a, p. 75; *Gaal*, a, p. 280.1.2.2.

h) *bnš mlk*.

j) *b'l.šd*, "field owner."

8. a) *ḥrš(m)*, "craftsmen"[18] "construction-workers".

b) KTU.4.103, 3, 58; KTU.4.141, III, 5, 7, 12, 13; KTU.4.155; KTU.4.207, 1, 3; KTU.4.214, I, 15; KTU.4.277, 9; KTU.4.216, 2; KTU.4.321, 1; KTU.4.547, 1; KTU.4.618, 12; 4.705, 2.

c) KTU.4.103; in both places *Yšn*, the *ḥrš*; KTU.4.141: respectively four, twelve, two, and two persons; KTU.4.155; thirteen persons mentioned by name; KTU.4.214, II, 13: only one *bn.ḥrš*, "son of a craftsman"; KTU 4.277: one person mentioned by name; KTU.4.216: a group; KTU 4.321: one person mentioned by name; KTU.4.618: three persons; KTU.4.705: a group.

d) Not clear; the appearance of *ḥršm* everywhere could be connected with their professional service work.

e) KTU.4.141:[19] "(5) four *ḥršm* (6) who worked at *(gt) Pḫn*"; "(7) twelve *ḥršm* who worked at (the *gt* of) Ugarit"; KTU.4.207: (9) [*b U*]*lm.bd.R*[-] "[at *(gt) U*]*lm* at the disposal of *R*[ ]"; (11-12) *ḥrš w*[.]*tlṯ.ḥršm*[ ], "[ ]*ḥrš* and three *ḥršm*."[20]

f) KTU.4.216, 2: *ṯlṯ (kdm yn).l.ḥr*[*šm*], "three (jars of wine) for the *ḥr*[*šm*]"; KTU.4.705, 1-2; *ṯlṯ.š'rt l.ḥršm*, "three (measures of) barley (or "wool") for the *ḥršm*".

h) KTU.4.141: *bnš mlk*.

i) KTU.4.214, II, 15: *bn ḥrš*, "son of a *ḥrš*"; KTU.4.135: in the *spr.ḥršm*, "list of *ḥršm*", we read (9) [*w*]*nḫlh*, "[and] his descendent", and (12) *Annmt.nḫlh*, "*Annmt* and his descendent".

j) KTU.4.103: *šd.bd.Yšn.ḥrš*, "a field at the disposal of *Yšn*, the *ḥrš*.

k) As seen from (e) the *ḥršm* worked at the *gt* — possibly participating in building or carpentry-work.

9. a) *ḥrš.anyt*, "shipwrights."

---

[18] Hebr. *ḥārāš*, "woodcutter," "stonecutter", "metal-worker"; cf. also Phoen. *ḥrš*. In some cases, ce include here *ḥrš*[ ], although the next word might have determined the category of *ḥršm* (*ḥrš bhtm*, *mrkbt*, *anyt*, *qšt*, etc.), possibly that the *ḥrš* in Ugarit was also the "carpenter" for we do not recognize among the texts of Ugarit a special term for it as also the Akkadian term *naggāru* is lacking, cf. also DISO, p. 97, Phoen. and IFPCO, p. 121, No. 39, l. 3, p. 143, No. 10, B, 4.

[19] Cf. the whole text Ch. I.

[20] The text may be dealing with a distribution of fields.

b) KTU.4.125, 1.

c) A group.

e) As we see from Excursus I, there existed in Ugarit a well-developed shipbuilding craft (including boats). So the *ḥrš anyt* "shipwrights" played a leading role there.

f) Received 6 GUR of grain. Among the recipients according to the text KTU.4.125 — this was the largest quantity given for one single group.

h) The text KTU.4.125 deals with various professional groups known as *bnš mlk* (Cf. Ch. I).

k) We have a considerable number of texts rendering the problems of shipbuilding and maritime supplies in Ugarit (Cf. Excursus I).

10. a) *ḥrš bhtm*, Akk. ^{LÚMEŠ}*bān bîtātī*^{MEŠ}, *itinnu*^{MEŠ},[21] "house builders".

b) KTU.4.38, 6; KTU.4.47, 10; KTU.4.35, I, 16; KTU.4.183; I, 1; KTU 4.609, 18; KTU.4.630, 8, 9; KTU.4.370, 14; KTU.4.545, II, 6: PRU, VI, 93, 11 (RS.17.131); 131, 1 (RS.19.35A); U,V, 99, 2 (RS.20.15).

c) KTU.4.38: a group; KTU.4.47: a group; KTU.4.35: ten persons mentioned by name; KTU.4.183: thirteen persons mentioned by name; KTU.4.609: ten or eleven persons; KTU.4.630: a group; KTU.4.545: at least five persons mentioned by name; PRU, VI, 93: three persons; PRU, VI, 131: a group; U,V, 99: a group.

d) PRU, VI, 131: distribution of weapons to various professional groups and villages of the kingdom, among them *bân bîtātī*.

e) It must be taken into account that conditions of Ugarit disallowed the use of special raw materials for building which would have to be imported, for in all mentions of ordinary (not especially luxurious building) building only local materials were used.

f) KTU.4.38: *ḥrš bhtm* receive 3 GUR of emmer (ZI.KAL.KAL), 6 shekels of silver (KU.BABBAR), and 6 sheep (UDU$^{ḪI.A}$); KTU.4.609: ration list (*ḥpr*) of the month of *Iṯtbnm*; KTU.4.630, 8-10; *ʿšr.ḥrš bhtm.lqḥ šʿrt*, "ten house-builders took barley" or "wool"; U.V. 99: "five jars of wine for the house-builders."

h) KTU.4.609: *bnš mlk*; KTU.4.370 *bnš mlk*.

i) KTU.4.35, I: (20) *Špšyn.nḥlh*; (22) *Nrn.nḥlh*, "(and) his heir".

j) KTU.4.183, I, 1: [*hrs.*]*bhtm.bʿl.šd* "house builders, owners of a field"; KTU.4.609: *bʿl šd*.

---

[21] U.V.99, 2: GIMÉ = *itinnu*; *bân bîtâti* = ^{LU}DIM É.MEŠ, PRU, VI, 93, 11; 131, 1.

k) Possibly providing the temples and royal palace economy, as well as all the other elements of the royal economy, with the necessary equipment.
l) It seems that there was a centralised organization of the group.
m) KTU.4.47, 10: the mention of the group as a whole is followed by the figure 2 (delivery or payment to the treasury); KTU.4.370: the headline of the whole text is: (1) *spr.bnš.mlk* (2) *d.taršn.ʿmsn*, "list of the king's men who solicit a *ʿmsn*."[22]

11. a) *ḥrš mrkbt/ʿrq*,[23] Akk. ^{LÚMEŠ}*naggārū* ^{GIŠ}*narkabti*[24] "cartwrights".
b) KTU.4.47, 8; KTU.4.46, 13-14; KTU.4.98, 6, 81; KTU.4.141, III.20; KTU.4.183, I, 12; KTU.4.243, 2; KTU.4.145; KTU.4.609, 28; KTU 4.339, 16; KTU.4.745, 9; PRU, VI, 93, 13 (RS.17.131).[25]
c) KTU.4.47: a group; KTU.4.46: one person; KTU.4.98: two persons by name; KTU.4.183: two persons mentioned by name; PRU, II, 98: a group; KTU.4.609: six or seven persons mentioned by name; KTU 4.380, 68: one person; PRU, VI, 93: two persons; KTU.4.145; a group.
d) KTU.4.141: the whole text refers to the work in certain *gt*.
e) KTU.4.145: (1) *ṯmn.mrkbt.dt* (2) *ʿrb.bt.mlk* (3) *yd.apnthn* (4) *yd.ḥẓhn* (5) *yd. trhn* (6) *w.l.ṯt.mrkbtm* (7) *inn.uṯpt* (8) *w.ṯlṯ.ṣmdm.w.ḥrṣ* (9) *apnt.bd.rb.ḥršm* (10) *d.šṣa.hwyh*, "(1) Eight chariots that (2) entered the king's house, (3) with their wheels, (4) with their arrows, (5) with their pole.[26] (6) And two chariots (7) lack the quiver. (8) And three yokes. And the *ḥrṣ*[27] (9) Wheels to the chief cartwright[28] (10) who delivered it to repairs.[29]
f) KTU.4.92: two persons receive two shekels (*ṯqlm*) each; KTU.4.609: delivery of food rations (*ḥpr*) to royal dependents; KTU.4.46, 13-14:

---

[22] *ʿmsn* is translated in UT, p. 457, No. 1872, by "shipment load (of supplies)".

[23] *ʿrq* cannot be related to talmudic Aramaic *ʿarqā* and to Arab. *ʿaraqīya* (as the author did it formerly, *Heltzer*, y). *ʿrq* = Akk. *ereqqu* "cart". Therefore, as proposed by *E. Lipinski* in *Heltzer*, c, p. 475, and *Dietrich-Loretz*, ZUL, II, OLZ, 62, 1967, p. 545 — *ḥrš ʿrq* = *ḥrš mrkbt* "cartwrights". There remains only one other question: *ereqqu* is more likely a 4-wheel waggon while *mrkbt* is a 2-wheel chariot (cf. *Salonen*, d, p. 18 and *Salonen*, c, p. 246.).

[24] PRU.VI.93, 13 — LÚ NA.GAR.GIŠ.GIGIR: Alalaḫ — *Gaal*, a, p. 290, 3.1.4.

[25] Cf. also the fragments where in all preserved texts appears *mrkbt* — KTU 4.447; 4.500; 4.527; 4.551; 4.602 and *ʿrq* in KTU.4.186.

[26] On the production of chariots (resp. waggons), Excursus II.

[27] Cf. Excursus II.

[28] *rb ḥrš* = *rb. ḥrš (mrkbt)* — without any doubt.

[29] Š-stem of YṢʾ; *ḥwyh* "for giving life to it" = "for reconstructions."

Atnb.ḥrš ʿrq šʿrt, "*Atnb*, the cartwright: 'barley' or 'wool'". KTU.4.243: *ḥpr bnšm* (passim), "food rations of the (king's) men"; at the month of *Iṯtbnm*; *l.ḥrš.ʿrq.ṯn.ʿšrh* (l. 2), "for the cartwrights, twelve (measure)".

h) KTU.4.141, 4.183; 4.243; 4.609; *bnš (mlk)*; KTU.4.339: *bnšm.dt.l.Ugrt*, "(king's?) men, who are (attached) to Ugarit."

j) KTU.4.183; KTU.4.609: *bʿl šd*, "field owners".

k) As seen from KTU.4.145 and other texts, the main supply was the military chariotry of Ugarit, but the word *ʿrq* (Akk. *ereqqu*) shows that 4-wheel carts were also produced for certain purposes.

l) The presence of a *rb* — elder — shows that there was a certain organization where the *rb* was responsible, to a certain degree, for the regular production.

m) KTU.4.78 and 4.745 where the mention of the professional group is followed by the figures 1 and 2, respectively, shows that it could be a delivery or payment to or from the treasury.

12. a) *ḥrš qṭn*, "*qatinnu*-makers."[30]

b) KTU.4.47, 9; KTU.4.98, 9; KTU.4.183, II, 6; KTU.4.609, 23; KTU 4.630, 12; KTU.4.370, 35; KTU.4.742, 12; 4.745, 8.

c) KTU.4.74: a group; KTU.4.99; one person; KTU.4.183: three persons mentioned by name; KTU.4.609: seven persons mentioned by name; KTU.4.630: four persons; KTU.4.370: nine persons mentioned by name;[31] KTU.4.745: a group.

f) KTU.4.98: *ʿpṯn.ḥrš.qṭn.ṯqlm*, "*ʿpṯn* (PN), the *qatinnu*-maker, two shekels"; KTU.4.600 "food rations in the month of *Iṯtbnm*"; KTU.4.630, 11-13: *arbʿ.ḥrš qṭn lqḥ šʿrt*, "four *qatinnu*-makers took barley" or "wool".

h) KTU.4.609: *bnš mlk*; see also KTU.4.370, 35.

j) KTU.4.609 and KTU.4.183: *bʿl.šd*, "field owners".

m) KTU.4.47 and KTU.4.745: the mention of the group is followed

---

[30] UT, p. 399, No. 93: "makers of *qṭn*"; RSP II, p. 49, No. 10: "makers of fine objects"; ZUL I, in BO, 23 (1966), p. 132, and ZUL VII, p. 100, compare rightly *qṭn* with Amarna, Nuzi, and Alalaḫ *k/qattinnu*, which is not to be confused with *LÚqaṭinnu/qaṭṭinu* who is a craftsman; *Freydank*, a, pp. 124-127, and it seems that the Middle-Assyrian *qatinnu*-maker (producer) is the exact Assyrian counterpart to the *ḥrš qṭn* in Ugarit. What the *qṭn/qatinnu* produced is still unclear.

[31] KTU.4.98, (9) *ʿpṯn* = 4.370, Rev. *ʿpṯn*.

respectively by the figures 1 and 2; possibly a delivery or a payment to the treasury. KTU.4.370: *spr.bnš.mlk d.taršn.ʿmsn.*[32]

13. a) *ḥrš qšt, psl qšt,*[33] *kṯtġl(m),*[34] *LÚsasinnu* (sàZADIM), "bowmakers".[35]

b) KTU.4.215; KTU.4.141, III, 18; PRU, VI, 93 (RS.17.131); 1; KTU 4.310, 2; KTU.4.643, 25-26.

c) KTU.4.215: six persons mentioned by name; 4.311, 1-2: group; PRU, VI, 93: two persons.

d) KTU.4.141: work at a certain *gt*.

h) KTU.4.141: *bnš mlk*.

i) KTU.4.215: *spr.ḥrš qšt*, "list of bowmakers"; in line 6: *Špšyn.nḥlh*, "*Špšyn* (and) his heir".

14. a) *yṣrm*, Akk. *LÚpaḫḫāru*, *LÚia-ṣi-ru-ma*, "potters".

b) KTU.4.99, 11; KTU.4.87, 3; KTU.4.46, 11-12; KTU.4.126, 28; KTU 4.367, 8; KTU.4.339, 24; KTU.4.358, 10; PRU, III, 15, 172; PRU, VI, 136,, 11 (RS 17.240).

c) KTU.4.99: a group; KTU.4.87: a group; KTU.4.46: two persons mentioned by name; KTU.4.126: a group; PRU, III, 15.172: a group by name; KTU.4.367: one person; KTU.4.339: one person mentioned by name; KTU.4.358: two persons; PRU, VI, 136: one person.

d) KTU.4.358: at a *gt*; KTU.4.367: at a *gt*.

f) KTU.4.46: two persons receive *šʿrt* ("barley" or "wool"); PRU, VI, 136: receipt of 1 shekel of silver.

---

[32] Ch. I, note 21.

[33] Lit. "producers of bows", "arch-formers."

[34] As pointed by *Dietrich-Loretz*, a, pp. 199-200, *-ġlm* gives us the Hurrian suffix of *nom. actoris*. The case of *-ġl(m)* in the place-name from Ugarit as *Ḫrbġlm* = *URUḪurbaḫulimi* which *E. Lipinski* (*Heltzer*, c, note 224) tries to compare with *kṯtġlm* and to show it as a place-name is irrelevant in this case; cf. *Laroche*, a, p. 139 *kštġl(m) *kaštuḫli(m)* "fabricants des 'arches'" the change *k/q* and *š/ṯ* is common and typical for semitic words in Hurrian despite the fact that *Dietrich-Loretz* (ZUL, VIII, p. 110, No. 37) retreat from their own formerly expressed opinion; cf. also *aškāpu ša qašti* — *Salonen*, g, p. 16, and above *aškāpu*.

[35] LÚ ZAZADIM (PRU, VI, 93, 28): is translated by *J. Nougayrol* (PRU VI, p. 87 and 152) with "lapidaire", and CAD, Z, p. 10, shows indeed that *zadimmu* = *purkullu*, "seal-cutter." However, both appear in PRU II, 93 (LÚBAR.GUL in l. 24) and CAD, Z, p. 10b, explains that, after the Ur III period, *zadimmu*, "lapidary", appears only in lexicographical texts. From the Old-Babylonian period on, one must read ZADIM as *sasinnu*, translated in AHW, p. 1032, by "Bogenmacher"; cf. Alalaḫ, *Gaal*, a, p. 290, 3.1.3; *Mayer*, a, pp. 186-187 — Nuzi.

h) KTU.4.367: *bnš mlk*; KTU.4.339, 17: *bnšm.dt.l.mlk*, "men, who (belong) to the king"; KTU.4.358: *bnšm*.

k) We have only archaeological, i.e., anonymous data about the existence of local production of ceramics.

m. KTU.4.99, 11; 4.87, 3; PRU, III, p. 205: the mention of the group is followed respectively by the figures 3, 1, and 3.

15. a) *kbs(m)*, "fullers".[36]

b) KTU.4.99; KTU.4.71, 19; KTU.4.125, 19; KTU.4.610, II; KTU.4.332, 13.

c) KTU.4.99: a group; KTU.4.71: three persons mentioned by name; KTU.4.125: a group; KTU.4.610: a group; KTU.4.332: one person mentioned by name.

d) KTU.4.125: connected with a *gt*; KTU.4.610; 8 shekels of silver paid by the *kbsm* as part of a great tribute due to the Hittite king: [*spr*.] *argmn Špš* (l. 1), "[inventory] of the tribute of the Sun", i.e., the Hittite king.

f) KTU.4.71, III, 5-8: three *kbsm* receive 4 (shekels) of silver each; line 9: ŠU.NIGIN KU.BABBAR.MEŠ 12, "total of silver: 12 (shekels)"; KTU.4.125, 19: the *kbsm* receive 4 GUR of grain.

g) KTU.4.332, 5: *b Qrt*[ ], "in (the village of) *Qrt*."

h) KTU.4.125: *bnš (mlk)* as also according to other texts.

16. a) *ksdm*/*kšdm*, "millers".[37]

b) KTU.4.99, 16; KTU.4.126, 15; KTU.4.125, 8; KTU.4.286, 1; KTU 4.332, 18.

c) KTU.4.99: a group; KTU.4.126: a group; KTU.4.125: ten persons; KTU.4.286: seven persons mentioned by name; KTU.4.332: one person mentioned by name.

d) KTU.4.125: work at a *gt*.

---

[36] UT, p. 417, No. 1193, translates "launderer", but "fuller" seems preferable. The Hebrew *kōbēs* has both meanings; cf. Akk. *kabāsu*, "treten" (AHW, p. 415). The fuller's work was done with his feet; cf. RSP II, p. 54, No. 17: "fuller"; but at the same time in Nuzi, *Mayer*, a, pp. 175-176. *ašlāku* "Wäscher, Walker"; if we are dealing here with fullers or the process of preparation of wool for further processing, we could compare the term with the terms of processing of wool in Alalaḫ — *Gaal*, a, p. 289-290, 2.5.

[37] UT, p. 121, No. 1278: "members of a certain guild"; ZUL I, in BO, 23 (1966), p. 130, "miller" (Akk. *kaṣṣ/zzidakku*); but it is highly doubtful if *alaḫinnu* designates a miller; we do not have any convincing material either concerning *alaḫinnu* or *kšdm* in reference to the distribution of grain for processing.

g) KTU.4.332, 18: *Ṣpr.ksd* [ ], "*Ṣpr*, the miller(?)", cf. line 5: one person mentioned by name.
h) KTU.4.125: work at a certain *gt*.
m) KTU.4.99: the mention of the group is followed by the figure 5; KTU 4.125, 8: *ʿšr.ksdm.yd.lmdhm.lqḥ*, "ten millers(?) with their apprentices took ..." it is clear that they had apprentices who were their subjects, i.e. that they were not on the lowest level in the system of *bnš mlk*, "royal dependents", in the kingdom of Ugarit.
17. a) *nsk(m)*, "smiths".[38] Akk. *nasikuma*.
b) KTU.4.98, 17; KTU.4.133, 3; KTU.4.261, 1; KTU.4.396, 20; PRU, VI, 136, 13 (RS.17.240).
c) KTU.4.98: one person mentioned by name; KTU.4.133: one person mentioned by name; KTU.4.29: nineteen persons mentioned by name; KTU.4.396: one person mentioned by name; PRU, VI, 136: one person.
e) KTU.4.261, 1: *spr.argmn.nskm*, "inventory of the tribute of the smiths."[40] Thereafter, the text mentions by name ninteen *nskm* from three villages. Each of them has to deliver from 500 (*ḫmš mat*) up to 2000 (*alpm*) shekels of metal. This might be the professional tax payable to the treasury and perhaps meant to be a part of the tribute due to the Hittite king.
f) KTU.4.98, 17: four shekels; PRU, VI, 136, 15: one shekel (of silver).
g) KTU.4.261, 2-12: *Rqdym*, "people (of the village of) *Rqd*." ten persons mentioned by name; lines 13-18: *Ušknym*, "people (of the village of) *Uškn*", four persons mentioned by name; line 19-22: *Lbnym*, "people (of the village of) *Lbn(m)*", three persons mentioned by name.
k) As we have seen (e), the production of the *nskm* was used for paying tribute by the king of Ugarit; Archaeological evidence about various metal artifacts of local origin.

---

[38] Here we are dealing only with "smiths" (*nskm*) whose specialization is not given. When the texts show that they work "copper" or "bronze" (*ṯlṯ*), we consider them as *nsk ṯlṯ*, "coppersmiths", and deal with them in the proper paragraph; the same when *ksp* "silver" is added to *nskm*; at the same time it is clear that these "smiths" liter. "casters", dealt with silver or copper (bronze) or with the casting of artifacts mentioned below; *Mayer*, a, p. 185, *nappāḫu* (SIMUG), "smith"; *Gaal*, a, p. 293, 3.7.1.

[40] *argmn*, "tribute"; cf. *Rabin*, b, pp. 113-139 (see pp. 116-118): Ugaritic *argmn* = Hittite *arkamman(u)*, "tribute". Cf. also *Pardee*, a, pp. 277-278.

l) The delivery of raw materials to groups gives evidence about a system of organization among them.

m) KTU.4.133, 3: *Ṯ'ly.tḥt.B'ln.nsk*, "*Ṯ'ly* instead of *B'ln*, the smith." Perhaps this is a change of appointment.

18. a) *nsk ḥḏm/ḥẓm*, "arrowsmiths".[41]

b) KTU.4.609, 25; KTU.4.630, 14.

c) KTU.4.609: eight persons mentioned by name; KTU.4.630: six persons.

f) KTU.4.609, 1: *spr ḥpr*, "list of food rations", ...*byrḫ Iṯtb*[*nm*], "in the month of *Iṯtbnm*"; KTU.4.630: *ṯṯ nsk*, *ḥẓm lqḥ.š'rt*, "six arrowsmiths took 'barley' or 'wool'."

h) KTU.4.609, 1: *bnš.mlk*.

j) KTU.4.609, 53: *b'l.šd*, "field owners."

k) Providing of the army with arrows, as we see from texts concerning military supplies (cf. Ch. VI).

19. a) *nsk ksp*, $^{\text{LÚ.MEŠ}}$*kuttimnu*, "silversmiths."[42]

b) KTU.4.68, 74; KTU.4.47, 6; KTU.4.99, 84: KTU.4.183, II, 22; KTU 6.20, 1; KTU.4.609, 32; KTU.4.745, 7: PRU, VI, 70, 4 (RS.17.50); 131 (RS.19.35A).

c) KTU.4.68: a group; KTU.4.47: a group; KTU.4.99: a group; KTU 4.183: four persons mentioned by name; KTU.6.20: a group; KTU.4.609: eleven or twelve persons mentioned by name; KTU.4.745: a group; PRU VI, 70: one person; PRU, VI, 131: a group.

d) KTU.4.68: together with the *mkrm* (*tamkārū*, "tradesmen"), the silversmiths provide the "archers" (*ṣābē*$^{\text{MEŠ GIŠ}}$*qašāti*^{MEŠ}) with one man; PRU, VI, 131: list of a delivery of arms to professional groups of royal dependents and to villages.

f) KTU.6.20: (1) *nsk.k*[*sp*] (2) *'šrt* (3) *wnṣp*, "silversmiths, ten and a half (shekels of silver?)";[43] KTU.4.609: food rations distributed in the month of *Iṯtbnm*.

g) KTU.4.609, 1: *bnš.mlk*.

j) KTU.4.183, 1, 1 and KTU.4.609, 53: *b'l.šd*, "field owners."

k) The archaeological finds provide us with a lot of jewellry, according to the stylistic analyses, of local origin.

---

[41] It seems that they cast and completed only the arrowheads for we know also of the *psl ḥẓm/ḫḏġlm* — *ḫḏm* — instead of *ḥẓm* under Hurrian influence.

[42] AHW, p. 518, "Gold und Silberschmied"; — KU.DIM.

[43] It is not clear whether this was a payment for work or raw material.

l) The collective obligations have shown us clearly that a certain inner organization existed among this group of professionals.

m. CTA, 73, 6; 74, 14; KTU.4.745; the mention of the group is followed by the figures 2, 10, and 2, respectively.

20. a) *nsk ṯlṯ*, Akk. *LÚ.MEŠnappaḫ erê MEŠ*, *LÚZAG.LU siparri*, *sbrdnm*, "coppersmiths".[44]

b) KTU.4.35, II, 8; KTU.4.43; KTU.4.126, 18; KTU.4.183; KTU.4.222, 8-11; KTU.4.181; KTU.4.272;[45] KTU.4.310; (PRU, III, 15.172, 10; PRU, III, 15.Y; PRU, III, 16.257, Tr. II; KTU.4.337; PRU, VI, 93 (RS.17.131), 23.

c) KTU.4.35: two persons mentioned by name; KTU.4.43: a group; KTU 4.125: a group; KTU.4.183: one person mentioned by name; KTU.4.202: five persons mentioned by name; KTU.4.181: three persons mentioned by name; KTU.4.310: five subgroups; PRU, III, 15.172: a group; PRU, III, 15.Y: one person; PRU, III, 16.257: eight persons mentioned by name; KTU.4.337: several persons; PRU, VI, 93: one person.[46]

e) KTU.4.31: (1) *ṯlṯ.d yṣa* (2) *bd.Šmmn* (3) *l argmn* (4) *l nskm* (5) *ṯmn.kkrm* (6) *alp.kbd* (7) [*m*]*itm.kbd*, "(1) Copper that was handed over (2) to *Šmmn* (3) for the tribute (40) (to be paid) by the smiths: (5) eight talents, (6-7) one-thousand two-hundred (shekels), in all" (ca. 250 kgs.4.181: (1) *spr. irgmn*, "inventory of the tribute."[47] The quantities of copper distributed between smiths dwelling in various villages follow. KTU.4.272:[48] (3) *ḫmš*.

---

[44] *ṯlṯ*, "copper" in Ugaritic. The terms referring to metalwork and metallurgy in Ugarit are examined by *Zaccagnini*, a, pp. 315-324; *sbrdnm* — *sipardannu* with the same suffix of Hurrian origin *dan/tan* — *den/ten* as in *kkrdnm* "bakers", "conditors" — cf. above. (2) *apym* and esp. notes 8 and 9; cf. also on Nuzi, *Mayer*, a, *nappāḫu* (SIMUG) "Schmied" pp. 105-186, the respective terms in Ugarit are not affected, as far as we know, in Nuzi or Alalaḫ — cf. *Gaal*, a, p. 293, 3.7.1; p. 294, 3.9.33; p. 295, 3.9.3.7; *Gicumakis*, a, p. 91, we see that in the texts of the XVth century B.C.E. "smith" was written phonetically *na-pa-ḫu* (AT.397:2).

[45] Since the text deals with large quantities of *ṯlṯ*, "copper", or "bronze", it is clear that the persons mentioned here, although not designated as *nsk ṯlṯ*, are coppersmiths.

[46] We have at least five texts in which the *nsk ṯlṯ* are mentioned by name. Unfortunately, the names in any single tablet do not coincide with the personal names of the other tablets.

[47] *irgmn*, variant of *argmn*.

[48] Lines 1-2 are obscure.

kkr.brr (4) *kkr.ḫmš.mat.kbd.ṯlṯ.šm[n]*, "five talents of tin,[49] (one) talent (and) five hundred (shekels), in all, of *šm[n]* copper," (5) *alp.mitm.kbd.ṯlṯ.ḥlb*, "(one) thousand five hundred (shekels), in all, of *ḥlb* "copper"; (6) *šb'.l.'šrm.kkr.ṯlṯ* (7) *d.ybl.Blym*, "twenty-seven talents (ca. 800 kgs) of copper which the people of (the village of) *Bly* brought," to the treasury. In the present case, the metals were tin and copper, i.e., the components of bronze. PRU, II, 137: "(1-2) (One) hundred (shekels) of copper, deficity (debited) against [51] the smiths of (the village of) *Kṯtġlm*,[52] (3-4) forty (shekels) of copper, the deficit of *Mtb'l*, man of (the village of) *Riš*; (5-6) thirty (shekels) copper, (debited) against the smiths of (the village of) *Ary*; (7-8) (one) thousand (shekels) of copper, (debited) against the smiths of (the village of) *Art*; (9-10) five hundred (shekels) of copper, (debited) against *Mtn*, man of (the village of) *Riš*."

KTU.4.337: (1) *spr.ḫṯbn.sbrdnm*, "Account list of the bronze-smiths.[53] (2-3) Five talents (and one) thousand (shekels) of copper, in all, for the smiths, people of (the village of) *Bir*, (4) at the disposal of *Urtn*, and six hundred (shekels) of tin ...; (6) five thousand (shekels) of copper for (the village of) *Ḫlby* (7) at the disposal of *Tlmi* ...". The text concerns a distribution of copper and of tin to bronzesmiths. According to PRU, III, 15.Y, line 16, *Tuppiyanu* "has to perform the duty of the smiths",[54] *pil-ka* $^{LÚ.MEŠ}$*ZAG.LU-ti ú-bal*. (Cf. Ch. III, p. 25).

f) PRU, III, 16.257: six persons received, each, a jar of oil (*karpat šamni*); one person received two jars, and another three jars.

g) KTU.4.181: one person in the village of *Maḫd*, one at *Ar(y)*, and one at *Ilštm'*; KTU.4.272: people of the village of *Bly* engaged smithery; KTU 4.310: two persons (ll. 4 and 10) from the village of *Riš*, a group from *Ary* (ll. 5-6), and a group from *Art* (ll. 7-8); KTU.4.337: smiths of the villages of *Bir* (ll. 1-2) and *Ḫlby* (l. 6); so we see that the coppersmiths dwelled in these nine villages of the kingdom, at least.

---

[49] *brr*, "tin"; cf. *Zaccagnini*, a, p. 317 ff.

[50] Possibly a designation of a special quality of copper.

[51] UT, p. 403, *ḫsr*. Perhaps the production did not correspond to the quantity of raw material received.

[52] Cf. *ḥrš qšt — psl qšt* etc. and the discussion around the word *kṯtġlm*.

[53] *Zaccagnini*, a, pp. 315-317: ^{LÚ}ZABAR DÍM, Ugar. *sbrdn*, and the discussion in note No. 44.

[54] *Zaccagnini*, a, p. 319.

h) PRU, III, 15, Y: text composed in the name of the king and dealing with a royal dependent, as well as from the other texts, it is clear that we are dealing with royal dependents.
j) KTU.4.183, I, 1: *b'l.šd*, "owner of a field"; KTU.4.222: distribution of fields by the authorities; four *nsk.ṯlṯ* receive each one or two fields (*šd*), as appears from the total 6 given in line 10; PRU, III, 15.Y: lands are given to *Tuppiyanu* for his service as smith (*pil-ka* $^{LÚ.MEŠ}$*ZAG.LU-ti*).
k) As seen from shipbuilding accounts, also arrowsmiths (*nsk.ḥẓm.* etc.), were provided with bronze. We have much archaeological data of supplies to the army of Ugarit (Ch. VI) as well as of the royal foreign trade of Ugarit.[55]
l) At least *Šmmn* (KTU.4.43) seems to have been a chief bronzesmith. Elders of other groups may have been responsible for the metal delivered to the villages for further treatment.
m) PRU, III, 15.172: the words $^{LÚ.MEŠ}$*nappaḫ erê* (l. 10) are followed by the figure 10.[56]
21. a) *ġzlm*, "spinners".[57]
b) KTU.4.368, 9.
c) Four persons.
d) Work at a *gt*.
h) The text deals with *bnšm (— bnš mlk)*.

---

[55] *Heltzer*, b, pp. 31-33, VII.

[56] A great number of studies, devoted to metallurgy in Ugarit and neighboring areas, are now in our possession. The summaries are given in *Curtois*, SDB, pp. 1233-1234; 1252-1253; *Liverani*, SDB, pp. 1331-1333; *Sznycer*, SDB, pp. 1423-1425; *Heltzer*, b, pp. 29-33; 59-61; 88-89; 93-98; 108-112, , etc.; *Zaccagnini*, a; on the possible use and trade with these metals, cf. also, *Bass*, a, pp. 163-167; *Muhly*, a, pp. 208-214, 258; *Muhly*, b, pp. 112-115; *Buchholz*, a, pp. 92-115; on archaeological evidence about metal-production and production of metal artifacts in Ugarit cf. *Schaeffer*, c, pp. 250-272; *Schaeffer*, d, pp. 276-279; *Schaeffer*, e, pp. 169-178; on the tribute, paid to the Hittites in metal, *Dietrich-Loretz*, i, pp. 266 ff.; cf. *Heltzer*, c, pp. 489-493. Metal workers with a certain organization on behalf of the royal authorities are also known from Alalaḫ and, especially in the period of the Ur III, dynasty in Mesopotamia (*Limet*, c, pp. 165-189; *Tjumenev*, a, p. 354). And we find a striking similarity between the organization of metallurgy and its personnel in Ugarit and Mycenaean Greece — *Poljakova*, a, pp. 147, and 231-234; *Pugliese-Carratelli*, a, pp. 242-254; *Chadwick*, a, pp. 139-147; *Hurst*, a, pp. 92-96.

[57] UT, p. 463, No. 1955 arab. *ġzl* "to spin" (wool or flax).

k) The large quantities of wool and flax, known from the texts of Ugarit, presuppose that spinners played a considerable role in the economy,[58] but it is also possible that the spinning was done as an *ilku*-service by the villagers of the kingdom.

22. a) *psl(m)*. "sculptors," "stonecutters."

b) KTU.4.68, 63; KTU.4.99, 18; KTU.4.103, 36; KTU.4.126, 8; KTU. 4.207; 7; KTU.4.370, 45; KTU.4.370, 45; KTU.4.412, III, 9.

c) KTU.4.68: a group; KTU.4.99: a group; KTU.4.103: one(?) person; KTU.4.126: a group; KTU.4.207: a group; KTU.4.370: one(?) person; KTU.4.412: five persons mentioned by name.

d) KTU.4.68, 63: mentioned with *yṣḥm*[59] and "singers" (*šrm*); they provide a man for the "archers" (*ṣābē*^{MEŠ} ^{GIŠ}*qašātī*^{MEŠ})

h) KTU.4.370: *spr.bnš.mlk d taršn.ʿmsn*, "list of the king's men who solicit a *ʿmsn*."

i) KTU.4.412, III, 11-12: *bn.Glʿd w.nḥlh*, "*bn Glʿd* and his heir(s)" (among the *pslm*).

j) CTA, 82, 36: [*šd.bd*].*Klby.psl*, "[field at the disposal of] *Klby*, the sculptor" (in a list of distribution of *ubdy*-fields).

k) The large number of stonecarvings, reliefs, statues, etc., confirm that they were made by the *pslm* of Ugarit. But they could work also with ivory and bone, etc.

23. a) *ṯrmn(m)*, akk. ^{LÚ}*u/išpāru*, "weavers".[60]

---

[58] Cf. all about the weavers and *Heltzer*, b, pp. 23-27.

[59] *yṣḥm* — cf. Ch. VIII, pp. 163-164.

[60] The etymology of *ṯrmn(m)* is not clear, but this term is connected with garments (*lbš*) in PRU II, 106, and the Akkadian text RS 11.732 B (PRU III, p. 181-182) mentions *šipātu uqnatu tarmani*, "blue *tarmani* wool". So we suppose that *ṯrmnm* could be connected with the weaving or dyeing of wool or woollen garments. For other opinions see UT, p. 507, No. 2749; RSP II, p. 89, No. 16, "diners", and p. 292, No. 48, connected only with toponyms.

There is another term in Ugaritic, appearing in a lot of lists of *bnš mlk* — *mḫṣm* — Akk. *māḫiṣu* (TAG) — PRU, VI, 10 (RS.17.390), 10 and VI, 168 (Rs.19.99) int. 4 — *ma-ḫi-ṣu ub-ru*, as *Nougayrol* translates "tisseur à domicile?". At the same time, although there are texts concerning the deliveries of silver, products etc. to the *māḫiṣu*, texts concerning various services of the *mḫṣ(m)*, etc., we have no one specific mention of the professional *pilku*-service of the *māḫiṣu* in Ugarit. In Alalaḫ the "weavers" are named *išparum*-^{LÚ}UŠ.BAR (*Gaal*, a, p. 291 — 3.3.1, as well as *māḫiṣum*, but *Gaal* adds, "we hardly find any reference to cloth"; cf. also *Giacu-*

b) KTU.4.182, 11, 13, 15, 20, 29, 31; KTU.4.168, 5; PRU, III, 15.172, 7; PRU, VI, 93 (RS.17.131), 23: U.V, 99 (RS.20.425), 5; *Thureau-Dangin*, b.[61]
c) PRU, VI, 93: one person; U.V, 99: a group; *Thureau-Dangin*, b, 29.
e) *Thureau-Dangin*, b — shows the delivery for weaving; cf. note 61.
f) U.V, 99, 5: three jars of wine for the LÚ.MEŠUŠ.BAR... *i-na* ITU.SAG.DU GEŠTIN.MEŠ, i.e., in the Ugaritic month of *riš-yn*, lit. "the beginning of the wine."
h) PRU, II, 106 and 107: various textiles are delivered to *ṯrmn(m)* and *ṯrmn mlk*. This might indicate that also they belonged to the *bnš mlk*.
k) The supply of the foreign trade of Ugarit, the textiles for shipbuilding, for the army, etc.[62]
m) PRU, III, 15.172 — the term *ušpāru* is followed with the figure 10.[63] The additional information on textile production comes mainly from the texts speaking about various textiles.[64]

---

makis, a, p. 80, *išparu* "weaver"; p. 86 — *māḫiṣu* — a profession, related to Ugaritic *mḫṣm*; *Klengel*, a, p. 439 and note 16, *ušparu* and *māḫiṣu* — as "weaver", without additional explanations; Nuzi, *Mayer*, a, pp. 169-179, does not find in Nuzi any of the two terms for textile-workers; in Mari in the XVIIIth cent. B.C.E. the term was *išpartum* "tissease" for a woman, ARMT, XVIII, p. 271 (glossary with the *Belegestellen*); CAD, M, I, pp. 102-103, *māḫiṣu* gives us the meaning connected always with the different contexts in which the word appears — "(1) weaver, (2) plowmen... (3) hunter (using the bow), etc.; AHW, p. 584 gives even more meanings; UT, p. 432, No. 1456. "numbers of a certain guild, perhaps 'butchers'"; WUS, p. 182, No. 1548, *mḫṣm* — without a definitive definition; *Yamashita*, a, p. 58, No. 22, "butcher"; *Salonen*, g, pp. 18-20, *māḫiṣu* "Bogenschütze", "archer" or "the hunter-archer", etc. The root *mḫṣ* has, in Ugaritic literary texts, always the meaning "to strike, smite, destroy", therefore, until there is additional information from the sources, we prefer to withhold making any statements about the *mḫṣm* in the Ugaritic texts as textile workers, and we will understand them as a kind of "guard" or "body-guard", possibly armed with a specific kind of weapon. Cf. Ch. VI, pp. 123-124.

[61] *Thureau-Dangin*, b. This text contains a special number count of 33 lines. 32 of them mention 29 weavers (without a designation of this profession) to whom certain quantities of purple wool" (*šipātu uknâtu*) were delivered (from 100-200 shekels for each one); the total (1) *bîltu 6 me-at šipātu uknātu napḫar* "2 talents, 600 (shekels) purple wool — the total."

[62] Cf. Ch. VI; also *Heltzer*, b, pp. 23-27 and 38-50.

[63] Possibly, there were some additional productive professions in Ugarit, but we have no means of identifying them at present, for no etymological explanations or knowledge about their professional activities are known to us.

[64] On the textile trade in Ugarit, *Heltzer*, b, pp. 23-27; 38-51 and the respective

The information concerning the craftsmen of the kingdom of Ugarit allows us to draw some conclusions about their organization. Naturally, many things remain unclear and we can only deduce by analogy with another group where we are better informed. One good example in this field is the fact that there were at least several thousands of wheeled vehicles in Ugarit and that presupposes that the general number of cartwrights was much larger than we are aware of. The same must be said about the shipwrights, for we know a widely developed vessel-building in Ugarit, but the shipwrights are mentioned only once and without designation of their number. We will try, in the future to approximate the number of *bnš mlk* in Ugarit based on various indirect calculations. Therefore, we must suppose that the information known about one group also concerns the others, and all this despite the fact that the lists are incomplete, broken, and that they may not have listed all the persons engaged in each particular profession at the time they were composed.

We must once again emphasize that from the point of view of the royal authorities of Ugarit the craftsmen did not differ from the most of the other groups of professional *bnš mlk*, "royal dependents" in the kingdom, and therefore representations of the productive professions is, to a certain extent, artificial. At the same time, we do not distinguish here between such productive professions as shipbuilding, builders, textile work, etc. which supplied the economy of the country, including the army and trade, in

notes, pp. 75-76, 81-83; 90-91 and 103. We are not sure that there were a kind of ergasterion-workshops for textile production in Ugarit. At the same time the presence of fullers (*kbsm*) and spinners (*gżlm*) shows a specialization of the working personnel, to a certain degree. Concerning the parallel situation in the vicinity, we know that a developed textile industry existed in the III millennium in Ebla (*Pettinato*, a, pp. 175-184) and that it was well-organized in the period of the Ur III dynasty in Mesopotamia (*Waetzold*, a, p. 91 ff.; *Tjumenev*, a, pp. 348-351), under state control. The contrary we see in the Old-Babylonian period, where the textile production, which was on a large scale, was sometimes in private hands (*Dalley*, a, pp. 155-159), or as in Mari, where it was in the hands of ergasterion-like workshops (ARMT, XVIII, pp. 121-140; ARMT, VII, p. 246, and texts 263, II, 1; ARMT, X, 11, 512, 9; 150, 5, etc., AHW, p. 804). In Nuzi, textiles were produced by palace-slaves and free people (*Mayer*, a, pp. 169-176). In the Old-Assyrian state it was in private hands (*Garelli*, a, *Veenhof*, a). In Mycenaean Greece women weavers appear, possibly semi-free, who supplied the needs of the palace and servicemen in textiles and worked on behalf of the palace economy (*Chadwick*, a, pp. 150-156; *Poljakova*, a, pp. 205-208).

general, and such professions which supplied only the needs of the court: bakers, (cooks), millers, etc. We see that the textile workers, metallurgists, shipwrights, cartwrights, etc. had to be provided with raw material for further processing. The same thing could not always be said about the potters and housebuilders, etc., for the raw material used in the exercise of their professions was always easily available.

Some things may be assumed with certainty:

1. All these artisans or people of the productive professions belonged to the *bnš mlk*.
2. The *ḥršm* of various kinds (*anyt*, *mrkbt*, (*ʿrq*), *qṭn*, etc.) and the metal workers (*nskm*, *nsk ṯlṯ*, *nsk ksp*, etc.) were the most numerous artisans. There is some evidence that the artisans (the *ḥršm* and, possibly, the *nskm*, "smiths", had elders (*rb*) who were, to a certain extent, responsible for the execution of the work, as well as for the quantity of raw material which the artisans received. Unfortunately, we do not know whether these "elders" were elected by the members of the group concerned or if they were royal officials. Possibly, they were nominated by the authorities from people of the respective professions, and possibly, at least among the metal workers, there were people who lived and worked in certain villages under the supervision of sub-elders who were responsible for the work.[65]

[65] Concerning the *rb*, "elder" in Ugarit, cf. Ch. IV, *rb nqdm* and *rb khnm* (Ch. IV and VII) as well as the mention of the *rb* (elder) in other texts from Ugarit — *rb ʿšrt* "elder or overseer of ten" = *ʿšrm* (KTU.4.714); (KTU.6.2, *l.rb*; 6.3 *l.rb.kṯkym*; 6.6-6.10. *rb.khnm*; 6.63 *rp śśwt* "the elder" (*rp* instead of *rb* of the "mares"); KTU.4.233 — *rb* is mentioned at the end of line 1. It is certainly a *rb* of a certain professional group, but we do not know which, and *rb* in a number of other texts. The term *rb*, except in Ugaritic, appears frequently in Phoenician and Punic texts and always as an elder, official or high functionary of some profession, or branch of administration or religious or temple life. They were also magistrates, but only the most recent times showed the functions of the *rb* in Punic texts being investigated (*Huss*, a, pp. 217-232); cf. also the Phoenician inscriptions where *rb* appears; Kition, B45, 4-5 *rb ḥzʾnm* "elder of the overseers"; B9.3 *rb ḥrš* "elder of the artisans"; *rb sprm* "elder of the scribes"; CIA, 14 and A.30, 2-3, B.45, 1, 2, 3 *rb srsrm* "elder of the traders"; *Magnanini*, a, (Umm el-Awamid) p. 20, No. 9, 1-2 *rb šʿrm* "elder of the gate-keepers"; p. 21, 11, 1 *rb*; Tyre, p. 26, No. 4, 1 *rb mat* "elder of hundred (men)"; Lapethos, p. 124. No. 2, 2, 6 *rb ʾrṣ* "elder of the land"; Pireus, p. 137, No. 2, *2 rb khnm*, (all texts, except those which appear for the first time in Kition are given according to CIS and RÉS also); cf. also DISO, *rb*, p. 270.

3. We also know that the artisans had no raw material of their own. They received it from the royal stores[66] and they had to deliver their products to the royal stores.
4. Craftsmen were considered as people performing the *pilku* of their profession. They usually worked in their profession. They usually worked in their specialty but the royal authorities sent them to work sometimes as an *ilku* at the *gt*. At various periods and in times of need, they had to provide the authorities with a certain number of men for other types of work, such as that of an archer. Artisans were taken into the royal service, bound to perform their *pilku*, which was connected with their land-allotment (cf. Ch. III, pp. 23-37).
5. The son could inherit his father's profession when the father remained on royal service. The "heir" (*nḥl*) might even receive an *ubdy*-field independently of his father's.
6. Thus, craftsmen might receive such tenures for their work, just like other "king's men". At certain intervals, perhaps monthly, or when they were working in the royal economy, they also received various supplies. Thus, craftsmanship was an integral part of the royal economy in Ugarit.
7. In certain cases, the artisans had to participate in the tribute (*argmn*) paid to the Hittite king. But it is not clear whether this was a special tribute paid by the professional groups, or if it was a tax imposed by the king of Ugarit on his subjects in order to pay the tribute due to the Hittites. It is also interesting to note that the royal artisans dwelt in various villages of the kingdom.

So we see that in Ugarit there was an organized system of supply of artifacts and a system of craftsmen, "royal dependents" (*bnš mlk*), who were not, at the same time, at the lowest state in the society, that of slaves. We do not recognize in Ugarit the working system of workshops where the

[66] Maybe the *yṣrm*, "potters", were excluded here, for we do not know of any place in the Ancient Near East which had a monopoly on clay; cf. also the view that in Pharaonic Egypt, especially at the time of the New Kingdom, artisans were mostly in royal service or were dependent on temples and other institutions of the establishment, while private artisans were almost completely missing. Also in Egypt, the artisans did not possess their own raw material. Cf. *Drenkhahn*, a, p. 133-161. It must also be said that completely private artisans working for trade appear in Mesopotamia in large numbers only in Neo-Babylonian times, and were possibly in Phoenicia and Carthage. Cf. also *Heltzer*, B, (in print).

working personnel was permanently concentrated. Sometimes, however, the workshops were concentrated at the temple-complex, as in the case of the cartwrights (*ḥrš mrkbt*).

Do we have another example of such organization of craftsmen in another society in the ancient orient? Despite the large amount of tablets from Nuzi, we see that the organization of craftsmen was on a much more primitive level there.[67] We also have much less knowledge about the system in Alalaḫ, for data is scarse, and the system seemed less developed.[68] When we take the Old-Babylonian period, we see, on the one hand, Mari,[69] and on the other hand the system of the Old-Babylonian state. We may say that there existed a system of royal dependency — where the *muškēnū(m)*-people were engaged, but this system was more dispersed,[70] at the time that in the Ugaritic Kingdom, taking into account its limitations in territory, it was more concentrated and centralized. In the Old-Babylonian state the state economy had to take into account also "private" interests.[71]

It seems that at the time of the Ur III dynasty the centralization of the royal economy and the degree of dependency of people on the authorities reached its highest degree. The workshops were concentrated and in the "ergasteria" worked often large number of slaves or people dependent in a very high degree.[72]

But concerning smaller political or territorial units, more or less contemporary with Ugarit, we see similar features on a large scale only in Mycenaean Greece, where a state-monopoly existed in the sphere of agricultural and craft-production.[73] And so we see that such a system is traced in the best manner in Ugarit and Mycenaean Greece. Possibly, the reason for this was the large-scale development of trade and the central maritime position of

---

[67] *Mayer*, a.

[68] *Gaal*, a; and *Klengel*, a, pp. 435-457.

[69] ARMT, XVIII, pp. 101-258.

[70] *Diakonoff*, b, pp. 37-62; *Renger*, a, pp. 249-256.

[71] *Komoroczy*, a, pp. 411-422; *Yoffee*, a (the whole monograph is devoted to this question).

[72] *Limet*, a; *Waetzold*, a; *Tjumenev*, a, pp. 341-359; recently also *Loding*, a, p. 33, where he points out that the crafts in Ur were a temple (resp. state) controlled segment of the economy. At the same time, we see (pp. 196-291) that the whole system was even more complicated and sophisticated than in Ugarit.

[73] *Chadwick*, a, pp. 135-158.

both countries, together with the international trade. But, at the same time, it is characteristic that in the I millennium, with the same geographical and economic conditions, when the process of development had gone further, free private artisanship in classical Greece and various forms of artisanship similar to the Greek was found in Phoenicia, Carthage[75] and, in Neo-Babylonian Mesopotamia.[76] We must therefore conclude that the specific developments in Ugarit and the development of its trade were dependent on the general development of the second half of the II millennium B.C.E., and the specific geographical and politico-economic position of this state in the framework of the Eastern Mediterranean.

[74] *Heltzer*, B, (in print); *Mendelsohn*, a, pp. 68ff.; *Mendelsohn*, b, pp. 17-21.
[75] *Weisberg*, a, and *Dandamayev, a, pp. 129-139.*

CHAPTER VI

THE MILITARY ORGANIZATION AND THE ARMY OF UGARIT

The problem of the general military organization of the kingdom of Ugarit in the XIV-XIIIth century B.C.E.[1] will be dealt with in this chapter. We do not pay special attention to the military organization of other societies, even those in close geographical proximity.[2] But, we will, for purposes of comparison use typologically similar societies insofar as they can help us to understand the same problems. These are: Middle-Assyria,[3] Nuzi-Arrapḫa,[4] Asia Minor,[5] and, to some extent, Egypt.[6]

Concerning the present subject, we have a number of special studies written by the author,[7] but we need to make some corrections in them. We also have the useful works of *F. Rainey*,[8] *M. Liverani*[9] and *Loretz-Dietrich*,[10] *J. Nougayrol*,[11] and others. Alalaḫ, which was very close to Ugarit,[12] must be taken into consideration where the economic and administrative texts allowed scholars to reconstruct its military organization in the

---

[1] On the warfare in the literary texts from Ugarit, cf. *Gibson-Driver*, a, Keret, pp. 19-23; Text, pp. 82-102; with the main literature previously given; cf. also *Calders i Artis*, a, pp. 168-175; *Vinnikov*, a, pp. 321-327; *Heltzer*, k, pp. 352-353, etc.

[2] *Yadin*, a, 1963; *Landsberger*, b, pp. 121 ff.; *Sasson*, b, 1967; *Faulkner*, a, pp. 32-47; *van Seters*, a, 1966.

[3] *Freydank*, a, pp. 110-124; *Freydank*, b, pp. 55 ff.

[4] *Kendall*, a, 1975; *Jankowska*, a, pp. 233-282; *Cassin*, a, pp. 225-236; *Cassin*, b, pp. 445-455.

[5] *Goetze*, b, pp. 124-130; *Korošec*, a, pp. 159-166.

[6] *Schulman*, a, 1964; *Schulman*, b, pp. 75-98; *Schulman*, c, pp. 51-69; *Yeivin*, b, pp. 12-16; *Helck*, b, pp. 127-134.

[7] *Heltzer*, a, pp. 18-23; *Heltzer*, g, pp. 125-132; *Heltzer*, k, pp. 245-253; with the previous literature given.

[8] *Rainey*, d, pp. 71-107; *Rainey*, f, pp. 17-27.

[9] *Liverani*, c, pp. 191-198.

[10] *Dietrich-Loretz*, j, pp. 39-42.

[11] *Nougayrol*, a, pp. 110-123.

[12] *Dietrich-Loretz*, k, pp. 57-97.

XVth century B.C.E. The Canaanite city-states of the El-Amarna period must also be considered.[13] Naturally, our main source remains the relatively rich documentation from Ugarit. We cannot limit ourselves here only to the military service of the "royal dependents" of the military professions, but we must also take into account the *bnš mlk* of non-military professions as well as the problems of the guard-service and general mobilization. We must deal separately with the various groups of military servicemen within the framework of the *bnš mlk*.

§1. Guard service

From the tablet KTU.4.68 we learn that professional groups of *bnš mlk*, as well as villages, which were listed separately, had to supply small numbers of archers[14] to serve in some kind of guard unit. The text lists sixty villages, of which fifty-five are legible. The parallel texts to KTU.4.68 are PRU, III, 11.841 and PRU, VI, 131 (RS.19.35A), written in Akkadian.[15] We learn from these texts that various *âlu/qrit* had to send a number of men varying from one bowman on behalf of three villages[16] to ten bowmen on behalf of one village.[17] Most frequently, we find 1-3 bowmen conscripted from a single village. The varying number of conscriptions was perhaps related to the population of each village. According to PRU, VI, 141, we read in the remaining parts of the text that $^{(6)}$ ^{URU}*Mu-lu-uk-ku* — received (if under consideration are armed people to whom the weapons were dis-

---

[13] *Helck*, a, pp. 109-173, 199-255, 338-341; *Yeivin*, c, pp. 27-32; *Yeivin*, d, pp. 59-78; *Malamat*, a, 1978; *Malamat*, b, pp. 25-52.

[14] Edge of the text: *ṭu[p]-pu ṣābē*^{MEŠ} *ša* ^{GI}[^{š}*qaša*]*ti*^{MEŠ} "tablet of archers", cf. *Heltzer*, g, pp. 125-131.

[15] Although the beginning and the end of the tablet are broken, the correspondence of the names of the villages in both texts which deliver one bowman conjointly with another village shows that the text deals with the same kind of conscription. KTU.4.68, $^{(49)}$ *Agm w Ḫpty* — 1-PRU, III, 11.841, $^{(13-14)}$ ^{URU}*A-gi-mu, Ḫu-pa-ta-u*-1; KTU.468, $^{(58)}$ *Ṣʿ* and *Šḥq*-1; PRU, III, 11.841, 11) *Ṣa-a-u* and *Ša-ḫa-iq*-1. At the same time we cannot agree with *Bordreuil-Caquot*, c, p. 313 (cf. also *Caquot*, ACF, 78, p. 577), that the IH 77/27 is similar in type to KTU.4.68 or PRU, III, 11.841 (resp. PRU, VI, 131).

[16] KTU.4.68, $^{(13-15)}$ *Dmt Aǵt w Qmnz*-1; $^{(17-19)}$ *Yknʿm, Šlmy w Ull*-1 PRU, III, 11.841, $^{(20-22)}$ ^{URU}*Uḫ-nap-pu,* ^{URU}*Šu-ra-šu,* ^{URU}*Ḫu-ri-ka*-1.

[17] PRU, III, 11.841, $^{(15)}$ ^{URU}*Ma-a-qa-bu*-10, $^{(22)}$ ^{URU}*Ra-aq-du*-10.

tributed). 1 ^{GIŠ}BAN (*qaštu*) 2 ^{KUŠ}*iš-[pa-tu]* 3 ^{KUŠ}*išp[ātu]* "1 bow and 2 (and) 3 quivers" $^{(7)}$ ^{URU}*Iz-pi* 1 ^{GIŠ}BAN 2 ^{KUŠ}*išpātu* "*Izpi* 1 bow (and) 2 quivers" $^{(10)}$ [^{URU}*A*]*-gi-mu* 1 bow, 1 quiver and x shields (*ga-ba-bu*); $^{(11)}$ *Ašar-Ba'ali-* 1 bow, 1 quiver +x?; $^{(\text{v. }1)}$ *Iluištam'i* 2 bows, 4 quivers $^{(2)}$ ^{URU}[ ] 1 bow 1 quiver. It seems that we have here the same number, for in fact we are dealing in every case with the armament of one or two warriors.

But texts KTU.4.68 and PRU, VI, 131 go further. According to the lines 60-62 *n'rm*, *md̠rġlm* and *kzym* give one bowman for these three groups; ll. 63-64 *mru skn*, and *mru Ibrn* — one bowman in two groups; ll. 65-67 the sculptors (*pslm*), singers (*šrm*) and heralds (*yṣḥm*) — 1 archer for these three groups; l. 68 the *'šrm-aširu* — 1 archer; the *mr'um* — 1 archer (l. 69); ll. 70-71 the *t̠nnm* — warriors and *nqdm* (shepherds) — one archer for both groups; ll. 72-73 the priests (*khnm*) and diviners (*qdšm*) — 1 archer for both groups and ll. 74-75 the silversmiths (*nsk ksp*) and *tamkars* (merchants, traders — *mkrm*) — 1 archer for both groups.

The same small numbers are seen in PRU, VI, 131:

1	^{LÚMEŠ}*bān bîti* (housebuilders, *ḥrš bhtm*) —	1 bow +x
2	^{LÚMEŠ}*kutimmu* (silversmiths)	1 bow +x
3	^{LÚMEŠ}*a-ši-ru-ma*	1 bow + 2[x]
4	^{LÚMEŠ}UN-*tu*	1 quiver + [x]
5	^{LÚMEŠ}*mur-u-ma*	1 bow, 2 quivers
8	^{LÚMEŠ}*aš[kāpu]* (leather-workers)	1 bow, 1 quiver
9	^{LÚMEŠ}*nāqidu* (shepherds)	1 bow, 1 quiver and 1 shield

Here we have a case where it is impossible to speak about a mass, or general, mobilization, but only the gathering of small groups of archers-guards provided by the village-communities as well as by all groups of royal dependents.

§2. Partial and General Mobilization

It is clear that in gathering a larger military contingent the royal authorities of Ugarit made a partial or general mobilization, calling in the various groups of "royal dependents" of military and non-military professions, as well as the villagers of the country. The term used in Ugarit for this purpose is *ḫrd* — corresponding to the Middle-Assyrian *ḫurādu,* and it seems to be of Hurrian origin.[19] This term appears in a number of texts from Ugarit.[20]

If we take the tablet KTU.4.179, we see the following:

1	*ṯnnm ṯṯ*			"*šanānu*-warriors — 6
2	*ʿšr ḫsnm*			10 dependents [21]
3	*nʿr mrynm*	4	*ḫmš*	servants (?) of the *maryannu* — 5
5	*ṯrtnm.ḫmš*			*šerdana*-people — 5 (cf. below)
6	*mrum.ʿšr*			*murʾu*-men — 10
7	*šbʿ.ḫsnm*			7 dependents
8	*mkrm*			*tamkars* (= traders) [22]
9	*mrynm*	10	*ṯlṯ.ʿšr*	*maryannu* — 13
11	*hbṭnm*	*12*	*ṯmn*	the *hbṭnm* (pl.) — 8 [23]
13	*mḏrġlm*	14	*ṯmnym ṯmn kbd*	the *mḏrġlm* (pl.) guards — 88 at all
15	*arbʿm.l.mit*	16	*ṯn kbd*	142 at all."

But we have, of the same type, at least four additional texts (KTU.4.137; 4.163; 4.173; 4.179), as was noted by *Liverani,* and also KTU.4.174. The concluding formula of these texts is very similar, despite the lack of the word *ḫrd* there. Thus, in KTU.4.137 (12) *ṯṯm[l].mit.ṯlṯ* (13) *kbd.[tg]mr bnš* (14) *l.b.bt.mlk* "163 at all in the house (palace) of the king" KTU.4.163 (14) *ḫmšm.l.mit* (15) *bnš l.d.yškb.l.b.bt.mlk* "150 men, which were placed to the royal palace (house)"; KTU.4.174 (13) *ḫmšm.l.mit* (14) *arbʿ.kbd* "154 at all" (without any further explanations).

---

[19] *Heltzer,* k, pp. 243-251 and *Freydank,* a, pp. 111-115; the main previous works; *Dietrich-Loretz,* j, pp. 39-42; *Diakonoff,* d, pp. 36, 66, etc.; *Liverani,* c, pp. 191-192; *Dietrich-Loretz-Sanmartin,* l, pp. 432-533; *Dijkstra,* b, p. 565; *Postgate,* a, pp. 496-502.

[20] KTU.4.179; 4.683; 4.230; 4.656; 2.16; 2.61; 2.47; 1.103; the full analysis of the term, *Heltzer,* k, pp. 243-251.

[21] *Liverani,* c, p. 195, "familiari" "(dependent) family-members", *Liverani* reaches the conclusion by comparison with Hittite texts.

[22] The lack of the figure seems to be a scribal error.

[23] Term obscure; *Liverani,* c, p. 195, note 5; *Dijkstra,* b, "to knock down", gives also only a non-definitive explanation.

From the concluding formulae of these texts we see that these people were called for palace service, or as palace guards. It is also important that there participated military persons as well as non-military professionals. We must compare the figures in all five texts.

Professional group	KTU. 4.137	4.163	4.173	4.179	4.174
ṯnnm "*šanānu* warriors"	5	9	7	6	5
ḫsnm "dependents" (?)	10	4	7	10	′10
mrynm *maryannu*-warriors	13	19	18	13	14+19=33
ṯrtnm "*šerdana*-warriors"	5	4	5	5	5
bn mrynm (cf. below)	3	3	5	5	—
mkrm "tamkars"	10	10	10	?	10
hbṭnm	9	9	10	8	19
mrum	10	10	10	10	10
(their) *ḫsnm*	7	7	7	7	—
mḏrġlm	96	83	90	88	90
(their) *ḫsnm*	21	17	24	—	—

We see here people of military professions as the *šanānu*-warriors (with their dependents (?)), *maryannu*-warriors (with their dependents) *šerdana*-warriors (cf. below) and the *mḏrġlm*-guards together with the representatives of the *muru(ma)* tamkars, etc. Therefore we can strengthen our impression that it was a mobilization for regular palace-guard service, as was pointed out by *Liverani* (c). At the same time, it seems to be a regular service, and since the texts are chronologically close to each other, that it was a monthly service. Thus, in order to get a more or less truthful idea of the number of people of respective professions mentioned in these texts, we must divide the total by 5 (the respective number of times mentioned) and to multiple the result by 12.

Accordingly, we get the following figures:

šanānu-warriors	32/ × 12 ≈ 80 persons,
(their *ḫsnm*)	41/5 × 12 ≈ 98
maryannu-warriors	96/5 × 12 = 230
their dependents	16/4 × 12 = 48
šerdana-warriors	24/5 × 12 ≈ 58
tamkars	43/4 × 12 ≈ 28
hbṭnm	55/5 × 12 = 132

mur'u-men	50/5 × 12 = 120
(their) *ḫsnm*	28/4 × 12 = 84
mdrġlm-guards	437/5 × 12 ≈ 1050
their *ḫsnm*	62/5 × 12 ≈ 149

In addition to the approximate figure of these servicemen we receive also the approximate figure of the number possible to mobilize at the time of general mobilization.

Next, we must deal with the tablet KTU.4.230. It is a list of wine-deliveries. According to lines 1-10, the *mrynm* receive "four (jars) of wine" (1) *[a]rbʿyn.l.mrynm* and other single persons from one to two jars, as well as the *mdrġlm* (l. 6) 2 jars (*kdm*). If we make the total up from these deliveries we receive fifteen. After the dividing line we read:

11 *arbʿm yn* 12 *l.ḫrd*

---

13 *hmsm.ḫmš* 14 *kbd tgmr* 15 *yn.d.nkly*

"(11-12) 40 (jars) of wine to the *ḫurādu* (men)"

"(13-15) 55 (jars) at all (is) the total of wine of supplies.[24]"

We must emphasize here that the total consists of 15+40 = 55 jars of wine. 15 jars receive *maryannu*, *mdrġlm* and single persons listed by name; 40 jars the mobilized warriors from various professional groups or villages. We see that these people mobilized to the army — the *ḫrd (ḫurādu)* — received wine at the time of performing their service of their profession. We must note that the *ḫrd* mentioned here are not divided according to their origin of villages and professional groups, as we have seen from KTU.4.179; 4.683, and other texts. They are taken here as one single body. It seems to be an additional proof that we must be dealing with mobilized people.[25]

This analysis of the official Ugaritic administrative documents gives us the opportunity to give a new look on the official or semi-official letters of the archives of Ugarit.[26] We have another text with no mention of the word *ḫrd*, which deals with arms deliveries to a professional group. It is

---

[24] *Milano*, a, pp. 83-97.

[25] Cf. also the fragment KTU.4.656, (1') [ ]*spr*[ ]. (2') [ ]*ḫrd*[ ], which gives no real sense, except the impression that also here we must deal with an official document.

[26] *Heltzer*, k, pp. 251-253.

KTU.4.624 (1) *nqdm.dt.kn.npṣhm* "The shepherds, whose equipment is well (in order)".[27] The text contained originally at least from 23 lines, but is only partly legible. (2) *[b]n.Lbn.arbʿ.qšt.w.arb[ʿ]* (3) *uṯpt. qlʿ.w, ṯṯ mr[ḥ]m* "*Bn Lbn.* 4 arches and 4 quivers, (1) sling and 6 spears."[28]
The next (ll. 4-5) receives 1 bow, 1 quiver, 1 sling and 6 spears.
Bn Šlmn (l. 6) receives 1 bow, 1 quiver, 1 sling and 3 spears.
Bn Mlṣ (ll. 7-8) receives 1 bow, 1 quiver, 1 sling and 4 spears.
Bn Ḫdmn (ll. 9-10) receives 1 bow, 1 quiver, 1 sling and 4 spears.
Additionally to these good legible lines, it seems that up to line 23 we have at least 10 other persons who received war equipment. So we have here at least 15 *nqdm* who were mobilized.

Concerning the texts about the *ḫrd* — mobilized people of various professions mentioned above, we see certain numbers of them. It seems not to be a general mobilization and the very similarity to other texts seem to show that these were possibly monthly data,[29] i.e. that the texts, concerning the *ḫrd*, reported about service or deliveries to the *ḫrd*-men for monthly periods.

By all means this important information gives us the possibility of reconsidering the mobilization of the people of the village communities, based on the existing tablets.[30]

The most important here is KTU.4.683,[31] (1) *spr.ḫrd.arr* "List of *ḫurādu*-men *arr*".[32] The text is badly damaged, but its standard formula helps us to

---

[27] Cf. Ch. IV, pp. 68-69; *kn*-hebr. *kēn* "in order", *npṣ* "equipment" cf. Excursus I, pp. 188-191.

[28] *mrḥ*, "spear", *WUS*, p. 195, No. 1670.

[29] Cf. former approach to this question *Heltzer*, a, pp. 18-23.

[31] The whole text is given in our reconstruction, *Heltzer*, k, pp. 249-250.

[32] *arr* — meaning obscure, cf. *Heltzer*, a, p. 9, where this word is given as the name of a village in the kingdom of Ugarit; also UT, p. 367, nr. 378 — place names, but ZUL, VII, p. 84, "name of a mountain", which explanation is based on the mythological text CTA, 10, III, 28-32; according to KTU.6.27, (1) *mṣmtʿbs* (2) *arr* (3) *ht* "The seal of *ʿbs arr* of the mountains (?)" (cf. another interpretation in Heltzer, a, p. 78); KTU.4.384 (1) *[ś]św.sgryn.arr* "[H]orse (or 'horses' pl. st. cstr.) *sgryn* (may be(?) pers. name UT, p. 449, N. 1738) *arr* (remains obscure)". It is interesting that further this text contains a list of *ṣmdm* "horse or ass pairs" in various villages of the kingdom; KTU.4.355 — the whole text relates to *bnšm* "persons" — in fact *bnš (mlk)* in at least 42 villages, but (32) *ṯ[xx]bnšm b.Mʿr arr* "3(?) (*ṯ[lṯ]*) men in the village *Mʿr arr*". So we see that *arr* is not a toponym, as not a "mountain". Maybe it is a designation written after the mention of a certain category of persons (?).

reconstruct it in part, and we learn that the *ḫrd*-men came from 30 villages. The exact numbers of men from one village are 40 from *Ap* (l. 2), 50 from *Pd* (*Padi*, l. 3) and 13 from *Gll.Tky* (l. 31). We have here much larger numbers than in KTU.4.68 and its kindred samples, speaking only about the archers-guard.

We have at this time the tablets KTU.4.63; PRU.VI.95 (RS.19.174).[33] We would add here the recently published photograph of RS.34.131,[34] where the introductory line designates ERIN.MEŠ = *ṣābē*^{MEŠ} "soldiers" and various numbers of soldiers from various villages are mentioned. As compared with the figures of *Ap* and *Pd* (40 and 50) we see in RS.34.131 ^{URU}*Ap-pu* 6 (soldiers) and *Pa-di* 25 respectively. According to this text more than 44 villages sent the men beginning from 1 (*Ya-ku-na'amu*, l. 49) and 2 men (44) *Šal-ri-bi* — 2; (41) *Mu-a-ri* — 2; (20) *A-gi-me* — 2; (17) *Ma-ra-il* — 2; (8) *Ḫu-ri-ka* — 2 up to more than 40 men from one village (20); *Ari* — 54; (49) *Šal-ma* — 40 (10) *Be-qa-ni* — 70). We also know that at least 30 villages were named originally in KTU.4.683; 10+x in PRU.VI.95 and in KTU.4.63 the villages *Ubr'y* — 61,[35] *M'r* — 6; *Arny* — 10; *M'rby* 21; *Ulm* — 21; *Bq't* — 7; *Ḫlb rpš* — 3; *Rkby* — 3; *Š'rt* — 8.[36] So it is possible to suppose that a thorough study of the mobilisation-lists gives us very important data for the demography of ancient Ugarit. Naturally, it is possible that not all texts were composed in the same year and there could be differences in the numbers of mobilised warriors from various villages, but there is no doubt that such mobilisations took place in the kingdom of Ugarit in wartime or in other situations. We are also not sure that in all the cases known to us all the men from the villages listed are designated. But we can be sure that we do receive a generally adequate picture of the mobilisation.[37]

---

[33] *Heltzer*, a, pp. 18-23.

[34] *Schaeffer*, b, Pl. XIII, "Liste de noms de lieux suivis de nombre de personnes" as defined by the editors. Preliminary reading of the author and Mr. *M. Parnas*.

[35] Col. III, 1-46; IV, 1-17, among them in Col. III, 32-46 and IV, 1-17; including 31 *ġmrm*; this word has various controversial interpretations. Now it is clear that it means "a special class of bowman." = ^{LÚ}*ḫa-am-ra-nu* according to *Boyd*, a, p. 85; and PRU, VI, 70 (RS.19.42), 9, 11, 13.

[36] *ġmrm* also in *M'rby* and *Ulm*.

[37] Cf. also KTU.4.611. (1) *Miḫdym* "people of (the village) *Miḫd*" apparently deals with the same subject. Only fifty names are legible, but the text originally listed no less than ninety people. The word *ḫlq* "perished" or "defected" appears after the

We also know that the coastal villages had to perform their service in the military navy of Ugarit, as we learn from KTU.4.40.[38] People from five villages are named as ship's crew. 58+x men are mentioned.

But the backbone of the military organization of Ugarit consisted of "royal dependents" (*bnš mlk*) of military professions. After the investigation made above, we can approach the question of these professional groups.

§3. The Military Professionals — "Royal Dependents"

We saw in Chapter I the whole system of *bnš mlk* — "royal dependents", as well as detailed data about them in Chapters IV and V. We also saw the *pilku/ubdy* system in Chapter III. Therefore we shall not return to the scrupulous analysis of all details of the data about the military professionals, which was partly covered in some of our previous studies.[39] We will treat some problems which are more commonly accepted somewhat briefly.

1. The *maryannu* (Ug. *mrynm*) — warriors.[40]

We find the *maryannu* mentioned in Ugarit in many texts.[41] They are listed as a whole group or by personal name, or according to their fathers'

---

names of the persons in I, 2, 4, 8, 9, 14 and II, 18. This may indicate that we have here a conscription list or a text concerning a contingent designated for conscription.

[38] *Heltzer*, a, pp. 21-23, where the text is analyzed; cf. also *Gaster*, a, pp. 105-121; *Sasson*, a, p. 131 and the text PRU, VI, 138 (RS.19.46) where [(20)] *napḫar 10+x ṣâbē*^{MEŠ} ^{GIŠ}*eleppē* "total: 10+x soldiers of the ship" (People from at least four villages are mentioned.), *Rainey*, b, p. 48.

[39] *Heltzer*, g.

[40] The etymology of the word, as shown by *Kammenhuber*, a, pp. 211-232 was of Hurrian origin; also *Diakonoff*, e, pp. 114-115 and cf. *Kammenhuber*, b, pp. 129-143; *Ivanov*, a, pp. 101-112 (with the previous literature). The former indo-arian etymology has now no linguistic or historical basis.

[41] KTU.4.69, I, II and IV, 1-5; lines 6-10 — *bdl mrynm* "the subjects of the *maryannu*); KTU.4.103, 7-10; KTU.4.126; 1; KTU.4.137, ll. 2 and 4 *bn.mrynm* "sons of *mrynm*"; KTU.4.140, 9-12; KTU.4.152, 3, 5; KTU.4.163, 5-7 and 8 — *bn mrynm*; KTU.4.173, 2 and 5 (*bn mrynm*); KTU.4.174, 5, 8; KTU.4.170, 3 — *n'r mrynm* and 9-10; KTU.4.216, 8, 12; KTU.4.230, 1; KTU.4.244, 16; KTU.4.322; KTU.4.377; KTU.4.416, 1; KTU.4.485, 1? and Rd. 2(?) KTU.4.528; KTU.4.561; KTU.4.623; PRU, III, 16.239; 15.155; 16.132; 12.34+12.43; 16.257, IV, 33-36(?); PRU, IV, 16.270, 27(?); 17.394; PRU, VI, 31 (RS.19.98); 93, 1 (RS.17.131); 90, 2 (RS.19.114); 136 (RS.17.240); U.V.68 (RS.20.246), 7.

names, or both. At least in one text (KTU.4.69) we find 48+x *mrynm* and in PRU.III.12.34 at least 51. The other groups are smaller. According to the calculation made in §2, there were about 230 persons among the *maryannu* in Ugarit. Some of the texts, as seen above, show us that their heirs (*nḥlhm*) could inherit the profession during the lifetime of the fathers.

There is no clear indication that the *maryannu* had to work elsewhere besides their professional service. According to PRU.III.16.234 the king, Arḫalba, frees *Abdu*, son of *Abdirergal* (ll. 14-19) from all obligations, except to be a *maryannu* and *mūdū* of the king. We also read in PRU III.16.137 that Ammistamru II (4) *ú-za-ak-ki* ^{I}*A-dal-še-ni ù mârē*^{MEŠ}*-šu* (5) *ù il-ták-na-aš-šu* (6) *i-na*^{LÚMEŠ}*mar-ya-an-ni* "Purified (freed from the former obligation) *Adalšenu* and his sons and put (nominated) them to be *maryannu*". Later, (16) ^{I}*A-dal-še-ni* [*la i-lak*] (17) [*a-n*]*a* [LÚ]^{MEŠ} *re-ṣi ù* [ ] "*Adalšeni* [has not to perform (to go)] to the help-service".(20) ^{amelM}*ub-ru*[*i-n*]*a bîti-šu u-ul e-ru-ub-ma* (21) *alpa-šu imêra-su immerat-šu šê*^{MEŠ} *šikāru*^{MEŠ} (22) *šam*[*nu*]^{MEŠ} ...*u gáb-bu mim-mu-šu* (24) *a-na ekallim ú-ul e-ru-ub-ma* "The *ubru*[42] shall not enter his house. His oxen, donkeys, sheep, grain, beer, oil... and everything he has not to bring to the palace." So we see here a freeing from various obligations and taxes and only the *maryannu*-service remains to be performed. As we have already seen in PRU.VI.31 (Ch. III, p. 24) *Quumilku* has to perform the *pilku* of his *maryannu*-ship.

According to texts KTU.4.69; 4.215; 4.230; PRU.III.16.257; PRU.VI. 135, the *maryannu* received pay or various distributions in silver, wine, oil and other products.

They were located in the territorial confines of various villages in the kingdom. According to the text KTU.4.244.16, ...*mryn Ary* "the *maryannu* of the village *Ary*"; according to PRU.III.12.34 the *maryannu* are in (1) ^{URU}*Be-ka-ni* — at least 21 people; (10) ^{URU}*A-ri* — 11 persons (26) ^{URU}*Ma-a-ra-pa* — 6 persons (39) ^{URU}*Mu-lu-uk-ku* — 2 persons (35) ^{URU}*A-tal-lig* — 3 persons (39) ^{URU}*Šu-ba-ni* — 1 person (41) ^{URU}*Riq-di* — 3 persons — in all 7 villages.

As we have also seen from Chapter I and III, the *maryannu* appear in various lists together with the other groups of the *bnš mlk*.

---

[42] *ubru* — AHW, p. 1399b, *ubārum-wabrum/ubru* "Ortsfremder, Schutzbürger", cf. also *Jankovska*, c, p. 44-46 the foreign merchants who were temporalily in Ugarit could enjoy the possibility of being temporarily placed at the houses of the Ugaritians, were the *ubāru-ubru*; cf. also *Cazelles*, a, p. 206 and *Astour*, e, pp. 70-76.

Besides the text PRU.VI.31, where the maryannu *Quumilku*, as well as other *maryannu* receive land-allotments for the performance of their *maryannu*ship-*pilku*, we have also general administrative lists where the allotments to the *maryannu* appear together with the other professionals (Ch. III — *ubdy*).

Another question is the connection of the *maryannu* with horses, harnesses and chariots. The texts give us the following data: KTU.4.377 (33) *ṯmn.l.ʿšrm* (34) *dmd*[43] *(=ṣmd).bd.mrynm* "28 harnesses[44] to the *maryannu* (pl.)." At the same time it is impossible to state whether the above persons were *maryannu* or not. Lines 1-22 list by name 22 persons, and next to the names of some of them (ll. 1, 5, 6, 17, 19) is written *ṣmd* team and in two cases *ṣmd w ḥrṣ* (Cf. Excursus II). The total follows (23) *ʿšrm.ṣ[md]* (24) *ṯṯ.kbd.b.h*[ ] (25) *w.arbʿ.ḥ[mrm]* "26 teams at all in *H*[ ] (place-name) and 4 donkeys." (26) *b.M*[ʿ]*rby* (27) *ṯmn ṣmdm* "in (the village) *Mʿrby* — 8 teams (of oxen, or horses)"; (28) *bd.Bʿlskn* (29) *bn*[45] *tdn.ʿšr* (30) *ḥmrm* "At the disposal of *Bʿlskn*, son of *Tdn* — 10 donkeys" (31) *ddm l.Ybr*[*k*] (32) *bd mr.Prs.l x m xx* "2 *dd*-measures to *Ybr*[*k*]... *parisu* (= $^1/_2$ kur) to...". Cf. also about the military chariots and their equipment and horses and their deliveries to the *maryannu* in Excursus II.

We must also consider KTU.4.169. (1) *arbʿm.qšt* (2) *alp.ḥẓm.w.alp* (3) *nṯq.ṯn.qlʿm* (4) *ḫmš.ṣmdm.w.ḥrṣ* (5) *ṯryn śświm* (6) *ṯryn.aḥd.d.bnš* (7) *arbʿ.ṣmdm.apnt* (8) *w.ḥrṣ* (9) *tšʿm.mrḥ.aḥd* (10) *kbd*. "40 arches, 1000 arrows and 2000 *nṯq*-arms,[46] 2 slings, 5 team harnesses (or "harnessed teams or yokes") and (1) cart-box;[47] (1) horse-armour;[48] and (1) human armour; 4 harnesses (or "yokes"), wheels and a cartbox; 91 spears at all." Despite these texts not mentioning the word *mryn(m)*, the horse-equipment and the chariot show

---

[43] In the text *dmd* and the correction of the editors of KTU; *ddm* — *dd*-measures", but we assume that  -*d* was written mechanically under the influence of the third radical *d* of the word, instead of *ṣ* ().

[44] St.cstr.plur.

[45] Scribal omission: *bd* instead of *bn* "son".

[46] Hebr. *nešeq* "arms" "ammunition", cf. WUS, p. 217, No. 1876; UT, p. 448, No. 1721, "a kind of weapon", perhaps "ballista, missile"; cf. also the same explanation *Margalit*, a, p. 65 — but the text lists concrete kinds of weapons, and the exact sense of the word is unclear. Cf. also *Del Olmo Lete*, c, p. 182.

[47] Cf. Excursus, II.

[48] Cf. *šir'ani ša sîsē*, *širiam*; hebr. *širyōn* "armour" *Salonen*, e, p. 146.

us clearly that the *maryannu* are under consideration. We see here the complete dependence of the *maryannu* on the royal stores and workshops. We have also seen that the *maryannu* were provided with all their spears, chariots and even horses from the royal stores (Excursus II).

As we saw in texts KTU.4.69.II.6-10, *bdl mrynm*; 4.137.4, *bn mrynm*; 4.163.8, *bn mrynm*; 4.173.4, *bn mrynm*; 4.179, *n'r mrynm*. We see first that because of the identical formulae of texts KTU.4.137; 4.163; 4.173 and 4.179, that there is not any doubt about the identity of the *bn/n'r — mrynm*. The same may be said about the *bdl* "at the disposal of..." the *maryannu*. So we see persons who were royal dependents and at the same time subjects of the *maryannu*.[49]

We have no concrete data about the elders of the *maryannu*, but according to the fact that they had their own subjects, we see that they were among those royal dependents who were in a privileged position. According to texts PRU, III, 16.157, 22; 16.239 and 16.250, 17 there existed the administrative serviceman *akil* ^{GIŠ}*narkabti* "overseer of the chariots." All these three texts tell us that the royal *mūdū* were freed from their power (jurisdiction).[50] From here we deduce that the *maryannu*, who were in a lower position than the *mūdū*, were subject to the *akil narkabti*. Possibly, this official appears in a small Ugaritic text (KTU.6.63) (1) *Gssn* (2) *rp* (3) *śśwt* "*Gssn*, the *rp* (instead of *rb* — elder) of the mares." So we have seen that the *pilku* of the *maryannu* was chariot-service in the royal army. They were in a relatively high position, but at the same time we see that they remained "royal dependents" and received lands, payments and all their arms and equipment, including chariots and horses, from the royal stables. Sometimes they were temporarily mobilized for certain palace services along with other royal dependents not necessarily of military professions. They also had the possibility of inheriting their profession during the lifetimes of their fathers. This shows us that, not only on etymological grounds, they did not belong to the indo-arian aristocracy, but were royal dependents of a relatively high rank. If we compare their position with societies in other neighboring states,

---

[49] Cf. Ch. I, pp. 3-15 the discussion on *bdl*-"subject", as well as *n'r* "subject, youth", but by no means "young aristocrat" as *Macdonald-Cutler*, b, pp. 27-35.

[50] *Heltzer*, h, pp. 338-341; we also know that *Abdu*, son of *Abdinergal* was also a *mūdū* and *maryannu* and therefore we assume that he was freed from the *akil narkabti* in his position as *mūdū*.

we must explain that in Alalaḫ we know that they received land-allottments, as well as chariots and equipment from the royal stores, and sometimes even had professions other than their *maryannu*ship.[51] But the data from Alalaḫ can only help to understand better this social group in Ugarit. Concerning Nuzi-Arrapḫa, as Kenwood points out,[52] there were *rakib narkabti* "chariot-rider" and *rakib-sîsî* "horsemen", and the *maryannu* were the charioteers of the king of Ḫanigalbat.[53] Possibly, we may accept the view of *Reviv* that the *maryannu* lost their essentially military character in the second half of the II millennium in Canaan, and became involved in administration, while the charioteers became part of the lower-ranking social groups.[54] This might be possible, and further analysis of the military groups may prove it, at least in part. But, at the same time, we see that the military *maryannu*-system was still alive in Ugarit, although maybe not in its original form. We know the Canaanite *maryannu* on a large scale also from Egyptian sources.[55] But we see one really important thing. The *maryannu* were an organic group of the whole region. In Ugarit we have the best data for defining their role and social status. The only case of *Abdu*, son of *Abdinergal*, who was the royal *mūdū* and *maryannu* at the same time, seems to strengthen the opinion of *Reviv*, but additional data is still lacking. The large number of horses in the royal stables (Excursus II) shows possibly that not only *maryannu*, whose numbers were not large, were engaged in chariotry.

2. The *mḏrġlm*-guards — LUMEŠUN-*tu*[56]

The *mḏrġlm* and UN-*tu* are frequently mentioned in the texts from Ugarit.[57] Their numbers are considerably larger than those of the *maryannu* and, as

---

[51] *Dietrich-Loretz*, k, pp. 57-97; *Salonen*, c, p. 210.

[52] *Kenwood*, a, pp. 128-141.

[53] *Kenwood*, a, pp. 64 and 75.

[54] *Reviv*, a, pp. 7-23; *Reviv*, c, pp. 218-228.

[55] *Helck*, a, pp. 522-526; *Epstein*, a, pp. 49-56; *Rainey*, c, p. 75. The depicting of the Canaanite chariotry on Egyptian monuments — *Curto*, a, pp. 18-27.

[56] On the etymology and meaning of the terms cf. below and also *Heltzer*, T (in print).

[57] KTU.3.7, 2-4; KTU.4.33; KTU.4.53; KTU.4.54; KTU.4.58, 61; KTU.4.69, VI, 6-16 and 17-20 *bdl mḏrġlm*; KTU.4.99, 17; KTU.4.102, 14; KTU.4.103, 54-56; KTU.4.137, 9; KTU.4.162, 9; KTU.4.174, 9-12; KTU.4.179, 13-14; KTU.4.183, II, 15-18; KTU.4.213, 28-29; KTU.4.216, 4, 11; KTU.4.230, 6; KTU.4.379;

we have seen above (§2) 96 *mḏrġlm* are mentioned in one text (KTU.4.137). At the same time we can suppose that their general numbers at one time could have reached even 1050 persons (§2). In the texts they appear either individually by their names or designations of their profession, or as a group.[58]

The *mḏrġlm* did not belong to the lowest rank of royal dependents. This is seen from the fact that the text KTU.4.69, II, 17-19 shows us that there were *bdl mḏrġlm* "subjects of the *mḏrġlm*". We also know that *mḏrġlm* received from 5-10 shekels of silver each and 3 *bdl mḏrġlm* "subjects of the *mḏrġlm*" received 2 shekels each, according to KTU.4.69, VI, 6-20, KTU.4.213 describes deliveries of wine from various *gt*'s[59] and among them (28) *mit.arbʿm.kbd.yn.mṣb* (29) *l.mḏrġlm* "140 (jars?) of lagered wine to the *mḏrġlm*."[60] Text KTU.4.387 speaks about distribution of grain

---

KTU.4.387, 9-10, 20, 24; KTU.4.635, 18; KTU.4.751; PRU, III, 16.249; 15.123; 16.257, IV, 7-16 and 17-20 LÚMEŠ*muš-ke-nu-tu* LÚMESUN-*tù* (= *bdl mḏrġlm*); PRU, VI, 93 (RS.17.131) 8; 131 (RS.19.35.A), 4.

[58] By comparison with the list of *mḏrġlm* KTU.4.33 and the groups of the personal names in the texts KTU.4.51 and 4.55 we get the following picture:

	KTU.4.33		*KTU.4.51*		*KTU.4.55*
3	*bn.Bʿyn Š[lmy]*	14	*bn Bʿyn Šl<m>y*	18	*bn Bʿyn*
5	*bn.Lṣn ʿrm[y]*	13	*bn.Lṣn ʿrmy*	—	
6	*Arśw.Bṣry*	11	*bn Arś[w.Bṣ]ry*	—	
9	*bn.Tgḏn.Ugrty*	—		29	*bn Tgḏn*
13	*bn.Glmn.Ary*	1	*bn.Glmn.Ary*	24	*bn.Glmn*
15	*bn.Śdy.Ary*	2	*[bn]Šdy*	23	*bn.Sdy*
22	*bn.Kdrn.Uškny*	—		26	*bn.Kdrn*
28	*bn.Ypy.Gbʿly*	5	*bn Ypy Gbʿly*	—	
29	*bn.Ġrgs Ilštmʿy*	9	*bn.Grgs*	—	
30	*bn.Ḫran Ilštmʿy*	10	bn.Ḫ*ran*	8	*bn Ḫran*
33	*bn.Gʿyn*	—			[*b*]*n Gʿyn dd* (one *dd*)
35	*bn Agynt*	—		12	*Agyt* (scribal error)
41	*ʿmn.bn.ʿbdilm*	—		16	*bn.ʿbdilm Hzpy*

We see that in 4.51 half of the preserved names are the same as in 4.33 and 9 names in 4.55. So we have clear evidence that KTU.4.51 and 4.55 relate to *mḏrġlm* also (cf. *Heltzer*, T and 4.55 deals with product-deliveries.

[59] Cf. Ch. III, p. 40.

[60] Cf. also KTU.4.216 where wine is distributed (4) *ṯlṯ.l.mḏr[ġlm]* "3 to the *mḏr[ġlm]*" (11) *kd.l.mḏrġl[m]* "1 jar to the *mḏrġlm*" also KTU.4.230, 6 "2 jars to the *mḏrġlm*".

(4) *b*[*yrḫ*. . .]. . . (9) *t̲t̲m dd.dd*.[*kbd*] (10) *l.md̲rġlm* "In the [month[... 60-*dd*-measures[61] to the *md̲rġlm*..." (13) *b.yrḫ* [*It̲t̲*]*bnm* . . . (19) *t̲mnym dd.kbd* (20) *l.md̲rġlm* "In the month [*It̲t̲*]*bnm* . . . 80 *dd*-measures at all to the *md̲rġlm*."[62] From this we learn that the grain deliveries were monthly.

The text KTU.4.751 relates about a delivery of various products (meat, poultry, flour, wine, spices and sweet dried fruits) to the *md̲rġlm*, possibly on the occasion of completing a period of service-duties.[63]

Texts KTU.4.33; 4.51; 4.53; 4.55, show us that the *md̲rġlm* lived in the territorial confines of the following villages of the kingdom of Ugarit: *Agn*,[64] *Ar(y)*,[65] *Art*,[66] *Ilštmʿ*,[67] *Ubrʿ(y)*,[68] *Uškn*,[69] *Ugrt*,[70] *ʿrgz*,[71] *ʿrm*,[72] *Bṣr*,[73] *Gbʿl*,[74] *Hzp*,[75] *Ḫbt*,[76] *Midḫ*,[77] *Mʿqb*,[78] *Mʿrb*,[79] *Mld*,[80] *Ndb(y)*,[81] *Rqd*,[82]· *Šlm(y)*,[83] *Ṣnr*,[84] *Šʿrt*,[85] *T̲lhn*,[86] *Yny*,[87] *Yʿrt*.[88] So there were at least 24 villages in which they dwelled.

---

[61] Double mention of *dd* possible scribal omission.

[62] Lines 21 and 24 (half-broken) also deliveries to the *md̲rġlm*.

[63] *Heltzer*, R (in print).

[64] KTU.4.379.9.

[65] KTU.4.33, 12, 13, 14, 15; 5.51, 1; 4.53, 4, 10; 4.55, 14; 4.379, 2, 7.

[66] KTU.4.33, 10, 11.

[67] KTU.4.33, 29, 30, 31; 4.51, 8.

[68] KTU.4.33, 18, 19.

[69] KTU.4.33, 21, 22, 23, 24.

[70] The capital city itself KTU.4.33, 8, 9.

[71] KTU.4.55, 27.

[72] KTU.4.33, 5; 4.51, 13.

[73] KTU.4.33, 6; 4.51, 11.

[74] KTU.4.33, 27, 28; 4.51, 5.

[75] KTU.4.51, 16.

[76] KTU.4.33, 39; 4.53, 3.

[77] KTU.4.33, 4.

[78] KTU.4.33, 16.

[79] KTU.4.33, 26.

[80] KTU.4.379, 10.

[81] KTU.4.33, 38; 4.55, 21.

[82] KTU.4.33, 32.

[83] KTU.4.33, 37; 4.51, 14.

[84] KTU.4.33, 36; 4.55, 22.

[85] SIG-KTU.4.33, 25; 4.51, 7.

[86] KTU.4.33, 17.

[87] KTU.4.33, 30.

[88] KTU.4.33, 7; 4.55, 9; 4.379, 4.

But KTU.4.54 also mentions: (1) *mḏrġlm.d.bt.B'lt Mlk*, "*Mḏrġlm* which (are) at the sanctuary (lit. "house") of the *Ba'alat* of (village) *Mulukku*." Ten persons are mentioned by their names and even that they had at their disposal: (4) *ṯlṯ.klbm* "three dogs", possibly watch-dogs. It seems likely that the *mḏrġlm* had to go to the sanctuary to perform their service.

As seen above (Ch. III) the *mḏrġlm* received silver-deliveries, along with other groups of the *bnš mlk*.[89] They also had at their disposal the *ubdy*-fields (*šd ubdy*), i.e., fields which were allotted for performing the service-obligations to the crown (Ch. III, pp. 26-30).[90]

According to text KTU.4.53, (1) *mḏrġlm.d.inn* (2) *msgm.lhm* "*Mḏrġlm*, who have no weapons." In lines 3-13 appear 10 persons and they receive (14) *ṯmn qšt* (15) *w.'šr uṯpt* (16) *d*-(illegible) "8 arches and 10 quivers, which...." It seems that for these *mḏrġlm*, who had no weapons, a delivery of weapons was received from the royal stores.

We also find in KTU.4.379 (1) *mḏrġlm.dt.inn* (2) *bd Tlmyn* "*Mḏrġlm* who are not at the disposal of *Tlmyn*". Names of 9 persons follow, together with the designation of their villages of origin. It seems that these people had to come to *Tlmyn*, but for some reason did not.

In text KTU.4.102 (14) [ ]*mḏrġlm*, as we see in a broken line. The tablet shows us a number of wives and children at [ ]*URU A-la-ši-ya*[KI] "[ ] town *Alašiya*" i.e. on Cyprus. Perhaps a part of the Ugaritic *mḏrġlm* were stationed there.[91] There were at least 27 households. Some of them had a "wife", (*aṯt*), some of them a "splendid" or "mighty" wife, (*aṯt adrt* — ll. 4, 7) and in some cases even 2 such wives (ll. 9.18, 28 — *aṯtm adrtm*).

So we can point out that the *mḏrġlm* were a relatively large group of the royal dependents. They were more numerous than the *maryannu* and the other groups of military servicemen. We see this from the above-quoted five service lists. They also received silver, products and land-allotments for their services, had families and lived in various villages of the kingdom of Ugarit. They had common meals on some occasions.

---

[89] KTU.4.99; 4.69; 4.99, 17.

[90] KTU.4.103, 54-56, 4.183, II, 15-18.

[91] Concerning the controversial interpretations of this text cf. *Liverani*, a, pp. 92-94; *Heltzer*, j, pp. 86-88; *Alt*, a, pp. 111-113; *Sanmartin*, a, p. 371, note 3.

This data is important in aiding us in clarifying the etymology of the term *mḏrġlm* which we have not found in this or any similar spelling in the cuneiform areas or where semitic speach was used.[92] In 1947 *A. Goetze*[93] expressed the opinion that they were *maẓẓaru*, "watchguard" and its proper meaning should be "(soldier of the) guard" and "the suffix *-uḫlu* (Hurro-Akkadian) that marks *nomina professionis*." Later, *M. Dietrich* and *O. Loretz*[94] accepted the opinion of *Goetze* adding that *maṣṣāru* "guard (soldier)" in Akkadian turned to *mḏr* in Ugaritic under Hurrian influence. The suffix is purely Hurrian. The author of this paper, as well as *Liverani*,[95] accepted these conclusions. We must add that the modern dictionaries give us the following translations: a) *Von Soden*[96] — *maṣṣartu(m)* "guarding" "guard" (*nom. collect*) and *maṣṣāru(m)* "Wächter" "guard" b) *Laroche*[97] reconstructs on the basis of the alphabetic Ugaritic spelling *mḏrġl* the *maṣṣaruḫli*(? and c) the CAD gives the meaning of *maṣṣartu* 1. (p. 333) as "watch, guard (as individual man and as a detachment), garrison"; and *maṣṣaru* (M., I p. 341) 1, "guardian, watchman, watch, garrison." As we have seen there is a large number of alphabetic texts from Ugarit where our term appears. We have no Akkadian parallel to it, at least not normally spelled. So it seems strange that such an important and frequently used Ugaritic term, with a partly Akkadian etymology, is lacking in the Akkadian texts from Ugarit.

We know from the Akkadian texts from Ugarit that a professional group of people, partly like the *bnš mlk* "royal dependents" in the alphabetic texts, are written by the sign UN and the phonetic sign *tù* — UN-*tù*.[98] We also learn the following concerning them: According to PRU.III.16.249, during

---

[92] It is impossible to bring all points of view of all the authors in all the years beginning from 1930. We have to limit ourselves only to those who promoted understanding of the problem.

[93] *Goetze*, e, p. 72.

[94] *Dietrich-Loretz*, SSAU, I, WO, III, 1966, pp. 198.

[95] *Heltzer*, s, p. 248; *Liverani*, c, p. 191; *Rainey*, f, p. 23, accepting the presence of the Hurrian suffix — *uḫlu*, considers *mḏr* as a certain *mḏrn*-weapon, as well as *Aistleitner* in WUS, No. 1701-2.

[96] AHW, pp. 620b-621b.

[97] *Laroche*, a, p. 169.

[98] *Labat*, a, No. 143/312; *Borger*, b, p. 127, No. 312. The sign UN has also the reading *nišū* — "people." Therefore, *Dietrich-Loretz*, ZUL, I, BO, 29, p. 129 compare it with alphabetically written professional group — *inšt*. But such an explanation does not clarify a nothing.

the reign of King Niqmepa three persons, *Ṭabiyanu*, *Abdinergal* and *Munaḫimu*, "made a grave sin. The counterfeit of the seal of the great king they made and tablets in the name of the king (lit. "royal") they wrote in Ugarit."[99] The text goes on to say, "the UN-*tù* seized them".[100] Later they were punished by the king.[101] So we may agree with *Speiser*, *Nougayrol* and *Yankovska* that the UN-*tù* had to perform some police-functions.[102]

In PRU.III.15.123, *Anatenu* and *Yayanu* exchanged their fields and *Anatenu* had "to perform the *pilku*-service of the UN-*tù*." (Ch. III, p. 25). PRU.III.16.257, IV.7-16 is a list of deliveries of "jars of oil" (*karpat šamnu*) to UN-*tù*-people. Nine people received from 2-4 jars each.[103] We also see from this text (IV.17-20) that three subjects of the UN-*tù* ^{amelMEŠ}*muš-ke-nu-tum* ^{amelMEŠ}UN-*tù* received also certain quantities of oil.

Another appearance of the UN-*tù* is found in PRU.VI.93 (RS.17.131), 8, where, besides the ^{LÚ}UN-*tu*, the figure 3 is given and the first line designates that persons are under consideration. the UN-*tù* are preceeded here by the ^{LÚ}*nāqidu* "shepherds" and followed by ^{LÚ}*mur-u* ^{LÚ}*sa-ki-ni* "the *mur'u* of the *sākinu* (vizier)." The text PRU.VI.131 (RS.19.35A) is a text of delivery of weapons to various professional groups. In line 4 ^{amelMEŠ}UN-*tù* appear as recipients of 1 quiver (1 ^{mašak}*i*[*špātu*]). The preceding group are the ^{amelMEŠ}*a-ši-ru-ma* (*ʿšrm* "overseers of (teams of) ten") and the UN-*tù* are followed by the ^{amelMEŠ}*mur-'u-ma*, i.e., again the *mur'u*. What is the real reading and interpretation of UN-*tù*? We cannot accept the above interpretation of *Loretz* and *Dietrich*. *J. Nougayrol*[104] translates the word "controleur (?)" without entering into the specific problems of the spelling. *Von Soden* translates the word, which he reads phonetically *undu III* "workman"[105] underlining that the word appears only in the Akkadian texts from Ugarit. In 1965, *Rainey* compared the *awîlu* UKU-*tu*, as he then read the word UN-

---

99 (15) *ḫi-iṭ-ṭa rabita*^{MEŠ} *i-te-ep-š*[*u*] (16) ^{aban}*kunukku mé-ḫé-er* ^{aban}*kunuk šarri rabi* (17) *i-te-ep-šu ù ṭup-pa-ti* (18) *šar-ru-ti i-na libbi*^{bi} (19) ^{al}*Ú-ga-ri-it i-ša-aṭ-ṭu-ru*.

100 (21) ^{amel}UN-*tù ik-ta-ša-ad-šu-nu-ti*.

101 *Speiser*, a, p. 157.

102 PRU.III, p. 237; *Jankovska*, c, p. 45, note 60.

103 The parts of the lines with the figures are broken. We must point out that the group of personal names does not coincide with any other group of personal names of any of the other professionals from Ugarit.

104 PRU.VI, p. 152.

105 AHW, p. 1420b "ein Arbeiter (?)".

tù, "guardsmen," with *awîli*^{MEŠ}UKÙ: *ma-ṣa-ar-ta* in the El-Amarna texts EA 136, 18 and 114, 31.[106] In his more recent work [107] he returns to the same comparison of EA 136 — LÚ.MEŠ UN *ma-ṣa-ar-ta*, where the term LÚ.MEŠ UN is interpreted phonetically *maṣṣartu* "guards." He also gives a newly reconstructed reading to EA 114.31 — [*ka-li* LÚ MEŠ]UN-*tù* "all the garrison," comparing this with PRU.VI.93.8, where the word UN-*tù* is written in the same way. At the same time we must point out that *Rainey* makes no identification of the UN-*tù* with the *mḏrġlm*. The recently published volume M, I of CAD, speaking about "guards" — *maṣṣartu* — proves that in the Hittite archives, as well as in Middle-Assyrian texts, it was written EN.NU. UN.[108] This forces us to suppose that in the El-Amarna texts, as well as in the tablets from Ugarit, we have a local abridged variant of EN.NU.UN, from which only UN remains and which in El-Amarna 136, 18 was glossated *ma-ṣa-ar-ta*. It seems possible, therefore, to propose the identity of the Ugaritic *mḏrġlm* with its Hurrian elements in its spelling with the UN-*tù* in the Akkadian texts from Ugarit.

The texts at our disposal do not, at present, give us any prosopographic grounds for identification. At the same time, we must emphasize that the known activities of the UN-*tù*, as well as the deliveries of weapons and products to them and the distribution of fields does not, at least, contradict the data received concerning the *mḏrġlm*. As seen above, the list in which the group of the UN-tù appear was always composed in such a way that they were in close proximity to the *mur'u*-men, in KTU.4.68, where the (60-62) *n'rm*, *mḏrġlm* and *kzym* together give one archer and in lines 63-64 the *mru skn* and *mru Ibrn* do it together. In KTU.4.69, the list of *mḏrġlm* is preceded by the *mru Ibrn*, and the *mrum* precede the *mḏrġlm* in KTU.4.137 and 4.173. So the formal connection in the lists of the UN-*tù* and *mur'u*, as well as the *mḏrġlm* and *mru(m)*, is the most frequent. Perhaps this can serve as an additional argument in favor of the identification of the *mḏrġlm* and the UN-*tù* who had to perform military, guard and police-functions.

---

106 *Rainey*, p. 25; printing error — instead of 136 — 316.

107 *Rainey*, b, p. 44.

108 CAD M, I, p. 333b — with references to KUB, 4, 64, 6 and KAR, 382, r. 21, etc.; as we see from various other texts given there, *UN — as the last element of maṣṣartu* — appeared also in other texts; cf. also p. 341a.

3. The *ṯnnm-šanānu*-warriors [109]

The *ṯnnm-šanānu*-warriors are mentioned individually by their names or the names of their fathers; they also appear in groups. As we saw above (§2), their numbers in Ugarit at a single time could reach about 80 persons. We know that they participated in the guard-service. Some texts (KTU.4.35; 4.66; 4.126; 4.405 and 4.745) show us that they performed their professional service (cf. also PRU.VI.93). We also have some texts (cf. 4.275) which speak about deliveries made to them. PRU.III.11.839 — text concerning silver deliveries to various persons named individually. (5) *89 kaspa* ^{MEŠ}*i-na qâti* ^{I}*Ia-an-ḫa-mi* ^{LÚ}*ša-na-ni* (6) *40 kaspa*^{MEŠ} *i-na qâti* ^{I}*Iltaḫmi* ^{LÚ}*ša-na-ni* ... (26) *1 me-at 9 kaspu*^{MEŠ} *ina qâti* ^{I}*Am-mi-na* ^{LÚ}*ša-na-ni* (5)" 89 (shekels of) silver to *Yanḫamu* — the *šanānu*; (6) 49 (shekels of) silver to *Iltaḫmu* — the *šanānu* (20) 109 (shekels of) silver to *Am-mi-nu* the *šanānu*." We see that the sums of silver were relatively high, even higher than for the *mḏrġlm* and *maryannu*, but we have no idea of how often or regularly they were made or the purpose of this particular delivery.

Generally, the *ṯnnm* appear together with all the other groups of *bnš mlk* (Ch. I). Besides the *ṯnnm* text KTU.4.35.II, 20-21, mentions also *nḥlh* "his heir", and according to 4.66, we also see the *nḥlhm* "their heirs" of the second generation of them (*nḥlh* — ll. 9-10). KTU.4.416, 4 treats deliveries of fields (GAN.ME) to these people (Ch. III).

According to the texts KTU.4.163; 4.173; 4.174 and 4.179 after the *ṯnnm* the *ḫsnm* appear (§2). Possibly, they were the dependents of the *ṯnnm*.

---

[109] Meaning of the word is not definitively clear. Cf. WUS, No. 2900, "spear-man" — based on Akk. from Mari *si-in-na-tum* "spear"; *Rainey*, f, p. 22, compares it with Eg. *śnn*, "archer". *Goetze*, b, p. 125, *šanānu*, the third warrior of the chariot, AHW, p. 1161, b, "chariot-archer" — concerning Ugarit and Alalaḫ. (Cf. UT, p. 504, No. 2708, also with Eg. *śnn*); against the Egyptian etymology is the appearance of the *ṯnn*-warriors in the Epic of Keret I, 91; cf. *Del Olmo Lete*, a, p. 101, that *ṯnn* was, in any case, a superior category of warrior. But, with no reason, *Macdonald-Cutler*, c, pp. 26-27, states that *ṯnnm* and *nqdm* are "producers and suppliers of sheep products." On *šanānu* in Alalaḫ, *Giacumakis*, a, p. 102, AT 145, 43; 183, 2; 226, 6, 11, etc.; *Dietrich-Loretz*, e, p. 117. The *ṯnn-šanānu* appear in the following texts: KTU.4.35, II, 11-23; KTU.4.66, 1; KTU.4.68, 70; KTU.4.126, 4; KTU.4.137, 1; KTU.4.163, 1; KTU.4.170, 1; KTU.4.174, 1; KTU.4.179, 1; KTU.4.275, 7; KTU.4.382, 5; KTU.4.416, 4; KTU.4.485, 7; KTU.4.745, 8; PRU, III, 11.839, 5, 6, 20; PRU, VI, 93 (RS.17.131).

We also know from the textfragment KTU.4.382,5 that a *rb ṯnnm* "elder of the *ṯnnm*" existed. Unfortunately, we do not learn anything about the real functions of the *šanānu-ṯnnm*, except, as shown above, their military functions were of the most trustworthy.

4. *mḫṣm* — *ma-ḫi-ṣu (ub-ru)* — guards[110]

The *mḫṣm*-guards appear less in our texts than the preceding groups. They are listed either by groups or by single persons, designated by their professions or by name. KTU.4.124 mentions at least 12 *mḫṣm* by name. Various texts (KTU.4.125; 4.128; 4.269) deal with deliveries of grain, and other products, as rations (*ḥpr*) to the *mḫṣm*. We learn from KTU.4.124 that the *mḫṣm* dwelled in the villages of *Šbn*, *Ilštmʿ*, *Šlmy*, *Ubrʿy*, *Gwl*, and *Miḫd* and (KTU.4.332) *Qrt*.

Ubdy-fields and the respective service were alotted and imposed upon them (cf. KTU.4.107, 57-58 and Ch. III). PRU.VI, 166 stands separately. In it the LÚ*ma-ḫi-ṣu* is designated as an *ub-ru*(?). Possibly, this person was a foreigner and, we see, possibly, that he was also something other than a military serviceman. PRU.VI.10 is a partly preserved letter. The preserved lines give the following information: (4′) *a-nu-ma* LÚ*š[a-ar-ra-q]u* (5′) *ša-a i-ša-ra-a[q]* (6′) *u-nu-tē*MEŠ *ša amêli-ia* (7′) *i-na-an-na e-nu-ma* (8′) *i-na* URU*Ra-a-ša-sa-ir* (9′) *a-ši-ib* "concerning the thief, who has stolen the objects of my man, now he dwells (or is) at *Rašasair*." (10′) *i-na-an-na* LÚ*ma[ḫi]ṣa [u]š-ši-ra* (11′) *a-na la-qá-i-šu* (12′) *ù at-ta la-a ta[k]à-la-šu* "And now, the *maḫiṣu*-guard you sent in order to take (arrest) him.[111] And you don't withhold him." We see from this text that there was a need to send to *Rašasair* a *maḫiṣu* for the purpose of arresting the thief and this may confirm that the *maḫiṣu* was

---

110 Cf. Ch. V, note 63 and, against the view of *Held*, a, pp. 169-179 and *Goetze*, c, pp. 34-38, "weavers"; *Salonen*, a, p. 147 Akk. *tamḫiṣu*, "a weapon for smiting and throwing,"; AHW, 1314, b. The literary texts of Ugarit give the meaning "to strike, smite" of *mḫṣ*, *Gibson-Driver*, a, p. 151; *Margalit*, a, p. 251. Canaanite EA *ma-aḫ-ṣu-*u_2 = *da-ku-šu* "he killed him". The *mḫṣm* appear in the following texts: KTU.4.99, 15; KTU.4.103, 57-58; KTU.4.124; KTU.4.123, 9; KTU.4.128, 3; KTU.4.182, 36; KTU.4.187; KTU.4.332, 14-17; KTU.6.48, 4; PRU.VI.10 (RS.17.390), 10′; PRU VI.166 (RS.19.99) int. 4.

111 Reading: *qá* instead of *dá* — *Rainey*, b, p. 36.

a military man, or guard,[112] and his task was to arrest the delinquent. Thus, we see that he had to perform a kind of police-function.

5. *n'rm*-"youths"[113]

It is not definitively clear whether the *n'rm* are identified with the *n'r mrynm* (*bn mrynm*; cf. above *maryannu*) or the *bdl mrynm* and *mḏrġlm*, the *ḫsnm* (cf. above) or the *lmdm* of the *mḫṣm*, or whether there was also a separate group of the *n'rm*.[114] But from the fact that they give 1 archer to the guard together with the *mḏġlm* and *kzym* (KTU.4.68, 60-62) and that the *nāḫiru* in PRU.VI.136.9 receive silver we can conclude that they could be a separate group of some auxiliary military personnel.

6. *kzy(m)* Akk. [LÚ]*kizū*-"Horsegrooms"[115]

The *kzy(m)* are considered as a particular group, but they are also mentioned individually. The *kzym* participated in the archers-guard (§1) and belonged to the *bnš mlk*. According to KTU.4.222, 3 at least the "elder of the *kzym*" (*rb kzym*) had at his disposal an *ubdy*-field (*šd ubdy*). The fact that their elder is mentioned is important. In Vir-Dan [LÚ]*ka-zi-ì-e ša bîti-ya* "the horsegrooms of my house(hold)", i.e., of the royal household are mentioned and it confirms their belonging to the royal dependents.

7. Other Terms Possibly Designating Military Servicemen.

a) *ḫb/pṯ* Akk. *ḫupšu*- : "soldiers (?) of a lower class."[116]

---

[112] Otherwise *Rainey*, b, p. 37, [LU]KIN = *mâr šipri* "messenger", but unacceptable on paleographic grounds; cf. *Labat*, a, *kin*$_7$ No. 206 does not present the form of the sign given by *Rainey*.

[113] KTU.4.68, 1; 126, 12; 4.745, 10; PRU.VI.136 (RS.17.240) [LÚ]*na-ḫi-ru-[ma]* — Akkadian spelling of Ugar. *n'rm*.

[114] Cf. also *na'arē śarē hammedīnōt* in I Reg. 20, 14, 19 and the *n'rm* in the battle of Kadesh, *Gardiner*, a, p. 37; *Helck*, a, p. 563, No. 136.

[115] WUS, p. 146, No. 1279; UT, p. 418, No. 1215 "(horse)grooms"; AHW, p. 496a "servant"; *Salonen*, e, p. 231 "Trossknecht" — "Horsegroom"; Alalaḫ, *Giacumakis*, a, p. 83 "youth, squire, attendant". Appears in KTU.4.68, 62; 4.99, 10; 4.126, 14; 4.222, 3 and in Vir. Dan., p. 23-26 — the collated reading *Lettinga*, a, p. 112.

[116] AHW, p. 35, 7a; CAD, Ḫ, p. 241, well-known from Byblos from the Amarna

b) *šmrm*-"guards".[117]

c) *mhr*-"warrior."[118]

d) *ḫsnm* (cf. above §2) and KTU.4.244, (15) ...*lḫsn.krm.aḥd*... "to the *ḫsn* — one vineyard...." So we see that they had their land-allotments. KTU 4.542, (1) [*spr.ḫ*]*snm.dt.b.gr*[ ] "[List of the *ḫ*]*snm*, which are at (the) *gr*[ ]." We see from here at least that they were sometimes treated as an individual group.

e) *trrm* — Akk. (from Ugarit only) *ta-ri-ru-ma*.[119] They belonged quite certainly to the *bnš mlk*, for it is well known (Ch. III) that they received *ubdy*-fields and other distributions.

§4. Foreigners in the Military Service of Ugarit

In this connection, the question of interest to us is that of the *sherdana*-warriors in Ugarit.[120] We can identify them with the *šrdn*-warriors in Egypt. In the Ugaritic alphabetic texts they appear as *ṯrtnm*[121] and *še-ri-da-nu* etc. in the Akkadian texts from Ugarit. PRU.III.16.251 is interesting for the better understanding of the question.

"(1) From the present day, (2) Niqmepa, son of Niqmaddu, (3) king of Ugarit, (4) took the fields of *Allan*, (5) the *sherdanu*, (^I*Al-la-an še-ri-da-nu*)[122] (6) in the (village) *Iluištam'i*, (7) and the fields of his inheritance(?) (8) an

letters. In Ugarit they are sometimes known as working personnel — KTU.2.17; 3.3; 4.360; 4.322; 4.430. On the military role of the *ḫupšu* in Alalaḫ — *Giacumakis*, a, p. 78; *Dietrich-Loretz*, k, p. 91; cf. *Rainey*, d, p. 103, No. 29.

117 Hebr. *šōmēr*; *Rainey*, f, p. 24 "patrol-men"; KTU.4.35, II, 10; 4.63, II, 48; 4.103, 26; 4.170, 24-25, but nothing is definitively clear here.

118 Possibly a more general term "warrior" without designation of the professional group. KTU.4.214, I, 4-5; *Rainey*, d, p. 101, No. 27; *Margalit*, b, pp. 181-188, esp. *Yṯpn mhr št Yṯpn* — "the *sūtū*-warrior."

119 UT and WUS as well as AHW, p. 1330a; *Helck*, a, p. 577 and all other authors without giving translation; KTU.4.7; 4.99.8; 4.103, 48-53; 4.126, 26; PRU. VI.93, 5 (RS.17.131).

120 A detailed study — *Heltzer*, D (in print).

121 §2 and *Liverani*, c, pp. 194-195 and *Liverani*, e, pp. 212-216; *Liverani*, SDB, pp. 1340-1341; *Dietrich-Loretz*, j, pp. 39-42.

122 Attention must be paid to the fact that before *Al-la-an* is the determinative sign of the masculine personal name () which was overlooked and misinterpreted by *Liverani*, e, pp. 194-195.

gave it (9) to Šawittenu. (10) And *Sawittenu* (11-12) shall honour the king, his lord with 100 (shekels) of gold. (13) Nobody shall take it (14) from his hands. (15) The seal of the great king. (16) Witness, *Šamaš-šarru*, the scribe."

Next we have to take PRU.IV.15.118:

"(1) From the present day, (2) Ammistamru, son of Niqmepa, (3) king of Ugarit, (4) took the fields of *Allan*, (5) the *Šerdanu* (*ᴵŠe-er-ta-an-ni*) with its vineyard, (6) in the (village) *Matiilu* (7) and gave it (8) to *Ibšali* (9) and *Ibšali* [x (shekels) of silver (?)] (10) shall give to the king. (11) In the future (12) nobody [ ] (13) shall take it (14) from *Ibšali*. (15) The seal of the king Ammistamru, son of Niqmepa. (16) Witness — *Iaširu*, the scribe."

The first text is written in the reign of Niqmepa, the second in the regnal period of his son Ammistamru II, and they are chronologically very close to one another. In both texts we see the usual legal formula *ittaši eqlā*ᴹᴱŠ "took the fields"[123] and this is the legal formula connected with the further redistribution of the lands by the king (cf. Ch. III, pp. 23-25). We also learn that *Allan* the *Šerdana* had at his disposal fields of two categories. There were fields received from the king, as well as inherited (PRU.III.16.251, 7 *eqlāt na-ḫa-li*). It is important that he received fields from the king as a serviceman (*bnš mlk*), but he also had inherited fields, which shows us that this *šerdana* was no mere foreigner in Ugarit. The fact, by itself, that the *šerdana*-people of obviously foreign origin, were in Ugarit, arriving there doubtlessly as mercenaries, is interesting by itself. The general number in Ugarit (§2) could not have exceeded 58-60.

We know some other text fragments concerning land transactions or allotments to the *šerdana*.[124] Under consideration is a salt-producing plot.[125]

There is also a fragment of an international legal text, PRU.IV.17.112, where [*x*] *mâr Mu-ut-ⁱˡBalal* ᴸᵁ́*še-er-da-n*[*a*] "[*x*] son of *Mutba'al*, the *šerdana*," appear. So we see that his father had a semitic name, but he inherited the profession of the *šerdana*, i.e., military serviceman.[126] We also see that they were considered as *bnš mlk*, from KTU.4.216, where wine is delivered, together with the carpenters (or builders) — *ḥršm*, the *mḏrġlm* and *maryannu*. (7) *kd.l.ṯrtn*[*m*] "(One) jar to the *šerdana*". So we have seen that

---

[123] Concerning this formula, *Greenfield*, a, pp. 189-191.

[124] PRU, III, 15.167 — cf. *Dietrich-Loretz*, j, p. 40; *Heltzer*, D, (in print).

[125] *eqil tâbti ṣí-ṣú-ma* — *Heltzer*, p, pp. 355-361.

[126] Cf. also RS.8.145, 27 in PRU, III, p. 277 and *Dietrich-Loretz*, j, and *Heltzer*, D.

without any regard to the origins of the *ṯrtnm/šerdana*,[127] they were foreigners in the royal service of Ugarit and were treated as other military servicemen (*bnš mlk* — royal dependents) in that kingdom.

§5. Questions of Organization and Equipment in the Military Forces

We have seen that the military organization of Ugarit was based on a) a very limited mobilization of guards and its division between the professional groups of royal dependents and the village-communities of the kingdom; b) on a partial mobilization of royal dependents for palace and other duties (*ḫrd*) and including possibly the villagers; c) on a general (or almost general) mobilization (or conscription) of the royal dependents and villagers of the kingdom. It is a complicated task to make even a limited attempt to estimate the numeral size of the Ugaritic mobilized army in the XIV-XIIIth century B.C.E. and such investigation must be the subject of a future study. Concerning some professions, we have seen (§2) that their numbers can be approximated.

In some cases, concerning chariots, we can see that they were supplied from the royal stores (Excursus II) as were their spares and equipment. At least a part of the chariot-horses came from the royal stables. The same thing is also seen with regard to other military equipment. So villagers received weapons from royal stores as did the *nqdm*-shepherds and *mḏrġlm*-guards. It seems, that practically all the basic armament and equipement came from the royal stores or workshops. Naturally, shipbuilding and metallurgical work were, in part used for military purposes. The large royal livestock stores could also supply the army when necessary.

---

[127] Cf. *Heltzer*, D and the text KTU.4.204 where quivers (*uṯpt*) are distributed to various persons, among them also quivers (of) *srdnnm (uṯpt srdnnm)* which could have been a special type of quiver characteristic of the *šerdana*. We must also note that the Egyptian wall-paintings and reliefs of the XIII-XIXth dynasties depicting foreigners, where the *sherdana* are given, do not show us any quiver in their armaments. If we assume that the *sherdana* are of sardinian origin, and we must connect them with the nuragic culture of perhaps the Late Bronze Age, we see a type of quiver of the bronze statuettes of the nuragic culture, which is a right-angled triangle from the bottom to the top (*Lilliu*, a, pp. 58-59, fig. No. 11 and 29-31, pp. 187-188, fig. 227-229; pp. 192-193, No. 101, fig. 336-337 — the arch of the last warrior is also extraordinarily big; cf. also *Buchholz*, c, pp. 151, N° 90-92.

Was the Ugaritic system a unique one? Or is it only a question of more concentrated information which is available for study and analysis, and there were similar systems also in neighboring countries, and perhaps it was common for the whole period.

Elsewhere we are dependent on the sources and the authors who investigated them. Egypt was the big power in the area, with a largely developed military organization, but, it seems, not dependent on general conscription and mobilization. This, recently studied by *Schulman*,[128] is not so widely known from the point of view of its conscription or mobilization-system. The Middle-Assyrian material studied by *Freydank*,[129] shows a similar system, where *ḫurādu* "conscripted" men participated. It also shows us the mobilization of various professionals and a logistic system, but the data is more scarse, and we do not see how the system of the general mobilization worked. The data we receive from the Hittite sources, gives us a lot about the military campaigns, but not about the completion and logistic side. Concerning Nuzi, we must say that the studies of *Kenwood*[130] and *Zaccagnini* and *Jankowska* (to some extent)[131] show us the system at work, but it seems that palace-servants and villages and districts (*ḫalṣu*) with their semi-autonomous local self-government organization played a role and the centralization was of a lower degree than in Ugarit. We also have some data about the military organization in Alalaḫ, where lists of men, obliged for conscription, and service, as well as the military organization of the villages is given.[132] But even here we cannot trace the system so widely as in Ugarit. In the military system of Ugarit we do not know only about the division of the army into the standing units.

It seems to us that the only known similar system at the second half of the II millennium B.C.E. existed in Mycenaean Greece, i.e., the states of Pylos and Knossos.[133] It is similar in regard to the armaments and their production and distribution,[134] as well as the completion and land-

---

[128] *Schulman*, a; *Schulman*, b, pp. 75-98; *Schulman*, c, pp. 51-69.

[129] *Freydank*, a, pp. 11-130; cf. also *Postgate*, c, pp. 210-213.

[130] *Kenwood*, a.

[131] *Zaccagnini*, c, pp. 21-38; *Jankowska*, a, pp. 233-282.

[132] *Dietrich-Loretz*, k, pp. 57-97.

[133] *Chadwick*, a, pp. 160-172; *Poljakova*, a, pp. 258-264.

[134] *Chadwick*, a, pp. 173-179; *Palmer*, b, pp. 35-62.

allotment system of the army.[135] Possibly, such similarity was influenced by the character of the material, i.e., the archives of Knossos and Pylos compared with the archives of Ugarit. Sometimes we see striking similarity in the formulas from the Aegean kingdoms and Ugarit. We see this in the texts concerning chariots and charioteers. Maybe whatever differences with it lay in the more highly developed tradition in Ugarit.

Now we must consider the last question about the employment of the army of Ugarit in various concrete situations. This we learn from the military correspondence, international treaties between the Hittites or Amurru, and the king of Ugarit. From these we learn about military contingents and other data.

Warfare in Ugarit was studied by *Nougayrol*[136] and *Rainey*. We are not concerned here with the political questions of the warfare, but the organization of the command.

First of all, we have to take U.V.20 (RS.20.33), the letter of the Ugaritic ^{I}*Šu-mi-*[*ia-nu*] who was the commander of the field army. We see that charge of the command was not always in the hands of the king. He asks from the king to send 6 chariots (3 pairs of chariots).[137] Further, he writes "[It is for] this five (months) that I have been located in the land of Amurru,"[138] i.e., southwards from Ugarit. So we see that the army of Ugarit left the country for longer periods.

He adds: "I am guarding them with half my chariotry placed on the coast and half my [chariotry] placed at the foot of Mt. Lebanon. I, myself, am stationed there on the plain."[139] This shows us an additional thing. The army was at the center and two wings were composed of chariotry.

That this was not the whole army of Ugarit under this general as we see from the following passage. (v. 15′) "So may the king and troops and chariots

---

[135] *Nougayrol*, a, pp. 110-123.

[136] *Rainey*, f, pp. 17-27; *Rainey*, c, pp. 73-80; *Rainey*, h, pp. 131-145; *Rainey*, i, pp. 280-282 and also *Heltzer*, E, pp. 164-165.

[137] (5) *...šu-uṣ-ṣi-šu-mi 3 ta-pal* ^{GIŠ}*narkabāti.*

[138] [*iš-tu (?)* IT]U^{ha} *5 a*[*n-nu-*]*ú i-nu-ma* ^{KUR}*Amurru aš-bà-k*[*u*] "I stay in Amurru for 5 months."

[139] (18) *a-na-aṣ-ṣa-ar-ša-nu mišil(MAŠ)* ^{GIŠ}*narkabāti*^{MEŠ}*-ia i-na a-ḫi ayabba ša-kín* (19) *ù mišil* ^{GIŠ}*na*[*rkabāti*^{MEŠ}]*-ia i-na i-ir-ti ḫuršan li-ib-la-ni šá-kín-ma ù a-na-ku i-na ra-ma-ni-ia-ma ul-*[*l*]*a-nu i-na tu-ša*$_{10}$*-ri aš-bá-ku* (according to the corrected reading in *Rainey*, 'h).

that will come up (16′) as replacements."[140] And later he says that the reinforcements have to be of (21′) "troops and chariots."[141]

The accord between Mursilis II and Niqmepa of Ugarit (PRU.IV.17.353) has the passage, where the Hittite king mentions the armed forces of Ugarit: (20) "And if you Niqmepa of your troops (*ṣâbē*^{MEŠ}*-ka* ^{GIŠ}*narkabāti*^{MEŠ}*-ka*) and your chariots..."[142] So we see that footsoldiers and chariots were the main composition of the military force, but a more detailed composition is not given.[143]

We see here, at least from the letter of *Šumi*[*yanu*], that not always the king personally was in command of the field army, and we learn from this text that, at least sometimes, forces remained in Ugarit to be sent as reinforcements. The army of Ugarit could remain outside its territory also for at least five months.

Some time before the destruction of Ugarit, its last king wrote to the king of Alašia (U.V.24; RS.20.238) "(20) All the soldiers of the lord, my father, (21) are in the land Hatti (22) and all my ships in (23) Lycia (*Lukka*)"[144]

Such was the situation in the last days of Ugarit, but we see again that the king remained in the country and other persons were in command of the army and navy. We learn from this that the military system of Ugarit could create a relatively mobile force, which could be used sometimes even far from its native country.

Naturally, the material given here about military organization is not definitive. But it is perhaps a real basis for a further study of this question.

---

140 (v. 15′) *ù li-wa-á᾿-ir šarru*^{ru} *ṣâbē*^{MEŠ}*-bu ù* ^{GIŠ}*narkabāti*^{MEŠ} *ša i-il-lu-ú* (16′) *te*$_{x}$*-diš-ti.*

141 *ṣâbē*(ERIN.MEŠ.BU) *ù* ^{GIŠ}*narkabāti*^{MEŠ}.

142 The same expression — l. 24; cf. also PRU.IV.17.351, A.5′; 17.79, 8′, etc.

143 Cf. also PRU.IV.17.59 where Tudḫalia IV frees Ugarit from its military obligations and declares that Ammistamru (II), king of Ugarit, must not come to his help, "with his footsoldiers and chariots"; cf. also 17.18 where, despite the fragmentary state of the text we recognize the mention of (6′) 300 soldiers of Ibiranu, king of Ugarit.

144 Corrected reading according to *Berger*, a, p. 220; the analysis — *Lehman*, a, pp. 55-59; (20) *...gab-bu ṣâbē*(ERIN^{MEŠ}) *bêli*(EN) ⸢*a-b*⸣[*i*]-[*ia*] (21) *i-na* ^{KUR}*Ḫa-at-ti* (22) *aš-bu ù gab-bu* ^{GIŠ}MA^{MEŠ}*-ia* (*eleppātija*) (23) *i-na* ^{KUR}*Lu-uk-ka-a* (24) *aš-bu ...*

CHAPTER VII

TEMPLE PERSONNEL, ITS ORGANIZATION AND THE QUESTION OF THE TEMPLE-ECONOMY IN UGARIT

The archaic mythological texts from Ugarit give us evidence that there were "houses" of the gods, i.e., sanctuaries. The existence of the temples is well known also from the archaeological and epigraphic sources from Ugarit.[1] Naturally, a temple organization also existed.[2] The question is, what connection did it have with the whole system of royal dependency in Ugarit in the XV-XIIIth century B.C.E. The existing studies, even the most recent ones, do not touch on this question and therefore we learn nothing from them about the role of the temple and its personnel.[3]

We are also speaking about large temple economies, as were the case in Mesopotamia during the Ur-III dynasty, or in the Neo-Babylonian times. We must take as possible parallels the temple organization in societies contemporary to Ugarit. The main question is: was the temple and its personnel an independent force in the kingdom of Ugarit, or did it belong to and was guided by the royal authorities according to the general system in that country.

On the one hand we know the village-sanctuaries (cf. note 2) and also property and something about the organization of the *mrzḥ*, which was perhaps, a non-royal cultic association. It seemed to possess a certain amount of immovable and movable(?) property.[4]

But when we consider texts such as KTU.1.39, which deal with various offerings to the gods (grain, cattle, poultry), we must suppose that these

---

[1] Cf. *Gibson-Driver*, a; *Courtois*, SDB, pp. 1156-1295.

[2] *Heltzer*, F, pp. 153-162, now partly out of date; *Heltzer*, a, pp. 71-74 treats the question of local sanctuaries of the villages of the kingdom (cf. also p. 48), *Rainey*, j, pp. 16-24.

[3] *de Tarragon*, a, pp. 131-148; also *Urie*, a, pp. 42-47; only *Rainey*, j, considers the question in a certain framework.

[4] *Heltzer*, G, pp. 366-367; *Fenton*, a, pp. 71-75; *Greenfield*, c, pp. 451-455; *Eissfeldt*, b, pp. 187-195 and recently *de Tarragon*, a, pp. 144-147.

products were, at least sometimes, stored in the temple stores.[5] Text KTU.1.41 shows us also the role of the king in the cultic practice. We see that: "at the thir[teenth] (day of the month) the king washes himself."[6] He did this for the offering ceremonial, for it is said that, "The king will make the offering to (name of deity)."[7] There are also various texts such as KTU.6.29 (1) *spr.ʿpsm* (2) *dt.št.* (3) *uryn* (4) *l.mlk.Ugrt*, "List of *ʿpsm*, which prepared (or put together) the *uriyannu*-priest for the king of Ugarit."[8] Thus, the king had certain contacts with a priest. As we learn from KTU 2.26, the king gave orders to prepare timber for the restoration of a certain sanctuary (*bt.Dml*).[9]

Another interesting text is KTU.1.91 (1) *yn.d.ykl bd k*[ ] (2) *l dbḥ mlk*, "(1) The wine which was supplied to ... (2) for the royal sacrifice."[10] Lines 2-3 speak about various gods and in lines 21-36 we have a list of 14 villages of the kingdom, each delivering from 2-10 jars of wine. This may show that the wine does not come from a temple-economy, but from the villages and the sacrifice is on behalf of the king.

We have no exact knowledge that there existed a separate temple-economy, at least no document does prove its existence. Another text is PRU III.16.267.[11] According to it the king Niqmaddu II gives to a certain *Kar-Kušuḫ*[14] and his wife *Apapa*, the daughter of the king, all the income from the village *Uḫnappu*. The concluding formula: (21) "The house (sanctuary) of Baal of Mount *Ḫazi*,[12] (22) and its prie[sts][13] (23) towards *Kar-Kušuḫ*.[14]

---

[5] *Caquot*, SDB, pp. 1403-1407; cf. also KTU.1.41.

[6] (3) *b.ṯlṯt.*ʿ[*šrt.yrtḥṣ mlk*]; cf. also KTU.1.43; 1.87, 2; 1.105, 5-6 ff.; 1.106, 25 ff.; 1.109 1 ff.; 1.112, 10 ff.; 1.119, 4 ff., and *Dietrich-Loretz-Sanmartin*, m, pp. 525-528; *Dietrich-Loretz-Sanmartin*, n, pp. 144-145; we deal here only with the ritual functions of the king, *de Tarragon*, pp. 31-32, 79-97, 113-120.

[7] (50) ...[*yd*]*bḥ mlk l*[ ]. We have another type of offering in KTU.1.115, (1) *id ydbḥ mlk*, "Then the king has to make the sacrifice."

[8] *ʿpsm* — meaning unknown. On the *uriyannu*-priest in Ugarit see *Liverani*, a, pp. 73-75.

[9] *Heltzer*, a, pp. 25-26.

[10] *nkl*/*ybl* — *Milano*, a, and *Fensham*, a, which is now preferable compared with our former translation. *Heltzer*, a, p. 40; nor a *molk*-sacrifice (*Eissfeldt*, a, p. 14).

[11] The full text and its interpretation, *Heltzer*, a, p. 48.

[12] Mount Ṣafān, Mons Casius of the classical times, modern Djebel-el-ʿAqra, *Albright*, c, p. 4 ff.

[13] LÚ*ku-um-*[*ra-šu*].

[14] *a-na* I*Kar-*il*Kušuḫ*.

(24) may have no claims." From here we see that there is no mention about an economy of priests. They had, formerly, only the right to collect income (taxes, etc.) from this village, in their favour. But, together with the royal letter KTU.2.26, we see that (in regard to the repair of a sanctuary) certain things were done by royal order and that the sanctuaries and their priests were subjects of the royal authorities.

This allows us to reconsider the temple personnel in Ugarit and to define their position in regard to the royal authorities.

1. The priests — Ug. *khnm* — Akk. ^{LÚ}*šangū*^{MEŠ}.[15] We read about them in a large number of texts.[16] We know that some of these texts mention groups, with no mention of individual persons. KTU.4.357 mentions even a family (?) of priests (*dr khnm*).

But the most interesting thing is the comparison of the various passages of texts KTU.4.69, VI, 22-31; KTU.4.633; KTU.4.761 [17] and PRU.III.16.257. In 4.69 and PRU.III.16.257 appear *mur'u Ibirana* and this means that these texts were written at the time when Ibirana was the heir to the throne, i.e., at the time of Ammistamru II.[18]

26	*KTU.4.69, VI, 22*		*KTU.4.633*		*KTU.4.761*		*PRU.III.16.257, IV*
22	*khnm* 10	4	*khnm*	1	*khnm*[ ]	1	^{LÚMEŠ}*šangū*
23	*bn Ṯ'y* 4						
24	*wnḥlh* 4						
25	*wnḥlhm* 4						
26	*bn.Nqly* 4	8	*bn.Nql*[*y*]	9	*bn Nqly*	42	^{I}*Ku-un-am-mu mâr Ni-qa-la-a*
27	*bn.Snrn* 8	9	*bn.Snr*[*n*]	2	*bn Sn*[*rn*]	45	*Ar.*^{il}*Tešub mâr Si-na-ra-na*

[15] Akk. phonetically *ša-an-gu/šan-gu* or ideographically SANGA. *khnm*- Hebr. *kohēn*; AHW, pp. 1163 *šangû* "Priester", "Tempelverwalter", "priest, head of sanctuary."

[16] KTU.4.29; 4.36, 1; 4.38; 4.68, 72; 4.69, VI, 22-37; 4.99, 9; 4.126, 6; 4.282, 5; 4.357, 24; 4.412, II, 1-5 (?) (the beginning of the column is broken, but the *qdšm* follow and usually they were preceded by the *khnm*); 4.416, 6; 4.633, 4-14; 4.745, 5; 4.761; PRU.III.16.257, III, 37; 16.186, 13′; PRU.VI.9.1 (RS.17.428 — corrected reading *Rainey*, b, p. 36); 93 (RS.17.131), 27; 136, 6 (RS.17.240); KTU 6, 6; 6.7; 6.8; 6.9; 6.10; 1.6.VI, 54-58; *Virolleaud* (V) 2, 4; KTU.2.4, 1-2.

[17] First published by *Bordreuil*, b, pp. 24-26.

[18] *Heltzer*, f, pp. 3-8; *Heltzer*, C, pp. 192-193.

28 bn.Ṯgd 6		11 bn.Ṯgd	46 Ia-an-ḫa-nu mâr Ši-gu-di
29 bn.D[x]tn 10			40 ^{I}Tak-^{il}$_{2}$Tešub mâr Da-ti-ni
30 bn.Amḏn 6	13 bn.Amd[n]	7 bn Amd[n]	38 $^{[I]}$Abdu mâr Am-ma-da-na
31 bn.Ṯmrn 3			49 ^{I}Ia-tar-^{il}Nergal mâr Ša-am-ra-an
32 bn.Pzny 6	10 bn.Pzn[y]	10 bn Pzty	41 ^{I}Ia-an-ḫa-mu mâr Pi-zu-ni
33 bn.Mglb 10	11 bn.Mgl[b]	4 bn Mglb[ ]	44 ^{I}A-bur$_{5}$-ša-nu mâr Na-ma-ag-li-bi
34 bn.[ ]b/d	5 bn.Ṯgr[b]		
35 bn.Š/ḏ[ ]r 3			
36 bn Š[ ] 2			
	6 bn.Ba/n(?)[ ]		
	7 bn.Ṯ'l[ ]		54 ^{I}Aḫi-mu-nu mâr Ša-a-la-na
	12 bn.Dbd/b [ ]		
	13 Annš[n]		
		8 Ngy bn[ ]	
		5 bn.Tbr[n]	51 ^{I}Ia-qub-ia-nu mâr Ša-ab-ra-na
		6 bn Nš[	
		8 bn.Tmy	
			39 ^{I}Abdi-an-ti mâr Ka-bi-iz-zi
			43 ^{I}A-kap-šeni mâr Ku-ni-ya
			47 ^{I}Mu-na-ḫi-mu mâr NIM (?)
			48 ^{I}Ili-milku mâr Ú-lu-na-a-ri
			48 ^{I}Abdi-^{il}Nergal mâr Ta-ak-te-na
			52 ^{I}Ar-te-nu mâr Ša-ša-na
			53 ^{I}At-te-ya mâr Iš-la-ma-na
			55 ^{I}A-ḫa-ma-ra-nu mâr Ma-ri-ma-na ^{LÚ}La-ba-nu

We can see in these four badly preserved texts at least 5 names coinciding in all four tablets, and 2 names also coincide in 3 tablets, and 4 names coinciding in two tablets. All four tablets are chronologically close. It is thus possible to conclude that the general number of *khnm-šangu*-priests in Ugarit at one time did not exceed 25-30 persons.

As we saw in Chapter I, the *khnm* appear in the same lists as a professional groups of *bnš mlk* "royal dependents" appear.[19] As we know from KTU.4.67, 72-73, the *khnm* have, together with the *qdšm*, to send one archer to the archer-guard. We know that according to 4.32-1 the *khnm* receive 3 GUR emmer (ZÌ.KAL.KAL), 6 shekels of silver and 6 sheep together with all professional groups who receive products according to this document.[20]

We also know that a certain *Aḫamaranu*, son of *Marimanu*, was from the village *Labanu* (PRU, III, 16.257, IV, 55). During the lifetime of the father the son could receive, as in other professional groups of *bnš mlk*, the same profession. We see this from KTU.4.69.VI. 23-25, where *bn Ṯʿy* received 10 shekels of silver and "his heir" (*wnḫlh*) — 4 shekels, and "his heirs" (*wnḫlhm*) — also 4 shekels. So we see three generations holding the same profession.

As described in Ch. III, the *ubdy*-fields were also distributed between the *khnm*.[21]

According to the colophone of the literary text KTU.1.6.VI [(54)] *spr Ilmlk Šbnry* [(55)] *lmd.Atn.Prln.rb* [(56)] *khnm rb.nqdm* [(57)] *ṯʿy Nqmd.mlk Ugrt* [(58)] *adn. Yrgb bʿl Ṯrmn.* "The scribe *Ilmlk* of (the village) *Šbn*, apprentice of *Atn. Prln*, elder of the priests (chief priest) elder of the shepherds, the noble of *Nqmd*, king of Ugarit, the Lord of *Yrgb*, the Master of *Ṯrmn*."[22] From this can be seen the high position which the *rb khnm* held; he was one of the nobles of the king of Ugarit. PRU.III.16.186, 13 — a text from the time of king Ibiranu, son of Ammistamru II, after the seal of the king follow

[19] Cf. KTU.4.36; 4.99; 4.126; 4.745; PRU.III.16.257, etc.

[20] Cf. also the texts where the *khnm* receive, collectively or individually, silver (KTU.4.69); 4.761 — oil; PRU.III.16.257 — oil; PRU.VI.136 — silver, etc.

[21] KTU.4.282; [(5)] *širm šd.khn*, "2 *šir*-measures of field (to the) priest (*šir* — WUS, p. 299, No. 2576; UT, p. 487, No. 2372 — without satisfactory understanding; AHW, p. 1219 b. *še/ir'u/m*, "Saatfurche" = "furrow" — possibly the basis for such a field measure-unit). KTU.4.357 — *šd bd.dr.khnm* "(one) field to (a) family of priests" KTU.4.416, 6 — field distribution to the *khnm*.

[22] Cf. *nqdm* — Ch. IV.

[*x mâr*^{l}...]^{LÚ}*sukallu* ^{LÚ}*akil šangi* "[ ] the *sukallu*,[23] the overseer of the priests" (possibly this position was the same as that of the *rb khnm*(?); KTU.6.6; 6.7; 6.8; 6.9 — inscription on a bronze axe — *l rb khnm* "belonging to the high priest." PRU.VI.9, a letter. (1) [*u*]*m-ma r*[*a*]*b* (RAB/p!) *šangi-ma* (2) *a-na* ^{LÚ}*sà-ki-ni a*[-*ḫi-ia*] (3) *qi-bi-ma* "So the elder of the priests (high priest) to the *sākinu* m[y], [bro]ther say." It is clear from this letter that the high priest was equal to the *sākinu* of the country, the highest official of the country.[24] KTU.2.4, (1) *l.rb.khnm* (2) *rgm*, "To the high priest say" — the beginning of a letter.

We see that the professional group of the *khnm-šangū*, "priests" had their *rb*, who was one of the highest officials in the land, even being on the same level as the *sākinu*, whom he could by right address as "my brother." But otherwise we do not see any difference in the social position of the priests and the other groups of *bnš mlk*.

2. *qdšm*, ^{LÚ}*qadšu* = ^{LÚ}*bârû* — "priests-diviners.[25] We know these from a number of texts,[26] and they are also listed in the texts as a whole group or individually. It even seems, according to KTU.4.412 that 26 persons -*qdšm*- were listed originally.

They (cf. above) participated with the *khnm* in the archerguard, received emmer, sheep, silver (KTU.4.38, 2) and other products and appear in common lists for the professional groups of the *bnš mlk* (cf. Ch. I).

According to KTU.4.412.II, 8 among *qdšm* we find (14) *bn Ṯrn* (15) *w.nḥlh* " *bn Ṯrn'* and his heir." So we see the inheritance of the profession in the father's lifetime. And the *qdšm* also appear as witnesses in legal documents (PRU IV.18.20; 17.231 and 18.02).

---

[23] *sukallu* — cf. Ch. VIII.

[24] *sākinu* — Ch. VIII.

[25] *qadšu* — Ugaritic word given in Akkadian spelling in PRU.VI.93, 26 (RS.17.131); *bârû(m)* — AHW, pp. 109b "divinator". *qdšm* — *bârûm* from the fact that, as in the alphabetic lists, the *qdšm* always follow the *khnm*, in the Akkadian lists from Ugarit the *bârû(m)* always follow the *šangû*; cf. PRU.IV.18.02 (10) ... ^{I}*Ša-mu-Addu* ^{LÚ}*bârû* ^{LÚ}*šangâ* ^{il}*Adad* (cf. PRU.IV.18.20, v. 14′; 17.231, 17), therefore we must not follow *Rainey*, f, p. 22, where the *qdšm* are connected with the female hierodules, and *de Tarragon*, a, pp. 138-141, where he connects the *qdšm* with a lot of factors.

[26] KTU.4.36, 2; 4.38, 2; 4.47, 1; 4.68; 4.29, 3; 4.126, 7; 4.412, II, 8-34; PRU.IV.18-20, v. 14′; 17.231, 17; 18.02, 16; PRU.VI.93, 26.

It seems that the *qdšm* were, according to their position, on a lower stage than the *khnm*.

3. *šrm* "(temple) singers",[27] known from a certain number of texts.[28] They appear in the lists individually and as a group. In KTU.4.141 15 persons are mentioned. According to KTU.4.68, 65-67, the *šrm* together with the "sculptors" (*pslm*) and "heralds" (*yṣḥm*) send one person to the archer-guard, and, according to KTU.4.610, had to participate in the tribute (Ch. I) paid to the Hittite king. The payment consisted of 20 shekels of silver, a relatively small sum. The text KTU.4.168, dealing with "rations of the (royal) dependents" (*ḥpr bnšm*) mentions (3) *ṯlṯm.l.mit.š'rt* (4) *l.šr.'ṯtrt* "130 (shekels) of wool[29] to the singer of (the goddess) 'Aštart." KTU.4.430 speaks about a (3) *...šr.d.yṯb[b...]*, "(a) singer, who dwells [at ...]." The tablets KTU.4.141 and 4.609 which are lists of various distributions of groups of *bnš mlk*, where this term is mentioned, show us without any doubt that they belonged to the royal dependents. This also explains the fact that, as seen from KTU.4.103, 41-43, the *šrm* "singers" receive the *ubdy*-fields (Cf. Ch. III). And this is not the only text about land-allotments to them.[30] We see, therefore, that they had an organization and PRU VI.93.24, where the word *nâru* is written in Akkadian, confirms that the *šrm* were "singers."

4. *mṣlm* "cymbalists" or "praying (priests)(?)".[31] We know only one mention of these among other groups of the *bnš mlk* (KTU.4.125, 30).

---

[27] Akkadian equivalent unknown from Ugarit from administrative texts but in the lexicographical tablets U.V.137 (RS.20.123+) III, (7) *za-am-ma-rum* = Ugar. *ši-i-ru* "song" and (20) *š]i-i-ru* "singer"; Non-realistic understanding in *Macdonald-Cutler*, c, pp. 22-23; cf. hebr. *šār*, 107, 42 ^{LÚMEŠ}*ši-ri-me*.

[28] KTU.4.68.66; KTU.4.35, I, 10-15; 4.103, 41-43, 4.126; 11; 4.141, IV, 1-2; 4.168; 4.183, II, 1-5; 4.309, 1, 10; 4.430, 2; 4.609, 17, 31; 4.610, Rs.II.3; PRU VI.93, 24.

[29] In this case "wool" and not "barley", for the other parts of the text deal with distribution of textiles (*ḥpn, mlbš, lbšm, pṯtm*, etc.).

[30] KTU.4.183, (1) *b'l šd* "field owners" II, (1) four persons, 4.399 (10) — 4 fields of the *šrm*; 4.609 — at least three *šrm*, who are *b'l šd*, "fieldowners."

[31] Hebr. *meṣiltayīm* "cymbals" *Gordon*, c, p. 143; WUS, p. 267, No. 2318 and UT, p. 436, No. 1528, but otherwise Arab. *ṣallā*, Aram. *ṣl'* and Ugar. *ṣly* "to pray".

5. *šib mqdšt* "water-drawers of the sanctuary,"[32] are known also from only one text (KTU.4.609, 15), where they received the rations (*ḥpr*), were "field-owners" (*b'l šd*) and three persons are given by name.

These are definite groups of people whom we can identify as temple- or cult-personnel on the one hand, and as *bnš mlk*. on the other. It is possible that there were other cultic professionals, but we have no confirmation of this. Except for the *uriyannu*-priests, about whose existence we know, all other data is hypothetical.[33]

The only sure conclusion that can be reached is that there was no independent cultic organization in Ugarit, and that the personnel belonged to the royal dependents, as did the other professionals. This does not exclude the fact that some groups of temple personnel were in a slightly higher position, as for example the "priests" — *khnm-šangû*, and the *rb khnm* "chief priest" was equal to the highest officials of the kingdom.

The fact that among the *gt* (Ch. IV) of the economy we see one *gt 'štrt* "*gt* of the (goddess) *'štrt*", does not prove any claims that there was a temple economy. There may have been certain stores, connected with the temples, but the role of the king in the cult and sacrifice may prove that the needs of sacrifice were also supplied through the royal economy.[34]

Was the temple-organization of Ugarit a unique phenomenon, characteristic only for this country, or a common feature of the whole region? Naturally, it is impossible to compare the temples of Ugarit with the highly developed temple-economy in Mesopotamia of the Ur III period.[35]

The question, in principle, is the following: Was there, in the Late Bronze Age in Western Asia, or in some of its kingdoms, an independent temple-economy, or was it dependent fully on the royal economy and administration?

Concerning Alalaḫ we have too little data for definitive conclusions, but, in fact, there did not exist any considerable temple economy and administration.

---

[32] *š'b* "to draw (water)"; WUS, p. 298, No. 2563; UT, p. 486, No. 2366.

[33] *de Tarragon*, a, pp. 131-148.

[34] The only priest who is mentioned in the text and not connected with the Ugaritic *bnš mlk* system was a foreigner. So, according to PRU.IV.18.02, Kiliya was a *šangû* of Ištar of Zinzaru. He redeemed slaves in Ugarit, but as we know Zinzaru (*Zinzar/Zinzira*) — modern Qal'at Seğar, northwest of Hama, outside the territory of Ugarit (RGTC, 6, p. 505).

[35] *Tjumenev*, a.

In the Hittite New Kingdom, the temple played a large role, had an expanding and developed economy and numerous personnel. But, as seen from the studies of *Güterbock* and *Klengel*,[36] it was closely connected with the palace and royal officials and even members of the royal family belonged to it. Compared with Ugarit, the temple-economy was more independent economically, but it seems that politically it was not.

In Kassite Babylonia, as well as in the preceding Old-Babylonian times, as shown by *Renger*, the temple was dependent on the central power, as well as on the local governor. But this was in the administrative sphere,[37] where economically the temple played a larger role than in Asia Minor and, naturally, Ugarit.

In the Middle-Assyrian period, in the time between Tukulti-Ninurta I and Tiglatpileser I the temples seemed to be directed by the central power and they were in a fully dependent status.[38]

The scarse data about the phoenician temples and their administration is only in the beginning stages of investigations.[39]

We must add that the egyptological view is, today, that in the period of the XIX-XXth centuries, B.C.E., there was a large-scale temple economy, but it was in a personal union (i.e. through the sacral and priestly functions) connected with the king and practically in his hands.[40]

We thus see that generally in the Late Bronze period, the temple and its personnel were in the hands of the royal power and possibly Ugarit was one of the most distinguished examples.

---

[36] *Güterbock*, b, pp. 128-132; *Klengel*, d, pp. 181-200.

[37] *Renger*, b, pp. 109-115.

[38] *Garelli*, b, pp. 116-124.

[39] *Delcor*, a, pp. 147-164.

[40] *Janssen*, b, p. 509.

CHAPTERS VIII-IX

These two chapters deal with the royal administration and the personnel of the royal palace. It is natural, that in so ancient times these two branches, the government and the court, were not absolutely divided. Thus our division here is, to some extent, artificial. In Chapter VIII we shall deal with the functionaries, who, in our opinion, participated mostly in the administration, and in Chapter IX with the question of the persons and professionals mostly engaged in palace activities.

CHAPTER VIII

THE ROYAL ADMINISTRATION OF THE KINGDOM

Concerning the administration in Ugarit, we must first begin with the higher functionaries. We have only a very short treatment of the question by *Liverani* (SDB, pp. 1337-1339). It must also be pointed out that in the texts from Ugarit, there are mentions of functionaries engaged from Karchemish and other neighbouring states. Their status is treated elsewhere and we will not pay attention to them.[1] Our task in this chapter is to try to derive from the sources information about the functioning of the administration and the officials in particular.

We shall begin with the highest official of the kingdom.

§1. *skn* — *sākinu*[2]

We know that the term is of Sumerian origin and the Canaanite spelling *skn* comes, possibly, from the Sumerian dialectical form *sakina*.[3] In the West-Semitic area we meet the *sākinu* in the XVIII-XVIIth cent. B.C.E. texts from Alalaḫ,[4] and later in the form of *su-ki-ni* in the El-Amarna letters from the first half of the XIVth century.[5] As was shown by *Buccellati*, in

---

[1] *Hawkins*, a, pp. 431-434; *Imparati*, b, pp. 154-159; *Goetze*, d, pp. 10-24; *Daddi-Pechioli*, b, pp. 169-191. Concerning the administrative system in Assyria and Babylonia including the II millennium B.C.E., cf. *Renger*, c, pp. 435-446; *Garelli*, c, pp. 446-452; *Deller*, a, pp. 639-653, esp. pp. 647-652.

[2] Hebr. *sōkēn*. The philological aspects of this term were studied recently exhaustively by *E. Lipinski*, b, pp. 191-207 with references to the previous bibliography.

[3] *Lipinski*, b, p. 195.

[4] On the date of these texts, cf. *Na'aman*, a, pp. 136-139 and *Collon*, a, pp. 27-131. According to the tablets *AT245; 248, 5; 253, 13; 256, 12; 264, 14; 275, 8 (autographs in AT, Pl. XXXI and *Wiseman*, a, pp. 17-20 and *Wiseman*, b, pp. 22-30). The [LÚ]*sá-ki-ni* is mentioned in these texts only as a recipient of barley and other food-stuffs (cf. also *Giacumakis*, a, p. 98 and *Tsevat*, a, pp. 20 and 123, "steward").

[5] EA, 265 — letter of Mut-Baalu [(9)] [amelut]*ra-bi-ṣi*//*su-ki-ni*; "commissioner (of the

Ugarit the sumerogramm MAŠKIM, usually read as *rābiṣu*, and the pseudo-logogramm SÁ-KÍN have to be always read *sākinu*.[6]

Approaching the texts of Ugarit we must remember that the meaning of the term was not homogeneous and designated a number of officials.[7]

A. According to a number of texts, there was a *sākin mâti* "*sākinu* of the country" in Ugarit. Thus, in the tablet, PRU, III, 11.730, the king of *Bîrûtu* ($^{(1)}$ *šar* ^{KUR}*Bîrûti*^{Mti}) addresses the "*sākinu* of (the land of) Ugarit" ($^{(2)}$ ^{LÚ}*sākin* (ŠÁ.KÍN) ^{KUR}*Ú-ga-ri-it*).

PRU, III, 19.19. The king of the (land) Parga (^{KUR}*Pár-ga*) "to the *sākinu*" ($^{(2)}$ *[a]-na* ^{LÚ}*sà-ki-ni*). There are also a number of other texts, where kings address the *sākinu* (cf. below). The most important seems to be RS.34.129 — containing a letter of the Hittite king:[8] "So (speaks) My Sun,[9] the great king: (To) the *sākinu* say: 'So it is (the case) with you. The king is little (an infant) and does not know nothing $^{(6)}$ *šarr[u] bêl-ka ṣe-ḫe-er* $^{(7)}$ *mi-im-ma la-a i-di*. And I, the Sun, gave him a task'." (In the following line the task is described and the *sākinu* is made responsible for its execution).[10]

There are also cases when not the king, but the *sākinu* of the neighbouring country addresses the sakinu of Ugarit. According to PRU, IV, 17.425, the "*sākinu* of Ušnatu" ($^{(4)}$ ^{LÚ}*sà-ki-in-ni ša* ^{URU}*Uš-na-ti*), your slave (*ardi-ka-ma*) writes to the *sākinu* of Ugarit "my lord" (*bêli-ia*). PRU, IV, 17.393 in a letter to the *sākinu* of Ugarit by a certain Epiqu "his servant". But, according to PRU, III, 15.33, a certain Hittite Ḫišmikušuḫ writes to

---

pharao) (cf. *Albright*, d, p. 11 and note 22); cf. also EA 362 MAŠKIM-*śu-ki-na* — *Thureau-Dangin*, d, pp. 91-94; 102-103; *Rainey*, k, pp. 18-19 and 90.

[6] *Buccellati*, a, pp. 223-228; *Lipinski*, b, p. 197, note 39; *Rainey*, a, pp. 426-428; *Rainey*, d, p. 86-87; *Fenton*, b, pp. 54-55.

[7] We also meet the *sākinu* of the neighboring kingdoms in the official correspondence of Ugarit. Cf. *Heltzer*, v, pp. 224-228, now partly out of date.

[8] U.VII, Pl.XI, XII. Autograph and reading *Dietrich-Loretz*, o, pp. 53-56.

[9] *Šamši-ia*. On the title of the Hittite king *Fauth*, a, pp. 227-264.

[10] PRU.IV, 17.288. The king of Ušnatu writes "to the *sākinu* of the land of Ugarit" $^{(2)}$ *a-na* ^{LÚ}*sākin*<*mâti*>^{ti} *ša* ^{KU}[^{R}*U-ga-ri-it*]); PRU.IV, 17.424C — Addu-dayyānu, king of Amqu writes to Uzakaptu, the *sākinu* of the land of Ugarit (*ša* ^{KURURU}*U-ga-[ri-it]*); U.VII, RS.34.137, Pl. XIX — The king of Hatti writes to the *sākinu* of Ugarit; U.VII, RS.34.146, Pl.XXVIII — The king of Qadesh writes to Uzzinu, *sākinu* of Ugarit; U.VII, RS.34.158, Pl. XXXVII — The king of Ušnatu writes to Uzzinu.

Ugarit (2) *a-na* LÚ*Sà-ak-ki-ni* (3) *aḫi-ia*... "to the *sākinu*, my brother."[11] And U.V.52 (RS.20.23) contains the salutation by a certain Madae (2) *a-na* LÚ*sà-ki-ni* "To the *sākinu*."

We also have letters to the *sākinu* from persons higher than he and it is noted there. Thus, in PRU, VI, 7A (RS.17.148) a woman Yabnienše writes (2) *a-na* LÚ*sà-ki-[n]iša* KUR*Ú-[ga-ri-it]* (3) *mâri-ia*... "To the *sākinu* of the land of Ugarit, my son...."

PRU.VI.9 (RS.17.428) contains the beginning of the letter of the high (chief) priest (*rab-šangi*) to the *sākinu*, "his brother."[12] We also have at our disposal letters, in which the *sākinu* of Ugarit addresses rulers and other functionaries.

U.V.54 (RS.20.23), (1) *um-ma* I*sà-ki-in* (2) *a-na* I*Rap-a-na*... "Here the *sākinu* to Rap'anu...." It seems that it was Rap'anu, one of the royal scribes.[13]

In PRU.VI.3 (RS.17.455) the *sākinu* turns to the addressée as "your servant" (*ardika*). Possibly, he was writing to his own king.

And, as we have already seen from the above-mentioned texts PRU IV.17.425; U.V.40; and probably PRU.III.15.33; 15.44; PRU.VI.4.5 and 6 and U.V.51, certain foreign *sākinu* write to the *sākinu* of Ugarit.

But we also know of letters in which foreign *sākinu* write to functionaries of Ugarit, or even to the king.

U.V.38 (RS.20.16) is a letter of Padiya, the *sākinu* of Kinza (Qadeš) written to the king of Ugarit (1) *a-na šarri* KUR*Ú-ga-ri-it* (2) *bêli-ia* "To the king of Ugarit, my lord".

U.V.22 (RS.20.18), (1) *um-ma* I*E-šu-wa-ra* (2) LÚ*sākinu* (MAŠKIM) *rabu*

---

[11] Cf. PRU.III, 15.24, where a certain Abušg[ama] (*sākinu* of Amurru?) writes to the *sākinu* (of Ugarit) "my brother" (*aḫi-ia*); U.V, 40 (RS.20.200B) the *sākin* of Kinza (Qadeš) writes to Uzzinu, the *sākinu* of Ugarit "his brother"; PRU.VI, 4 (RS.17.142) a certain Lullu writes (2) *a-na* I*sà-ki-in-ni* (3) *aḫi-ia* "To the *sākinu*, my brother". Other letters "to the *sākinu* the brother (of me)", cf. PRU.VI, 4 (RS.17.452); VI, 7B (RS.17.148); VI, 6 (RS.17.144) — cf. *Heltzer*, i, pp. 4-8; U.V, 41 (RS.20.158) — again a letter to U.V, 41 (RS.20.158) — again a letter to Uzzinu, who is designated as "brother"; possibly, the same Uzzinu also U.VII, RS.34.172; Pl. I and KTU.4.10 and 4.11 in Ugaritic — cf. *Caquot*, b, pp. 389-398.

[12] Cf. Ch. VII, pp. 133-136.

[13] PRU.VI, 98 (RS.17.239) — the *sākinu* addresses a certain Ta'azi.

(GAL) *ša* ^{KUR}*A-la-ši-ia* "Here Ešuwara, the great *sākinu* of Alašia" (on Cyprus) addresses the king of Ugarit.[14]

From the texts brought above we see that the "*sākinu* of the land of Ugarit" participated, along with the king, in the foreign politics of his country. We also see that the *sākinu* had the right to receive and accept letters even from rulers of foreign countries.[15] And from U.VII (RS.34.129) we see that the *sākinu* of Ugarit received orders from the Hittite king and that he was possibly acting as the regent at a time when the king was a child and could not rule alone.

We also learn from the texts that the *sākinu* of the neighboring states were, from the point of view of protocol on an equal level with the *sākinu* of Ugarit. We sometimes see the full title of the *săkinu* — thus, in PRU.III, 15.182 $^{(6)}$ *Uzzinu* appears a ^{LÚ}*sākin (ŠÁ.KÍN)mâti*^{ti}*(KUR*^{ti}*)*.[16] We may conclude that all the letters of this kind were written to or by the *sākinu* of the country (*sākin mâti*).

The administrative and legal texts show us some of the functions of the *sākinu*.

KTU.4.342 mentions "20 talents of [ ] to the *skn*" ($^{(1)}$ *skn ʿšrm kk*[*r*]) and KTU.4.361 "Flour of consuming supplies at the house of the *sākinu*" $^{(1)}$ *qmḥ.d.kly.b.bt.skn*.[17] So we see that the *sākinu* was connected with deliveries of food products and artifacts.

In the international sphere we must remember that Ugarit was a vassal of the Hittite great king and also of the Hittite rulers of Karchemiš.[18] And we see that in legal cases between Ugaritians and subjects of the Hittite zone of influence, Ugarit was represented by its *sākinu*.

Thus, according to PRU.IV.17.346, the *sākinu* of Ugarit and a certain Mašanda "raised a legal case" (*a-na di-ni iš-ni-qu*). It took place before Initešub, king of Karchemiš. The *sākinu* of Ugarit demanded, in the name

[14] Cf. the corrected reading of the text *Berger*, a, p. 217.

[15] Cf. also *Kümmel*, a, p. 160.

[16] Cf. also U.V, 40 and 51; and PRU.IV, 18.04, 4.

[17] Cf. also KTU.4.184 where some goods are mentioned in the house of then *skn*; KTU.4.592, 3.

[18] *Liverani*, a, *Klengel*, b, pp. 325-421; on the principles of the Hittite indirect rule, cf. *Alt*, b, pp. 99-106.

of his king, 4000 shekels of silver, which Mašanda refused to pay. Mašanda had to return the silver to the king of Ugarit, according to the verdict.[19]

Another case is seen in PRU.IV.17.111. The *sākinu* again represented the king of Ugarit, who lost the case and 140 shekels of silver which had to be handed over by the *sākinu* of Ugarit to a certain Zimrilim and Puritešub.

PRU.IV.19.66 + PRU.VI.35 (RS.27.051) before Initešub, the king of Karchemiš $^{(2)}$ ^{I}*Tul-pi-šeni it-ti* ^{LÚ}*sà-ki-in-ni* $^{(3)}$ *ša* ^{KUR}*Ú-ga-ri-it a-na* [*d*]*i-ni iš-ni-qu*. "Tulpišenni raised a legal case with the *sākinu* of Ugarit." The complaint is that "The *sākinu* seized my brother (of Tulpišeni) by force and put him to the prison and he died in the prison." The *sākinu* denies the accusation (lines 8-10).[20]

PRU.IV.17.129 is a legal case before Initešub. One of the parties is even the king Ammistamru II (ll. 2-3). But he was there represented by the *sākinu*, for the text says, "and the *sākinu* took 5000 shekels of silver."[21]

But we also see the intervention of the *sākinu* of Ugarit before the King of Karchemiš in political issues. In PRU.IV.17.341 the *sākinu* complains that "the sons of Siyannu cut our vineyards."[22]

The role of the *sākinu* in legal cases is strongly underlined in PRU IV.17.288, where the king of Ušnatu (cf. above) writes: "Not the king, but you, in the legal cases of the sons of (the village) Araniya have to decide."[23] The king of Ušnatu proposes to the *sākinu* "If my servants are thieves, they have to compensate the sons of Araniya" (lines 21-23). This text explains also the fact that the *sākinu* of Ugarit, not the king, dealt with cases involving foreigners in Ugarit.

Another letter, PRU.IV.17.393, written by a certain Epiqqu, pleads with the *sākinu*, "My lord, please free the sons of [Ušn]atu, for you seized the sons of Ušnatu."[24] The *sākinu* promised, also, to Madae, a foreigner (U.V.52 (RS.20.239)) to liquidate the case concerning his stolen cattle.[25]

---

[19] *Nougayrol*, PRU.IV, p. 175.

[20] Further, the text is broken and only the last four lines of the reverse show that the verdict of Initešub was that Tulpišeni and the *sākinu* of Ugarit had to denounce mutual demands and accusations.

[21] *ú* ^{LÚ}*sá-ki-in-nu 5 li-im šiqil kaspa il-te-qi-ma*. It ends with the mutual liquidation of claims.

[22] *ma-a mârē*$^{\text{MEŠ URU}}$*Si-ia-an-ni* ^{GIŠ}*karāni*^{MEŠ}*-ni it-tàk-sú-ni.*

[23] $^{(7)}$ *úl-ul šarru ú at-ta* $^{(8)}$ *dînūtē*^{MEŠ} *š*[*a*] *mârē*$^{\text{MEŠ URU}}$*A-ra-ni-ya* $^{(9)}$ *ip-ru-šum-mi* — *Heltzer*, a, p. 8, No. 13 and p. 63.

[24] $^{(7)}$ *bêli-ia ki-i-me-e mârē*$^{\text{MEŠ KUR URU}}$[*Uš-n*]*a-ti* $^{(8)}$ *tu-muš-šar ú* [*mâ*]*rē*$^{\text{MEŠ URU}}$*U*[*š-n*]*a-ti ti-iṣ-ṣa-bat*; similar legal cases in U.V, 51 (RS.20.158).

We see from these texts that judicial power, as well as police-functions were concentrated in the hands of the *sākinu* in Ugarit, especially where foreigners were concerned.

The same seems to be true about foreign commercial relations. According to PRU.IV.17.78 (cf. above) the foreign *sākinu*(?) Ebinae, concerning the voyage of his "son" (*mâru*) or "subject" pleads with the *sākinu* of Ugarit to assure that "nobody shall make any obstacle for him. The customer (*mākisu*) shall not impose on him custom-duties."[26] We see that here we are dealing with a standard formula of international commercial relations.

The unique document from Ugarit written in Hittite — U.V.RS.17.109[27] is a demand on behalf of the *sākinu* from the *mākisu* — customer Atalli — for 800 shekels of silver. The *sākinu* has his witness, a certain Pallariya, confirming his demands. Again we see that the "customer" was one of the subordinates of the *sākinu*.

The *sākinu* was also personally engaged in "indirect" foreign trade, which was formally an exchange of gifts with *sākinus* and other high officials in other countries.[28] These activities reached from Amurru and the neighboring countries to Asia Minor. Among the so-called gifts and counter-gifts were textiles, slaves, gold and silver objects. We even know that the *sākinu* of Ugarit received slave-boys and an iron dagger from Asia Minor.[29]

We learn from all the above-given material, that the *sākinu* was a wealthy and relatively independent official. We must add that he also certainly received something from the treasury of his kingdom. We also have some evidence about this from PRU.IV.17.129. The *sākinu* took (*il-te-qí-ma*) 5000 shekels of silver and did not return (*la-a it-ta-di-in-šu*) this sum. PRU.III.15.182 relates that the well-known Uzzinu bought land *i-na 95 šiqil*

---

25 A detailed analysis of the text, *Heltzer*, a, pp. 63-65 and 79.

26 (12) *ma-am me i-na pa-ni-šu* (13) *lu-ú la i-pár-r*[*i*-]*ik* (14) *LÚma-ki-su mi-ik-su-šu* (15) *lu-ú* [*l*]*a* [*i*]*-ma-ki-is*. Possibly similar issues in PRU.III, 15.33, where a Hittite Ḫismikušuḫ writes to the *sākinu* that a person is sent to him to clear a problem on the spot. And there we also read the same formula as given above (lines 12-15 of the text, PRU.IV, 17.288).

27 *Laroche*, d, p. 769 ff.; *Kümmel*, a, pp. 158-162; *Haase*, a, pp. 71-74.

28 *Zaccagnini*, d, esp. pp. 149-193.

29 *Zaccagnini*, d, p. 150; *Heltzer*, i, pp. 4-7; PRU.VI, 7B (RS.17.148); U.V, 40 (RS.20.200B), etc. According to PRU.VI, 8 (RS.17.239) the *sākinu* of Ugarit asks a certain Ta'azi to send him "seeds of *ḫuratu (zêr ḫurati)*; cf. also *Heltzer*, b, pp. 10, 27 and notes 134-135.

kaspe^{MEŠ} "for 95 shekels of silver." According to PRU.IV.17.251, 2 persons, Tagišarruma and Talpišarruma, sons of Ḫaštanuru (all Hittites), "sold to Uzzinu the *sākinu* of Ugarit Taršazida, for 40 (shekels) of silver."[30] It is thus clear that the *sākinu* could also be a slaveowner. This seems to be confirmed by the text KTU.4.102 (16) *[ṯ]lṯ.aṯṯ.adrt.w.ṯlṯ ġzr[m].w.ḫmš.nʿrt. b.bt.skn* "3 wellborn(?) wives and 3 slaves (males) and 4 (slave)-maidens in the house of the *sākinu*."[31] But this seems to be the private side of the life of the *sākinu*.

The official functions of the *sākinu* inside the country put him into a special position. He had the right to carry the royal seal, as we learn from PRU.III, 16.145 — a legal document where "Upsānu, the *sākinu*, who seals with the royal seal,"[32] appears as a witness.

People belonging to the *bnš mlk*, "royal dependents", were at the disposal of the *sākinu*; they were the *murʾu* of the *sākinu* (cf. below). There were, perhaps, other persons "at the disposal of the *sākinu*" (*bd skn*), as we see from KTU.4.635.[33]

We have already seen (Ch. III) that certain *ubdy*-fields were at the disposal of the *sākinu (bd skn)*.[34] In PRU.III, 16.190, king Niqmaddu II declares that he "gave the fields of Tibranima (*gt Tbrn*(?)) to Iribilu, his *sākinu*," And he adds, "(It is) a gift of Niqmaddu, the king, to Iribilu forever."[35] It is an important fact that this was a royal gift and not a field given into conditional landholding.

The tablet PRU.III, 15.70 relates that the *sākinu* took (bought) the house of the *marzeʾu (mrzḥ)* of the cultic association of (the god) Šatranu. This transaction was also sanctioned by the king.[36]

---

30 (5) *ip-šur-ru-nim* ^{I}*Tar-ša-zi-da* (6) *a-na Uz-zi-na* (7) ^{LÚ}*sākin* ^{KUR}*[U-ga]-ri-it* (8) *i-na 40 kas[pe*^{MEŠ}*]*.

31 *Heltzer*, p, pp. 86-88.

32 (24) *(sîbu)* ^{I}*Up-sa-nu* ^{LÚ}*sākinu* (25) *ša uš-te-ṣi* ^{nu_4}*kunuk* (26) *šarri*.

33 At least lines 8, 11, 12, 15, 37 and 75. The other persons are at the disposal of the king *(bd.mlk)* or the queen (*bd mlkt*); cf. also the letter KTU.2.17 where the writer speaks to "his lord, the *skn* (8) *bʿly.skn* and semi-dependent(?) *ḫb/pṯ* = *ḫupšu*-people are considered.

34 Cf. also KTU.4.357, (30) *ṯn.šdm.bd.skn* "Two fields at the disposal of the *skn*."

35 (10) *ni-id-nu* ^{I}*Niqma-*^{il}*Addu šarri* (11) *a-na* ^{I}*I-ri-bi-li a-na da-ri-ti*.

36 On *marzeʾi* — *mrzḥ* — cf. *Fenton*, a, pp. 71-75; *Greenfield*, b, pp. 451-455; *Eissfeldt*, b, pp. 187-195; *Eissfeldt*, c, pp. 171-176.

Texts KTU.4.132, 4-5 and KTU.4.165 tell about various quantities of precious garments, partly of Tyrian production (*ktn.d.Ṣr*) delivered to the *sākinu*.[37]

In PRU.III.16.267,[38] we see another interesting feature. King Ammistamru II frees one of his slave-maids from slavery. "If this Šaia dies, so, all her property, her house, fields, everything that she possesses is for Šaittenu, the *sākinu*, her husband" (13) (*a-na* *ᴵŠa-it-te-na* (14) *ᴸᵁsākini mu-ti-ša*). This could be a case where the king tried to bind through the court the *sākinu* giving him his freed slave-girl for a wife, with a rich dowry, and making the *sākinu* the heir to her possessions.

It is not excluded that the *sākinu* sometimes had cultic functions. The text KTU.6.14, incribed on a stela (1) *pgr.d.š'ly* (2) *'zn.l.Dgn b'lh* [*š w a*]*lp.b.mḫrt* "Stela, which Uzzinu erected to (the god) Dagan, his Lord [(1) sheep and o]x in the morning." As *E. Lipinski* supposes, it is the *sākinu* Uzzinu, known from other texts.[39] On behalf of the *sākinu* a cultic object was erected.

After reviewing all the main functions and occupations of the *sākinu* of the kingdom of Ugarit, and possibly in the neighboring small countries during the same period, we must accept the opinions of *Alt*[40] and *Boyer*[41] who regard the *sākinu* as the highest official of the country, the "vizier". Therefore, we cannot go along with *Jankowska*[42] who interprets *sākin mâti* as "appointée of the country." But none of this clarifies the social stratum from which the *sākinu* came. Only one text, U.V.38 (RS.20.16), written by the *sākinu* of Kinza (Qadeš), says the following (8) *...a-na pa-ni* (9) *amêlē* (*LÚ.MEŠ*) *rabūtē*(*GAL.MEŠ*) *aḫḫē*(*ŠEŠ.MEŠ*)*-ia a-kán-na* (10) *aq-te-bi* "In the presence of the great men, my brothers, so I spoke."[43] Possibly, this means that the *sākinu* had, in important matters, to consult "his brothers," i.e. persons who were more or less equal to him in rank and that they were

---

[37] *pḫm* "purple." *Heltzer*, b, p. 26, No. 31 and note 119.

[38] More about this text, *Heltzer*, j, p. 89 ff.

[39] *Lipinski*, b, p. 201, note 69; cf. also U.V, 39 (RS.20.172) where the king of Kinza (Qadeš) writes to the king of Ugarit about certain offerings he has to make in Ugarit. For this purpose he sends his *sākinu* Bidiilu.

[40] *Alt*, c, pp. 1-11.

[41] *Boyer*, b, p. 165.

[42] *Jankowska*, a, p. 262, 280 ff.

[43] Cf. also (38) *ù a-na-ku a-kán-na a-na aḫḫe*(*ŠEŠ.MEŠ*)*-ia* (39) *aq-te-bi*.

designated as *rabû* "great (men)". As we have already seen (Ch. VII), the *sākinu* and the *rab šangû* "chief priest" were "brothers". It also seems that the letter U.V.54 (RS.20.23), which was written by Rap'anu, a very high courtier and scribe (cf. below), to the *sākinu* addresses him as an equal, but does not use the expression "brother." From here we get the clear impression that the *sākinu* belonged to the highest social group in the kingdom. At the same time, having enough information about the numbers of royal family, royal princes, etc. (cf. Ch. X), we cannot connect the *sākinu* with the royal family. On the other and, we also have no information telling us a particular person was promoted to *sākinu*. The answer to this question must wait until new data becomes available.[44]

B. But the *sākin mâti* "*sākinu* of the country" was not the only official with the title *sākinu*. There was also the title *skn bt mlk* "*skn* of the house of the king (i.e. the palace)", as well as *sākin bît šarrati* "*Sākinu* of the queen (mother)".[45] It is not always possible to recognize where the *sākin mâti* or *skn bt mlk* are mentioned, especially when after the word *sākinu/skn* no additional explanation is given. Obviously, the functions of *skn bt mlk* exceeded those of managing the palace personnel and we will bring here the information concerning them.

In the fragment KTU.4.63 (4) *B'lṣdq* (5) *skn.bt* (6) *mlk.ṯġr* (7) *mlk*... "*B'lṣdq*, *skn* of the royal palace, gatekeeper of the king...," we see that the first office was preferable or higher than the second one.[46] U.V.161 (RS.17.325) is a land-transaction. The queen of Ugarit, Šarrelli (Hurrian equivalent of her Ugaritic name Aḫatmilku)[47] purchases 8 *ikû* of field-land. Among the witnesses appears (21) ...*[I]Ma-te-nu sākin* (ŠÁ.KÍN) *bît šarrati*. "Matenu, the *sākinu* of the palace of the queen."[48] A certain "Gilben,

---

[44] Cf. also *Henshaw*, a, I, pp. 517-525; II.451-483 with a comprehensive bibliography mostly concerning the I millennium B.C.E.

[45] Cf. Ch. X and *Donner*, a, p. 105-145.

[46] The text PRU.III, 15.89, where in line 15 a certain *sākin bîti* is mentioned. We are not sure if the text speaks about a *sākinu* in the royal service or if he is the majordomo of a large private household; cf. also PRU.III, 16.149; 16.197; *Liverani*, a, pp. 99-100 and 139; *Klengel*, b, II, pp. 373, 378, 386-387, 416.

[47] *Nougayrol*, U.V, pp. 261-262.

[48] Cf. the similar land-transaction texts of the queen U.V, 159 (RS.17.80) where (18) [*sîbu* *[I]Ma-t*]*e-nu* *[LÚ]a-ba-ra-ku ša šarrati* "[witness Mat]enu, the *abarakku* (majordomo) of the queen", appears. We learn from here the identity of the terms *sākin*

sākinu (MAŠKIM), of the palace of the queen (*bît šarrati*) appears also in RS.8.208.[49] He frees his slave-girl Eliava. So we see that this official could also have his own slaves. It seems to us that this official was the major-domo, i.e. the manager of the royal economy as a whole and the economy of the queen-mother, in particular. Unfortunately, the chancellory of this *sākinu* is not yet at our disposal.[50] It is only clear that he was a royal official.

C. We also know about the *skn qrt/sākin âli*, the *sākinu* of the town/village in the kingdom of Ugarit.[51]

In KTU.4.288, (1) *spr blblm* — "List of *blblm*".[52] Lines 2-5 mention *skn Uškn, skn Šbn, skn Ubr' skn Ḫrṣb'*, i.e. the *sākinu* of four well-known villages of the kingdom. Lines 8-10 mention a certain number of *kt*[*t*] "chitons," delivered to them. This may prove that they were royal officials. KTU.4.160 is also a "list" (1) *spr*[ ]). In l. 6 we read *skn Ulm* "the *skn* of (the village) *Ulm*." And as we have seen from KTU.4.609 (Ch. I), dealing with distribution of rations to royal dependents" (*bnš mlk*), in the lines 10-11 *2 skn qrt* are listed.

From U.V.9 (RS.17.61) we learn about a certain Iribilu, *sākinu* (MAŠKIM) of the village Riqdi,[53] who acts as a representative of the authorities, depriving two *nayyālu*-women of their lands. We also learn from the texts about the *sākinu* Ukullilanu, of the village Miḫi (PRU.III.16.244), appearing as a witness and Entašalu, the *sākinu* of Bêru (*Bir*). So, from all the available sources, we know of only 8 *sākinu* from certain villages. The question is whether these *sākinu* were only from those villages which were designated in the texts, or were these villages the central settlements of

---

bîti = *abarakku*; cf. AHW, p. 3b "Haus-Palastverwalter" and 2), 3); CAD, A, I, pp. 32-35 esp. 3c) 1′ MA "chief steward for the royal estate"; 2′ of other estates; d) 2′b′ — of the queen (or queen-mother) (neo-Assyrian).

[49] *Thureau-Dangin*, a, p. 248 and 253-255; cf. Ch. IV *namû*.

[50] Possibly the counterpart of *skn bt mlk* in Nuzi-Arrapḫa was *sākin bîti* — cf. *Jankowska*, a, p. 235.

[51] Cf. *Heltzer*, a, pp. 82-83, but we must now alter our previous opinion.

[52] Meaning unclear; WUS, p. 49 No. 518; UT, p. 372, ZWL, I, BO, 23, 1966, possibly "people (?)", delivering grain tax (??)".

[53] Full treatment of this text *Heltzer*, a, pp. 55-56.

certain districts.[54] Only further publications of texts will help solve this question.

But it is now possible to solve another question, that of the relationship of the *skn/sākinu* of the village *âlu/qrt* to the *ḫazannu* (*ḫazanu âli*), known from the texts of Ugarit and otherwise.[55] Was he identical with the *skn/sākinu* of the village, or was he a special representative of the local self-governement. *Ḫazannu* is usually translated as "mayor", "Bürgermeister".[56] But in Alalaḫ in the XVth century B.C.E. the *ḫazannu* belonged to the lower groups of royal servicemen.[57] In the El-Amarana texts the word *ḫazannu* is regarded as a "governor" imposed by the Egyptians.[58] *H. Otten* regards also *ḫazannu* in the Hittite Empire as the "mayor".[59] The exhaustive investigation of *Daddi-Pecchioli*, dealing with all known Hittite texts, shows us that the *ḫazannu* was a high royal official in the capital, Ḫattusa and other Hittite towns.[60] We also see in Ugarit that the *ḫazannu âli* acted as a royal official and we have no data that he was a representative of an elected or traditional body. So we are sure that he was an official. In this context we bring a text from Nuzi, HSS, 15, 1, widely treated by *Jankowska*[61] and *Zaccagnini*.[62] The text contains orders and instructions of the king to the *ḫazannu* of the town (URU) Tašuḫewe. In lines 8-10, we read that, "Inside the territory of his town no robberies must be committed, nor must be (encountered) enemies who kill or plunder." But, if such events do occur, the responsibility rests with the *ḫazannu*,[63] as it does if somebody flees from the country. We see clearly, then, that the *ḫazannu* was a royal official and

---

54 *Aistleitner*, b, p. 34.

55 *Heltzer*, a, pp. 80-82; cf. also Ch. VII, *maryannu* and *mūdū* below.

56 CAD, Ḫ, pp. 163-165; AHW, p. 338b-339a.

57 *Dietrich-Loretz*, k, pp. 88-89.

58 *Albright-Moran*, e, pp. 164-165; *Klengel*, b, II, p. 434; *Rainey*, k, p. 64 "chief magistrate of a town, mayor of a city": is unacceptable, contrary to ^{LÚ}MAŠKIM-*ḫazanika* (your *ḫazannu*) shows that *ḫazannu* was identical to the *sākinu*-official.

59 *Otten*, a, pp. 91-95.

60 *Daddi-Pecchioli*, a, pp. 93-136, esp. 130-134.

61 *Jankowska*, a, pp. 273-276.

62 *Zaccagnini*, b, pp. 17-20. We will follow the reading and interpretation of *Zaccagnini*.

63 Line 19 and 23-24 — we find twice *ù* ^{LÚ}*ḫa-za-an-nu pè-ḫa-as-sú na-ši* "and the *ḫazannu* will bear the responsibility."

possibly we can find some support for our opinion about the *ḫazannu* in Ugarit.

We have clearly seen that the term *skn/sākinu* must be distinguished in Ugarit. We see here the *sākinu* of the whole country, the "vizier," the royal majordomo (*skn bt mlk*) and the *skn qrt (ḫazannu âli)*, the royal official exercising statepower in one or several villages. The question of the *sākinu* must still await comprehensive investigation in the whole west-semitic area.[64]

As was pointed out above, the *mākisu* "customer" was dependent on the *sākinu* and received instructions from him. The Ugaritic word for designating this term is unknown or unrecognized so far. We know about the *mākisu* as a subject of the *sākin mâti* from the texts PRU.IV, 17.78; PRU.III, 15.33; PRU.IV, 17.75; 17.314; 17.139; 17.232[65] and the Hittite tablet.[66] So, the *mākisu* belonged to the staff of the *sākinu*.

§2. The *ašīru* = Ug. *ʿšr(m)*

First of all, we have to emphasize the fact that the *ʿšrm-ašīru* are by no means identical with the Akk. *asīru* — "prisoners," known from a great number of Old-Babylonian texts.[67]

We see in Ugarit the *ʿšrm* Akk. ^{LÚMEŠ}*a-ši-ru-ma* = *rb ʿšrt* "overseers of ten (man-teams)."[68]

---

[64] Cf. the *skn/sākinu* in the west-Semitic area: a) *skn*, following the mention of the king (*mlk*) in the Aḥiram inscription from the Xth century B.C.E. from Byblos, KAI, No. 2, 2; b) (8) *Ṣry* (9) *bn ʾšmnšlm* (10) *skn* «*Ṣry*, son of *ʾšmnšlm* the *skn*," from the ostraca from Sidon from the VIth century B.C.E. (*Vanel*, a, pp. 61-67; *Lipinski*, b, p. 207); c) *ʾdnlrm skn* from Hamath in Syria, IXth century B.C.E. — KAI, II, p. 201; d) CIS, I, 5 = KAI, 31 *skn Qrt-ḥdšt ʿbd Ḥrm mlk ṣdnm* "*skn* of *Qrthdšt* (on Cyprus) servant of Hiram, the king of the Sidonains," VIIIth cent. B.C.E. (*Masson-Sznycer*, a, p. 38); (3) *ʾšmnʾdn bn (son of) ʾšmnʾdn skn* [placename?] (*Masson-Sznycer*, a, pp. 69-70; *van den Branden*, a, p. 98; *Guzzo-Amadasi*, Kition, F.6, Pl. 38, 3); f) Hebr. *sōkēn*, Jes. 22, 15; *Yeivin*, e, pp. 54-575 and *śar hāʿīr* "city-governor" *Avigad*, a, pp. 178-179 (= *skn qrt*) and *Barkay*, c, pp. 69-71.

[65] CAD, M. I pp. 129-130; AHW, p. 589; *de Jong Ellis*, a, p. 230, note 75.

[66] *Kümmel*, a, p. 161; *Haase*, a, p. 71; concerning the Hittite officials, connected with the *sākinu* of Ugarit, cf. *Pecchioli-Daddi*, b, pp. 169-191; *Imparati*, b, pp. 154-159, *Goetze*, d, pp. 1-24.

[67] *Leemans*, a, pp. 56-57; *Rainey*, c, pp. 296-301; *Loretz*, d, pp. 121-160.

[68] *ʿšr* = "10"; cf. CAD, A, II, p. 440a, "supervisor, helper" and p. 440b *aširīma*;

We meet them in a large number of texts from Ugarit.[69] As with the other *bnš mlk*, these texts mention individuals, listed by name, and sometimes their number is given or a group is mentioned. Among the texts is PRU.VI.72, where at least 40 persons are mentioned.[70]

We also know (cf. Ch. VI) that the *ʿšrm* sent, together with other professional groups of *bnš mlk* and the villagers of Ugarit, very small numbers of archers to the guard.

As we saw above, the *ʿšrm/ašīru* received lands for their services, given into conditional holding — *pilku/ubdy* (Ch. III). The *ʿšrm/ašīruma* received, along with the other professional groups, deliveries of silver and products (cf. Ch. III) and these were called *ḥpr* "rations" to the *bnš mlk*.

We also see the hereditary character of the members of professional group, i.e. that the sons of an *ašīru* could become *ašīru* in the royal service during the lifetime of their father. The best example of this is found in PRU, III, 16.257, III B, (according to this text, the *ašīru* receive jars of oil (*karpat šamnu*) (1) *a-ši-ru-ma* (6) *ᴵAbdi-ilu mâr* (son of) *E-ri-ia-na* (7) *ᴵMa-aš-šu-ú-mâr* MIN.MIN ("the same"), (8) *Ša-mu-ma-nu mâr E-ri-ia-na* (9) *ᴵTup-pi-ia-nu mâr ᴵE-ri-ia-na*. So we see here four sons of the same father who became *ašīru* during the lifetime of their father, or after his death. According to PRU.III.16.247, Arsuwanu and his sons have to perform the *ašīru*-service. According to PRU.III.15.127, king Ammistamru II alienates (*ú-na-kir-šu*) Abdiḫagab and his sons from the *ašīru*-service and made them "to the *mūdū* of the king" (*i-na* ^{LÚMEŠ}*mu-de*$_4$ *šarri*).

---

we cannot agree with *E. Lipinski* (in *Heltzer*, c, note 171) — Hebr. *ʿašīrīm* "landholders of lower rank" than the ^{LÚMEŠ}*mūdū šarra(ti)*"; cf. Nuzi *rab ešri* = *emantuḫlu* — *Cassin*, a, pp. 234-235; *Kenwood*, a, p. 60, 68-69, 71-75 and esp. 99-109; but contrary to Nuzi, in Ugarit it is not a military rank; *Nougayrol*, PRU.VI, p. 150, note 2 accepts our opinion. (*Heltzer*, C, p. 193 notes 20-22) "overseer of ten, 'dizenier'." *Nougayrol*, PRU.VI, 72 (RS.19.65) instead of U.MEŠ-*(te)* (lines 2, 5, 7, 9, 11, 13, 15, 17, 19) as *i-na ašīrū-te*.

[69] KTU.4.68, 66; 4.99, 2; 4.103, 30 ff.; 4.125, 3; 4.392, 4; 4.415, 3; 4.412, III, 15-25; 4.609, 2, 5, 7, 8; 4.714; 4.745, 2; PRU.III.16.257, III, 1 and 30 (*muškēnūtu* ^{LÚMEŠ}*a-ši-ru-ma*); 15.137, 9; 15.242, 12; PRU.VI, 93, 4 (RS.17.131); 115, 4 (RS.17.64); 131, 3 (19.35A); 72 (RS.19.65).

[70] KTU.4.412 — originally 9 persons were mentioned by their names, but only 2 of them are legible — *bn ʿbdmlk* and *P*[ ]. At the same time in KTU.4.714 among 5 names we meet (6) *bn ʿbdmlk* and *bn.Pndr* and they are designated as *rb.ʿšrt*. This may confirm once more the identity of *ʿšrm/rbʿšrt*.

Besides the numerous mentions of the *pilku/ubdy* fields in the hands of the *ašīru*, we also know that they had at their disposal dependents, designated in PRU.III.16.257.III, 30-36 as the *muškênūtu* LÚMEŠ*a-ši-ri-ma* "the *muškēnu* of the *ašīru*." But, like dependents of the other professional groups of the *bnš mlk*, these also received deliveries from the royal storehouses individually, and not via the *ašīru*-people.

We know from the text KTU.4.392, a certain *bt ʿšrm* "house of the *ašīru*", but what its functions were we do not know.

We see that in reality the *ašīru/ʿšrm/rbʿšrt* were also not on the lowest level of the royal administration and, most likely, they were the overseers of the royal works.

§3. THE *mur'u*-MEN

We know the following terms: a) *mrum* — Akk. *mur-'u* (*mur-'u šarri*); b) *mru skn* Akk. *mur-'u sākini;* c) *mru Ibrn* Akk. *mur-'u Ibirana, mur-'u ušriyanni* — Ug. *uṯryn*).[71] According to their etymology and functions, the *mur'u* of the king, the *sākinu* and Ibirana, i.e. the prince Ibirana, the son of Ammistamru II, who later became the king Ibirana, or *mru uṯryn (ušriyanni)* "the heir of the throne",[72] we see that they were something like liaison-men or officers of the king, the *sākinu* and the heir to the throne.

We know about them from numerous documents.[73] From these documents we see that sometimes three separate kinds of *mur'u* appear in one

---

[71] The etymology of *mru(m)* comes from the west-semitic (attested in Aramaic and Ammonite) root *mr'* (*Heltzer*, I, in print); cf. *Noel-Giron*, a, pp. 63-65; *Galling*, a, p. 181, No. 61a; *Hammond*, a, p. 41. The root *mr'* "to command, to lead" appears also in Ugaritic literary texts (*Ullendorf*, a, p. *23); CAD, M II, p. 228b (an official).

[72] *Liverani*, a, pp. 74 and 125; *Heltzer*, f, pp. 3-8; *ušriyannu* "heir", UT, p. 369, No. 426 "crown prince"; AHW, p. 1442, a "Kronprinz (?)".

[73] KTU.4.36, 3 — *mru skn;* 4.47 (2) *mru skn*; (3) *mru Ibrn*; 4.69, III, (11-13) *mrum*, V, (6-16) *mru skn*; (17-26) *mru Ibrn*; 4.68, (63) *mru skn*, (64) *mru Ibrn*; (69) *mrum*; 4.92 — *mru skn*; 4.99, (12) *mru Ibrn* (13) *mru skn*; 4.103, (20-29) *mrim*; (37-38) *mri Ibrn*; 4.105, (1) *mru Ib[rn]*; 4.126, (2) *mrum*; (23) *mru skn* (24) *mru Ibrn*; 4.137, (7) *mrum*; 4.163, (3) *mrum*; 4.173, (6) *mrum*; 4.174, (3) *mrum*; 4.179, (6) *mrum*; 4.207, (4) *mrum*; 4.212, (2) *mri* (pl.st.cstr.); 4.332, (9) *mru*; 4.416, (2) *mrum*; 4.610, (58) *mrum* Rev. 44. *mr[u I]brn* (45) *mru skn*; 4.745, (1) *mrum*; PRU, III, 16.348, (5) LÚMEŠ*mur-'i* I*I-bi-ra-na*; 11.839, (21-22) LÚ*mur-'ú*; 16.257, IV, (21-32) LÚMEŠ*mur-'u uš-r[i-ya-]ni*; PRU.VI, 93 (RS.17.131) (2) L[Ú*mu]r-ú šarri*; (9) LÚ*mur-'ú* LÚ*sà-ki-ni*; (10) LÚ*mur-'ú* I*I-bi-ra-na*; PRU, III, 16.139 (14) LÚMEŠ*mur-'ú* LÚ*sākini (MAŠKIM); PRU, VI, 116 (RS.17.64)*, (5) LÚ*mur-ú-ma*; 131 (RS.19.35A) (5) LÚ.MEŠ*mur-ú-ma*; 136 (RS.17.240) (14) LÚ*mur-ú-[ma]*.

text, i.e. that these were not identical groups. In all the texts the *mrum* usually appear as individuals or as particular groups. As seen already from the text KTU.4.137; 4.163; 4.173; 4.174 and 4.179, the general number of *mrum* in Ugarit might have been approximately 120 (Ch. VI, §2). This does not include the *mru skn* and *mru Ibrn*. We also know that the *mru(m)* had at their disposal dependent persons — *ḫsnm* (Ch. VI, §2). We might also suppose that the same services which the *mrum* gave to the king, the *mru skn* and *mru Ibrn* gave respectively to the *sākinu* and heir to the throne.

We know about the guard-service of the *mrum* of all kind (Ch. VI, §§1 and 2). According to KTU.4.610, at least the *mru skn* and *mru Ibrn* participated in paying tribute to the Hittites.[74] We also know from PRU.VI.116 (cf. Ch. IV) that the *mrum* had to pay for their pasturing rights to the king.

As seen above (Ch. III), the *mur'u* of all kinds had their *ubdy*-fields and performed their *pilku* service. They received, according to a large number of texts (Ch. III) silver and natural deliveries for their professional services. Sometimes they received even non-military equipment (KTU.4.92, ⁽¹⁾ *npṣm* ⁽²⁾ *bd.mri* ⁽³⁾ *skn.* ⁽⁴⁾ *ʿšrm* ⁽⁵⁾ *ḫmš* ⁽⁶⁾ *kbd* "equipment[75] to the *mru skn* — 25 at all").[76].

We may suppose that the *mrum* lived in various villages of the kingdom, but we know only about *Qrt* (KTU.4.332, 5) and Šammeqa (*Ṯmqy*) — PRU.III.16.139.

In PRU.III.16.139 and 16.348, the *mur'u* is mentioned together "with his sons" (*qadu mârē^{MEŠ}-šu*) and from KTU.4.69.III where *mrum* are mentioned by name we see among them ⁽¹⁷⁾ *bn.Pity* — 6 (shekels of silver) ⁽¹⁷⁾ *w.nḥlh* — 6 "and his heir — 6". So we see that a son of a *mur'u* could become a *mur'u* also during the lifetime of his father.[77]

We also see, according to PRU.III.16.348, Ammistamru II alienated (*unakiršu*) a *mur'u Ibirana* from his status and "established him to the *mūdū* of the queen" (⁽⁶⁾ *iš-ku-un-šu i-na mu-de$_6$-šarrati^{ti}*) (*mūdū* cf. below). Naturally, certain changes of status occurred also regarding redistribution of the *ubdy*-

---

74 *Heltzer*, a, pp. 41-43; cf. also KTU.4.745, where a certain payment (?) had to be made by professional groups including *mrum*.

75 Cf. Ch. IV *nqdm* and Excursus I.

76 Cf. also KTU, 4.212 ⁽¹⁾*apl* (= *alp*) *kspm* ⁽²⁾ *l.mri* ⁽³⁾ *ṯmn.kbd* ⁽⁴⁾ *arbʿm* "1048 in all (shekels) of silver to the *mrum*."

77 In PRU.III, 16.257, IV, 29-30 we see also two sons of the same person.

fields (KTU.4.103, 32-33).[78] Concerning their movable property, we know that the *mur'u*-people possessed cattle, for according to PRU.VI.116 they had to pay for their pasture-rights (cf. Ch. IV *nqdm*).

From the text PRU.16.348, where Yanḫamu is transferred by the king from being the *mur'u* of Ibirana to the being the *mūdū* of the queen (*šarrati*), we see that as a *mūdū* he must not (9) *i-na eqli šarri ul e-r*[*u-ub*] (10) LÚ*ḫa-a*[*z-z*]*a-na a-na bîti-šu ul* [*errub*] (11) *šikar-*MEŠ*-šu*[ ] *bîti-šu*[ ] (12) *ul i-n*[*a-ad-din(?)*] (13) *a-na ši*[*pri ekllim/šarri(?)*] (14) *ul i-*[*la-ak*] "The field of the king he shall not enter (i.e. not go to the royal economy for working there), the *ḫazannu* shall not [enter] his house, his beer [ ] (he shall not pay?), to the royal wor[k he must not [go]". The fact that the *mūdū* is freed from these things shows that the *mur'u* was subject to various royal works, including some in the royal economy, as well as being subject to the control or interference of the *ḫazannu* (possibly *ḫazannu âli*). He also had to pay various taxes.

So we can see that all three kinds of *mur-'u* belonged, in the same degree as the other professional groups, to the system of *bnš mlk*. We also learn some of the things they were engaged in but, except for the fact that they belonged to the king, sakinu or heir to the throne, their principal task is unclear.

§4. *Sukallu*

This term is known in Ugarit only from the Akkadian texts. Since the term has various meanings in various areas and periods,[79] we can only briefly describe the known data from Ugarit concerning it.

We see the *sukallu* appearing as witnesses in PRU.IV, 17.137; PRU.III, 15.136; 8.207; 16.178, 15′ — but in the last case, as well as in PRU.III, 8.098 and PRU.III, 15.113; PRU.VI.43 (RS.17.77), 45 (RS.18.26), the *sukallu* is also a "scribe" LÚ*tupšarrum*. Thus, the *sukallu* had a second

---

[78] Cf. also PRU.III, 16.139; KTU, 4.416, 2 — distribution of fields to the *mrum*.

[79] AHW, p. 1055, *sukallu* = *šukallu* and also pp. 1263b-1264a = "Minister, Wesir" (7) Ug. "ein Beamter mittleren Ranges," Assyria — *Garelli*, c, p. 448; *sukallu* in the texts from Ugarit PRU.III, 11.732; PRU.IV, 17.227, 34-35; 17.382, 47 — belong definitely to the Hittite kingdom; in Ugaritic *skl* only PRU.IV, 11.772, 37′ — a Hittite official.

profession. Such a feature is not unique in Ugarit, for in the fragmentary text PRU.III, 16.168, we read [PN] ^{LÚ}*sukallu* ^{LÚ}*akil šangi*... "[PN] *sukallu* overseer (elder) of the priests."

Additionally, we see that the witness Karranu (PRU.IV, 17.137 $^{(6')}$ *šîbu* ^{I}*Kar-ra-nu*) was the "*sukkal* of the king of Ugarit" (^{LÚ}*sukkal šàr* ^{URU}*Ú-ga-ri-it*), as well as in PRU.IV, 18.20, a certain Iltaḫmu appears as the "*sukkallu* of the king." (*sukkal šar*[*ri*]).[80] From all of the above we learn little, except that the *sukallu* was mostly connected with the scribe. Therefore, we will not deal with him any further.

§5. The Scribe

In Ugaritic there is the usual West-Semitic word *spr* and Akk. *tupšarru* (DUB.SAR). The matter of the scribe was exhaustively dealt with by *Rainey*, taking into account the publications up to 1967.[81] It seems that the scribes who wrote the literary tablets in Akkadian and Ugaritic were not always identical with the scribes of the royal office. We know that the scribe *Ilmlk*, at least, was an apprentice (*lmd*) of the *rb khnm* (cf. Ch. IV *nqdm* and Ch. VII), and that he even had the title *ṯ'y* "noble".[82] But, at the same time, Rap'anu was a royal scribe in a very high position, who had close connections with the *sākinu* (cf. above) and he kept in his home copies of very important political and legal documents (U.V.).

We also know a *tupšarru emqu* "specialist scribe"[83] — possibly identical to *rb sprm* (KTU.1.75.10).[84] We know well that the legal formulae in all the documents were written in Akkadian or in a literal Ugaritic translation.[85] The scribe, of course, had to perform the public function of the "notary", and he was always connected with the royal authorities.

---

[80] Cf. *Heltzer*, J, pp. 89-93, and also PRU.IV, 18.100, 5'; PRU.VI, 132 (RS.19.85).

[81] *Rainey*, g.

[82] *Rainey*, g, pp. 2-3; *Hurwitz*, a.

[83] *Rainey*, g, pp. 3-4, note 13. At the same time we cannot follow the reading of the name UTU.LUGAL as Šamaš-šarru. He was an Ugaritian and we must read it Šapši-milku.

[84] *Rainey*, g, p. 4; note 17; cf. also Kition, *rb sprm* — A, 30, 2-3 and C.1.A14.

[85] *Rainey*, g, pp. 8-11.

As *Rainey* pointed out, the scribes Ḫuṣanu and his son Yaṣiranu, were connected with the royal service.[86] So perhaps they were included in the system of *bnš mlk*.

It is important to note that we do not find scribes in the lists of distributions, nor in those of military service. Possibly, the scribes performed only the important scribal service as *bnš mlk*. Almost from the time of the king Niqmaddu II until Niqmaddu III or ʿAmmurapi (i.e. from ca 1360-1200 B.C.E.), we know of at least 35 scribes, including those whom we know engaged only in literary texts.[87] We find now that the scribal art was

---

[86] *Rainey*, g, p. 19.

[87] The names of the scribes are taken from the legal and administrative texts:

Abdianti	PRU.III, 16.182, 21 possibly PRU.VI, 52.
Abdiḫamanu	PRU.III, 16.348, Rev. 6′ — time of Ammistamru II.
Abdiyaraḫ	U.V, 159.19 — queen Šarelli, possibly identical to Arad-Sin, *Thureau-Dangin*, a, 8.213, 35.
Abimalku	PRU.VI, 50, 27.
Anatešub	U.V, 161, son of ^{I}*Ir-su-ya-nu*.
Burqanu (Brqn)	KTU.3.89; PRU.IV, 17,256, 27; *Thureau-Dangin*, a, 8.145.
Bṣmn (spr)	KTU.4.183, 29.
Eḫlitešub	PRU.VI, 45, 35 — Niqmaddu III.
Ḫuṣanu	PRU.III, 15.138, 25; 16.206, 10; 16.239, 4; 16.283, 8; 16.153 — Niqmepa, Ammistamru II and Arḫalbu (father of Iaṣiranu).
Ilišapaš	U.V, 7, 12.
Iltaḫmu	PUR.III, 16.353, 34; 13.140.26; PRU.IV, 17.299, V.2′; PRU.VI, 32, v. 8′; 37, v. 5′; 38, 21′; 39, 17′; 41, 2′ — Ammistamru II and Ibiranu.
Ilumilku	U.V, 9.21; 16, 15′ *Thureau-Dangin*, c.
Iluramu	PRU.VI.20 — Ammistamru II.
Karranu	PRU.III, 15.119, 20′; 16.284, 20′; 16.207, 18 — Niqmepa
Munaḫimu	(son of Yarimmu) PRU.III, 15.145, 22; 15.147, 20′; 15.196, 8′; 16.86, v. 4′; 16.243, 24-25; 16.255D, v. 14′; 16.386, v. 19; 16.255H; PRU.VI, 40, 31; U.V, 5, 29; 6, 9 and 31 — Ammistamru II
Naʿamrašap	PRU.III, 15.143, 14; 15.168, 20; 13.131, 5′; PRU.IV, 18.02, 17; 18.20, v. 16; PRU.VI, 42, 8′; 43, 13′; 44, 4′; U.V, 167, IV, 5′; — son of Abaya, — Ammistamru II, Ibiranu, Niqmaddu III.
Naḫešišalmu	PRU.VI, 18, 2.
^{I}Nir-^{il}Nabū	PRU.VI, 18, 1 — possibly not from Ugarit.
Numenu	PRU.IV, 17.251, 23.
Rapʾanu	U.V, 88, 19′.

taught and cultivated in Ugarit,[88] and that the scribe Rap'anu even possessed his own "library"[89] of tablets and sometimes he copied for himself official texts and international letters. We find in his archive 2 different texts on one tablet.[90] From the literary and non-legal or economic texts we know that certain scribes named themselves "disciples" (^{LÚ}A.BA.KAB.ZU.ZU) of other scribes,[91] as is the case with the scribe Ilumilku, the disciple of *Atn.Prln*, the "high (chief) priest" (*rb khnm*).

We see in Ugarit multilingual glossaries in which we find Hurrite, Hittite, Egyptian and Cypro-Minoan texts. A number of Akkadian texts were translated into Ugaritic and from Ugaritic into Akkadian. Thus there had to be translators (interpreters) among the scribes. In fact, PRU.IV, 17.251, 23 mentions a scribe who was a *tar-gu-um-ia-nu* "interpreter."[92]

As seen above, a certain number of scribes were also *sukallu*.

There is a lack of much documentary evidence about the involvement of the scribes with the *bnš mlk* system in Ugarit. Therefore, all data shedding

---

Šapaš-milku	PRU.III, 16.114, 14; 16.203, 26; 16.133, 12; 16.156, 22; 16.283, 17; 16.142, 16; 15, V, 18; 16.254, D, 18; 16.143, 30; 16.157, 29; 16.250, 25; 15.88, 12; 16.147, 19; 16.208, 5; 16.254, v.13; 16.207, 16; 16.191, 1, 7′; Pt.383G; PRU.VI, 26, v.3; Niqmaddu II, Arḫalbu, Niqmepa.
Šunailu	(possibly from Ura) — PRU.IV, 17.319, 24.
Tamartenu	PRU, VI, 51, 13′.
Yadidu	PRU.III, 16.204, v.15; 15.136, 22; 16.138, 39; 16.261, 29; PRU.VI, 31, 27 — Ammistamru II.
Yadlinu	PRU.VI, 65, Tr. 4.
Yarimmu	PRU.III, 16.156, 21; 16.145, 22; 15.147, 20′-21′; 15.190, v.4′-5′; 16.243, 24-25; 16.384, 22; 16.386, 19′; 16.253H father of Munaḫimu — Ammistamru II.
Yaṣiranu	(son of Ḫuṣanu) PRU.III, 16.206; 16.239; 16.153, 6; 16.205, 26; 16.282, 16; 16.193 — Ammistamru II.
Yaširu	PRU.III, 15.118, 16 — Ammistamru II.
Yašmu	U.V, 81, 45. Cf. also PRU.III, 16.166, 21; 16.353, v.15′; 8.098, v.2′-3′ 15.113, 3′; U.V, 165, 16′-17′.

[88] *Rainey*, g; *Horowitz*, a.

[89] Texts from the Rap'anu archive, U.V, No. 18-158.

[90] U.V, 49 (RS.20.13) — two letters of a certain Yanḫamu to two different persons; 54 (RS.20.23) two letters to Rap'anu sent by different persons; 55 (RS.20.178); cf. also PRU.VI, 7 — containing 2 different letters to the *sākinu*.

[91] U.V, 163 (RS.22.439); U.V, 143-152.

[92] *Liverani*, SDB, p. 1328; *Gelb*, d, pp. 93-104.

some light on the nonprofessional involvement of the scribes is very interesting.

In KTU.4.690, which is a "list of *mdm (mūdū)*" (cf. below), (1) *spr mdm.* Seven persons are listed. Each one received 2 shekels (*ṯqlm*) of silver and then (12) *Tkyn Agmy* (13) *mitm.ṯlṯm.kbd* (14) *aḥd.kbd* (15) *Ri.ʿbd.Ṣtry* (16) *w.ḫmšm.ʿl* (17) *l.pwt* (18) *k sprhm.Ṣdqn.* "*Tkyn* of (the village) *Agm* — 231 in all. *Ri*, servant (slave) of *Ṣtry*, And 50 on(?) for *pwt*,[93] for (*k*) their scribe is *Ṣdqn.*"[94] If our understanding is correct, at least one thing is clear, *Ṣdqn* was the scribe of the group of people, possibly the *mūdū*.

The position of the scribe becomes clearer concerning Yaṣiranu, son of Ḫuṣanu. According to PRU.III, 16.239, king Arḫalbu took the house of ^{I}Yaṣiranu, son of Ḫuṣanu and gave it to Abdu, son of Abdinergal, the royal *mūdū.* His successor, king Niqmepa, according to PRU.III, 16.206 took lands from a certain person "and gave them to Yaṣiranu, son of Ḫuṣanu, the scribe. And Yaṣiranu shall give 115 (shekels) of silver to Sinara(nu), son of Siginu, the *tamkar* ...".[95] We see that the transaction went through Sinaranu, the chief royal commercial agent.[96] Therefore it seems to be a payment for *ubdy*-land. But we also see that the same Yaṣiranu was in a high position in Ugarit, for he received from Ammistamru II the village *E*[*xx*]*iš* and "its grain and beer, the tithe and the sheep for pasturing-tax to Yaṣiranu (he gave)."[97] Thus, this scribe even received the right to collect taxes from a whole village.

According to PRU.III, 16.269, king Niqmaddu relates that a certain Gabanu killed Yatarmu, the scribe (*Yatarmu* ^{LÚ}*tupšarru*),[98] who committed a crime. It seems that Yatarmu had had the right to collect the taxes from the village, Beqa-Ištar, for Gabanu now received this privilege.

The scarce data concerning the scribes shows that at least some of them belonged to the top level of the society of Ugarit. All of them were royal

---

[93] Word unclear; cf. *Macdonald-Cutler*, c, pp. 21-22.

[94] Or "*Ṣdkn* counted them."

[95] (8) *ú id-din-šu a-na* ^{I}*Ya-ṣi-ra-na* (10) *mâr Ḫu-sa-na* ^{LÚ}*tupšarru* (11) *ù Ya-ṣi-ra-nu* (12) *1 me-at 15 kaspe*^{MEŠ} (13) *a-na qâtē* (14) *Si-na-ra* (15) [*mâr*]*Si-gi-na* ^{LÚ}*tamkar* (15) [*i-n*]*a-din*[ ].

[96] *Heltzer*, b, pp. 29 and 132-135.

[97] *Heltzer*, a, p. 51; PRU.III, 16.153.

[98] *Heltzer*, a, p. 49.

subjects, but to what degree they belonged to the system of *bnš mlk* is unknown.

§6. The *md(m)-mūdū* "Friend(s) (of the King)"

Ugaritic *md(m)*, Akk. ^{LÚMEŠ}*mūdū*.[99] They are known from numerous texts[100] and they appear as individuals, performing their obligations (*pilku*), and as a whole group. We can sometimes divide the general term *mūdū*/ *mdm*, for we know that there existed *mūdū šarri* "*mūdū* of the king." (PRU.III, 16.239) and *mūdū-šarrati* "*mūdū* of the queen" (PRU.III, 16.348, etc.).

From a number of texts (PRU.III, 16.239; 16.157; 16.143; 16.250; 16.254D; 15.137; 16.353; 16.148; 16.386) we learn that the *mūdū* had to pay to the king (resp. to the "queen" (queen-mother)) from 5-20 shekels of silver yearly for their *mūdū*-ship.[101].

The *mūdū* received flour and other products together with the other professional groups of the *bnš mlk*. KTU.4.383, [(1)] *b yrḫ* "in the month" *mūdū*, despite their having to pay the "silver of their *mūdū*-ship" also received silver. Thus, in KTU.4.690, [(1)] *spr mdm* "list of *mūdū*-people" 5 persons are mentioned by name as having received 2 shekels each (cf. "scribe" above).

We also see that the *mūdū* lived in various villages of the kingdom. KTU.4.690 designates the villages *Bir* and *Agm*. PRU.III, 16.239 relates that the *mūdū* Abdu had fields in Kannabiya and Napakima (also 16.157), his

---

[99] *Heltzer*, h, p. 351, where the term is explained from the root *y/wdd* "to love" "to be friendly"; such etymology is now accepted by *Liverani*, SDB, p. 1340, and by *Nougayrol*, PRU.VI, 151 note 1. Other opinions, CAD, M.II, pp. 162b-164a; but *mūdē šarri* "friends of the king pl. *mūdū* ugar. pl. *mu-du-ma*. CAD, M.II, 167 [(2b)] *mūdū šarri*, "Friend of the king (RS.only). The etymology cannot be connected with *yd'* "to know", for in the Ugar. spelling there is no *'('ayyin)*.

[100] KTU.4.38, 4; 4.54.13; 4.47, 4; 4.99, 4; 4.103, 1-6; 4.188, 7, 17, 19; 4.245, I, 1, II, 1; 4.387, 12(?), 25; 4.690; PRU.III, 16.239; 16.143; 16.157; 16.250; 15.137; 16.353; 16.348; 16.386; 16.148; PRU.VI, 93 (17.131) ^{LÚ}*mu-du-me*.

[101] Cf. *Jankowska*, c, pp. 40-41; *Haase*, b, pp. 13-16; *Haase*, c, p. 201, *Heltzer*, h, p. 343; Example; PRU.III, 16.157, [(20)] ^{I}*A-zi-ru* ^{LÚ}*mu-du-ú šarri* [(10)] *10 kaspa i-na šanāti*^{MEŠ} *ú-bal* "Aziru is the *mūdū* of the king, 10 (shekels) of silver yearly he has to deliver." PRU.III, 16.348, [(7)] *20 kaspa ú-bal mu-da-at-šu* [(8)] *i-na qātī šarrati*^{ti} *bêlti-šu* "20 (shekels) of silver he shall deliver (for his) *mūdū*-ship to the queen, his lady."

son Kalbu in Ullami and his son Ilimilku in Rîšu. And they also may have resided in some other villages of the kingdom.

We must repeat that the *mūdū* appear in the texts together with the other *bnš mlk* (cf. Ch. I and III).

We also see that Abdu, son of Abdinergal (PRU.III, 16.234) is a *mūdū* and *maryannu* of the king and his sons also had to be *mūdū*. Thus we see the hereditary character of the position (PRU.III, 16.157; 16,143; 16.250). As we saw above, we know that the king alienated a certain Abdiḫagab from the *ʿšrm/ašīru* and made him a "*mūdū* of the king."[102]

We also saw that the *pilku/ubdy* service and lands were distributed to the *mūdū* for services performed by them, as was the case with the other professional groups of *bnš mlk*.[103] At the same time we have no data concerning some kind of dependent persons at the disposal of the *mūdū*, but this might have been an occasional feature.

The *mūdū* also had special privileges — the *ubru* (cf. above) and various overseers (of the chariots, of the fields and the *ḫazannu*) could not enter their houses. Here we see the difference between the *maryannu* and the *mūdū*, for the *maryannu* were not freed from these overseers.[104] According to PRU.III, 15.286 the *mūdū* were even "freed from the service to go to Egypt and to Hatti and to *sisaḫallima*, to the palace and to the overseer of the palace he shall not do his service."[105]

So we see that on the one hand the *mūdū* were privileged persons and were freed from the jurisdiction of the overseers of the fields, chariots and the *ḫazannu* — local governors. They also did not have to accept the *ubru*, i.e. they could not be enslaved for debts to foreign *tamkars*, as was the case with the enslavement of Ugaritians by the *tamkars* of Ura.[106] They were also freed from messenger service to Egypt and Hatti. We see here two

---

[102] PRU.III, 15.137; cf. also 16.348, where Ammistamru II changes the status of a person from the *mur'u* Ibirani to the *mūdū* of the queen; cf. PRU.III, 16.386.

[103] Cf. *Heltzer*, n, pp. 47-55 and texts KTU.4.103; and the texts given above and in Ch. III.

[104] *Jankowska*, c, pp. 46-47, note 71; *Cazelles*, a, pp. 208-212; *Astour*, e, pp. 74-76; *Heltzer*, b, pp. 137-138.

[105] (4′) *iš-tu ḫarrânāti*$^{\mathrm{MEŠ\ KUR}}$*Mi-iṣ-ri* (5′) *ú iš-tu ḫarrânātē*$^{\mathrm{MEŠ\ KUR}}$*Ḫa-at-ti* (6′) *ù i-na sí-sà-ḫal-li-ma* (7) *a-na ekallim ù a-na* ^{LÚ}*akil ekallim* (8′) *ši-ip-ra* [*mi*]*m-ma* (9′) *la-a e-pu-šu*; *sisaḫallima*, *Liverani*, SDB, p. 1328 "cavalier"(?).

[106] *Heltzer*, b, pp. 137-139.

things: There was a change of status; some persons of a lower group of *bnš mlk* became *mūdū* by order of the king. But the sons of a *mūdū* could become *mūdē* in the royal service then during the lifetime of their fathers.

A *mūdū* could also possess some private property. We see this in PRU.III, 16.239, where Abdu, son of Abdinergal, the *mūdū*, handed over to Kalbu, his son, "a house of horses (stable) and 5 (*ikū*) field-land in the same *dimtu*, 1 bronze basin, which weighed 200 (shekels) and 12 bronze kettle of 200 shekels weight."[107] Thus, the *mūdū* had more than the possessions donated by the king and as we see from PRU.III, 16.143 he also had purchased fields.[108]

But we cannot really derive the obligations, privileges and possessions of the *mūdū* from the obligations he was freed from. We stated that they were the "friends of the king" (resp. queen). At the same time we have no idea what their obligations as *bnš mlk* were and must wait for the publication of new sources which may be helpful.

We also know of some additional professions which were connected with the royal administration, possibly of lower rank.

§7. The "Herolds" — *ysḥ(m)* Akk. ^{LÚ}*nāgiru*[109]

We know of the herolds from a number of texts in Ugaritic and Akkadian.[110] They appear as single persons or groups. The most interesting among

---

[107] (22) *...bît^{HA} sisî* (23) *ú 5 eqlu i-na dimti um-ma-ti* (24)*1 allalû siparru 2 me-at šuqultašu* (25) *1 sa-ap-lu siparru 2 me-at šuqultašu; dimti ummati* — AHW, p. 1415a and *Heltzer*, K, p. 11, note 44. Translation according to *Harris*, a, p. 154, "the same *dimtu*."

[108] Cf. also PRU.III, 16.143, Abdu receives various fields from the king and (8) *it-ta-ši-šu* (9) *qa-du eqli ša ši-ma-ti* "he took them together with the purchased fields"; cf. similar features in PRU.III, 16.250, 8-13, where Ilimilku receives fields and goods from his father Abdu; we know also, that the *mūdū* Takḫulinu bought fields for 1000 shekels of silver. (PRU.III, 16.353).

[109] *yṣḥm* — from the root *ṣwh* "to shout, to cry"; UT, p. 413, No. 1140; "members of a certain guild"; WUS, p. 134, No. 1225, "Standes-oder Berufsbezeichnung". *E. Lipinski* in *Heltzer*, c, p. 480 and note 189 proposes "torch-bearers(?)" from Arab. *waḍaḥ* "light" (*wḍḥ/yḍḥ*). We take it with an analogy as *yqšm* "fowlers" (Ch. IX) and *yṣrm* (Ch. V) against the view of *Lipinski;* akk. *nāgiru* "herold", AHW, p. 711, cf. AHW, p. 886b. *qabiānum* "Sprecher", "Speaker" known

the tablets is KTU.4.151, which is partly preserved. But Col. II concludes the text "Total (of the) herolds — 31 in all — royal dependents."[111]

The *yṣḥm* (KTU.4.69, 65-67) participate together with the *pslm* ("sculptors") and *šrm* ("singers") in the archers guard, giving jointly 1 person (cf. Ch. VI, §1).

We know from PRU.III, 16.238 that the house of the most important royal *tamkar*, Sinaranu, was freed from the approaching of the "herold" (*nāgiru*), i.e. from his anouncements.[112]

We also know that, as with the other professional groups, there were deliveries of various products and silver, designated as *ḥpr bnšm* "rations of the *bnš (mlk)*" (KTU.4.626, 1) "The request of the herolds[113] (23) 4200 (at all) copper (or bronze); (4-5) 4 talents 800 (shekels) (at all) (6) *pwt* (red purple dye) (7) 800 (shekels) flax (8-9) 2 talents 2800 (shekels) in all of refined stone".[114]

In almost all the texts the *yṣḥm* appear together with the other professional groups of the *bnš mlk*. We see also from KTU.4.609 and 4.692 that the *yṣḥm* "herolds" received *ubdy*/fields (cf. Ch. III). So we see that their professional service was a certain *pilku*/*ubdy* service.[115]

§8. The *šatammu*

We do not know the Ugaritic counterpart of this Akkadian term, and if we examine it in various areas and periods we see that it had many different meanings.[116]

---

only from Assyria, pp. 889-890, *qabū(m)* "sagen, befehlen" cf. from Ugarit, PRU. VI, 136, 8 *qa-bi*[*xx*].

[110] KTU.4.47, 7; KTU.4.68, 67; 4.99, 19; 4.105, 2; 4.126, 10; 4.147, 5; 4.207, 5; 4.141, II, 1-6; 4.609, 9; 4.626; 4.692; PRU.III, 16,238, 14 (*nāgiru*); PRU, VI, 136, 8 (RS.17.240).

[111] II, (1) *tgmr* (2) *yṣḥm* (3) *ṯlṯm* (4) *aḥd* (5) *kbd* (6) *bnš mlk*.

[112] (14) *LÚnāgiru a-na bîti-šu la-a* (15) [*i-q*]*ar-ru-ub*.

[113] *iršt yṣḥm* — UT, p. 363, No. 379.

[114] Cf. *puwatu*, *Heltzer*, b, p. 69, note 410; *abn ṣrp*, p. 61, note 214.

[115] Cf. also the *LÚḫa'iṭu* (PRU.III, 16.147) and *LÚḫa-i*[*t*] *bîti-* "the *ḫa'iṭu* of the house (palace(?)"; possibly identical or connected with the *akil ekallim* "overseer of the palace."

[116] AHW, p. 1199, "Verwalter, Verwaltungsdirektor" is a very general term. The

The *šatammu* is known from several Akkadian texts.[117] From the lists in PRU.VI, 93 and 136, where the *šatammu* are listed together with the other professional groups of *bnš mlk* "royal dependents" we see that they belonged to these groups, and the tablet PRU.III, 16.173 preserved the line 5′ "and he put him into the *pilku*-service of the *šatammu*-ship."[118]

Text PRU.VI, 27 relates about the redistribution of certain lands by king Ammistamru II in various villages and he gave it to a certain Abbanu: "And Abbanu 400 (shekels) of silver, the honoring of the king, his lord shall give. And the *pilku*-service of the *šatammu* he shall perform."[119] And again the *šatammuship* is designated as a *pilku*. Possibly, the 400 shekels were a symbolic payment, and "honorary gift." But in such a case the land-plot had to be a large one!

According to PRU.III, 16.174 (Ch. III) Niqmaddu takes lands of a *nayyālu* and hands them over to the *šatammu* Tuppiyanu. But the latter pays for this 135 shekels of silver. And again in PRU.III, 15.122, Ammistamru II takes lands of a *nayyālu* and gives them to Kabityanu. Among the lands given to Kabityanu are also the fields of "Kilpibri, the *šatammu* in Uḫnappu."[120] In the partly broken part of the texts, 200 shekels of silver are mentioned in connection with Kabityanu. Perhaps he had to pay this sum. And then Kabityanu has to perform "his *pilku*-service of the *šatammu*-ship."[121] Abdu, son of Abdinergal, according to the text PRU.III, 16.143,

---

word is of Sumerian origin (ŠA.D/TAM) and we find it up to the Seleucid period. AHW, p. 1199b (3) Alalaḫ — *šatammu* of the king; (4) Ugarit — in connection with fields; *šatammūtu* — *šatammu*-office. *Giacumakis*, a, p. 103 "steward"; *Dandamayev*, b, p. 590, "estate mangaer"; RlA, I, p. 449 "official dealing with royal lands"; *Landsberger*, d, p. 48 — high priestly official in Babylonia, but also mayor of a town; *Rainey*, c, p. 85 — an official responsible for the royal stores in Ugarit, *E. Cassin* in FWG, III, explains that in Arrapḫa the *šatammu* was a manager of the temple.

117 PRU.III, 16.173; 16.178; 16.174; 15.122; 16.143; 16.148; 15.141; 16.201; PRU.VI, 27 (RS.17.01); 37 (RS.17.88); 93, 20 (RS.17.131); 136, 4 (RS.17.240); 18 (RS.19.53).

118 (5′) [*ù*] *il-ta-kán-šu* (6′) [*i-n*]*a píl-ku* ^{LÚMEŠ}*šatammūti*$^{\text{mu-ti}}$.

119 (26) *ù* ^{I}*Ab-ba-nu* (27) *4 me-at kaspa kabudat šarri be-li-šu* (28) *it-ta-din*... (30) *ù píl-ka* ^{LÚMEŠ}*šatammi ú-bal*; cf. also PRU.III, 16.178 where the *šatammu* Tagirašap receives lands from the king.

120 (17) *ša* ^{I}*Ki-il-pi-ib-ri* ^{LÚ}*šatammi* (18) *i-na* ^{URU}*Uḫ-nap-pi*.

121 (30) ... *píl-ka-šu ša* ^{LÚ}*satammūti*^{MEŠ}.

received lands taken away from Tešubmati, the *šatammu* in the village Ullami.[122]

We also have additional mentions of the *šatammu*. Of special interest are PRU.VI, 93 and 136 where we have deliveries of small quantities of silver and service of small quantities of people of the professional groups. This may prove that the presence of the *šatammu* as a professional group in the Akkadian texts shows us that they also had to be in the Ugaritic texts. The difficulty is that we cannot identify them.[123]

The *šatammu* appear also as witnesses,[124] and one letter is sent to "*DU-Šapaš* the great *šatammu*" while this person had a "scribe" as well. It seems that the letter was addressed to Ugarit.[125]

But all positive information which we have shows that the *šatammu* were "royal dependents" with all the typical features of such. However, their real functions are not clear to us.

§9. Other Administrative Professions

The other administrative professions are less known than those given above.

a) ^{LÚ}*dayyānu* (DI.KUD) is known only in Akkadian.[126] Once (PRU.III, 16.156) a certain ^{I}*Ili-yanu* ^{LÚ}*dayyānu* appears as a witness and in PRU.III, 16.132 where fields are mentioned: $^{(28)}$ *ša i-na Ra-aḫ-ba-ni* ^{LÚMEŠ}*dayyāni*^{MEŠ} which are in the "Raḫbanu of the judges (area)."

b) We also know various PA (*aklu*) "overseers" which belonged to the

---

[122] $^{(4)}$ ...*ša* ^{Iil}*Tešub-ma-ti* ^{LÚ}*šatammu* $^{(5)}$ *i-na* ^{URU}*Ul-la-mi*.

[123] Cf. PRU.III, 16.148, where the *mudu* Takḫulinu, receives lands (according to a broken text) of $^{(5')}$ [ ]*DIR-*^{il}*im* ^{LÚ}*šatammu* $^{(6')}$ [*ša i-na Na-*]*pa-ki-ma* "of DIR-^{il}IM, the *šatammu*, which is in Napaki(ma)"; PRU.III, 15.141 where Ammistamru II takes away the fields of "Yaquru, the *šatammu*, which are in the fields of Ṣa'u"; PRU.III, 16.201, where Ammistamru II deprives from his lands Sigilda(nu), the *šatammu* in the village of Marabu (*M'rb*).

[124] PRU.VI, 37 $^{(\text{v. }3')}$ *šîbu* (witness) ^{I}Zu-[*l*]*a-la-nu* ^{LÚ}*šatammu* $^{(4')}$ *šîbu* ^{I}*Ar(i)-pa-ba-nu* ^{LÚ}*šatammu*.

[125] PRU.VI, 18 (RS.19.53). A scribe Nir-Nabū writes to Naḫešišalmu... "the scribe of DU-Šapšu the great *šatammu*" ($^{(3)}$ $^{\text{LÚ}}{}_{2}$*tupšarri ša* ^{I}*DU-*^{il}*utu* ^{LÚ}*šatammu rabī*...).

[126] Ugaritic parallel unknown. *Ṯpṭ* — in the mythological texts (?).

"royal dependents" (*bnš mlk*). PRU.II, 11.787 lists 10 ^{LÚ}*aklu* and each one received 4-12 $^{2}/_{3}$ shekels.

1) ^{LÚ}*akil kāri*: "overseer of the quai." According to PRU.IV, 17.424,10 it was Abdu, son of Ayaḫḫu; we know that such functionary was also Rašapabu, whose texts are preserved in U.V. We also know that the latter had his personal lands, and that he received certain products. It seems that they controlled maritime trade and the archive of Rašapabu shows that he was a rather wealthy man.[127]

2) ^{LÚ}*akil* ^{iṣ}*narkabti*: (PRU.III, 16.250) (cf. above on the *maryannu* and *mūdū*). It seems that they had something to do with the chariot-conscription and the care for the chariotry.

3) *akil e[q]lāti*^{ti}: "overseer of the fields" (cf. above Ch. IV, and this chapter on the *mūdū*). This is possibly the same as *nġr mdrʿ* and *nġr krm* "guard of the sown" and "guard of the vineyard" and he was the royal overseer of the *gt*.

4) ^{LÚ}*akil ekallim*: "overseer of the palace", PRU.III, 16.386. The *mūdū* were freed from his jurisdiction. Possibly, he mobilized people for certain kinds of service.

5) ^{LÚ}*akil šangi:* (cf. Ch. VII) "overseer of the priests."

6) ^{LÚ}*akil li-im*: "overseer of thousand" possibly a functionary. We know him from PRU.VI, 52 (RS.19.78) lines 4 and 9 and they are liberated from something, but we do not know exactly from what. In U.V.42 (RS.20.239), 27 the ^{LÚ}*akil li-im* appears as a member of the council of elders of the village Rakba.[128].

---

127 U.V, No. 1-14; *Heltzer*, b, pp. 146-47.

128 *Heltzer*, a, pp. 64-65 and 79.

CHAPTER IX

THE PALACE PERSONNEL

The present chapter is a continuation of the preceding one. We must still keep in mind that, to a certain degree, the division between the administration and palace personnel is artificial. We must also keep in mind that most of the professionals described in this chapter belonged to the *bnš mlk*.

We will be making another, possibly artificial, division between the professions which could belong to the palace administration (not the administration of the kingdom) described in Ch. VIII, and between the personnel which had the task of personal service of the king and those of high rank in the palace.

§1. Persons Possibly Belonging to the Palace Administration

1. We know the term *mâr šarri*, "son of the king", *ušriyannu* Ug. *uṯryn*[1] and *tard/tennu*[2]. It seems that the latter terms refer to the real son of the king. The term *mâr šarri* does not always mean the real son of the king, but designates a certain palace, or royal, official.[3]

We know that according to PRU.III, 16.204 king Ammistamru II distributes land-allotments and gives them to a certain Abdimilku. And "Abdimilku and his sons have to perform the *pilku* of the sons of the queen forever." In PRU.III, 16.138 the same king grants lands, with the same conditions, to Ilitešub and his sons.[4] In these two cases, at least, we see that

---

[1] Cf. Ch. VIII — *mur'u ušriyanni, mru Ibrn*; *Liverani*, a, p. 74, *Heltzer*, f, p. 38; UT, p. 369, No. 426; AHW, p. 1442a, "Kronprinz".

[2] *Liverani*, a, pp. 74-75; 103-106; 125; *Wilhelm*, a, pp. 277-282; AHW, pp. 1329, 2b) Bo. Ug. Nuzi "Krnzprinz"; *ta/erd/tennūtu/uttu*, Ug. Bo. "Kronprinzstellung".

[3] *Brin*, a; *Brin*, b, pp. 433-463 accepts the view that almost always it was an official. At the same time, *Imparati*, c, pp. 80-85, accepts the necessity of considering every case according to its context; *Heltzer*, L, p. 183 and below.

[4] Cf. Ch. III, pp. 23-48; possibly the queen-mother is concerned.

certain officials are considered, not real royal sons.[5] We by no means know the number of such persons in Ugarit and their real functions. Even the well-known title "king's-son", from Egypt, does not clarify this question.[6]

2. *ṯġr(m)*, Akk. LÚ*atû* "gatekeepers".[7] We know these individuals from several texts,[8] where they are mentioned individually or as a whole group. Sometimes they are mentioned by name. Among those mentioned in PRU.V, 93, 17 is a gatekeeper *atû*, together with a "tailor"(?) (LÚ.TUG.LÁ). There was even one *gt* in Ugarit (Ch. IV) named after the "gatekeepers" (*ṯġrm*).

According to KTU.4.195, 14, *w.ptḥ.ḫdr.ṯġr* "and the door-opening of the room"(?)[9] or "and the gatekeeper opened the room"(?). In KTU.4.224, both persons mentioned appear as *ṯġr hk*[*l*] "gatekeeper of the palace" and this may be the full designation of the word *ṯġrm* "gatekeepers". In this connection we must take KTU.4.63, (4) *B'lṣdq* (5) *skn.bt.mlk.ṯġr* (7) *mlk bny*... "*B'lṣdq*, the *sākinu* of the palace, gatekeeper of the king, my son...".[10]

KTU.4.128, a text dealing with product-deliveries, mentions *dd.l.ṯġr* "(one) *dd*-measure to the *ṯġr* (gatekeeper)" and the *ṯġrm*, listed in KTU.4.609 (cf. Ch. I), together with the other *bnš mlk*, received the "rations of the royal dependents" (*ḫpr* bn*šm*) in the month *Iṯtbnm*.[11]

Both texts KTU.4.103, 39-4 and 4.609 show us that the *ṯġrm* had their *ubdy* (*-pilku*) fields (Ch. III) and according to PRU.VI, 93, we see that they had to participate in certain collective service.

---

[5] Cf. PRU.IV, 17.423 where the king of Karchemish speaks about "the brother of Upparmuwa, who is a son of the king." Cf. also cases where clearly non-Ugaritians are mentioned, with such titles — PRU.III, 15.77; PRU.IV, 17.314; 17.28; 17.247; *Brin*, a and b; *Imparati*, c.

[6] *Schmitz*, a.

[7] Hebr. *šo'ēr* WUS, p. 34, No. 2914; UT, p. 404, No. 2721; Akk. spelling NI.DUḪ; *Nougayrol*, PRU.VI, p. 130; AHW, p. 88 "Pförtner" "Türhüter".

[8] KTU.4.103, 39-40; KTU.4.126, 22; 4.128, 11; 4.141.III, 2; 4.195, 14; 4.224, 8-9; 4.609, 13-14; 7.63; PRU, IV, 93, 17.

[9] The text is heavily damaged. In the partly preserved lines we see often *ptḥ* "door' and *ḫdr* "room".

[10] Possibly a third person addressed *B'lṣdq*. Correct interpretation of the tablet, *Liverani*, a, p. 68; UT, p. 505, No. 2721, "King of the gate" is incorrect.

[11] KTU.4.103; 4.126; PRU.VI, 93 are also texts dealing with various groups of *bnš mlk*.

It seems to be clear that we are dealing here with the gatekeepers of the palace. The proof of this can be the following case in which they are even mentioned in such a capacity;[12] a) that their number was relatively small b) the gatekeeper-ship was a permanent occupation at the royal palace and therefore there is no mobilization of the *ṯġrm* to monthly service at the palace, as we have seen in the *ḫrd* (*ḫurādu*)-texts (Ch. VI, pp. 105-108). At the same time we see that at least one of the *ṯġr(m)* could also be the major-domo of the palace-economy. Thus we may conclude that the *ṯġrm* did not belong to the lower ranks of the palace-personnel.

3. *rêšu* (SAG) var. *ša rêšu.*[13] "eunuchs" (LÚMEŠ*(ša)rêši*).[14] The spellings are LÚMEŠ*ša rêši*; LÚMES*rêš(*SAG)*šarri*(LUGAL); (or *ša re-ši šarri*); LÚ*ša re-ši ekalli* (É.GAL-*li*), (i.e. "the king" and "the palace" respectively) and sometimes simply *re-šu* or (SAG).[15]

Some of the *rêšu*/*ša rêši* appear as witnesses in business texts. According to PRU.IV, 17.251, p. 236, a slave was sold to Uzzinu, the *sākinu* of Ugarit. Among the witnesses we find: (21) [IG]I *Bin*(DUMU)-*ia-ri-mi* (22) LÚ*ša-a rêši* (SAG) *šarri*(LUGAL), "[witne]ss, Bin-Yarimu, royal eunuch."

PRU.IV, 18.20 and 17.373, pertains to the *kartappu* of Karchemish and king Niqmaddu III(?) of Ugarit. On verso line 13′, we find: IGI I*Ta-gu-uḫ-li-nu* LÚ*ša rêši* (SAG) [*ekalli* (E.GAL)?], "Witness, Taguḫlinu, eunuch of the [palace?]." The text Ug V, 161 (17.325), records a purchase of land by the queen of Ugarit, Šarelli, the wife of Niqmepa. *šîbu* (IGI) I*Ibri(*EN-*ri)-dun* LÚ*rêšu* (SAG), "Witness Ibridun, the eunuch" (line 20).

---

[12] *ṯġr hk*[*l*] "gatekeeper of the palace" and *ṯġr bt mlk* "gatekeeper of the palace (lit. 'royal house')".

[13] Ugaritic parallel unrecognized. Cf. *Heltzer*, i, pp. 4-111. We cannot agree with the translation of *Nougayrol*, PRU.VI, p. 7, No. 1, "chef". *Heltzer*, i, p. 6; cf. also *ša rêš šarri* in the harem instructions of the Middle Assyrian period in *Weidner*, b, pp. 264-265. AHW, p. 974. About differences in the status and meaning of *rêšu* cf. *Renger*, c, p. 446; *Garelli*, c, pp. 447-448.

[14] PRU.III, 16.162, 24; 15.238, 17; PRU, IV, 17.112, 4; 17.251, 22; 17.231, 9; U.V.16 (RS.17.325), 20; 33 (RS.20.212); 167 (RS.22.421), IV, 6 (here a literary text) ⌜SAG⌝ dSU.GAR.DURU$_2$ NA.

[15] The presence or absence of *ša* before SAG (*rêšu*) does not alter the meaning and the text PRU.VI, 6 (RS.17.452) where a certain Zullanu writes to the *sākinu* of Ugarit about a *rêšu* (SAG, l. 11) sending him a youth (*apla* — IBIL, l. 15) whom he shall (10) ... *a-na* LÚ*rêšūti* (SAG *ut-ti*) (17) *li-pu-šu-šu* "to turn him into a *rêšu*" i.e. "to eunuchize him", *Heltzer*, i, p. 7.

There are also some texts pertaining specifically to eunuchs (*rêšu*). Thus the legal text PRU.III, 16.162, relates that the king, Ammistamru II, took away the land from a certain Bin-ilu and from some others and awarded it: *ana Amataruna ú ana mârišu adi dāriš*, "to Amataruna and his sons forever" (lines 8-10). After the royal seal: *pilkušu ša* ^{LÚMEŠ}*ša re-ši ubbal; šanu pilku yanu ina eqlāti annati*, "He must perform the *pilku* of the eunuchs; there is no other service on these fields" (lines 24-26). So we see that Amatarunu and his sons had to perform "the *pilku* service of the eunuchs." Amatarunu received a land-holding in accordance with the practice regarding other men in royal service. It is also interesting that he had children. Possibly they were adopted. Such practice is known in the Ancient Near East,[16] or we must suppose that, at least in some cases, the *rêšu*-ship was only a formal designation and not all *rêšu* were real eunuchs. In any case this Amatarunu held a relatively high position and received no less than three service-allotments.[17]

In PRU.IV, 17.112 we have a passage dealing with a certain "Kilu'û, the man of (the town) Ḫišiššiba, the *kar*[*tappu*], who leads the r[oyal] eunuchs".[18] from here we see that the eunuchs were possibly an organized body within the *bnš mlk* framwork in Ugarit.

PRU.IV, 17.231 is also very interesting.[19] It pertains to the queen of Ugarit.

(1) *iš-tu ûmi(UD-mi) an-ni-i* (2) *a-na pa-ni* $^{LÚ.MEŠ}$*ši-bu-ti* (3) *šarrat(MI.LUGAL) mât(KUR)* ^{URU}*Ú-ga-ri-it* (4) *tu-un-te-ed-di aras-(ÌR)-sa* (5) *mâr(DUMU) māti(KUR)-ša*$_{10}$*(SA)* (6) ^{I}*U-ri-*^{d}*Tešub(IŠKUR) šum-šu* (7) *iš-tu(!) bîti(É-ti)*

---

16 Cf. CḪ §187, where we have the *mâr* (DUMU) *gerseqqim* (GÌR.SÌ.GA) *mu-za-az ekallim* (É.GAL), "son of a *gerseqqum* (eunuch?) a courtier ...".

17 An additional text, PRU.III, 16.238, 17, where *Nougayrol* reconstructs $^{LÚ.MEŠ}$*ša* ⸢*re*⸣[-*ši*], which is very doubtful. The text concerns Sinaranu, the son of Siginu, one of the most privileged royal commercial agents, *tamkāru*, who was not an eunuch. It must also be pointed out that in the texts about eunuchs (*rêšu*), there is no mention of the name of their father. Sinaranu, on the contrary, is known as the son of Siginu and Siginu, the son of Milku-aḫu (PRU.III, 15.138, 4, p. 101); for more details about Sinaranu, *Heltzer*, b, pp. 132-134.

18 (2) ... ^{I}*Ki-la-'e*[*-e* (3) *amil(LÚ)* ^{URU}*Ḫi-ši-iš-ši-ba* ^{LÚ}*kar-t*[*ap-pi*] (4) [*š*]*a(?) i-la-kam a-na pa-ni* $^{LÚ.MEŠ}$*rêš(SAG) š*[*arri* (*L*[*UGAL*]*à?*]. Cf. CAD, K, pp. 225b-226b; *Daddi-Pecchioli*, b.

19 Full text and interpretation, *Heltzer*, i, pp. 8-11.

(8) *ᴵTab-ra-am-mi* (9) *ᴸᵁša re-ši ekalli(E.GAL-li)* (10) *ù tal-te$_9$-qe-šu* (11) *i-na 70 kaspi(KU.BABBAR.MEŠ)* "From this day in the presence of witnesses, the queen of Ugarit has recognized her slave, a son of her country,[20] Uri-Tešub by name, from the house of Tabrammu,[21] the palace eunuch. And she bought him for 70 shekels of silver." Later, the same text providing the validity, mentions (15-16) "The seal of Tabrammu, the palace eunuch."

(15) *^{na_4}kunuk(KIŠIB) ᴵTab-ra-am-mi* (16) *ᴸᵁša re-ši ekalli(E.GAL-li)* It would seem that the slave recognized by the queen of Ugarit as her compatriot had come from Amurru, from whence the Ugaritic queens were also taken.[22] He was the slave of the "palace eunuch" Tabrammu and it would appear from this text that the queen bought and released him. The transaction is confirmed by the seal of Tabrammu. So the "eunuch of the palace" could possess a seal and even own slaves. Furthermore, as discussed above with their appearance as witnesses, they could also act in legal cases.[23] The other mentions of the rêšu deal with foreigners who came to Ugarit in certain diplomatic capacities.[24]

On the basis of their data, the following conclusions may be drawn: The original status of the *rêšu* was that of a slave-eunuch. This is clear from PRU.VI, No. 6, and also from the fact that not one of them is mentioned by his patronymic. But during their *rêšu*-service (*pilku ša rêši*) the eunuchs could become "royal dependents" (*bnš mlk*), and even reach a privileged position among them. In some cases they appear as witnesses, possess a personal seal, have their own property and appear as one of the parties in a sale-contract, as well as receive land-allotments for their service to the king. The tablets concerning Amatarunu and Tabrammu (PRU III, 16.162, and PRU.IV, 17.231), show us that a *rêšu* could achieve a relatively high position and accumulate wealth at the royal court. All these facts are not contradictory to our knowledge of the *rêšu* in Middle Assyria.[25] There were,

---

[20] T.m. "her compatriot."

[21] Perhaps the scribe has omitted a line here; it ought to say something like, "And she took him from the house of Tabrammu."

[22] *Heltzer*, j, pp. 85-96.

[23] It is not clear whether there were any differences in such cases between the "royal eunuchs" and "eunuchs of the palace."

[24] Ug. V, 33, where (27) *ᴵA-li-zi-[ti] rêš*(SAG) *šarri*(LUGAL) from Hatti is mentioned.

[25] *Weidner*, b, pp. 264-265; another view of the *rêšu* in Ugarit cf. *Oppenheim*, a, p. 325 ff., but later *Oppenheim* accepted our view- *Oppenheim*, b, 95.

possibly, other functionaries belonging to the palace administration, but we do not recognize them.

§2. Auxiliary and Personal Serving Personnel of the Palace

Naturally, we do not possess the definitive knowledge of the functions and obligations of this kind of personnel. But, in general, the data allows us to conclude that they were, in general, attached to palace-service.

1. *yqšm*.[26] Akk. LÚU.DAB.MUŠEN [27] as well the Ugaritic word in Akkadian script LÚ*ya-qi-š[u-ma]* (PRU.VI, 136, 12),[28] "fowlers". They are mentioned in the texts as single individuals or as a group. According to KTU.4.99, the *yqšm* receive two units of a certain delivery. From this text, as well as from KTU.4.126, and PRU.VI, 136, we see that under consideration are professional groups of *bnš mlk*. Possibly, they participated in the royal hunt, or brought birds caught by them to the royal kitchen.

2. LÚTÚG.LÁ (PRU.VI, 93, 17) "tailors" which, as we know, appear together with the *atû(ṯġrm)* "gatekeepers". Possibly, they had to serve the royal family and the court.[29] They also certainly belonged to the *bnš mlk*.

3. LÚ*ḫuppu* (ḪUB.NITA) "acrobat".[30] (PRU.VI, 93, 21). We have to add once more that even if we have the Ugaritic counterparts of this and related terms we cannot recognize them, as yet. We must also take into account that the Ancient Oriental royal courts had special staff for cultic and

---

26 WUS, p. 135, No. 1232 Vogelsteller(?) Hebr. *yāqeš*; UT. p. 414, No. 1145 "fowlers" Hebr. *yāqōš*, *yāqūš*.

27 *Salonen*, g, p. 49, LU.MUŠEN.DU_3 "Vogelfänger." It is also not excluded that we are talking about the poultry-breeders.

28 KTU.4.99, 6; 4.114, 8; 4.126, 25; PRU, VI, 136, 12 (RS.17.240); U.V.96 (RS.20.12), 9(?).

29 *Nougayrol*, PRU.VI, p. 87 and 152 "tailleur" (?) — possibly *mukabbû* or *kâṣiru*; *kâṣiru* — AHW, p. 458a, *kāṣirum* "Knüpfer, Gawandschneider(?)" — LÚ*túg-ka*-KIŠ*kés* = *ka-ṣi-ru*; CAD, K, p. 264, "(a craftsman producing textiles by a special technique)", but according to CAD, K, p. 265, *kāṣiru* B it could be an official; *mukabbû* — AHW, p. 669b, "Näher, Flickschneider" LÚ*túg*.KAL.KAL, CAD, II M, p. 181 "clothes mender", but known only from the Neo-Babylonian period.

30 *Nougayrol*, p. 87, 130, 161, "Danseur acrobatique"; AHW, p. 365, LÚ*ḫub*, "Kulttänzer"; CAD, Ḫ, p. 240, "acrobat", known also on the contemporary Hittite texts.

entertainment purposes, and the *ḫuppu*, who belonged to the *bnš mlk*, could be one of them.[31]

4. *aluzinnu* — "jester" (PRU.VI, 93, 22).[32] As we see, he also appears in a list of various groups or individuals of *bnš mlk*. We must derive the word from *lezēnu* "to jeer", "to scoff".[33] Possibly this was the court jester of the king.[34]

5. ^{LÚ}*parkullu* (BAR.GUL) (PRU.VI, 93, 24) "seal-cutter" appears as one single person in the text, mentioning *bnš mlk*. Beside him appears the

6. ^{LÚ}*nâru* (NAR) "singer" possibly this time not temple- but palace-singers.[35]

7. In PRU.VI, 93, 19 we find also ^{LÚ}*[g]ipári(?)* ^{URU}*Sí-na-ri* (GI.PAR.A)[36] and three persons are mentioned. We would suppose that these were "tomb-builders" for the purposes of the royal court and that we have to read the signs as *qi-bar-a*.[37]

---

[31] *Römer, a, pp. 43-68, esp. p. 48,* (2) *ḫub-bé* = *ḫu-up-pu-u* "ein Kulttänzer."

[32] The reading of *Nougayrol*, PRU, VI, p. 87 is a misunderstanding. The spelling here is according to the autograph ALAN.ZU, as it appears also in the Boghazköi texts and in Alalaḫ (*Römer*, a, p. 50) and we know also the *aluzinnu* from contemporary Middle-Assyrian texts (*Freydank*, a, p. 117).

[33] *Römer*, p. 46; *Freydank*, a, p. 117, note 35; AHW, p. 548; CAD, L, p. 162.

[34] *Römer*, a, shows us that such a feature was possible. (Cf. also *Foster*, a, pp. 69-85) but another view *Gelb*, c, pp. 43-76). There also exists a Phoenician counterpart of the *aluzinnu*, — *lṣ*, as he appears on a bronze-bowl from the VIIIth cent. B.C.E., from Nimrud (*Heltzer*, M, p. 409, and *Heltzer*, V, pp. 1-6). Taking into account that the *aluzinnu* was known in Ugarit and Hittite Asia Minor, i.e. in the areas having close connections with the Aegean world in the second half of the II millennium B.C.E. we can suppose that the word ἀλαζών "charlatan" "quack" "braggart" "boaster" (*Liddel-Scott*, I, pp. 59-60) cf. *Passow*, a, p. 91 and *Alazon Greece huic nomen est comediae* in ThGL, I, pp. 1390-1391 is connected with *aluzinnu*. As is well-known, the ἀλαζών was a typical personnage in the Old Attic Commedy. The existing etymologies of this greek word derive it from the ethnonym of a Thracian tribe Ἀλαζόνες (*Bonfante*, a, pp. 77-78), but we can now propose the connection of this greek word with *aluzinnu*.

[35] In the same text, l. 25 appear also the *nuḫatimmu* "cook" "baker" *Ugar. apy(m)*, (cf. Ch. V) and the *ma-ṣi-lu* "cymbalist" cf. Ch. VII).

[36] *Nougayrol*, PRU.VI, p. 86 and 151. "Hom[me du *g*]*ipâru* de (la ville de Sinaru)."

[37] Cf. *qi-bar* "tomb" "grave" in U.V. 20 (RS.20.33, v. 31) and the reading in *Heltzer*, E, pp. 164-165 accepted also by *Nougayrol*, b, p. 95; CAD, G, pp. 83-84 *gipāru* does not designate a person and has a different spelling.

8. *gallabu* — "friseur" (PRU.VI, 136, RS.17.240, 10)[38] is receiving 1 shekel of silver among other professionals of *bnš mlk*.

There could, of course, be other professionals, but we have no possibility to recognize them.

The important thing here is that the general number of these professionals was very small and this speaks in favor of putting them in the auxiliary personnel of the palace. We must also see that they belonged to the *bnš mlk*.

---

38 ^{LÚ}*qa-la-p*[*u*?] *Nougayrol*, PRU.VI, p. 107 leaves it without translation. We suppose *ga-la-b*[*u*].

GENERAL REMARK TO CHAPTERS IV-IX

In all of these chapters we dealt only with the professional groups of *bnš mlk*, "royal dependents", which were identifiable with a certain profession whose occupation was understandable, or about which we have at least some data about their integration into the framework of the *bnš mlk* (cf. *trrm* Ch. III). At the same time, we know of some professions about which data is lacking and only new material can aid in greater understanding about them. Such professions are the *krtm* (KTU.4.126, 29), *tknm* (KTU 4.126, 31), *blblm* (KTU.4.288, 1), *btwm* (KTU.4.320, 13) *ʿtrgm* (KTU.4.420, 7, 12); *ʿpsm* (KTU.6, 29, 1) and others such as *qrṭym*, *bdl qrṭym* (Ch. I and III), or LÚTIBIRA.GÍD (PRU.VI.93, 12) which cannot be identified satisfactorily with their Ugaritic parallels.

Together with a number of other questions, this remains open in understanding the social structure of Ugarit.

CHAPTER X

THE ROYAL AUTHORITY

In the preceding chapters we have seen the internal functioning of the organization of Ugarit under royal authority. This, in addition to the rural community and the supervision of the royal authority over it, and the organization of international trade, where the royal authorities were also the organizing power.[1]

We may now summarize the results of the preceding chapters and consider some aspects and prerogatives of the members of the ruling dynasty besides the king.

We shall not enter here into questions about the origin of royal power in Ugarit, which can be drawn from the literary texts whose composition belong to an earlier period.[2]

We must point out that the pioneering work, studying the functions and essence of royal power in Ugarit, belongs to *M. Liverani*,[3] in the same way as the same work concerning Nuzi-Arrapḫa and Alalaḫ was done by *E. Cassin* and *H. Klengel*.[4]

Despite the sometimes striking similarity in the internal organization of the royal economy and system of dependent people in Ugarit and Mycenaean Greece, we cannot, as yet, find such similarities in the organization of the royal power. This may possibly depend on the lapidary character of the Linear B early Greek documents.

We must now consider the data concerning the king and the members of the royal family.

---

[1] *Heltzer*, a, and *Heltzer*, b.

[2] *Ginsberg*, a, which remains still one of the outstanding works in this field; *Aistleitner*, c, pp. 87-108; *Gibson-Driver*, a, pp. 19-23 and 82-102; as well as the abundant literature and bibliography in UF, concerning the Epic of Keret; cf. also *Heltzer*, N, Introduction and Ch. IV, where the historical background of the Ugaritic dynasty is given; *Kitchen*, a, pp. 131-142 and *Klengel*, b, II, pp. 332-333; *Caquot*, c, pp. 425-429.

[3] *Liverani*, f, pp. 329-356.

[4] *Klengel*, c, pp. 273-282; *Cassin*, c, pp. 373-392.

§1. The King

Ug. *mlk* Akk. *šarru*

As is widely known, the king held in his hands the international relations of Ugarit, sometimes aided by the *skn (sākin mâti)*.

We know that among his titles there appeared the expression *adn Yrgb b'l Ṯrmn*, "The Lord of *Yrgb*, the potentiate of *Ṯrmn*." These two words were toponyms and we do not know exactly where they were located, but they hint that in a certain period the territory of the kingdom of Ugarit was expanded to include them.[5] In most of the texts the king is named *mlk* Ugarit, and in the Akkadian texts, *šar* ^{KUR}*Ugarit*, "king of the country of Ugarit", or ^{URU}*Ugarit*, "the town of Ugarit," or both of these designations appear together.[6] In the documents, the name of the ruling king is given together with the name of the father. But sometimes the name of an ancient king Yaqarum appears, as it does in PRU.III, 16.145 $^{(1)}$ *iš-tu u-mi an-ni-i-im* $^{(3)}$ ^{I}*Ya-qa-ru šàr* ^{URU}*Ú-ga-ri-it* "From the present day, Yaqaru, king of Ugarit."[7] As we know now, Yaqaru was a real king, possibly founder of the state, in the XIXth cent. B.C.E. and his dynastic seal remained acceptable on documents issued by the royal authorities.[8] In the XIV-XIIIth cent. B.C.E. Yaqarum might also have been one of the royal titles in Ugarit, such as *Labarna/Tabarna* was in the Hittite Empire.[9] The fact that almost all documents have the formula "in the presence of x, king of Ugarit" (*a-na pani x šar* ^{KUR}*Ugarit*), seems to demonstrate that this presence had a certain notarionic significance, besides the appearances of the witnesses and the scribe.[10]

As *Liverani* points out, the royal power tried to be the "judge of justice" in every case and interfered actively in the entire way of life of the *bnš mlk* — "royal dependents".[11]

---

[5] *Buccellati*, b, p. 33.

[6] *Buccellati*, b, p. 66.

[7] *Kitchen*, pp. 138-142, *Schaeffer*, U.III, pp. 66-67; *Liverani*, a, pp. 27-56; 129, 137; *Klengel*, b, II, pp. 333, 343-358; 396-398. *Haase*, b, pp. 13-15; cf. also the texts KTU.3.2 and 3.5.

[8] *Rainey*, c, pp. 22-24.

[9] *Boyer*, a, pp. 115-152; *Boyer*, b, p. 157; *Bucellati*, b, p. 67, *Haase*, b, pp. 12-13; cf. also *Millard*, a, pp. 139-140.

[10] *Liverani*, f, p. 333.

[11] *Heltzer*, a, pp. 18-47 and Ch. II-V of the present study.

Concerning the royal prerogatives, we see from the previous chapters, and our previous works, the following:

1. The king collected taxes from the rural communities as well as from private family-properties and from various groups of "royal dependents" (not connected with their professional service). Sometimes it was connected with the tribute paid to the Hittite king. The taxes were paid in silver, products and sometimes by performance of corvée-work.[12]

2. The military authority was in the hands of the king. This concerns the conscription and mobilization of the villagers and professional groups, as well as the full control of the "royal dependents's" military service. Sometimes, as seen in Chapter VI, the king could delegate his command to other persons.[12]

3. As we have seen above, all groups of the "royal dependents" were dependent on royal authority, and even various degrees of privileges of single groups were in the hands of the king. (But, some of the privileges of the groups may have been dictated by tradition.)

4. The royal authorities (the king) possessed a large economy consisting of agricultural and cattle-breeding branches. In the royal hands were also the pasture lands of Ugarit. The artisanship known to us was also part of the royal economy.

5. The king possessed, or at least had at his disposal, according to the tradition, a large land-fund which he distributed and redistributed as land-allotments connected with special professional service of "royal dependents". Lands of persons not connected with royal service, but unable to perform their obligations and to pay taxes were alienated from them and handed over to this fund.[13]

6. The king, through his commercial agents — *tamkars* — held in his hands the main part of the international trade of Ugarit and regulated, on the basis of international mutual treaties, the commercial activities of foreign *tamkars* in the Kingdom of Ugarit.[14]

7. The king offered, in several cases, whole villages to certain persons, i.e.

---

[12] U.V.22 (RS.20.18) and 24 (RS.20.238) where we learn also that the king remained in Ugarit at the time of the invasion of the "peoples of the sea"; cf. *Berger*, a, pp. 217-220.

[13] *Heltzer*, b, pp. 125-139.

[14] *Heltzer*, b, pp. 125-139.

the right to collect taxes from these villages, along with performance of various services.[15]

8. Possibly on a traditional basis, the king of Ugarit had the prerogative to give special rights, and deprive of special rights, members of the royal family,[16] with the exception of the queen-mother (cf. below).

9. The extradition of fugitive slaves and political refugees on the basis of mutual international agreements was also in the hands of the king.[17]

10. In legal cases, the decisions of the king of Ugarit, concerning the litigation between his subjects, or his subjects and the authorities, were obligatory for all sides, as we see from the documents.[18]

11. The king supervised the restoration of sanctuaries and ordered various special works for this, if necessary.[19]

12. In connection with the above, we know from a great number of cultic texts that the king was heavily involved in cultic actions. Possibly, this was based on more ancient tradition.[20] So KTU.1.87, as well as numerous other texts, relates about the sacrifices, performed by the king, *dbḥ mlk* "royal sacrifice", and some other texts connected with cultic actions.[21]

In various prayers such as KTU.1.40 or 1.141, we see some kind of pleas for the wealth and security of the country, where help from the gods against the enemies is demanded.[22]

We also know that, along with the gods of the whole kingdom, the king had also his personal protecting gods.[23]

---

[15] *Heltzer*, a, pp. 42-51.

[16] Cf. esp. PRU.III, 16.144, *Tsevat*, b, pp. 237-243.

[17] *Heltzer*, a, pp. 4-6; *Boyer*, b, p. 160; *Liverani*, g, pp. 313-336; esp. PRU.VI, 17.79 where the Hittite king Mursilis II gives the instruction to Niqmepa of Ugarit (38) *šu[m-m]a iš-tu* KURURU*Ḫa-at-ti* LÚ*mu-nab-tu in-n[a-bi-iṭ]* I*Niq-me-pa li-iṣ-bat-šu-ma a-na šár* KURURU*Ḫa-a[t-ti li-id-din]*. "If from the land of Hatti a fugitive de[fects] let Niqmepa seize him — to the king of Hat[ti] he shall deliver him."

[18] Cf. *Heltzer*, a, p. 49; PRU.III, 16.269; 16.356; 16.245; 16.205 and also *Rainey*, c, pp. 28-31.

[19] KTU.2.26; 6.29; *Heltzer*, a, pp. 25-27.

[20] On archaic traditions from the cultic and epical texts, cf. *Gray*, a; *Gray*, b, pp. 79-108; *Liverani*, f, pp. 338-341. The main texts, KTU.1.90; 1.106; 1.109; 1.111; 1.112; 1.119 and Ch. VII.

[21] KTU.1.43; 1.39; 1.46; 1.24, etc.

[22] *Aistleitner*, c, pp. 105-107 with another interpretation; *Heltzer*, N, pp. 7-8.

[23] PRU.III.15.24, (6) *ilāni ša* KUR*Ú-ga-ri-it* (7) *ú ilāni*MEŠ *ša-a šarri bêli-ka a-na šul-*

In addition, we know that the whole administrative apparatus of the kingdom was subdued to the king. Naturally, there had to be a certain interrelation between the local authorities and the self-government, in the measure which existed there.[24] At the same time, we also see a number of limitations of royal power and prerogatives. Their definition belongs to *M. Liverani.*[25] It was, first of all, the political dependence from the Hittite Empire and its chief vassal, the king of Karchemiš. Then, as *Liverani* remarks, we see that certain persons received exemptions from various obligations[26] and this was a certain (possibly based on some tradition) self-limitation of royal power. We do not find any hints that the royal power was limited by the local self-government, but its existence was recognized by itself. Another feature was, naturally, the fleeing of fugitives, which was, at least, a kind of passive resistance against the king.[27] And, as we have seen above (Ch. VIII) in the case of the juvenile king, the *sākinu* had executive power in his hands, at least in some cases.

§2. The Queen-Mother

The queen-mother seems to be the next, after the king, in the power-hierarchy of the royal family. We know that the *g^{e}bīrā* is well-known also from the Old Testament,[28] the *tawananna* of the Hittite Empire and various other examples from the Ancient Oriental world.[29] But, concerning Ugarit, we have only one study by *H. Donner*, based on the documented sources, published up to 1957,[30] and the role and influence of the queen-mother in Ugarit was underlined by *Boyer*[31] and *Liverani.*[32]

---

ma-ni liṣṣuru^{ru}-ka "may the gods of Ugarit, and the gods of the king (of Ugarit) your lord, protect you for peace."

[24] *Heltzer*, a, pp. 75-83 with the correctives concerning the local administration in Ch. VIII.

[25] *Liverani*, f, pp. 348-350.

[26] *Liverani*, f, p. 350.

[27] *Liverani*, f, pp. 352-356; *Kestemont*, b and c.

[28] *Urman*, a, pp. 402-403 with the bibliography given.

[29] *Bin-Nun*, a; *Cassin*, c, pp. 379-381.

[30] *Donner*, a, pp. 105-145.

[31] *Boyer*, b, p. 164; cf. also *Rainey*, c, pp. 38-42.

[32] *Liverani*, a, pp. 107-109; *Donner*, a, pp. 106, 113 and the data from El-Amarna given there.

A special term, designating the queen-mother is lacking, but in several letters a royal prince or the king addresses here a *mlkt um(y)*, "The queen, (my) mother". That this referred to the queen-mother is seen clearly from the letter in KTU.2.34, (1) *tḥm.mlk* (2) *l. Ṯryl.umy rgm*, "The message of the king. To *Ṯryl*, my mother, say!?"[33] Also important in this context is KTU.2.30 (1) *l mlkt u*[*m*]*y* (2) *rgm tḥm mlk bnk*, "To the queen, my mother, the message say of the king thy son."[34] The letters to the queen-mother by the king concern various political and administrative issues and it seems likely that they were written by the king at moments of his absence from Ugarit. This may mean that at these periods a part or full-scale executive power remained in the hands of the queen-mother.[35] It is also possible that a number of the letters of the queen, and to the queen, belong to the queen-mother.[36] The queen-mother possessed landproperty and she was able to buy lands, as we know from U.V. No. 159-161.[37] She also had here *bunušu-bnšm* "men, dependents" (cf. Ch. I) and her separate economy in which we know of "the *gt* of the queen" — *gt mlkt*.[38] The letter, KTU.2.21, which is also addressed to the queen of Ugarit mentions... "say to the *sākinu* of the *gt* of the queen of Ugarit."[39] We also know from U.V. 159-161 about the *sākin bît šarrati* "the *sākinu* of the house (palace) of the queen" (cf. Ch. VIII *sākinu, skn*). I.e., the queen had her majordomo who was in charge of the economy of the queen. As we know (Ch. III), the queen had at her disposal "sons of the queen" (*mârē šarrati*), who were not her sons at all, but were certain officials and the title was the designation of their rank. We also learn from the texts (Ch. VIII) that

---

[33] *Ṯryl* = *Šarelli* cf. *Nougayrol*, U.V, pp. 261-262 — possibly Aḫat-milku, the mother of king Ammistamru II; *Liverani*, a, pp. 137-138.

[34] Cf. also KTU.2.13 (1) *l.mlkt* (2) *umy.rgm* (3) *tḥm.mlk bnk*, "To the queen, my mother the message say of the king, your son." Additional letters to the queen-mother from Talmiyanu, a royal prince KTU.2.16 and possibly 2.17 and 2.12. Cf. *Caquot*, SDB, pp. 1413-1417; and *Kristensen*, a, pp. 143-158.

[35] An exhaustive study about the functions and prerogatives of the queen-mother in Ugarit is waiting its scholar.

[36] U.V.48 (RS.20.19); 49 (RS.20.13), etc. Cf. *Nougayrol*, a p. 117, note 47; *Donner*, a, p. 114.

[37] *Heltzer*, a, p. 103.

[38] KTU.4.143 (1) *B.gt.mlkt.b.Rḥbn* (2) *ḫmšm.mitm.zt*, "At the *gt* of the queen in Raḫbanu — 250 (measures) of olives (or olive-trees)." On *gt*, cf. Ch. IV.

[39] (8) ...*rgm.l.skn gt* (9) *mlkt Ugrt*.

besides the *mūdū* of the king, there were also *mūdū* of the queen (*mūdē šarrati*). As in the case of the king these were males. Often, the queen of Ugarit originated from Amurru, and we know that she had the right to redeem an Amurrite she found enslaved in Ugarit.[40]

This preliminary data about the role of the queen-mother needs additional investigation.

§3. The Queen

Under consideration here is the wife of the king, who is the mother of the heir to the throne. As said above, the queens of Ugarit mostly came from Amurru. We see this from the text which was the "tablet of the dowry of the queen Aḫatmilku" (from the period before she became the queen-mother),[41] sealed by the seal of Dutešub, king of Amurru.

We have first a border case. It is the text PRU.IV, 17.352. This is a text composed "at the presence of Initešub," the king of Karchemish, to whom Ugarit was subject. Aḫatmilku, known as the queen-mother from the time of Ammistamru II (cf. above) was the wife of Niqmepa, his father. Two of the brothers of Ammistamru, Ḫišmišarruma and Aradšarruma, committed a sin against their brother Ammistamru. Their mother (*ummu-šu-nu*) Aḫatmilku gave them a part of her property and banned them to Alašia (on Cyprus). It is possible that the text was composed when Ammistamru was not yet an adult and the regency was in the hands of the queen, who became queen-mother, with all the prerogatives of the queen-mother, at the beginning of the factual reign of Ammistamru II.[42]

Among the divorce texts we must consider PRU.IV, 17.159.[43] They are written in the name of Tutḫalia IV, the Hittite king and Initešub, the king of Karchemish. They sanctioned the banishment by Ammistamru II of his wife, the daughter of the king of Amurru, Bentešina.[44] At the same time, her son Utrišarruma remains in Ugarit as the heir to the throne. But this is

[40] PRU.IV, 17.231; the analysis of this text, *Heltzer*, i, pp. 9-10.

[41] PRU.III, 16.146, (1) *ṭup-pu an-nu-ú ša ú-nu-te*^{MEŠ} *Aḫat-milki šarrati*; cf. *Liverani*, a, p. 99.

[42] *Liverani*, a, p. 101; *Klengel*, b, II, p. 387.

[43] Cf. also PRU.IV, 17.396 and 17.348.

[44] Cf. *Nougayrol*, PRU.IV, p. 125; *Liverani*, a, p. 104; *Klengel*, b, II, p. 384-385.

followed by the clause, "If Ammistamru will die (lit. 'go to his fate') and Utrišarruma will take his mother to Ugarit and will put her to the queenship, so Utrišarruma may put his garments on the throne, and he may go where he wants."[45] So we see that the wife of the king could become, in certain cases, the queen-mother, and she could also have been prevented from this. We see from this that the wife of the king, even the mother of the heir, did not have the significance and importance of the queen-mother. Whatever happened there, we know that during the lifetime of Ammistamru II, the heir became Ibiranu and not Utrišarruma.

We also have a case of divorce with the king Ammistamru, which is widely illustrated in the existing literature. We know that the case ended even with the execution of the queen, who committed adultery, and her brother, the king of Amurru was involved.[46] All this shows us that the role of the wife of the king, even when she was the mother of the heir, could not reach the influence of the queen-mother.

§4. The Heir to the Throne

As we saw above, it was in the hands of the king to decide who the heir would be. The heir to the throne was designated by the term *tardennu*,[47] despite that fact that in the cuneiform texts from other areas this term designated the second son of the king. The other term known to us was the Ugar. *uṯryn* — Akk. *ušriyannu* — appearing in a number of texts.[48] Concerning its etymology, we have to reject the former interpretations[49] and to regard the term as a Hurrian one.[50] As we saw above, the prince

---

[45] (31) *... šum-ma* (32) *[Am-mis-tam-]ru arki ši-im-ti-šu* (33) *il-lak-[ma] ú* *ᴵUt-ri-ⁱˡšarru-ma* (34) *umma-šu i-li-qi-ma* (35) *i-na Ú-ga-ri-it* (36) *a-na* SAL.LUGAL-*ut-ti* (37) *u-ta-ar-ši* *ᴵUt-ri-ⁱˡšarru-ma* (38) *ṣubat-šu i-na ⁱˢlitti li-iš-ku-un* (39) *a-šar libbi-šu lil-lik*.

[46] PRU.IV, 17.348; 17.159; 17.372, A, etc. as well as *Fischer*, a, RS.19.57, 1, pp. 12-13; *Liverani*, a, pp. 104ff.; *Klengel*, b, II, pp. 373-374; 385-386; *Fisher*, a, pp. 14-18 with the literature given.

[47] *Liverani*, a, p. 74, 106; *Buccellati*, b, p. 68; *Wilhelm*, a, pp. 277-282; AHW, p. 1379; *ta/erd/tennūtu* Ug. ... "Kronprinz."

[48] PRU.III, 16.257, B, IV, 21; *uṯryn* — KTU.2.67, 2; above *mur'u ušriyanni* = *mur'u Ibirana*.

[49] *Loretz-Dietrich*, i, p. 299; WUS, p. 41, No. 476, etc.

[50] AHW, p. 1442a; *Laroche*, a.

Ibiranu, being the heir to the throne, had, along with the king and the *sākinu*, his *mur'u*-men. As we see from PRU.IV, 17.159, the king Ammistamru nominated one of his sons to be the heir and changed, during his regnal period, his nomination at least once.

§5. Other Members of the Royal Family

Our knowledge in this area is very limited. From the text PRU.III, 16.276 (cf. Ch. III) we know that a certain Karkušuḫ was married with Apapa, the daughter of the king, and this gave him the privilege of using the income from the village Uḫnappu.

We also know from a number of texts in Akkadian that a certain Nuriyanu was the brother of the king Niqmaddu II and that he, according to a number of documents, received lands in various villages of the kingdom of Ugarit.[51] In some cases Nuriyanu had to pay the king some of what he received from the lands.[52] He was also freed from *pilku*,[53] which seems to be natural in his position.

Thus, as we have seen, in Ugarit the role of the king was enormous and there did not exist considerable limitation of his power inside the country. At the same time we see that except for the queen-mother, the other members of the royal family played a relatively small part in the governing of the kingdom.

---

[51] PRU.III, 16.150; 16.166; 16.248; etc.

[52] PRU.III, 16.263; 16.275.

[53] PRU.III, 16.140 formerly the lands were in the hands of a certain Abdinikal (11) ... *za-ki* *ᴵNu-ri-ya-nu iš-tu pí-il-ki bît ᴵAbdi-ni-kal* "Nuriyanu is free (pure) from the *pilku*-service of the house of Abdinikal" (we understood the expression "house" here, as the "family of the serviceman"). Cf. also PRU.III, 16.272.

GENERAL CONCLUSIONS

We have seen that a widely developed system of the royal economy existed in Ugarit, alongside the economy of the village community which utilized the labor of the peasant-households [1] and, in wealthy families, slave-labor.[2] The royal economy was dispersed all over the kingdom and its local units were named *gt (dimtu)*. In the *gt* were concentrated the agricultural work, manpower and beast of burden, cattle and stores of seeds and products for delivery and maintaining the palace, army and other branches of the government.[3]

Craftsmanship was also government-managed and the artisans worked for the treasury, supplying it with almost all products needed by the court, army and other branches of the royal economy.

We see that the manpower, except for certain corvée-service of the rural communities, belonged to the special category of the "royal dependents" (*bnš mlk*, lit. "royal men") to which belonged numerous professional groups with their own internal organization.

The "royal dependents" worked not only in the economy, but there were professional groups in the military field, administration, auxiliary personnel of the palace and even the temple-personnel had their specific *bnš mlk* groups.

This system was the dominant one in the state and economic organization of Ugarit. We see in Ugarit a very specific and complete socio-economic organization. The royal dependents were not slaves. They received land-allotments for their service, had families and descendents, but they were dependent on the royal authorities. Between these dependents there was not equality and there were groups of lower and higher position in the society of Ugarit.

We must also point out that this was a very large group of people who made up a very considerable part of the male population of Ugarit and

---

[1] *Heltzer*, a; *Liverani*, i, pp. 146-164.

[2] *M. Heltzer*, Private Property in Ugarit (in press).

[3] Cf. also *Liverani*, h, pp. 57-72.

involved themselves continuously in the various works and deeds of royal service. As *Liverani* supposes,[4] this could have caused a general social and economic crisis in Ugarit, as well as in neighboring kingdoms, and it may have been one of the causes of the easy destruction of Ugarit by the "peoples of the sea" at the beginning of the XIII-XIIth centuries B.C.E. But this question needs additional data and investigation.

At least the major part of foreign trade was run by the royal authorities of Ugarit through the *tamkar* (royal trade-agent) system. Such organization of the society has its closest parallel in Mycenaean Greece, and the comparison based on documents of these two societies, is a task for further investigation.

---

[4] SDB, pp. 1346-1348.

EXCURSUS I

SHIPBUILDING IN UGARIT AND ITS ORGANIZATION

Ugarit was closely connected with the sea. The kingdom possessed one big harbor at Ugarit, and a number of smaller ones. It had a large commercial fleet and military navy, as well as smaller vessels at the disposal of the villagers of the maritime villages.[1] The latter had small boats, but we know that there were also relatively large ships in Ugarit.

According to the text U.V, 33 (RS.20.213) the Hittite king ordered the king of Ugarit to organize the transportation of 2000 GUR (ca. 500 metric tons) of grain, which were to be purchased in Mukish-Alalaḫ and says to him: "And you (i.m. king of Ugarit) on a large ship (22) and the crew of sailors, which shall this grain transport to their country (the Hittite Empire); may be in two times they shall carry it".[2] Contrary to the previous views,[3] we know now that as *H. Frost* points out as a result of the investigation of the stone-anchors of Ugarit, "a half-ton anchor presupposes a wooden ship of at least 200 tons and a length of 20 meters."[4] So it is possible that to transport 2000 GUR in two freighters did not create special difficulties. It is also noteworthy that the half-ton anchors, as Frost points out, are characteristic of Ugarit and are much heavier and larger than the Byblian ones. This would indicate a larger port in Ugarit[5] and we would also assume larger scale shipbuilding. But the known anchors of Ugarit, as investigated by *Schaeffer*,[6] had the weights from about 100 to 400+x kg. This, alone, shows the large-scale development of shipbuilding in Ugarit. We must take into account that a large number of the anchors known were found in temples as votive offerings and in other places not on the shore.

---

[1] On the harbors of Ugarit, *Astour*, c, pp. 113-127; *Borger*, a, pp. 1-3. On the fleet of Ugarit, *Sasson*, a, pp. 126-136; *Heltzer*, a, pp. 21-24; *Heltzer*, b, pp. 150-156, etc.

[2] Cf. *Heltzer*, b, pp. 151-152, as well as the fragmentary text U.V, 175 (RS.26.155).

[3] *Klengel*, b, II, p. 395.

[4] *Frost*, a, p. 235 ff.; *Heltzer*, A, p. 210.

[5] *Frost*, b, p. 38, cf. also *Frost*, c, pp. 137-162 and *Frost*, d, pp. 425-442.

[6] *Schaeffer*, a, pp. 371-381.

This shows us the importance allotted to anchors by the Ugaritians. Thus, the existence of "shipwrights" (*ḥrš anyt*) is a normal feature in this kingdom.

There are also texts which relate directly about subjects connected with shipbuilding. One of them is KTU.4.689.

1	*spr.npṣ.any*	"List of the equipment of the ship.[7]
2	*tš'.mṯṯm*	Nine oars (or "pairs of oars")[8]
3	*mšlḥ.ḥdṯ*	(One) new anchor (??)[9]
4	*w.mṣpt.ḫrk*	and ....[10]
5	*w.trn*[.]*w.ḫbl*	and (one) mast[11] and (one) rope (tow)[12]
6	*w.kpṯ*	and a *kpṯ*."[13]

[7] Such translation is preferred for the texts list the equipment of only one ship; *npṣ*-equipment, cf. Ch. IV concerning the *nqdm*; the word *npṣ(m)* is used concerning garments, weapons and other specimens, which are included into "equipment" — depending upon whom it concerned. In this case we have *npṣ* — pl.st.cstr.

[8] If 9 oars are mentioned here we have 4 pairs and one rudder-oar; if we understand *mṯṯm* as the dual form we have 9 pairs of oars; *mṯṯ* — Hebr. *māšōṯ*, Ez. 27, 6, 9 "oar"; cf. Akk. *gumuššu* "oar" or "rudder", *Salonen*, b, p. 104.

[9] Cf. Hebr. *šelaḥ*, "missile, javelin," but it never appears in the OT in connection with ships or the sea, as well as never in Ugaritic texts. As a naval term, the word is also unknown from Akkadian. I can only explain this in that *mšlḥ*, from the root *šlḥ*, could mean a new (*ḥdṯ*) artifact, which had to be thrown — possibly an anchor.

[10] This is a naval term. *Salonen*, b, p. 126, *erkû* — a kind of vessel. Hebr. *ḫărakkīm* — Ct. 2, 9 — "Gitterfenster", but in later Hebrew also *ḫarāk* "Luke" — *Levy*, a, II, p. 111, and this can be the luke of a ship. But such explanations have no satisfactory foundations. Otherwise, cf. CAD, K, p. 217b, TÚG *muṣipēti kar-ke-ti ša* SIG.SAG — "*muṣiptu* garments of twined (?) thread of first quality wool"; also CAD, M, II, pp. 242-243 and esp. f), where the *muṣēptu* is connected with fishermen. It is unclear whether this is the Ugaritic word for sail, or not, but it seems to be a textile artifact.

[11] Hebr. *tōren*, Is. 33, 23; Ez. 27, 5.

[12] Hebrew, *ḥebel*.

[13] Cf. AHW, p. 443b, *kapāšu(m)?*, "Deutung unklar" = "meaning unclear," according to *Salonen*, b, p. 131. *kappāti* is something connected with the hiring of a ship; at the same time, Hebr. *kāfīs*, Aram. *k^{e}fas* — in Mishnaic times "to tie, to put together", etc. — *Levy*, a, II, p. 382, but it also has the meaning of some iron tools. *Levy*, a, II, p. 390; cf. also *Laroche*, a, p. 155, the hurrian word from Alalaḫ ^{LÚ}*ku-up-šu-ḫu-li*, i.e., *kupšu*-makers. Although all the explanations are unsatisfactory we cannot accept the translation of *Gordon*, UT, p. 422, No. 1291a, *kpṯ* "earth", for this could not be one of the items of ship equipment.

The words of this text which are understandable obviously concern the equipment of a naval vessel. These words, which are quite clear, *mšṭ* "row" and *trn* "mast" — are wooden artifacts, the "tow" — "rope" *ḫbl*, is made of some kind of fibers.[14]

Of no less interest is the text PRU.VI, 73 (RS.19.107), concerning various ships and especially PRU.VI, 126 (RS.19.28) where textile equipment was delivered (9) *qât* ^{I}*A-bi-ḫi-li* (10) *a-n[a]* ^{URU}*Gu-ub-li* (11) *napḫar 2[5] ṣubâta*^{HA} *qât* ^{I}*A-bi-[ḫ]i-li* "Into the hands of *Abiḫili* to Byblos: Total 25 garments/textiles to *Ahiḫili*". More interesting is the line (1) *7 ṣubât*^{MEŠ} *elippâti*^{MEŠ} *ma-aš-ḫa-tu-ma* "7 garments of ships (ship-garments) — *mašḫāṭu*."[15] It is clear that *mašḫāṭu* was a type of cloth, but whether it was a sail or something else is an open question. The fact that it is a ship-garment speaks in favor of such a proposal.[16] By all means we see textile artifacts in the shipbuilding and equipment of Ugarit. In PRU.VI, 141 (RS.19.112) we read (3) *2* ^{URUDU}*ḫa-ar-me-ša-tu* ^{iş}*elippāti*^{MEŠ} (4) *4* ^{URUDU}*ul-ma-tu rabâtu*^{MEŠ} *ša* ^{iş}*eleppi* (5) *20* ^{URUDU}*ul-ma-tu ṣeḫrêtu*^{MEŠ}. "(3) 2 (bronze/copper) sickles[17] of ships, 4 (bronze/copper) hammers (or axes) of ships[18] 20 (bronze/copper) small hammers."

We see that the shipwrights in Ugarit had to deal with wood, textile and metal artifacts. It is not clear if they worked on all the details of the ship or only used tools made of these materials in the production of the vessels, but it is clear that shipbuilding was very highly developed. The best and most outstanding evidence we have in this area comes from the unique text RS.34.147.[19]

---

[14] Cf. also the text KTU.4.399, (1) *mit ʿš[r]* (2) *[t]lṯ.abd* (3) *b.anyt*, "100+x+3 *abd* at the ship (vessel)". We have also texts dealing with various types of vessels.

[15] *mašḫāṭu-ma, ma* the Plur. suff. in Ugaritic.

[16] *Boyd*, a, p. 212, a cloth for a boat, perhaps a sail; but at the same time in KTU.4.167, 12, 15, *mšḫṭ* is connected with "chariots" *mrkbt*; cf. also AHW, p. 625 *mašḫaṭu* "Treppchen" "ladder"; CAD, M, I, p. 365 — without translation; *Veenhof*, a, p. 169, "a kind of textile."

[17] Cf. Ch. IV, p. 49-79, where we see the *ḫrmṯ* is an agricultural tool. Here it is important to emphasize that the *ḫarmešatu* is made from metal. Possibly, it was some kind of a sharp metal-tool or weapon used by shipbuilders or in the warships.

[18] *ulmatu* — AHW, p. 1410, b, "eine Axt", *Nougayrol*, PRU, VI — "grand marteux" "big hammers".

[19] *Schaeffer*, b, pp. 399-479, Pl. 39; on this text cf. *Heltzer*, P, (in print).

In this tablet we learn that even the king of Karchemish had vessels in Ugarit. They were sometimes dragged, possibly using the smallest waterways to Karchemish. This proves that shipbuilding was on a very large scale in Ugarit. But, at the same time, the organizational side of such industrial activities as shipbuilding is not yet clear. We do not yet know whether there was the same kind of prototype of the later Athenian trierarchy,[20] under the guidance or supervision of the authorities, or not.

---

[20] *Jordan*, a.

EXCURSUS II

THE DATA ABOUT CHARIOT AND WAGGON PRODUCTION IN UGARIT

The problem of chariot and waggon construction in Ancient Mesopotamia has been investigated by *A. Salonen*[1] and recently by *W. Farber*[2] and *Littauer* and *Crouwel*.[3] *Zaccagnini*[4] dealt with the same problem in Nuzi. Some works have also appeared on the construction of vehicles in Ugarit.[5]

We have a number of texts from Ugarit dealing with chariots and waggons. From them we learn about the construction and restoration of these items in the royal workshops, as well as about the various parts and details of the vehicles and their equipment. The texts are the following: KTU.4.145; 4.167; 4.392; 4.88; 4.89; 4.136; 4.169; 4.363; 4.368; 4.377; 4.384; 4.618. From these texts we can learn the following about the details of a chart. They consisted of wheels — *apnm*, and also had a pole — *tr*,[6] yoke — *ṣmd*[7] and the cart-box — *ḥrṣ*.[8] We also learn that the common armament of the chariots consisted of quivers — *uṯpt* and arrows — *ḥẓm*.[9] These details are taken from 4.145. But tablet KTU.4.167 gives us some uncommon details.

---

[1] *Salonen*, f.

[2] *Farber*, a, pp. 336-344.

[3] *Littauer-Crouwel*, a, pp. 344-351.

[4] *Zaccagnini*, c, pp. 21-38.

[5] *Del Olmo Lete*, b, pp. 47-51; c, pp. 179-186; *Calders*, a, pp. 167-193; *Dietrich-Loretz*, p, and *Amadasi*, a.

[6] *Calders*, a, p. 181; *Del Olmo Lete*, c, pp. 179-186; KAI, 161; DISO, p. 335, *tr*$_1$.

[7] We must differentiate, according to the context, between the words *ṣmd* — Hebr. *ṣemed*, Akk. *ṣimdu* "yoke" and *ṣmd* "pair (of oxen)", cf. *Calders*, a, p. 182, note 58; *Pini*, a, p. 110; *Zaccagnini* c, p. 30.

[8] In KTU.4.145 by mistake *ḫrṣ*; the autograph in PRU, II shows *ḥ*; *Heltzer*, c, p. 486, e, also not correct, *Calders*, p. 182 and 190, *ḥrṣ*; *Salonen*, f, p. 133. ^{GIS}*ḫi-ir-ṣum ša narkabtu*; we do not accept the explanation of *Del Olmo Lete*, c, and *Dietrich-Loretz*, p.

[9] In some cases we see a similar organization of the production of chariots in Mycenaean Greece; cf. *Poljakova*, a, pp. 133, 146 and 173.

We meet here *mrkbt ṣpyt bḫrṣ*, "chariots, covered with gold (plates). These were royal chariots (*mrkbt mlk*) and among their armanent we see "slings" (*qlʿm*), *mḏrn* — weapons,[10] hammers(?) — *mšḫṭ*[11] and *msg*-weapons.[12] We also learn from KTU.4.392[13] that [(1)] For five chariots — fifteen trained horses (*l ḫmš mrkbt ḫmš ʿšrh prs*) were given.[14] There was also a chariot (store) house (*bt mrkbt*) and the text deals with the tires of the chariots — *šant*.[15] All the texts given at the beginning of this excursus relate the same details about chariots or waggons, but only a few of them give us additional information about the chariots, their details, equipment or armament.

KPU.4.136 relates about "9 yokes of bronze" (*tšʿ ṣmdm ṯlṯm*) given to a certain *Ibrtlm*, and it is underlined that "one of their front-sides was lacking" (*w.pat.aḥt.in.bhm*).[16] KTU.4.169 shows us that the military stores of the kingdom of Ugarit stored the production of the *ḥrš mrkbt* — cart-wrights.

KTU.4.363 informs us about additional equipment. Mentioned are 13 tunics (*ktnt*),[17] neck-armor — *grbz*,[18] of the charioteers, *ḫpnt*-garments of horses (*ḫpnt śśwm*),[19] *pldm-palidu*-garments,[20] as well as inventory already known from the above referenced texts.

---

[10] UT. No. 1435, "kind of weapons."

[11] *Calders*, a, p. 183 and note 68, but such translation is not reliable, cf. Excursus I.

[12] *Calders*, a, p. 183, note 69, Ch. VI, pp. 103-130.

[13] *Dietrich-Loretz*, p, p. 191 (with the previous literature); *Del Olmo Lete*, a, p. 49; *Calders*, a, pp. 188-189; *Watson*, a, p. 497.

[14] *prs* — "trained horse," a word of Hurrian origin, cf. *Loretz*, e, pp. 188-191.

[15] *Del Olmo Lete*, a, p. 50; AHW, p. 1213-1214; CAD, H, 48b; *Zaccagnini*, c, p. 29-30; *šēnu* "Radreifen" in the Nuzi texts; *Salonen*, f, pp. 117-118; *Dietrich-Loretz*, p, p. 191.

[16] *pat* — WUS, p. 252, No. 2181, "Saum, Grenze, Gefielde", UT, p. 465, No. 1994, "without any *pēʾā(h)* of them." So we see that *Gordon* connects it with harvestable land. In our opinion we have to take into account Akk. *pātu/pūtu* — which always appears as the front side of vehicles or harness — *Salonen*, f, pp. 82-83, 92-94, 124.

[17] *Heltzer*, b, p. 41, No. 94.

[18] Akk. *gurpisu*, possibly made from wool and protecting the neck — *Zaccagnini*, c, p. 31, *Salonen*, e, p. 141.

[19] There appear also *tkyġ* and *llḫ*, whose meaning is unclear.

[20] *Heltzer*, b, p. 47, No. 109.

Besides horses we also see with the *ṣmdm* (yokes) donkeys (*ḥmrm*) and oxen (*alpm*) in a number of texts. We learn that carts or waggons were in these cases being referred to.

All the above shows us that the work of the Ugaritic cartwrights (*ḥrš mrkbt*) and possibly craftsmen in related specialities was not a very simple job.

The data about the number of vehicles is very uncertain. We have learned above that three horses were given to a war-chariot. Possibly, there were pairs of horses as we learn from U.V.105 (RS.20.211 A/B+...). The better preserved lines of this text show that in most cases 1, but sometimes 2 and 3 "pairs of horses to PN" (*ta-pal* sīsi a-na x(PN)) were listed. It was a distribution of horses from the royal stables.[21] At least 200 pairs of horses were counted originally in this text. We must also take into account the letter KTU.2.33.[22] (22) *w.mlk.bʿly* (23) *lm.škn.hnk* (24) *lʿbdh.alpm śśwm* (25) *rgmt ʿlyṯh*... "And, O king, my lord, why has he imposed this on his servant? 2000 horses has then assigned as my share." And further (31) ...*hn* (32) *alpm.śśwm hnd*, "behold, the 2000 horses are here..." (37) ...*hn* (38) [*a*]*lpm śśwm* (39) [*hnd*... "Verily, behold, the 2000 horses [are here." So we see that at least 2000 horses are mentioned at one given moment. Such a number shows that the chariotry of Ugarit nqmbered at least 700-1000 chariots and the ox or donkey carts were also numerous. This brings us to the conclusion that the cartwrights in Ugarit were a relatively large group, permanently working in cart production and their restoration.

---

[21] Cf. also Ch. VI, pp. 103-130.

[22] The interpretation according to *Albright*, b, pp. 36-38.

INDICES

* Mrs. Sh. Yaron participated in the indexation.

I. Cuneiform texts.

a) Ugaritic

b) Akkadian

II. *Personal names.**

* Here and further we follow the general order of the latin alphabet, but there are some specific features, connected with the transliteration of Ugaritic, Phoenician and Akhadian:

a) a, as also the Ugaritic $'_1$ = a, the Phoenician '- is given in the same order as a̱; the west-semitic ʻ (ʻaiyyīn) is also given in the same order.
b) The Ugaritic $'_2$ = i and is given in the order of the letter i̱.
c) The semantic ġ (ghain) follows after *g*.
d) h is followed by ḥ and ḫ.
e) s is followed by ṣ and š.
f) d is followed by ḏ.
g) t is followed by ṭ and ṯ.

Abbanu – 25, 165.
ʻbd – 4, 6-7.
ʻbdadt – 5-6.
Abdʻl – 5.
ʻbdʻnt – 4, 6.
Abdianti – 134.
Abdiḫagab – 23, 25, 153, 162.
ʻbdil – 33.
Abdiilu – 153.
(bn)ʻbdilm – *116*.
ʻbdilt – 5, 7.
Abdinergal – *25*, 112, 114, 120, 134, 160, 162-163, 165.
Abdinikal – *185*.
ʻbdmlk – 4-6, 24, *153*, 168.
ʻbdrpu – 5, 7.
Abdu – 112, *114*, 134, 160, 163, 165, 167.
ʻbdyrḫ – 5, 7, 44.
Abġl – 5, 6.
Abiḫili – 190.
Abmn – 63.
Abṣn – 4, 6.
Aburšanu – 134.
Abušgama – *143*.
Abutenu – 25.
Adad – *136*.
Adalšennu – 20-21, 112.
Addudayyānu – *142*.
ʻdn – 4-7, 43, 45.
Adnʻm – 8, 77.
'dnlrm – *152*.
ʻdnm – 13, 58, 64.
Adrdn – 32, 33.
ʻdršp – 5-6, 32, 45, 48.
ʻdy – 5, 7.
(Bn)ʻgltn – 44.
(bn) Agpṯ – 64.
Agyn – 5, 8.
(bn) Agy(n)t – *116*.
Agytn – 4.
Aḥiram – *152*.
Aḫamaranu – 134-135.
Aḫatmilku – 149, *182*, 183.
Aḫimunu – 134.
Aḫmlk – 5, 7.
Aḫmn – 59.
Akapšeni – 134.
Alḏy – 5, 7.
Aliziti – *172*.
Allan – 125-126.
Amataruna – 24.
Ammadanu (Amd/ḏn) – 134.
Amminu – 122.
Ammistamru II – 4, 20-21, 23-25, 27, 50, 82, 112, 126, 133, 135, 145, 148, 153-155, 160, *162*, 165-166, 168, 171, *182*-184.
Ammurapi – 158.
ʻmn – *116*.
Amtrn – 4, 5, 7, 74, 172.
Ananiyana – 72.
Anatenu – 72.
Annḏr – 4.
Annmn – 5, 7.
Annmt – 85.
Annšn – 134.
Anntn – 11, 25, 45.
Ansny – 5, 7.
Apapa – 132, 185.

III. *Geographic and Ethnic names**

(Including the names of gt)

* The name Ugarit (Ugrt), appearing on almost every page is not included.

IV. *Terms designating professions, offices or certain social status*

The terms appearing on every page as bnš, bnš mlk (king) and mlkt (queen) etc. are not included.

sâḫit šamni – *82*.
Sākin āli – 150-152.
Sākin bît šarrati – 149-150, 182.
sākin bîti – *149*, 150.
Sākin māti – 142-149, 178.
sākinu – 11, 26, 56, 136, 141-152, 170, 181-182, 185.
^{LÚ}sasinnu – 89.
sbrdnm – 93-95.
sġrm – 13, 15, 41, 46, 69, 71.
sisaḫallima – 162.
skn – 11, 26, 62, 141-152, 178.
skn bt mlk – 149-150, 169.
skn.qrt – 4, 150-152.
sōkēn – *141*.
*spr – 157-161.
srdnnm – *127*.
sūkini – *141*.
sukallu (skl) – 136, 156-157, 159.
ṣabē eleppē – *111*.
ṣbu – 3.
ṣbu anyt – 111.
śnn – *122*.
ša naqi – 40.
šanānu-ṯnnm – 14, 28, 37-38, 68, 105-107, 122-123.
šangū – 133-136, 138.
ša rêšu – 24, 170-173.
šarraqu – 123.
šatammu – 21, 25-26, 164-166.
šatammu rabū – *166*.
šerdana/ṯrtnm – 40, 106-107, 125-127.
šib.mqdšt – 5, 138.
šmrm – 125.
šrm – 5, 9, 18, 27-28, 77, 96, 105, 137, 164.
tamkarā/mkrm – 18, 19, 25-26, 31, 40-41, 105-107, 160, *171*, 179, 187.
tard/tennu – *168*, 184.
targumyanu – 159.
taršuwanni – 181.
tdgr – 57.
tdġlm – 5, 12.
^{LÚ}TIBIRA.GID – 176.
tknm – 176.
tmrym – 67.
trrm/tariruma – 27, 38, 125.
^{LÚ}TUG.LÁ – 169, 173.
tupšarru emqu – 157.
*tupšarrum – 156-161, 166.
turuḫi – 2.
ṯʿy – 157.
ṯġr mlk – 149, 169.
ṯġrm – 5, 27, 32-34, 40, 169-170.
ṯrmnm – 96-97.
U.DAB.MUŠEN – 173.
^{LÚ}U.DAB – *70*.
UKU-tu – 120.
undu – 120.
UN-tu – 25, 40, 105, 115-121.
uriyannu (uryn) – 132, 138.
ušriyannu (uṯryn) – 168, 184.
yqšm/yaqišuma – 38, *163*, 173.
yṣḥm – 4, *11*, 28, 32-34, 38, 96, 105, 137, 163-164.
yṣr – 5, 10, 11, 13, 44, 58, 73, 78, 89-90, *100*, *163*.
zadimmu – *89*.
ZAG.LU – 20, 25, 40, 93-95.
zikaru – 2.

* (A complete list with all references on pp. 158-159, note 87).